WHY BUDGETS MATTER

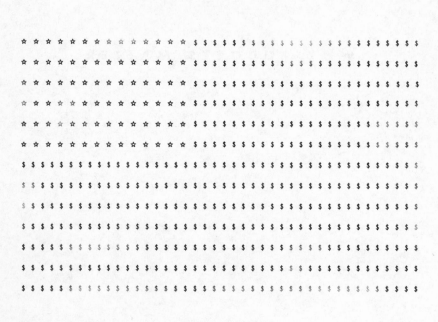

WHY BUDGETS MATTER

BUDGET POLICY AND AMERICAN POLITICS

DENNIS S. IPPOLITO

THE PENNSYLVANIA STATE UNIVERSITY PRESS
UNIVERSITY PARK, PENNSYLVANIA

Library of Congress Cataloging-in-Publication Data

Ippolito, Dennis S.
Why budgets matter : budget policy and American politics /
Dennis S. Ippolito.
p.   cm.
Includes bibliographical references and index.
ISBN 0-271-02259-0 (cloth : alk. paper)
1. Budget—United States.
2. Budget—Political aspects—United States.
I. Title.

HJ2051 .A5I66 2003
320.973—dc21   2002154502

FOR MY FAMILY,

Fide et caritas

CONTENTS

FIGURES AND TABLES

PREFACE

Americans have an unusual aversion to "big government." While this term can refer to many different characteristics of government, one of its clearest and most concrete applications involves the powers to tax, spend, and borrow. "Big government" in this sense means heavy taxation, expansive domestic spending programs, and the routine use of deficits and debt to help finance federal programs.

During the past two centuries, this fiscal dimension of big government has been at the heart of key political battles over the size and role of the federal government. The framers of the Constitution conferred on the federal government broad and largely undefined fiscal powers. Political leaders and parties ever since have competed to impose their preferred definitions—what to tax and how heavily, how much to spend and for what purposes, and whether to borrow and accumulate debt. The collective outcome of these policy controversies is found in the federal budget, and this book examines the development of federal budget policy from the nation's founding through the modern era of the welfare state. Its purpose is to illuminate the political significance of budget policy—what budget policy tells us about the outcomes of past struggles over the size and role of the federal government and how budget policy is likely to shape the parameters of future ones.

Since the budget is a measure of political reality that uses money, this book makes extensive use of historical budget data to demonstrate why and how government has grown. It also uses conventional benchmarks—particularly the size of government in relation to the size of the economy—to measure the relative size and shape of budgets over time and to compare budget policy trends in the United States to those in other industrialized democracies. These historical data and cross-national comparisons will, I hope, provide some useful insights into our long-standing debates over big government.

In the course of writing this book, I have incurred many debts and would like to acknowledge several of them. Louis Fisher and James D. Savage provided thorough and constructive critiques of the original manuscript and are responsible for much of its subsequent improvement. Christine Carberry has been an invaluable and integral part of this project from the beginning. Southern Methodist University provided a research leave and research support that helped me to complete the project. My sincere thanks to all.

Note: Numbers in the text and tables that follow may not add up to totals because of rounding.

PERSPECTIVES ON BUDGET POLICY

In recent decades, conflicts over federal budget policy have monopolized the nation's political agenda. During the 1970s and 1980s, the partisan and ideological deadlock over spending and taxation was especially severe, resulting in chronic deficits and soaring debt. Between 1980 and 1990, the publicly-held federal debt more than tripled, to $2.4 trillion.[1] Then, over the next decade, the budget outlook changed dramatically. A series of deficit-reduction measures, and an unusually favorable economy, produced the first balanced budgets in nearly three decades.[2] In January 2001, budget surpluses of $5.6 trillion were projected for the first decade of the twenty-first century, and policymakers were debating how to allocate these surpluses and to prepare

1. The federal debt has two components. The publicly-held debt is debt that is in the hands of nonfederal investors, including individuals, corporations, the Federal Reserve System, state and local governments, foreign governments, and central banks. Debt held by federal government accounts comprises debt held by federal trust funds, deposit insurance funds, and other federal accounts. The net interest payments recorded in the budget represent the costs of servicing the publicly-held debt. Publicly-held debt and debt held by federal accounts total gross federal debt.

2. The technical definition of a balanced budget is when spending (outlays) equals revenues (budget receipts) during a fiscal year. Since perfect equality is obviously a rarity, the term "balanced budget" applies to any surplus of revenues over spending.

for future demographic pressures on federal retirement and healthcare spending.[3]

Before long, however, another fiscal turnaround occurred. Tax cuts enacted in 2001, defense increases that followed the September 11 terrorist attacks on the United States, and a weak economy brought the budget back into deficit. In January 2002, ten-year surplus projections were $4 trillion less than the previous year's, and Congress and the executive branch were once again seriously at odds over the size, shape, and balance of the federal budget.

The history of federal budget policy provides a useful context for analyzing these contemporary struggles over fiscal politics. More than two centuries ago, Alexander Hamilton made clear the critical importance of the federal government's "power of the purse." "Money," Hamilton wrote, "is, with propriety, considered as the vital principle of the body politic; as that which sustains its life and motion and enables it to perform its most essential functions."[4] From the Federalist-Jeffersonian Republican battles of Hamilton's day to the present, the budget has served as the principal determinant of the size and scope of government. The extent and use of federal taxing powers, the constitutional reach of federal spending, and the management of deficits and debt have defined the federal government's role in the social and economic lives of its citizens.

The challenge of determining the appropriate size of government is a common feature of the eras, or stages, of budget policy development in the United States. There are, however, important distinctions between these eras as well. Extraconstitutional fiscal norms, particularly regarding peacetime deficits and debt, have changed a great deal over time, as has the composition of federal spending. During the nineteenth and early twentieth centuries, federal spending was limited to traditional public goods, such as internal improvements, government services, and national defense. Since the New Deal and World War II, the budget has been dominated first by Cold War defense requirements and more recently by social welfare programs. On the revenue side, the transition from the limited indirect taxes of the nineteenth century to the comprehensive income taxation of the post–World War II period has been equally far-reaching. Finally, as the president and Congress

---

3. On the changing surplus projections between January 2001 and January 2002, see Congressional Budget Office, *The Budget and Economic Outlook: Fiscal Years 2003–2012* (Washington, D.C.: CBO, 2002), xiv.

4. Alexander Hamilton, James Madison, and John Jay, *The Federalist Papers* (New York: New American Library, 1961), 188.

have competed over spending and tax policy, the institutional parameters of the budget process have changed.

Chronicling these changes and their impact comprises the approach of this book. The history of federal budget policy is divided into eras that reflect distinctive conceptions of the size and scope of government. Within each era, budget policy is examined in terms of major spending and tax issues, the institutional arrangements of the budget process, and the effectiveness of budget control. Comparing these eras helps to illuminate the policy and political bases of government growth and provides insights into how and why fiscal problems develop and the means through which legislators and presidents attempt to resolve them.

The History of the Balanced-Budget Rule

A good starting point in understanding budget policy and budget control is the balanced-budget "rule." The belief that the federal government should balance its budget has been a powerful force in American politics. Webber and Wildavsky, who identify a number of important differences between American and European budgeting during the nineteenth century, find the clearest example of "American exceptionalism" in a balanced-budget belief that was "almost a religion."[5] Against this backdrop, our modern-day difficulties with deficits and debt might suggest a serious decline in fiscal responsibility, but the reality is more complex.

Deficits and debt are not modern inventions. The United States began with a substantial Revolutionary War debt; deficit spending during wartime and periodic economic recessions produced comparable debt levels after the Civil War and World War I (Fig. 1.1).[6] The balanced-budget rule, then, has always accommodated emergency deficits (notably war) and cyclical deficits

---

5. Carolyn Webber and Aaron Wildavsky, *A History of Taxation and Expenditure in the Western World* (New York: Simon and Schuster, 1986), 360.

6. Gross national product (GNP) and gross domestic product (GDP) are commonly used measures of economic performance and production. GNP is the monetary value of all goods and services produced by the labor and capital of residents of a country; GDP is the monetary value of these goods and services produced domestically. The difference between the two is minor, and older historical data are usually based on GNP. Both measures are employed to assess the relative size of government spending, revenues, deficit, and debt. Thus, spending-GDP ratios would provide a comparison of the size of the U.S. government over time and a comparison between the size of the U.S. government and other governments.

(temporary imbalances during severe economic downturns). In addition, the rule had contradictory political applications during our early history.

Before the Civil War, for example, the balanced-budget rule was used by Jeffersonians and Jacksonians—by the 1830s, Thomas Jefferson's Republican party had become Andrew Jackson's Democratic party—to limit the federal government's role in domestic politics. State governments, by comparison, borrowed freely and accumulated much larger debts than the federal government. Then, after the Civil War, the balanced-budget rule accommodated a different set of political concerns. The Republican majority that dominated national politics during this period was committed to high protective tariffs. Armed with the abundant revenues from these tariffs, Republicans initiated expensive spending programs. Thus, during this latter period, the balanced-budget rule was employed to expand rather than limit government.

Modern Deficits: Causes

Since the New Deal, deficits have certainly been more common than they were earlier. During the Great Depression, federal spending rose sharply, the budget was in deficit each year, and the relative size of deficits was approximately three percent of gross domestic product (GDP) (Table 1.1). The deficits that helped finance World War II were enormous, averaging about 25 percent of GDP from 1943 to 1945. By the end of World War II, the publicly-held federal debt was almost 110 percent of GDP, the highest level ever recorded. Despite their unusual scale, the deficits of the 1930s and early 1940s were, like prior deficits, driven by a weak economy and by war. After World War II and through the 1950s, the commitment to balanced budgets resurfaced. The Truman administration achieved a budget surplus from 1947 to 1949, and the Eisenhower administration balanced three of its peacetime budgets after the Korean War.

The transition to large and chronic deficits began during the 1960s, as economic policy prescriptions and nondefense spending growth undermined the balanced-budget rule. In 1963, the Kennedy administration proposed large tax cuts and planned deficits to boost economic growth. Its rationale was that fiscal stimulus, in the form of deliberate deficits, would revitalize a sluggish economy; the budget could then be brought into balance at high levels of growth and employment.[7] When growth surged and

---

7. In his budget message to Congress, John F. Kennedy declared, "Our present choice is not between a tax cut and a balanced budget . . . [but] between chronic deficits arising out of a slow

Fig. 1.1 U.S. Federal Debt Held by the Public, 1790–2000 (as a percentage of GNP)

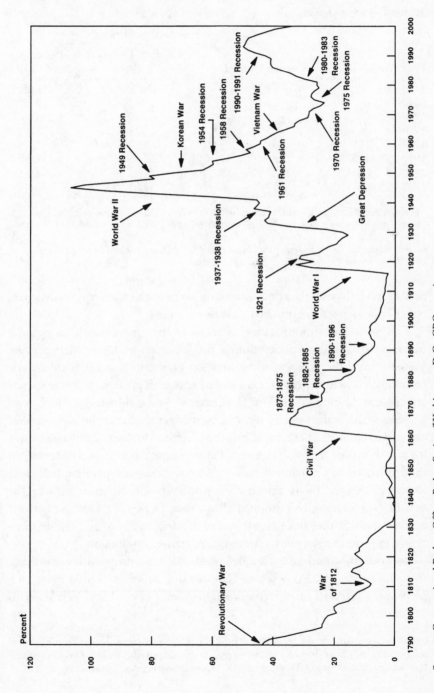

Source: Congressional Budget Office, *Budget Options* (Washington, D.C.: CBO, 2001), 14.

Table 1.1 Budget Deficits, 1930–1999 (in billions of dollars)

| | | Annual Average Deficits* | |
Fiscal Years	Current Dollars	Constant Dollars (FY 1996)	Percentage of GDP
1930–39 (9)	$ 2.1	N/A	3.0%
1940–49 (7)	17.8	149.1	9.7
1950–59 (7)	1.8	10.0	0.4
1960–69 (8)	5.7	26.7	0.8
1970–79 (10)	35.1	91.7	2.1
1980–89 (10)	156.5	221.5	3.9
1990–94 (5)	247.9	274.3	4.0
1995–99 (3)	19.9	22.3	0.3

* For each decade, these figures are average net deficits (i.e., deficits minus surpluses). The numbers in parentheses for each fiscal period are the annual deficits in each period.

SOURCE: *Historical Tables, Budget of the United States Government, Fiscal Year 2002* (Washington, D.C.: Government Printing Office, 2001), 23, 25–26.

deficits fell following the administration's tax cuts, this more aggressive fiscal policy approach was legitimized, at least for a time.

The second and more lasting element of the 1960s transition was the reshaping of spending policy during the Johnson presidency. Despite the Vietnam War, the Johnson administration pursued an ambitious domestic policy agenda, and the result was a sharp break with previous wartime spending patterns. During World War II, defense spending absorbed as much as 90 percent of the budget, while the defense budget share for the Korean War climbed to almost 70 percent. When the Vietnam War began, defense spending was still more than 40 percent of federal outlays, but the wartime peak in the late 1960s was not much higher, because domestic spending had risen along with defense. By the time the Vietnam War officially ended in 1973, the defense budget share had dropped to just over 30 percent. Defense budgets declined even further through the end of the decade, but total spending continued to grow in response to domestic program commitments.

Between 1965 and 1980, the defense-GDP ratio dropped by one-third, from 7.4 percent to 4.9 percent. Total outlays, however, soared from 17.2 percent of GDP to 21.6 percent, the highest level since World War II. With

---

rate of economic growth, and temporary deficits stemming from a tax program designed to promote a fuller use of our resources and more rapid economic growth." *Budget of the United States Government, Fiscal Year 1964* (Washington, D.C.: Government Printing Office, 1963), 10–11.

Table 1.2 Budget Deficits vs. Structural Deficits, 1981–1989 (in billions of dollars and percentage of GDP)

Fiscal Year	In Current Dollars (Billions)		As a Percentage of GDP	
	Budget Deficit	Structural Deficit	Budget Deficit	Structural Deficit
1981	$−79	$−17	−2.6%	−0.5%
1982	−128	−52	−4.0	−1.5
1983	−208	−120	−6.0	−3.3
1984	−185	−144	−4.8	−3.7
1985	−212	−177	−5.1	−4.2
1986	−221	−212	−5.0	−4.8
1987	−150	−155	−3.2	−3.3
1988	−155	−127	−3.1	−2.5
1989	−152	−115	−2.8	−2.1

SOURCE: Congressional Budget Office, *The Budget and Economic Outlook: Fiscal Years 2002–2011* (Washington, D.C.: CBO, 2001), 139.

revenue levels lagging well behind, deficits grew rapidly during the 1970s and even more rapidly during the 1980s. Under Ronald Reagan, annual deficits averaged almost 4 percent of GDP.

Moreover, the deficits that took hold during this period were "structural"—had the economy been at optimum levels of growth and employment, the spending and tax laws in place would still have yielded deficits. Structural deficits for the 1980s were generally lower than actual deficits, but the structural deficit "policy gap" between spending and revenues was still extremely large (Table 1.2). Efforts to reduce these deficits were frustrated by sharp differences between the Reagan administration and Congress over spending and tax policy. While both sides endorsed the balanced-budget rule, there was no consensus on the level of federal spending at which the budget should be balanced.

The Spending Problem. The impasse over budget policy that emerged during the 1970s and deepened under Reagan was directly related to the changes that had occurred in the composition of spending. The shift in the spending side of the budget began with the social welfare initiatives of the Johnson presidency and accelerated with their expansion during the 1970s. From the end of World War II through the early 1960s, defense and nondefense discretionary spending—that is, spending determined by the annual appropriations process—accounted for about two-thirds of the budget. The remainder consisted of mandatory spending for social welfare programs and interest

Table 1.3 Outlays by Major Spending Category, 1965–1990 (as a percentage of GDP)

Fiscal Year	Discretionary		Mandatory		Offsetting Receipts	Total Outlays
	Defense	Nondefense	Entitlements	Net Interest		
1965	7.4%	3.9%	5.8%	1.2%	−1.1%	17.2%
1970	8.1	3.8	7.2	1.4	−1.1	19.3
1975	5.6	4.5	10.9	1.5	−1.2	21.3
1980	4.9	5.2	10.7	1.9	−1.1	21.6
1985	6.1	3.9	10.8	3.1	−1.1	22.9
1990	5.2	3.5	10.9	3.2	−1.0	21.8

SOURCE: Congressional Budget Office, *The Budget and Economic Outlook: Fiscal Years 2002-2011* (Washington, D.C.: CBO, 2001), 147, 149.

payments on the federal debt.[8] By the 1980s, the budget shares for discretionary and mandatory spending had been nearly reversed (Table 1.3).

Retirement and healthcare entitlements accounted for much of this change. In 1960, Social Security outlays were less than 2.5 percent of GDP. Two decades later, Social Security along with the Medicare and Medicaid programs enacted in 1965 had risen to 6 percent of GDP. These and other social welfare expansions more than offset the modest decline in discretionary spending levels during this period. During the 1970s, for example, the defense-GDP ratio dropped by more than three percentage points, but nearly half of this reduction was absorbed by higher spending for discretionary domestic programs. Under Ronald Reagan, the latter were cut back, but defense levels rose. In effect, Congress was unwilling to restrain domestic spending during the 1970s; Reagan was equally unwilling to cut defense, and he was unable to reverse the growth of major entitlements. The result was the highest spending levels since World War II.

The Revenue Problem. During World War II, when spending was almost 45 percent of GDP and the political barriers against high taxes were weak, revenues were only marginally higher than 20 percent of GDP. After the war, revenue levels fell and, in contrast to spending, remained within a narrow range (Table 1.4). In addition, the composition of revenues shifted toward direct taxes over the postwar period. In 1950, about one-half of total revenue was produced by individual income taxes and social insurance taxes (primarily

8. The classification of spending into discretionary and mandatory categories was part of the Budget Enforcement Act of 1990 and is now used in executive branch and congressional budgeting. Mandatory spending is based on budget authority from laws other than annual appropriations acts. Its largest components are various entitlement programs and net interest on the public debt.

Table 1.4 Revenues, 1950–1989 (as a percentage of GDP)

Fiscal Years	Annual Average Percentage of GDP
1950–59	17.2%
1960–69	17.8
1970–79	17.9
1980–89	18.3

SOURCE: *Historical Tables, Budget of the United States Government, Fiscal Year 2002* (Washington, D.C.: Government Printing Office, 2001), 23–24.

payroll taxes for Social Security). By the 1980s, this share had grown to approximately 80 percent, making it more difficult to raise revenue levels without imposing higher tax burdens on individuals.

The Reagan administration's tax program was directed toward lowering, not raising, tax burdens on individuals. The 1981 tax cut that the administration sponsored contained large reductions in income tax rates, and the 1986 Tax Reform Act cut marginal rates still further. When deficits soared after the 1981 tax cut, Reagan signed tax bills that boosted corporation income taxes and payroll taxes, but he adamantly opposed efforts to raise tax rates on individuals.

The revenue levels in place during the 1980s were only slightly above those of prior decades, but spending levels were substantially higher. The yawning gap between the two could not be narrowed without a significant increase in the federal government's largest revenue source, individual income taxes, and these increases were unacceptable to Ronald Reagan.

Modern Deficits: Solutions

The severity of structural deficits led many observers, including leading scholars, to conclude that the modern deficit problem was intractable. Numerous studies argued that the defining features of contemporary American politics—divided party control, congressional decentralization, ubiquitous and powerful interest groups—and the constitutional separation of powers between the president and Congress posed formidable, perhaps insuperable, barriers to effective fiscal control.[9] A 1996 study concluded that

9. The literature here is vast. For a summary of the basic arguments, see William R. Keech, *Economic Politics* (New York: Cambridge University Press, 1995), chap. 7.

institutional limitations and expansive policy commitments had undermined the federal government's ability "to pursue coherent and rational [fiscal] objectives," resulting in "a rising trend in deficit spending that shows no signs of abating."[10]

Even more sweeping indictments questioned whether modern budgets should "be left adrift in the sea of democratic politics."[11] For some critics, the answer to this dilemma was amending the Constitution to prohibit deficits except during wartime or recession. By restricting the options for deficit financing, a constitutional balanced-budget rule would force the public and its representatives "to take account of the costs of government as well as the benefits, and to do so simultaneously."[12] While various balanced-budget amendments had been introduced in Congress for decades, the fiscal problems of the 1980s and early 1990s served to intensify support for a constitutional change. In 1995, when Republicans gained control of the House and Senate, their constitutional balanced-budget proposal was a top legislative priority, and Congress failed by the narrowest of margins to send the amendment to the states for ratification.

The debate over a constitutional remedy soon lost its urgency, when it became apparent that policy changes during the early 1990s were moving the budget toward balance more quickly and decisively than anyone had expected. In 1990, President George H. Bush had broken the long-standing partisan deadlock over deficit reduction by signing a multiyear package of tax increases and defense cutbacks. Unlike Reagan, Bush finally accepted the necessity for higher taxes on individuals and substantially higher revenue levels in narrowing structural deficits. On the spending side, the end of the Cold War had allowed Bush to make important concessions on defense. Then, in 1993, the Clinton administration had persuaded Congress to pass another five-year deficit-reduction package of tax increases and spending cuts.

Both the Bush and Clinton budget agreements contained tight limits on discretionary spending and complementary deficit-reduction controls on entitlements and revenues. Policy changes, multiyear enforcement provi-

---

10. G. Calvin Mackenzie and Saranna Thornton, *Bucking the Deficit: Economic Policymaking in America* (Boulder, Colo.: Westview Press, 1996), 162, 144.

11. James M. Buchanan and Richard E. Wagner, *Democracy in Deficit* (New York: Academic Press, 1977), 175.

12. Buchanan and Wagner, *Democracy in Deficit*, 11. For a discussion of a constitutional rule limiting spending, see Dennis S. Ippolito, *Congressional Spending* (Ithaca: Cornell University Press, 1981), chap. 11.

Table 1.5 Components of Deficit Reduction, 1990–2000 (in billions of dollars and percentage of GDP)

FY 1990 = −$221			FY 2000 = +$236		
Revenues	= 18.0%	GDP	Revenues	= 20.6%	GDP
Outlays	= 21.8%		Outlays	= 18.2%	
Deficit	= −3.9%		Surplus	= +2.4%	

	FY 1990	FY 2000	Change
Revenues	18.0% GDP	20.6% GDP	+2.6% GDP
Individual	8.1	10.2	(+2.1)
Corporation	1.6	2.1	(+0.5)
Payroll	6.6	6.6	(+0.0)
Other	1.6	1.6	(+0.0)
Outlays	21.8%	18.2%	−3.6%
Discretionary Defense	5.2	3.0	(−2.2)
Discretionary Nondefense	3.5	3.3	(−0.2)
Mandatory Programmatic	9.9	10.5	(+0.6)
Deposit Insurance	1.0	0.0	(−1.0)
Net Interest	<u>3.2</u>	<u>2.3</u>	<u>(−0.9)</u>
	22.8	19.1	−3.7
Offsetting Receipts	<u>−1.0</u>	<u>−0.8</u>	<u>+0.2</u>
	21.8	18.2	−3.6

Source: Congressional Budget Office, *The Budget and Economic Outlook: Fiscal Years 2002–2011* (Washington, D.C.: CBO, 2001), 142–51.

sions, and an unexpectedly strong economy moved the budget into surplus in 1998. Two years later, the surplus exceeded $235 billion. As shown in Table 1.5, the structural deficit problem was solved by two basic policy adjustments. First, revenue levels were raised substantially between 1990 and 2000, with more than 80 percent of this revenue growth supplied by individual income taxes. Second, discretionary spending fell by 2.4 percent of GDP, with more than 90 percent of this reduction in defense. Defense cuts, the elimination of deposit insurance outlays that had funded savings and loans insolvencies in the early 1990s, and interest savings from lower debt levels combined to bring the outlay-GDP ratio to its lowest level in more than three decades.

It took time, then, for the causes and consequences of the modern deficit problem to be fully understood. Policymakers then needed additional time, and different circumstances, to implement the policy changes and budgetary controls that altered spending and revenue growth rates. The combination of Cold War defense requirements and social welfare state commitments had created very powerful spending pressures, and this spending dynamic had to be broken to control and finally eliminate structural deficits.

The deficit problem of the post-Vietnam period was caused by basic political disagreements over spending and tax policy. Similar disagreements over the appropriate level of taxation and the balance between defense and nondefense spending have resurfaced since 2001. President George W. Bush's $1.35 trillion tax cut in 2001 was aimed at lowering revenue levels and thereby limiting spending growth. The war on terrorism that was launched after the September 11 attacks on the United States has sharply increased defense budgets. As projected surpluses give way to deficits, the Bush administration and Congress must struggle once again to reconcile the desire for balanced budgets with the political pressures of modern budget policy.

Cross-National Comparisons

An additional perspective on budget policy and budget control in the United States is provided by past and future fiscal trends in other democracies. During the past century, the relative size of government has increased in all of the industrialized democracies, and, since the 1960s, the composition of their spending has shifted toward social welfare entitlements. [13]Moreover, this latter shift has caused similar structural deficit problems. A critique of U.S. fiscal policy during the 1980s attributed the explosive growth of deficits to "intellectual error of the first magnitude . . . [or] deliberate moral irresponsibility on a truly astonishing scale."[14] This condemnation, however, ignored the fact that deficits in the United States were not isolated events. Other industrialized democracies were encountering deficit-control problems of comparable severity and for similar reasons: "The fiscal deficits of the 1980s were rooted in decisions made in the 1960s and 1970s to create and enlarge public programs. Governments . . . increased spending under the presumption that the high economic growth rates of the 1950s and 1960s would continue. By the time economic growth rates slowed in the mid-1970s, many of these programs were entrenched."[15]

13. See Vito Tanzi and Ludger Schuknecht, *Public Spending in the 20th Century: A Global Perspective* (Cambridge: Cambridge University Press, 2000), 30–45.

14. Benjamin M. Friedman, *Day of Reckoning: The Consequences of American Economic Policy Under Reagan and After* (New York: Random House, 1988), 24.

15. General Accounting Office, *Deficit Reduction: Experiences of Other Nations* (Washington, D.C.: GAO, 1994), 28.

These entrenched programs, in the United States and elsewhere, "involved social welfare commitments."[16] New benefit programs had been established, existing ones had been expanded, and automatic benefit adjustments, such as indexing, had been introduced at a time when budgetary projections were optimistic. When economic growth began to slow and deficits appeared, it was widely assumed that the imbalances were temporary and would not require major fiscal adjustments. By the time governments recognized that budgetary problems were more severe, they "found themselves overcommitted and facing even larger deficits."[17]

The expansion of government budgets in the industrialized democracies paralleled spending trends in the United States. Traditional or "defining" programs, such as defense, diminished in terms of relative importance, while social welfare programs proliferated in number and rose sharply in cost.[18] For a time, these cost increases were financed through budgetary growth and transfers from other sectors of the budget, such as defense. When growth slowed and the margin for transfers narrowed, governments were confronted with "a structural budgetary fault . . . [caused by] demands that cannot be reduced and supplies of revenue that cannot be raised sufficiently to satisfy them."[19]

By the early 1980s, all of the Group of Seven (G-7) countries had deficits (Fig. 1.2). Over the next fifteen years, virtually all of the larger group of developed countries included in the Organisation for Economic Co-Operation and Development (OECD) faced chronic and, in some cases sizable, structural imbalances. From 1980 to 1995, structural deficits for the OECD countries averaged approximately 3 percent of potential GDP annually; structural deficits in the United States over this period were at or below the OECD average.[20] Then, by the late 1990s, fiscal consolidation efforts in the United States and in most industrialized democracies had either eased or reversed structural imbalances.[21]

The trend in public debt levels in the United States was also part of a broader pattern. After World War II, the publicly-held federal debt-GDP

16. General Accounting Office, *Deficit Reduction*, 28.

17. General Accounting Office, *Deficit Reduction*, 30.

18. See Tanzi and Schuknecht, *Public Spending in the 20th Century*, chap. 2.

19. Webber and Wildavsky, *A History of Taxation and Expenditure in the Western World*, 493.

20. These data include total government spending and revenues—that is, government at state or regional and local levels, as well as the national level. Congressional Budget Office, *The Economic and Budget Outlook: Fiscal Years 1997–2006* (Washington, D.C.: CBO, 1996), 108–9.

21. Tanzi and Schuknecht, *Public Spending in the 20th Century*, 63–64.

Fig. 1.2 Total Government Surplus or Deficit in the G-7 Nations, 1982–1998 (as a percentage of GDP)

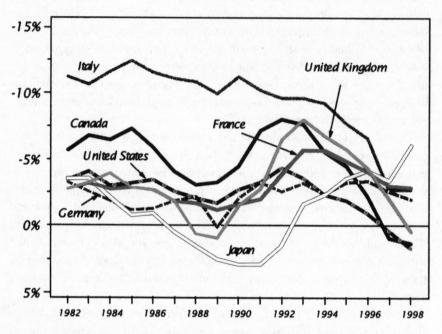

SOURCE: *A Citizen's Guide to the Federal Budget, Fiscal Year 2001* (Washington, D.C.: Government Printing Office, 2000), 24.

ratio dropped by more than three-fourths before stabilizing during the 1970s and then rising during the 1980s and 1990s. By the mid-1990s, publicly-held debt was nearly 50 percent of GDP. Rising debt-GDP ratios similarly afflicted other countries beginning in the 1970s. By 1995, the average OECD gross public debt was over 70 percent of GDP, and net debt was close to 50 percent.[22]

These cross-national comparisons reflect the substantial convergence in the fiscal problems faced by the advanced democracies. These countries have long-established and costly social welfare systems that enjoy strong public support, and the programs that provide retirement and health benefits across virtually the entire population are the most entrenched. Past rates of growth in these programs have been unusually high, making it necessary

22. Organisation for Economic Co-Operation and Development (OECD), *Reforms for an Ageing Society* (Paris: OECD, 2000), 33–35.

for governments to create new macrobudgetary rules to achieve fiscal consolidation. Under the Maastricht Treaty, for example, European Union members must comply with budgetary limits on deficits and debt. While other financial criteria must be satisfied as well, "deficit and debt targets clearly have taken center stage in recent European politics."[23] In the United States, macrobudgetary rules have been even more restrictive in terms of spending controls and tax policy changes. This common effort to strengthen fiscal discipline "suggests the critical role of budgeting and public administration in contemporary international affairs, as well as what might be called the internationalization of budgeting."[24]

There is also a prospective dimension to this internationalization of budgeting. Funding requirements for social welfare systems will intensify over the next few decades because of demographic trends. Population aging, caused by the confluence of longer life expectancy and low birth rates, means there will be fewer and fewer workers to support a growing number of beneficiaries. In the face of "these relentless pressures on public finance," governments will be forced to consider additional fiscal reforms.[25]

Similar budget policy problems among the industrialized democracies have produced similar fiscal policy strategies, with budget planning geared to structural-deficit control and to debt-to-GDP ratios that can be sustained indefinitely. Neither of these fiscal goals can be achieved in the future without social welfare retrenchments that, given demographic patterns, extend over many decades, but the necessity for long-term budget discipline creates an obvious dilemma for democratically elected governments having limited political tenure. The European Union has attempted to provide some electoral protection for its member governments by setting uniform limits on deficits and debt. The United States will be attempting to exercise much the same discipline without a fixed standard, albeit with less severe demographic pressures and a narrower social welfare system.

The Budget Process and Centralization

The framers of the Constitution conferred on Congress the powers to tax, spend, and borrow. One of the persistent problems that Congress has faced

23. James D. Savage, "Budgetary Collective Action Problems: Convergence and Compliance Under the Maastricht Treaty on European Union," *Public Administration Review* 61 (January/February 2001): 43.

24. Savage, "Budgetary Collective Action Problems," 51.

25. OECD, *Reforms for an Ageing Society*, 33.

in exercising its "power of the purse" is how to organize the budget process to protect its institutional prerogatives, while producing acceptable fiscal outcomes. In the modern era, Congress has faced the additional difficulty of controlling large spending programs that operate outside the regular appropriations process. An effective budget process must be congruent, in terms of procedural controls, with the types of spending programs and revenue policies that drive the budget. For the past few decades, this requirement has led Congress to centralize its internal procedures and to rely on macrobudgetary rules and controls. The result is a budget process that is extremely complex and time-consuming and often depends heavily on presidential direction.

Microbudgeting and Incrementalism

During the early history of the United States, there were no formal mechanisms in Congress for coordinating spending and revenues nor, until 1921, was there a presidential budget. Yet, as Wildavsky explains, "Calculations were made, conflict diffused, and . . . budgets were passed on time while revenues and expenditures stayed within hailing distance."[26] This microbudgeting, or bottom-up, approach allocated spending to individual programs and agencies without the need for overall totals, because there was "widespread agreement on the norms of balance and comprehensiveness."[27] The former rested on a "de facto spending limit," while the latter meant that "neither substantial revenues nor expenditures were outside the purview of the political authorities for ratcheting up or down."[28]

Whereas much of the historical literature on classical budgeting stresses the effectiveness of incrementalist, decentralized decision making, the reality was more complex. Wartime financing presented serious problems throughout the nineteenth century, forcing Congress to cede authority to the executive branch and especially the Secretary of the Treasury. The requirement that wartime debt be quickly retired also meant centralized controls were required for spending, with the post–Civil War Appropriations Committees providing a model reform of this type. In addition, balanced budgets did not

26. Aaron Wildavsky, *The New Politics of the Budgetary Process* (Glenview, Ill.: Scott, Foresman, 1988), 424.

27. Wildavsky, *The New Politics of the Budgetary Process.* For an explanation of the theoretical differences between micro- and macrobudgeting, see Roy T. Myers, *Strategic Budgeting* (Ann Arbor: University of Michigan Press, 1994), 10–12.

28. Wildavsky, *The New Politics of the Budgetary Process,* 424.

guarantee financial stability. Federal credit and debt management, for example, often created financial dislocations, because Congress could not adequately coordinate fiscal and monetary policy.

Perhaps the key element in classical budgeting, however, was the limited scope of federal spending. With the exception of interest on the debt, most spending during the nineteenth and early twentieth centuries was what we now classify as discretionary. The locus of control was the annual appropriations process, which allowed Congress to enforce spending discipline as needed. Moreover, since state and local governments were responsible for many of the largest and fastest-growing spending programs during this period, Congress was not confronted by relentless pressures to spend.

Macrobudgeting and Coordination

The decline of incrementalism as both a descriptive and prescriptive norm for budgeting can be attributed to a variety of economic and political changes that have made budget policy less stable and consensual. The changing composition of spending policy, however, has clearly had an enormous impact on the perceived need for centralization and coordination in the budgetary process. As mandatory social welfare entitlements displaced discretionary spending as the largest share of the federal budget, the congressional appropriations process could not effectively control either spending totals or spending growth. A parallel decline affected presidential budgets, since the president's leverage over mandatory spending was limited.

These new forms of spending commitments necessitated the implementation of macrobudgetary rules and procedures. Since the 1970s, both Congress and the executive branch have worked to make budgets more comprehensive, predictable, and controllable through enforceable, multiyear limits on spending and through formal coordination of spending and revenue levels. The federal budgetary process is now highly centralized, allowing Congress and the president to negotiate multiyear budget agreements and to use expedited legislative processes to implement those agreements.

Budget Reform

The balanced-budget principle in American politics is not self-enforcing. A degree of centralized control has always been necessary to balance spending demands against one another and to keep them in line with available revenues. Periodic attempts to reform the budget process have therefore been directed toward centralizing spending authority within the House and Senate and, in the twentieth century, with providing fiscal policy coordination through presidential budgets.

Budget reform efforts have typically been spurred by deficit and debt concerns. Until recently, these concerns were tied to wartime debts, with the Civil War, World War I, and World War II being followed by congressional budget process reforms that met with varying degrees of success. The deficit and debt problems that surfaced more recently were different in terms of causes and severity, and the corresponding reform efforts were more complex and comprehensive than in the past. In particular, the 1974 Congressional Budget and Impoundment Control Act mandated annual legislative budgets that governed both spending and revenue levels. Prior congressional reforms had focused on spending, notably appropriations bills, rather than on formal coordination of spending and revenue decisions.

The major reforms of the budget process have a shared emphasis on centralization. The difficulty has been in designing reforms that would protect the legislative power of the purse against executive encroachments and would resolve budget policy problems, such as excessive spending, inadequate revenues, or persistent deficits and growing debt. Institutional arrangements are a complicating feature in federal budget control, and concerns have been raised about the institutional costs to Congress of centralization. A leading constitutional scholar has argued that the 1974 Budget Act has compromised congressional accountability to the public and increased Congress' vulnerability to presidential leverage.[29] Since it is likely that even more centralized and comprehensive fiscal controls will be proposed to deal with future entitlement financing pressures, these concerns about constitutional prerogatives and institutional balance will need to be addressed in budget reform debates.

The Politics of Budget Policy

The budget represents a crucial set of political decisions. Much of what we consider politically important—what the government does, who decides what it does, and who benefits from it—can be translated into the financial language of budget policy. The chapters that follow trace the evolution of budget policy from the nation's founding through the modern era, and the

29. Louis Fisher, *Congressional Abdication on War and Spending* (College Station: Texas A&M University Press, 2000), 173–84.

purpose of this historical analysis is to document the growth of government over time and to explore the factors that have shaped that growth.

The central debate about the appropriate size of government is not an abstract argument. Rather, this debate involves competing ideas about what the federal government should do in terms of its spending commitments and the tax policies to support that spending. The size of government debate also involves competing ideas about deficits, debt, and the importance of balanced budgets. Today, for example, it is generally accepted that governments cannot, indeed should not, balance budgets during major wars or recessions. At other times, however, the crucial question is whether budgets should be balanced at high or low spending levels. Battles over balanced budgets, today as in the past, are battles over the size and shape of budgets. The size and shape of budgets, in turn, define the role of the federal government in carrying out its constitutional powers to tax, spend, and borrow to "provide for the common Defence and general Welfare of the United States."

☆ ☆

THE "SMALL GOVERNMENT" ERA

(1789–1860)

Most historical analyses of budget policy agree that "until a few decades ago the federal budget was viewed mainly in terms of money costs. Governmental activities were widely thought to be a burden. . . . A balanced federal budget was believed to be a prerequisite for financial stability and economic growth."[1] Nevertheless, important conflicts over spending policy, deficits, and debt can be traced to the earliest days of the Republic, when financial controls and budgetary procedures were first implemented.

From 1789 to 1860, there was general acceptance of the balanced-budget rule, but this rule was not entirely straightforward. National emergencies, notably war, could make deficits unavoidable. It was expected, however, that the federal debt accumulated under such circumstances would then be retired through budgeted surpluses. The federal debt from the Revolutionary War and the War of 1812, for example, was entirely paid off by the mid-1830s, although a dozen deficits over the next twenty-five years created a nearly $65 million federal debt before the Civil War began.

In addition, the balanced-budget rule during this era was aimed chiefly at the federal government by opponents of national power. Alexander Hamilton,

1. Lewis H. Kimmel, *Federal Budget and Fiscal Policy, 1789–1958* (Washington, D.C.: Brookings Institution, 1959), 1.

the nation's first Secretary of the Treasury, defended the federal government's right to borrow and accumulate debt as a way to bolster its legitimacy and credibility. Hamilton was committed to using the powers to tax, spend, and borrow as expansively as possible, not simply as a hedge against wartime exigencies but to strengthen and develop the American economy.[2] For Hamilton's chief opponent, Thomas Jefferson, federal borrowing and debt were a threat to limited government and a prescription for political and social inequality. State deficits and debt, however, were viewed very differently by Jefferson and his followers. This double standard was a reflection of the Jeffersonians' attachment to state powers, and their political ascendancy after the 1790s meant that the balanced-budget rule was directed toward limiting the size and role of the federal government.

The strength of fiscal discipline in the pre–Civil War period can easily be exaggerated, since there was no "unified, orthodox 'balanced budget' mentality applying to all levels of government."[3] Moreover, the balancing of federal spending and revenue levels did not require inordinate political sacrifices. The burden of financing internal improvements fell largely on the states, which limited spending pressures on the federal government. In addition, the federal government's revenues were chiefly supplied by indirect taxes, primarily tariffs. Raising additional revenues through higher tariffs had substantial political benefits in terms of protection for domestic interests.

This unusual juxtaposition of spending and revenue policy also undercut efforts to develop an executive budget or to centralize controls in Congress. The budget process in Congress was concerned with details of expenditure rather than the direction of budget policy. Congressional distrust of the executive branch made it impossible to assign that responsibility to the president. Under normal conditions, this fragmented and uncoordinated system produced acceptable outcomes, but it caused serious problems during wartime and economic crises.

National Debt and Centralization

"Our present Constitution," declared a nineteenth-century financial historian, "owes its origins to the financial embarrassments of the Government

2. See John Steele Gordon, *Hamilton's Blessing* (New York: Wallace and Company, 1997), 22–41.

3. James D. Savage, *Balanced Budgets and American Politics* (Ithaca: Cornell University Press, 1988), 106.

formed under the Articles of Confederation."[4] The Revolutionary War was financed largely through borrowing, and the Confederation Congress found itself unable to service its debt.[5] It lacked the authority to impose taxes directly or to compel the states to raise revenues on its behalf. The Congress itself "was a feeble institution from its inception—especially on the financial side—[and] by the mid-1780's it was rapidly approaching complete impotency."[6] The much broader financial powers that the Constitutional Convention subsequently conferred on the federal government were directly related to this initial experiment with borrowing and debt.

The Revolutionary War Debt

For nearly a century, colonial governments had issued paper currency to meet wartime and other financial exigencies and also to facilitate trade.[7] Gold and silver specie supplies were inadequate for these purposes, while taxing powers were very limited and actual tax collections slow and unwieldy. Therefore, the governments in the colonies created various forms of paper currency, including bills of credit and loan bills. Since these currencies were rarely secured, severe depreciations in value were common. By the time the Revolutionary War began, the Continental Congress almost immediately found itself relying on paper currency as well.

The "Continental" dollars issued during the Revolutionary War held their value for only a short time. By 1777, the trading value of paper currency to specie was 1.25 to 1, but during 1779 paper's value dropped precipitously, falling to 30 to 1 by the end of the year.[8] Two years later, the ratio was 167.5 to 1. Similar declines in the value of paper currencies also affected the state governments. One alternative to paper currency financing was taxation, but the Continental Congress had no power to tax, and the state governments typically lacked the means and the will to impose taxes of any significance.

4. John Watts Kearny, *Sketch of American Finances, 1789–1835* (New York: G. P. Putnam's Sons, 1887), 1.

5. The sale of public lands would eventually be used to pay off wartime debt, but there were immediate needs for revenues to pay interest and to refinance expiring debt. See E. James Ferguson, *The Power of the Purse: A History of American Public Finance, 1776–1790* (Chapel Hill: University of North Carolina Press, 1961), 221.

6. Kimmel, *Federal Budget and Fiscal Policy, 1789–1958*, 2.

7. On colonial finance, see Davis Rich Dewey, *Financial History of the United States*, 6th ed. (New York: Longmans, Green and Co., 1918), 1–32.

8. Donald R. Stabile and Jeffrey A. Cantor, *The Public Debt of the United States* (New York: Praeger, 1991), 13.

Attempts by Congress to force the states to levy taxes through formal requisitions were unsuccessful. Of an estimated $95 million in requisitions apportioned among the states from 1777 to 1779, less than $13 million was paid, and the specie value of the payments was less than $1 million.[9]

As a consequence, the Continental Congress turned to borrowing. The first substantial authorization for borrowing took place at the end of 1776, with $5 million in domestic loan certificates placed with loan-office commissioners in the states.[10] When this initial issue was not fully subscribed, interest rates were raised, but again the supply of domestic credit outstripped the demand. In 1777, however, Congress received the first of a series of loans and subsidies from the French government. During the next several years, loans from France, Holland, and Spain totaled nearly $8 million.[11]

The management and servicing of this growing debt proved troublesome throughout the war. The Continental Congress experimented with a variety of committees, offices, and boards to administer the government's financial affairs, but none of these worked especially well, in large part because Congress refused to delegate to them the necessary independent authority. In 1780, interest payments on a portion of the existing debt were suspended. Congress was finally forced in 1781 to establish a Department of Finance, headed by Robert Morris, and to confer on Morris broad authority to establish a coherent system of financial administration. Under Morris, the collection of state requisitions was improved and the use of specie payments expanded. Centralized controls were instituted for revenues and expenditures, and annual treasury reports were prepared. Morris also persuaded Congress to charter the Bank of North America, which proved extremely useful in providing short-term loans to the government and in lending greater flexibility to treasury operations.

Of necessity, Morris concentrated much of his effort on restoring the central government's credit. On January 1, 1783, the total public debt was estimated at $43 million—$7.9 foreign-held and $35.1 domestic.[12] Interest payments on nearly one-third of the latter were past due by two years.[13] While Morris was able to stabilize government credit through creative use of the Bank of North America and his own resources, the improvements

9. Ferguson, *The Power of the Purse*, 34.
10. Dewey, *Financial History of the United States*, 46.
11. Dewey, *Financial History of the United States*, 47.
12. Ferguson, *The Power of the Purse*, 136–37.
13. Stabile and Cantor, *The Public Debt of the United States*, 14.

were only temporary. To meet the mounting requirements for scheduled interest and principal payments, the government needed predictable sources of revenue. But the Confederation Congress, like its predecessor, could not raise revenue independent of the states, nor could it compel the states to raise revenues on its behalf.

Under the Articles of Confederation, Congress was authorized to spend "for the common defence or general welfare" and permitted to borrow money and issue bills of credit.[14] The Articles specified, however, that "[a]ll charges of war, and all other expences" were to be "defrayed out of a common treasury, which shall be supplied by the several states, in proportion to the value of all land within each state." The taxes necessary to pay for these apportionments, however, were to be "laid and levied by the authority and direction of the legislatures of the several states." The Confederation "instrument for national government," concluded Davis Rich Dewey, "brought little succor to the treasury."[15] When states failed to cooperate, as they routinely did, Congress had no recourse.

The difficulty of enforcing requisitions, or apportionments, on the states plagued the Confederation Congress. On October 31, 1781, an $8 million annual requisition was imposed on the states. Two years later, less than $1.5 million had been paid, with most states having satisfied only a small part of their apportionment and several having contributed nothing at all.[16] In 1784, the Confederation Congress appointed a "Grand Committee," headed by Thomas Jefferson, to devise a plan for state requisitions that would cover interest payments on the debt.[17] Jefferson's committee recommended that the original state requisitions be reduced to encourage compliance, and Congress agreed to cut delinquent obligations by one-half. But most states still refused to meet their obligations. From 1781 to 1786, Congress actually received only $2.4 million of the $15.7 million in outstanding state requisitions.[18] Complicating these problems were the substantial debts that the

14. Henry Steele Commager, ed., *Documents of American History*, 6th ed. (New York: Appleton-Century-Crofts, 1958), 113.

15. Dewey, *Financial History of the United States*, 49.

16. Calvin Jillson and Rick K. Wilson, *Congressional Dynamics: Structure, Coordination, and Choice in the First American Congress, 1774–1789* (Stanford: Stanford University Press, 1994), 262.

17. Grand committees were "open to all members of the Congress, though only members of Congress appointed to such a committee could debate and vote in it." The appointed members included one member from each state, and state delegations were responsible for nominating their representatives. Jillson and Wilson, *Congressional Dynamics*, 58, 98.

18. Savage, *Balanced Budgets and American Politics*, 72–73.

states had themselves incurred during the war, amounts that were estimated at more than $20 million.[19] In response to these financial pressures, a number of states had begun to issue large amounts of their own paper currency, thereby exacerbating the problems with money and credit.

The Tariff Battle

Since state requisitions could not be relied on, Robert Morris, along with others seeking to strengthen the central government, pressed Congress to impose a national tariff or other national tax. Under Article IX of the Articles of Confederation, however, the states alone had the power to levy tariffs: "The united states in congress assembled, shall have the sole and exclusive right and power of . . . entering into treaties and alliances, provided that no treaty of commerce shall be made whereby the legislative power of the respective states shall be restrained from imposing such imposts and duties on foreigners, as their own people are subjected to, or from prohibiting the exportation or importation of any species of goods or commodities whatsoever."[20]

In 1781, Congress approved a 5 percent import duty to be collected by federally appointed officers, but the unanimous consent of the state legislatures was necessary for what was, in effect, a constitutional amendment. Rhode Island blocked this effort, objecting to what it claimed was the disproportionate burden on commercial states and to the appointment of collection officers not responsible to the state governments. Other proposals by Morris for federal revenues included a land tax, a poll tax, and an excise tax on liquor, none of which was approved by Congress.

In 1783, Congress revived the national tariff plan, seeking to make it more acceptable to the states by restricting its coverage to certain types of goods, limiting its duration to a maximum of twenty-five years, and pledging all revenues exclusively to interest and principal payments on the federal debt.[21] In a further concession to the states, state officials rather than federal officers were to be responsible for collecting the tariff, an abrogation of national authority that Morris and his allies believed was especially unwise. Congress approved this compromise plan, but the requirement for unanimous agreement by the states again proved insurmountable. In 1786, three years after Congress had acted, four states were still opposed. While three of

19. Dewey, *Financial History of the United States*, 56.
20. Commager, *Documents of American History*, 113.
21. Dewey, *Financial History of the United States*, 50–51.

these eventually yielded, New York's continued objections and reservations kept the tariff plan from going into effect.

Lacking dependable sources of revenue, Congress could not meet its obligations. The domestic debt created severe financial pressures that threatened economic stability. Widespread speculation in debt instruments, currency devaluation, and inflationary pressures continually buffeted the states. The national government faced the collapse of its foreign credit.[22] In 1785, interest payments on the debt to the French government were suspended, followed two years later by a formal default on principal repayments. Loans from Dutch financiers and banks were refinanced in 1786 and 1787, permitting the continuation of interest payments, but the prospects for avoiding default on scheduled principal installments were grim. There was a special urgency connected to the credit problems with Holland, since "it was feared that the Dutch would retaliate in case of default by seizure of American ships."[23]

The postwar debt that the national government confronted was estimated at nearly $40 million, while the wartime and other debts incurred by the states totaled an additional $21 million (Table 2.1). The interest on the national government's foreign and domestic debt was estimated at more than $1.8 million in 1784, well above the state requisitions that Congress managed to collect.[24] As interest payments were suspended or missed, the size of the outstanding debt grew accordingly. Between 1783 and 1789, the principal of the foreign and domestic debt rose by less than $2 million, but arrears in interest increased by nearly $10 million.[25]

When Robert Morris became Superintendent of Finance, he wrote that the "political existence of America" depended on "permanent revenues sufficient to discharge the interest of our public debt. . . . A public debt, supported by public revenue, will prove the strongest cement to keep our Confederacy together."[26] For Morris and others in the emerging Federalist movement, the failure of the tariff and other national tax initiatives during the Confederation period represented more than a temporary setback in efficient debt

22. Ferguson, The Power of the Purse, 234–38.
23. Ferguson, The Power of the Purse, 235.
24. Dewey, Financial History of the United States, 56.
25. Dewey, Financial History of the United States, 57.
26. Letter of Robert Morris to Nathaniel Appleton, April 16, 1782. Francis Wharton, ed., The Revolutionary Diplomatic Correspondence of the United States (Washington, D.C.: Government Printing Office, 1889), 5:311.

Table 2.1 Estimated National and State Debts, 1784

National:	
Foreign Loans (principal and arrears of interest)	$ 7,921,886
Loan Office Certificates	11,585,000
Unliquidated Certificates of Indebtedness	16,708,000
Domestic Debt Arrears of Interest	3,109,000
Total	$39,323,886
State:	
Wartime Debt	18,271,787
Other	2,728,213
Total	$21,000,000

SOURCE: Davis Rich Dewey, *Financial History of the United States*, 6th ed. (New York: Longmans, Green and Co., 1918), 56.

financing. The political weakness of the national government was so serious, in their view, that constitutional reform was necessary. Moreover, the key to successful reform was the centralization of fiscal powers in the national government—spending, taxation, borrowing, and coinage.

From this perspective, the wartime debt could facilitate political and economic development, if the lessons of the Confederation period were properly learned and applied. When the war had begun, Thomas Paine had written, "No nation ought to be without a debt. A national debt is a national bond."[27] After the war had been successfully fought, the bond holding the states together began to weaken, and the infirmities of the Confederation Congress further eroded the ties between the states and the national government. Indeed, some members of Congress were prepared to distribute the national debt among the states, a move that probably would have fractured the union. Instead, the financial chaos being fueled by the debt was converted into a powerful argument for centralization. If all wartime debts, national and state, could be consolidated in the central government, the political loyalties and economic interests of creditors and property owners might be transferred as well. And with a consolidated debt, the rationale for enlarged federal power would become much stronger, since there would be "an economic motive for supporting the central government . . . [that] justified the demand for federal taxes."[28]

27. Thomas Paine, *Basic Writings of Thomas Paine: Common Sense, Rights of Man, Age of Reason* (New York: Willey Book Co., 1942), 44.
28. Ferguson, *The Power of the Purse*, 143.

Constitutional Revision

The weaknesses of the Confederation Congress extended beyond fiscal matters. The central government lacked adequate powers to ensure the nation's security against foreign attack, while trade and commercial regulation were chaotic in the absence of uniform national rules. The Confederation could not resolve political disputes between the states, nor could it respond effectively to rebellions and uprisings within the states. Time and time again, the Confederation Congress found itself stymied, unable to act decisively even within the narrow confines of its authority. And on those rare occasions when Congress was able to settle on a course of action, it could not easily impose its will on the states. Finally, Congress authorized a meeting in Philadelphia in May 1787 to consider revisions in the Articles.

In presenting the Virginia Plan to the Constitutional Convention on May 29, 1787, Edmund Randolph explained that the Confederation had been drafted "in the then infancy of the science, of constitutions, and of confederacies."[29] At that time, declared Randolph, "[T]he inefficiency of requisitions was unknown—no commercial discord had arisen among any states—no rebellion had appeared as in Massachusetts—foreign debts had not become urgent—the havoc of paper money had not been foreseen—treaties had not been violated—and perhaps nothing better could be obtained from the jealousy of the states with regard to their sovereignty."[30] Later that day, Alexander Hamilton observed that the Virginia Plan and its accompanying critique of the Articles of Confederation posed the inescapable question of "whether the united states were susceptible of one government, or required a separate existence connected only by leagues offensive and defensive and treaties of commerce."[31]

For Hamilton and other committed proponents of "one government," the states ultimately would have to yield the sovereignty they enjoyed under the Articles. As Hamilton later described this "melancholy situation" in *The Federalist* 15: "While [the states] admit that the government of the United States is destitute of energy, they contend against conferring upon it those powers which are requisite to supply that energy. They seem still to aim at things repugnant and irreconcilable; at an augmentation of federal authority

29. Max Farrand, ed., *The Records of the Federal Convention of 1787* (New Haven: Yale University Press, 1911), 1:18.

30. Farrand, *The Records of the Federal Convention of 1787*, 1:18–19.

31. Farrand, *The Records of the Federal Convention of 1787*, 1:27.

without a diminution of State authority; at sovereignty in the Union and complete independence in the members."[32] Hamilton was especially insistent on national fiscal powers, principally taxation, which would substantially reduce the independence of the states. The national government, he asserted, needed a "complete power . . . to procure a regular and adequate supply of revenue."[33] Its power to spend should be equally generous, extending beyond the direct support of the military to the "support of the national civil list; for the payments of the national debts contracted, or that may be contracted; and, in general, for all those matters which call for disbursements out of the national treasury." The Convention's decisions about the national government's fiscal powers were among its more radical departures from past practice and understandings. There were, in the end, few restrictions on the powers to tax, to borrow, and to spend.

Taxation

Since the Confederation Congress lacked authority to impose tariffs and enforce requisitions, the Convention could simply have remedied these deficiencies. The New Jersey Plan, submitted to the Convention on June 14, 1787, proposed a modest revision of the Articles of Confederation that would confer on Congress authority to levy stamp taxes and "a duty or duties on all goods or merchandizes of foreign growth or manufacture imported into any part of the U. States . . . [and] to make rules and regulations for the collection thereof."[34] If requisitions became necessary, Congress could apportion them based on population and, if any states did not cooperate, could "direct the collection thereof in the noncomplying states and for that purpose to devise and pass acts authorizing the same."[35] As John Lansing, a New York delegate who favored the New Jersey Plan, pointed out, the New Jersey and Virginia Plans presented the Convention with "two systems . . . fairly contrasted. The one now offered is on the basis of amending the federal government, and the other to be reported as a national government, on propositions which exclude the propriety of amendment."[36] Gouverneur Morris, on the other side of the debate, stressed this same distinction between a federal and a national government: the former a

---

32. Hamilton, Madison, and Jay, *The Federalist Papers*, 107–8.
33. Hamilton, Madison, and Jay, *The Federalist Papers*, 188.
34. Farrand, *The Records of the Federal Convention of 1787*, 1:243.
35. Farrand, *The Records of the Federal Convention of 1787*, 1:243.
36. Farrand, *The Records of the Federal Convention of 1787*, 1:246.

"mere compact resting on the good faith of the parties; the latter having a compleat and *comprehensive* operation."[37]

Although most delegates apparently shared Hamilton's view that "indirect taxes . . . must for a long time constitute the chief part of the revenue raised in this country," there were strong objections to his further assertion that the "federal government must of necessity be invested with an unqualified power of taxation in the ordinary modes."[38] Hamilton admitted that indirect taxes might suffice during peacetime but claimed they might prove grossly inadequate during "the very first war in which we should happen to be engaged."[39] The likely result, he predicted, would be "the destruction of public credit at the very moment that it was becoming essential to the public safety."[40]

The Convention agreed, in the end, to grant the federal government authority to impose and collect both indirect and direct taxes. To preclude discriminatory legislation against particular regions or states, indirect taxes were to be uniform throughout the United States, and export taxes were prohibited. Still, these checks were relatively minor, and the primacy of national commercial regulation and tariff powers was protected by forbidding the states to levy any taxes on imports or exports without congressional consent.

On direct taxing powers, the Convention was more divided, and the constitutional language more ambiguous. Whether and how slaves were to be counted was the subject of an intense and extended debate over the apportionment of seats in the House of Representatives. According to James Madison's notes, Gouverneur Morris had suggested the "proportioning of direct taxation to representation," a compromise that eventually proved acceptable to the slave-holding states and the free states.[41] This solution, however, precluded direct taxation based on wealth, a restriction that concerned Morris and that he later sought, albeit unsuccessfully, to eliminate.[42] Since indirect taxes were expected to provide the bulk of federal revenues for the foreseeable future, the lack of clarity regarding direct taxation and its illogical method of apportionment did not immediately create serious problems. When revenue demands eventually necessitated substantial direct taxation, however, these constitutional constraints had to be removed.

37. Farrand, *The Records of the Federal Convention of 1787*, 1:34.
38. Hamilton, Madison, and Jay, *The Federalist Papers*, 143, 195.
39. Hamilton, Madison, and Jay, *The Federalist Papers*, 191.
40. Hamilton, Madison, and Jay, *The Federalist Papers*, 192.
41. Farrand, *The Records of the Federal Convention of 1787*, 2:106.
42. Farrand, *The Records of the Federal Convention of 1787*, 2:106.

Another important compromise on taxation was the requirement that the House originate revenue bills. In addition to following English precedent, according to which the House of Commons had the sole authority to originate money bills, House origination provided the larger states with a counterweight to the Senate's powers over treaties, appointments, and the trying of impeachments. Language that would have prevented the Senate from amending House-passed revenue bills was adopted but later dropped. Nevertheless, the power to originate revenue measures buttressed the House's fiscal influence as the new Congress was developing its internal dynamics and organization.

Under the proposed Constitution, federal taxing powers were neither complete nor exclusive but were nonetheless superior to those of the states. Indirect taxes could be levied and collected by the central government, while the states could not tax imports or exports without congressional consent. Thus, federal power predominated with respect to the primary source of revenue at the time. It also extended to direct taxation if and when that became necessary. Each of these provisions was attacked by the Constitution's opponents in state ratifying conventions: "Every state which subjoined amendments to its ratification of the Constitution proposed that federal revenues be restricted to indirect taxes, that additional sums be raised by requisitions, and that federal collection of direct taxes be permitted only in case of default."[43] When the first Congress proposed amendments to the states, however, none of these revenue restrictions was included.

Borrowing

The constitutional language on borrowing and credit was another victory for the Federalists. The Convention conferred on Congress the power "to borrow money on the credit of the United States," an authority "well-nigh complete; there is no limitation as to time, manner, place, amount, security, payment, or interest."[44] The Convention did not approve an express grant of authority to issue bills of credit, but neither did it include a prohibition against bills of credit in the proposed Constitution. This ambiguity in effect permitted the federal government to finance deficits with paper money. By comparison, the framers of the Constitution made state borrowing much

43. Ferguson, *The Power of the Purse*, 291.
44. Dewey, *Financial History of the United States*, 67.

more difficult. The states were barred from issuing bills of credit, from coin-
ing money, and from allowing debts to be paid in anything but gold and silver
specie. Under the Articles of Confederation, the states had used these options
to finance deficits and debt. The Constitution not only withdrew these
options, but made the prohibition absolute.

The Constitution established, quite deliberately, a federal borrowing
authority in accord with Hamilton's principle that "[a] government ought to
contain in itself every power requisite to the full accomplishment of the
objects committed to its care, and to the complete execution of the trusts for
which it is responsible."[45] In response, both the New York and Rhode Island
ratifying conventions called for a constitutional amendment requiring two-
thirds majorities in the House and Senate to authorize any federal borrowing.[46] Neither this proposal nor efforts to restore the states' powers to issue
bills of credit made any progress in the first Congress. The federal government enjoyed, as a result, an unfettered borrowing authority and an independent power of taxation to support borrowing. The Antifederalists believed,
with good reason, that this concentration of fiscal powers amounted to a
fundamental and perhaps irreversible transfer of political authority, but their
efforts to weaken or curb these powers proved futile.

Spending

The Convention's decisions defining the scope and exercise of the federal
spending power were dealt with rather routinely when compared with the
debates on taxation and borrowing. Congress was authorized to spend to
"provide for the common defence and general Welfare of the United States."
Under the Articles of Confederation, the authorization had been similar.
The crucial distinction between the two was not the scope of the spending
power, but the independent authority of taxation or borrowing to support
spending. Since the federal government could raise revenues as needed, the
"general welfare" clause proved to be enormously elastic. Although there
have been repeated conflicts over the constitutionality of appropriated spending for purposes not enumerated in the Constitution, beginning with the
disputes over the national bank and internal improvements early in the nineteenth century, a decidedly broad construction of congressional powers has
prevailed.

45. Hamilton, Madison, and Jay, *The Federalist Papers*, 194.
46. Savage, *Balanced Budgets and American Politics*, 83.

The Convention never seriously considered anything but a legislative power of the purse. A formal presidential role in the budgetary process, beyond the power to veto revenue and appropriations legislation, is a comparatively recent statutory creation. The framers saw the power of the purse as "the core legislative process—underpinning all other legislative decisions and regulating the balance of influence between the legislative and executive branches of government."[47] The question with which they struggled was whether to grant the House superior or even exclusive power over appropriations. Early drafts of the Constitution provided that all bills "apportioning money . . . shall originate in the first branch of the legislature and shall not be altered or amended by the second branch; and that no money shall be drawn from the public treasury, but in pursuance of appropriations to be originated in the first branch."[48] These restrictions on the Senate were eventually removed, but the House soon established the precedent of originating all appropriations bills.

Because the fiscal defects of the Confederation were so glaring, the framers of the Constitution were understandably eager to establish a government free of these incapacities. With the Constitution conferring on the national government very broad powers to tax, spend, and borrow, the checks on its fiscal powers were essentially political. Accordingly, federal financial policy under the Federalist majority in power for the Constitution's first decade was very different from policy under the Republican majority that succeeded it.

Federalist "High Finance"—1789–1801

Alexander Hamilton's tenure as Secretary of the Treasury lasted from 1789 to 1795, but his influence over federal financial administration has been enduring. Hamilton's two reports on the public credit defined how the government would fund and service debt. His "Report on a National Bank" established the first central bank in U.S. history and validated a liberal interpretation of federal powers under the Constitution. Other reports, dealing with manufactures and with national mint and coinage issues, prescribed an active federal role in promoting economic stability and development.

47. Richard F. Fenno Jr., *The Power of the Purse: Appropriations Politics in Congress* (Boston: Little, Brown and Company, 1966), xiii.

48. Farrand, *The Records of the Federal Convention of 1787*, 1:523.

Hamilton's vision of fiscal policy was an aggressive one, managing borrowing and debt so that the public credit would be "immortal."[49] Hamilton argued as well for the centralization of fiscal authority—in the federal government as opposed to the states and in the executive branch rather than the legislature. His financial strategy, while successful for a time, also spurred Thomas Jefferson and James Madison to build an opposition party that displaced the Federalist majority and instituted a very different financial program.

The Hamilton Program: Debt

The Treasury Department was established on September 2, 1789. Hamilton was appointed Secretary shortly thereafter and, on January 19, 1790, submitted to the House of Representatives his famous "Report Relative to a Provision for the Support of Public Credit." Article VI of the Constitution provided that "All Debts contracted and Engagements entered into, before the Adoption of this Constitution, shall be as valid against the United States under this Constitution, as under the Confederation." Hamilton's plan for fulfilling this obligation included two extremely controversial provisions: first, that the federal domestic debt, like the foreign-held debt, would be honored at its original or par value, and, second, that the federal government would assume the wartime debts incurred by the states.

For years, there had been widespread speculation in various federal debt instruments, with old bonds eventually trading at a fraction of their original value. Madison and others in the House objected to Hamilton's redemption scheme, arguing that it would provide unconscionable profits to speculators, while in effect punishing those who had initially purchased bonds at full value and then been unable to hold their securities through the travails of the Confederation. Madison insisted there be discrimination between original and current holders of debt; original holders would receive par value, but others would be compensated according to prevailing market value rather than the considerably higher face value of the debt they held. Hamilton maintained that such discrimination was impractical and would inevitably impair the free trading of government debt securities on which a sound system of public credit was based. Hamilton wanted to ensure that the federal government would be able to borrow to meet any future emergencies and

49. Albert S. Bolles, *The Financial History of the United States from 1789 to 1860*, 2d ed. (New York: D. Appleton and Company, 1885), 179.

could do so at favorable rates. Then, as now, potential creditors would take into account the risk of lending to the federal government as they calculated their necessary return, so that the unquestioned repayment of debt had to be ensured.

Hamilton's arguments against discrimination were endorsed by a heavy majority in the House, but a more protracted and divisive quarrel broke out over his recommendation that the federal government assume the wartime debts incurred by the states. Here again, heavy speculation had created opportunities for substantial profits if state debts were treated in the same way as federal debt. In addition, some states, notably Virginia, had already redeemed much of their wartime debt and were not anxious to assume the collective burden of assisting those states whose fiscal affairs were in disarray.

The practical advantages of federal assumption were, in Hamilton's view, complemented by an even weightier political benefit. The legitimacy and authority of the federal government would be greatly strengthened "by rendering all the creditors of the several States dependent on the Union."[50] These creditors were the "prosperous men of business, commerce, and agriculture—the oligarchs. . . . Although they had largely supported the creation of the new Union, Hamilton had every reason to suppose that their support would quickly fade away if their self-interest dictated it."[51] With Madison once more leading the opposition in the House, federal assumption of state debts was voted down several times. The measure was finally passed on August 4, 1790, but only after Madison and Jefferson secured Hamilton's support for moving the capital from New York City to the Potomac. The new location of the capital was, for many Southern members of the House, a prize that overcame their scruples about federal assumption.

The consolidated debt the federal government had assumed amounted to nearly $80 million (Table 2.2). Estimated interest on this debt was nearly $4.6 million annually.[52] These debt and interest obligations posed what Hamilton termed an "interesting problem."[53] It might be possible for the government to fund the debt as scheduled and to fund at the same time the "current service of the government," but this approach "would require the extension of taxation to a degree, and to objects, which the true interest of

50. Bolles, *The Financial History of the United from 1789 to 1860*, 39.

51. Gordon, *Hamilton's Blessing*, 30.

52. Jacob E. Cooke, ed., *The Reports of Alexander Hamilton* (New York: Harper & Row, 1964), 21–22.

53. Cooke, *The Reports of Alexander Hamilton*, 22.

Table 2.2 Consolidated Debt of the United States, 1790

Foreign Debt:	Principal	$ 10,070,307.00
	Arrears of Interest	1,640,071.62
		11,710,378.62
Domestic Debt:	Principal	27,383,917.74
	Arrears of Interest	13,030,168.20
		40,414,085.94
Continental Bills of Credit (estimated)		2,000,000.00
Public Debt of the States (estimated)		25,000,000.00
	Total Debt	$ 79,124,464.56

SOURCE: Jacob E. Cooke, ed., *The Reports of Alexander Hamilton* (New York: Harper & Row, 1964), 19–21.

the public creditors forbids." Furthermore, there were those unanticipated exigencies that "may, ere long, arise, which would call for resources greatly beyond what is now deemed sufficient for the current service." The answer to this problem, stated Hamilton, was to renegotiate the debt "into such a shape, as will bring the expenditure of the nation to a level with its income. 'Til this shall be accomplished, the finances of the United States will never wear a proper countenance."[54] The funding plan he designed contained new borrowing in the form of bonds, with varying maturities and interest rates, which would allow the Treasury to reschedule interest payments on a manageable, long-term basis.

With new securities authorized and quickly subscribed, immediate interest obligations were greatly reduced, but to ensure that these obligations would be met, and to enhance the attractiveness of federal securities, Congress incorporated into the funding acts of 1790 dedicated revenues from tariffs and other duties. The first funding act directed that revenues in excess of a specified sum for current expenses be "pledged and appropriated for the payment of the interest on the stock issued by the government."[55] Furthermore, any proceeds from Western land sales were also assigned to debt redemption. The second funding act provided that "all surplus revenue should be applied to the purchase of the debt of the United States, 'at its market-price, if not exceeding the par or true value thereof.'"[56] Interest on redeemed debt held by

54. Cooke, *The Reports of Alexander Hamilton*, 31.
55. Bolles, *The Financial History of the United States from 1789 to 1860*, 43.
56. Bolles, *The Financial History of the United States from 1789 to 1860*, 43.

the government and any surpluses on sums appropriated for interest payments were also dedicated to retiring debt. The pledging of revenues to debt service and management, or sinking-fund approach, was followed in all but one of the many funding acts enacted during Hamilton's tenure.[57]

The Bank of the United States

Hamilton's financial program assigned great importance to a national bank. The particular institution he proposed was a private bank, modeled on the Bank of England, to be operated under a federal charter. The federal government would own a portion of the bank's capital stock and would have limited supervisory powers over its operations. The benefits of a properly designed central bank were, in Hamilton's view, economic and political. Credit and liquidity for commercial purposes would be improved, as would regulation of the money supply through a national paper currency. The government could use the bank as a secure depository for its funds and, more important, as a source of ready credit when necessary. In his "Opinion on the Constitutionality of the Bank," Hamilton stated:

> A Bank has a direct relation to the power of borrowing money, because it is an unusual and in sudden emergencies an essential instrument in the obtaining of loans to the government. A nation is threatened with war. Large sums are wanted, on a sudden, to make the requisite preparations. Taxes are laid for the purpose, but it requires time to obtain the benefit of them. Anticipation is indispensable. If there be a bank, the supply can, at once be had; if there be none loans from Individuals must be sought. The progress of these is often too slow for the exigency: in some situations they are not practicable at all.[58]

A central bank would also buttress the authority of the federal government, as Hamilton's opponents well understood. Within Congress, Madison led the fight against legislation authorizing a federal charter for the bank, attacking its constitutionality and its potential for facilitating excessive government borrowing. Congressional passage, however, was easily secured, albeit on a heavily sectional vote, and the battle then shifted to the Washington administration's cabinet. Jefferson, President George Washington's Secretary of

57. Bolles, *The Financial History of the United States from 1789 to 1860*, 179.
58. Cooke, *The Reports of Alexander Hamilton*, 105.

State, and Attorney General Edmund Randolph submitted written opinions calling for a presidential veto of the bank legislation based on constitutional objections. The federal government's enumerated powers, they contended, provided no express authorization for a national bank, and a proper construction of the "necessary and proper clause" disallowed any federal action not strictly and directly related to the exercise of an enumerated power.

Hamilton's response was an aggressive defense of the "necessity and propriety of exercising the authorities intrusted to a government on principles of liberal construction."[59] Implied powers should be judged, in terms of constitutionality, according to one fundamental criterion: "If the end be clearly comprehended within any of the specified powers, and if the measure have an obvious relation to that end, and is not forbidden by any particular provision of the constitution—it may safely be deemed to come within the compass of the national authority."[60] The immediate struggle for President Washington's support was won by Hamilton, as was the more important long-term contest over constitutional interpretation. The Bank itself remained a contentious issue for several decades, even though its initial performance clearly evidenced the practical advantages Hamilton had claimed on its behalf.

Executive Authority

The financial system that Hamilton erected was characterized by another form of centralization—strong executive authority. When Congress established the Treasury Department in 1789, it recognized that the sorry record of treasury boards and commissions under the Continental and Confederation Congresses could best be cured by a single secretary. Nevertheless, Congress was reluctant to confer broad fiscal powers on the Treasury secretary and the executive branch. Thus, the secretary would "prepare" rather than "report" plans "for the improvement and management of the revenue."[61] Financial information and budget estimates from other executive departments were to "be made directly to the treasury department without going to the president," and then submitted without revision to Congress.[62] This directive did not entirely preclude presidential intervention but did

---

59. Cooke, *The Reports of Alexander Hamilton*, 90.
60. Cooke, *The Reports of Alexander Hamilton*, 91.
61. On the establishment of the Treasury Department, see Louis Fisher, *Presidential Spending Power* (Princeton: Princeton University Press, 1975), 10–13.
62. Dewey, *Financial History of the United States*, 86.

"place the responsibility of the budget upon Congress instead of upon the executive as in European countries."[63]

Under Hamilton, these attempts to circumscribe executive powers were largely ineffective. Hamilton's spending estimates, for example, were organized into several very general, or lump-sum, appropriations that conferred wide latitude on Treasury and other executive officials in the expenditure of funds. The transfer of unexpended appropriations was commonplace, and, in 1793, the president was granted authority "to borrow money in anticipation of the revenue."[64] On occasion, the treasury warrants required for the expenditure of funds were ignored as were the requirements for advance appropriations.[65] In addition, Hamilton's financial reports to Congress were neither regular nor systematic.

Hamilton's domineering approach led Congress to curb executive spending discretion through increasingly specific, or line-item, appropriations. Anther counterweight was specialized committees. In 1789, the House had established a Ways and Means Committee to handle fiscal matters, but the committee lasted only one session. When Republicans gained control of the House in 1795, Albert Gallatin was able to revive Ways and Means by decrying "the existing bias in favor of increasing as far as possible the power of the Executive branch."[66] The buttressing of congressional authority through line-item spending bills and organized expertise was the ostensible goal of Hamilton's Republican critics, but their real target was Hamilton's record on deficits and debt.

Debt Retirement

Under Hamilton and his successor, Oliver Wolcott, the Federalist era of high finance yielded higher budgets, periodic deficits, and increased debt (Table 2.3). From 1789 to 1801, the single largest expenditure each year was interest on the public debt, and over the entire period interest represented nearly one-half of total outlays.[67] But expenditures for the Army and Navy, which accounted for less than 15 percent of spending from 1789 to 1791,

63. Dewey, *Financial History of the United States*, 87.

64. Bolles, *The Financial History of the United States from 1789 to 1860*, 183.

65. Bolles, *The Financial History of the United States from 1789 to 1860*, 185.

66. Henry Adams, *The Life of Albert Gallatin* (New York: Peter Smith, 1943), 157. The Ways and Means Committee was officially designated as a permanent, or standing, committee in 1802.

67. *Historical Statistics of the United States, Colonial Times to 1970, Part 2* (Washington, D.C.: U.S. Bureau of the Census, 1975), 1114–15.

Table 2.3 Federal Budget Totals, 1789–1801 (in thousands of dollars)

Fiscal Year	Total Revenues	Total Outlays	Deficit (−) /Surplus	Debt
1789–91	$ 4,419	$ 4,269	$ 150	$ 77,228
1792	3,670	5,080	−1,410	80,359
1793	4,653	4,482	171	78,427
1794	5,432	6,991	−1,559	80,748
1795	6,115	7,540	−1,425	83,762
1796	8,378	5,727	2,651	82,064
1797	8,689	6,134	2,555	79,229
1798	7,900	7,677	224	78,409
1799	7,547	9,666	−2,120	82,976
1800	10,849	10,786	63	83,038
1801	12,935	9,395	3,541	80,713

SOURCE: *Historical Statistics of the United States, Colonial Times to 1970, Part 2* (Washington, D.C.: U.S. Bureau of the Census, 1975), 1104.

rose sharply in response to a series of military challenges—Indian wars, the Whiskey Rebellion, Algerine pirates, and strained relations with England and, especially, France. In 1794 and 1795, expenditures for the Army averaged more than $2.5 million. From 1798 to 1800, outlays again averaged more than $2 million, with Congress authorizing a standing army of 50,000 men. The Department of the Navy, which had essentially no funding in 1792, absorbed $3.4 million of the $10.8 million budget in 1800.

With such pressing spending demands for interest and defense, Hamilton and the Federalist Party were able to enact a sweeping program of federal taxation. The first tariff bill was passed by Congress in 1789 before the Treasury Department was established, but Hamilton subsequently persuaded Congress to increase import duties and to impose excise taxes as well. There was strong opposition to excises in general and to whiskey taxes in particular, but, with Hamilton continually pressing for additional revenues, excises were extended to a wide range of commodities. In 1796, proposals were introduced in Congress to levy direct taxes in the event that customs duties were interrupted by the growing turmoil in Europe. In 1798, with military expenditures growing, a direct tax of $2 million was apportioned among the states, with levies on houses, land, and slaves.[68] Throughout this period, customs duties were, as expected, the primary source of federal revenue, providing

68. Dall W. Forsythe, *Taxation and Political Change in the Young Nation, 1781–1833* (New York: Columbia University Press, 1977), 53.

almost 90 percent of total receipts, but tariff policy extended beyond revenue needs to protectionism for American industries. Hamilton's 1791 "Report on Manufactures" was a comprehensive assessment of existing and potential industrial capabilities, with proposals for developing these capabilities through government assistance. Tariff protections were strongly advocated, and many of Hamilton's specific recommendations were adopted in tariff bills.

The spending and tax initiatives of the Federalist-dominated 1790s demonstrated how budget policy could be directed toward political and economic goals. Restoring public credit required that the federal government tax and borrow to service its own debt. The assumption of state debts made the financial problem considerably larger but provided a rationale for exercising federal revenue powers aggressively. The federal government, wrote Hamilton, should "lay hold" of the excise "before it was generally preoccupied by the State governments."[69] Federal authority over internal taxation should be exercised quickly and decisively, before the states could "beget an impression that it was never to be exercised, and next, that it ought not be exercised."[70] Moreover, a sound system of centralized financial administration, promoting economic development and growth, would establish support for the federal government among those influential segments of the population whose economic interests were being served.

The Republican critique of the Federalist policy pointedly targeted this expansive interpretation of the authority and role of the federal government. When the Jefferson administration took office in 1801, it substituted a much narrower fiscal approach to the federal budget, emphasizing the negative effects of deficits and debt to force cutbacks in federal power. The Republican ascendancy of the next several decades yielded numerous surplus budgets and, for a brief time, a nation free from debt. It also produced a good deal of chaos and confusion in fiscal policies, as well as an enormous amount of what would now be termed "hidden spending."

Republican Vacillation

Thomas Jefferson's first inaugural message called for "a wise and frugal Government . . . [which] shall leave [people] otherwise free to regulate their own

69. Letter of Alexander Hamilton to George Washington, August 18, 1792. John C. Hamilton, ed., *The Works of Alexander Hamilton* (New York: Charles S. Francis and Company, 1851), 4:256.

70. Hamilton, *The Works of Alexander Hamilton*, 4:256.

pursuits of industry and improvement, and shall not take from the mouth of labor the bread it has earned."[71] The chief fiscal goal of the Jefferson administration was the elimination of deficits and debt, and Secretary of the Treasury Albert Gallatin designed a budget program to achieve this goal through spending cuts, heavily tilted toward the military, and reductions in internal taxes. The Jefferson administration succeeded in retiring a large portion of the debt it had inherited, and, although substantial borrowing took place during the War of 1812, the debt was entirely retired in the mid-1830s. Wartime spending and economic dislocations over the next quarter century then raised the total—if not the relative size of the debt—close to pre-Jefferson levels.

The extraordinary significance assigned to the balanced-budget principle during the early 1800s owes a great deal to the Jeffersonian notion that deficits and debt were corrupting influences. Corruption in this sense went beyond mere thievery or bribery; it signified the "political decay eating away at the foundations of republican and parliamentary governments, with England serving as the prime example of a corrupt state."[72] From this perspective, republicanism and debt were antithetical; the fear was that "speculators, bankers, and the moneyed aristocracy would benefit from the unearned financial leverage and profits derived by financing the national debt, [and] the government would spend its added revenues by promoting an industrialized economy through Hamiltonian policies that resembled those of mercantilist and corrupted England."[73]

Despite these concerns, Jeffersonians were not opposed to having state governments borrow, which they did, or to providing federal subsidies to the states in the form of land grants, or to maintaining protective tariffs. In addition, Jeffersonian fiscal policy in practice was not nearly as restrictive as Jefferson's earlier arguments about balanced budgets and limited government suggest. His oft-cited letter to John Taylor in 1798 seemed unequivocal: "I wish it were possible to obtain a single amendment to our constitution. I would be willing to depend on that alone for the reduction . . . of our government to the genuine principles of it's [*sic*] constitution; I mean an additional article, taking from the federal government the power of borrowing."[74] By his second inaugural, however, Jefferson endorsed a broader vision of

71. James D. Richardson, ed., *A Compilation of the Messages and Papers of the Presidents* (New York: Bureau of National Literature, 1917), 1:311.

72. Savage, *Balanced Budgets and American Politics*, 93.

73. Savage, *Balanced Budgets and American Politics*, 95.

74. Quoted in Savage, *Balanced Budgets and American Politics*, 106.

Table 2.4 Federal Budget Totals, 1801–1809 (in millions of dollars)

Fiscal Year	Total Revenues	Total Outlays	Deficit (−) /Surplus	Debt
1801	$ 12.9	$ 9.4	$ 3.5	$ 80.7
1802	15.0	7.9	7.1	77.1
1803	11.1	7.9	3.2	86.4
1804	11.8	8.7	3.1	82.3
1805	13.6	10.5	3.1	75.7
1806	15.6	9.8	5.8	69.2
1807	16.4	8.4	8.0	65.2
1808	17.1	9.9	7.1	57.0
1809	7.8	10.3	−2.5	53.2

SOURCE: *Historical Statistics of the United States, Colonial Times to 1970, Part 2* (Washington, D.C.: U.S. Bureau of the Census, 1975), 1104.

what the federal government could accomplish: "[R]edemption once effected, the revenues thereby liberated may, by a just repartition among the States and a corresponding amendment of the Constitution, be applied *in time of peace* to rivers, canals, roads, arts, manufactures, education, and other great objects within each State."[75]

Jefferson and Gallatin

Under the Federalists, federal spending had more than doubled, reaching a peak of nearly $11 million in 1800. The Jefferson administration proceeded to cut spending by nearly 20 percent in its first two years. While expenditures then began to increase, total spending was usually well below $10 million annually. Since customs duties continued to grow until the ill-fated Embargo of 1807, Gallatin was able to apportion substantial sums toward debt retirement. Only one deficit, in 1809, interrupted a series of very large surpluses that reduced the total public debt by more than one-third (Table 2.4). This reduction was accomplished despite the more than $11 million in new long-term borrowing for the Louisiana Purchase. By 1808, Treasury reserves were nearly $14 million, compared to $3 million in 1801.[76]

Gallatin's fiscal program depended on systematic budgeting and control over estimates. Like Hamilton, Gallatin wielded considerable influence over budget policy, but he provided Congress with more detailed spending infor-

75. Richardson, *A Compilation of the Messages and Papers of the Presidents*, 1:367.
76. Forsythe, *Taxation and Political Change in the Young Nation, 1781–1833*, 57.

mation. Gallatin's efforts were not entirely successful, since Congress and some executive departments at times undercut the controls Gallatin sought to impose. In 1802, Gallatin's proposals for sharply reducing military spending were rebuffed by Congress, which then proceeded to repeal excise taxes without adjusting spending levels.[77] Only an unexpected surge in customs duties kept the budget from going into deficit. Then, as the war with the Barbary States became more costly, Congress was forced to raise customs duties to supply additional revenues. Despite Gallatin's insistence on specific, line-item appropriations, enforcement was haphazard. The Treasury Department "adhered rigidly to the law, [but] the Departments of State, War, and Navy could not or did not so adhere."[78] The War and Navy Departments were also able to exceed their appropriations by circumventing the statutory controls on unexpended balances.[79]

In 1803, Jefferson impounded funds that Congress had appropriated for Navy gunboats, but this action was only temporary. The next year, after studying "the most recent models of gunboats," Jefferson notified Congress that the program was proceeding.[80] Several years later, Jefferson recommended to Congress that two hundred gunboats be built, roughly triple the number Gallatin had proposed and considerably more than many Navy officers believed were necessary.[81] Jefferson also ignored Gallatin's warnings about the budgetary impact, and efficacy, of the 1807 embargo.[82] The comparatively stable aggregate spending budgets during the Jefferson administration were somewhat misleading. Between 1801 and 1809, interest payments on the debt dropped by more than one-third, to $2.9 million. Total spending rose by less than $1 million over this eight-year period, but, given the reduction in interest, military and civilian expenditures actually grew by almost 50 percent, to more than $7.4 million in 1809.

A related and intriguing development of the Jefferson years concerned federal aid for internal improvements. In 1802, Congress pledged a portion of the proceeds from the sale of public lands in the newly admitted state of Ohio to the building of public roads. This legislation set the stage for the

---

77. Bolles, *The Financial History of the United States from 1789 to 1860*, 206–7.

78. Arthur Smithies, *The Budgetary Process in the United States* (New York: McGraw-Hill, 1955), 54.

79. Smithies, *The Budgetary Process in the United States*, 54.

80. See Fisher, *Presidential Spending Power*, 150.

81. Bolles, *The Financial History of the United States from 1789 to 1860*, 211.

82. Bolles, *The Financial History of the United States from 1789 to 1860*, 212.

Cumberland Road project, which cost an estimated $2.5 million over the next twenty-five years, and for other road-building programs in states and territories.[83] When the Treasury Department reported that its debt-reduction program might soon free up "a considerable portion of the revenue now appropriated for [debt service]," the administration determined that the surplus should be diverted to other purposes.[84] Jefferson recommended that the Constitution be amended to permit federal spending for internal improvements "within each state."[85] Gallatin prepared plans for a $20 million federal appropriation to establish a permanent revolving fund to build roads and canals.[86]

These ambitions were soon eclipsed by the specter of war during Jefferson's second term. As the United States found itself embroiled in the conflict between France and England, optimism about budget surpluses evaporated. In 1807, Gallatin informed Congress that "should the United States, contrary to their expectation and desire, be involved in a war, . . . receipts of the year 1808 will not be materially affected."[87] He warned, however, that the "revenue of the United States will, in subsequent years, be considerably impaired" and that "resources . . . should be selected for supplying the deficiency and defraying the extraordinary expenses."[88] He proposed that borrowing be used for extraordinary war expenses but that taxes be raised to finance nonwar expenditures and the interest on new and old debt.[89] There was little opposition to increased borrowing and additional debt, but Congress resisted for a long and dangerous time the war taxes needed to secure that debt.

The fiscal record of the Jefferson presidency is more complex than the small-government, balanced-budget model suggests. The deficit reduction that was achieved involved little or no sacrifice. The comprehensive tax system that the Federalists had put into place provided such abundant revenues that their Republican successors were able to eliminate internal taxes and still register large surpluses. They could do so, moreover, even though the strict economies in civil and military expenditures Gallatin had initially proposed were not realized.

83. Dewey, *Financial History of the United States*, 212–13.

84. Adams, *The Life of Albert Gallatin*, 348.

85. Richardson, *A Compilation of the Messages and Papers of the Presidents*, 1:367.

86. Bolles, *The Financial History of the United States from 1789 to 1860*, 210.

87. *Reports of the Secretary of the Treasury of the United States* (Washington, D.C.: Government Printing Office, 1828), 1:359.

88. *Reports of the Secretary of the Treasury of the United States*, 1:360.

89. Henry C. Adams, *Public Debts: An Essay in the Science of Finance* (New York: D. Appleton and Company, 1887), 112–13.

The sinking-fund mechanism that Gallatin put into place in 1802 used permanent appropriations to accelerate debt retirement in accordance with Jeffersonian rhetoric concerning the evils of debt finance. Still, the administration's ambitious plan for federal domestic programs and its willingness to amend the Constitution suggest that the commitment to "frugal government" was less than wholehearted. Finally, the growth in non-interest spending during the Jefferson presidency shows how difficult it was, and is, to maintain spending discipline on the basis of abstract principles.

The War of 1812

To protect the government's ability to borrow during wartime emergencies, interest payments must be secure and currency controls reliable. The Revolutionary War violated these principles, presenting the nation with its first fiscal crisis. The War of 1812 presented the second. The absence of fiscal responsibility in the first case was understandable, given the government's constitutional limitations and lack of experience, but the War of 1812 was launched by a government suffering neither of these impairments. Its limitations were entirely self-imposed.

The first Republican program for wartime financing was set forth in Gallatin's 1807 Treasury report, which recommended that any extraordinary expenses resulting from war be supported by new loans. Gallatin did not propose that new taxes be levied to support the war directly but insisted that tax revenues be adequate to fund the "annual expenses on a peace establishment, the interest of the existing debt, and the interest on the loans which may be raised."[90] This last point was extremely important, since it meant that interest payments on wartime loans would be serviced by taxes rather than additional borrowing. In Gallatin's subsequent reports, nothing materially changed. In 1811 and 1812, he recommended to the Ways and Means Committee that new taxes be imposed, because customs duties could not be depended on to fund ordinary expenses along with old and new interest obligations.[91] The chairman of the Ways and Means Committee, Ezekiel Bacon, supported the call for war taxes, warning his colleagues, "[I]f we suffer ourselves to yield to the new theory of borrowing both principal and interest, we have no data by which to judge upon what probable terms loans may be obtained at all, or how long it will be before we must wind up business. This

90. *Reports of the Secretary of the Treasury of the United States*, 1:360.
91. Adams, *Public Debts*, 114.

is an experiment which it is believed no regular or provident Government . . . has of late been presumptuous enough to attempt."[92]

Congress rejected new taxes, despite the heavier than anticipated borrowing necessary to finance the war and the mounting difficulties in securing new loans. The first loan authorization of $11 million took place on March 12, 1812, and almost half of the authorization remained unsubscribed two months later.[93] Similar problems were encountered with additional authorizations in 1813 and 1814. The credit problems encountered during the war were made worse by Congress's refusal to re-charter the Bank of the United States in 1811. Although James Madison had opposed the Bank's establishment two decades earlier, his administration supported an extension of the Bank's charter, with Gallatin insisting that the Bank was essential in securing loans and regulating the currency if war did occur. Congress was pushing the administration toward war, but it was not willing to provide the administration with the Bank or the taxes necessary to finance the war. The entirely predictable consequence was a financial debacle. The federal government issued massive amounts of treasury notes when borrowing proved inadequate, in a replay of the Revolutionary War experience. The Bank's demise also encouraged state banks to expand their issuance of non-specie-backed notes. The Treasury had no real control over the money supply and indeed was forced to accept state banknotes as payments for taxes or other revenues.[94]

By 1814, the federal government's military situation was deteriorating rapidly, and its financial position was, if anything, even worse. The new Secretary of the Treasury, Alexander Dallas, concluded that the "theory of defraying the extraordinary expenses of the war by successive loans had already become inoperative."[95] The government's credit had been nearly destroyed, he stated, not because of any "want of resources" but because of the "inadequacy of our system of taxation to form a foundation of public credit, and the absence from our system of the means which are the best adapted to anticipate, collect, and distribute the public revenue."[96] Not until the latter part of 1813 did Congress begin to enact the internal taxes and direct taxes needed to prevent a complete financial collapse. At this juncture, the Committee on Ways and Means went so far as to consider, but finally

---

92. *Annals of Congress*, 12th Cong., 1st sess., 1098.
93. Adams, *Public Debts*, 117–18.
94. Stabile and Cantor, *The Public Debt of the United States*, 34.
95. Quoted in Adams, *Public Debts*, 122.
96. Adams, *Public Debts*, 122–23.

reject, a tax on salaries.[97] Most of these new levies were designated as "war taxes," with automatic expiration one year after the war's conclusion. Those that were extended followed the precedents of earlier sinking funds, with revenues pledged to interest and principal payments.

The United States was able to negotiate a treaty of peace with Britain at the end of 1814, and the Treasury Department then undertook to repair the nation's finances. The public debt had nearly tripled, from $45 million in 1812 to more than $127 million at the end of 1815. The process of debt reduction began almost immediately, with budget surpluses of more than $28 million in 1816 and 1817. In 1816, total receipts were more than $47 million, roughly three times greater than the highest levels reached before the war. The schedule of duties in the 1816 tariff bill was set more than 40 percent above prewar levels.[98] Internal taxes were kept in place after the war, and sales of public lands were stepped up for several years. In a belated concession to fiscal realities, the Second Bank of the United States was chartered in 1816, with a $35 million capital stock authorization.

The War of 1812 returned the debt issue to a prominent place on the political agenda, even as it demonstrated the impotence of a balanced-budget philosophy divorced from fiscal discipline. Republicans held large majorities in the House and Senate during the war but were unwilling to impose in a timely manner the taxes needed to protect the government's credit. The refusal to re-charter the Bank of the United States in 1811 was another triumph of ideology over practical necessity. The Jefferson and Madison administrations also evidenced mounting congressional resistance to executive branch control of budget policy. Gallatin was eventually forced from office, as Hamilton had been, by congressional attacks that ostensibly concerned matters of personal integrity but were in reality contests over policy and influence.

Balanced Budgets and Policy Conflicts

Between 1815 and the Civil War, the balanced-budget rule acquired the status of dogma. Each administration during this period made clear its abhorrence of peacetime deficits and its allegiance to debt retirement, while the arguments in favor of this approach became more encompassing.[99] The

97. Bolles, *The Financial History of the United States from 1789 to 1860*, 258.
98. Forsythe, *Taxation and Political Change in the Young Nation, 1781–1833*, 70.
99. See Kimmel, *Federal Budget and Fiscal Policy, 1789–1958*, 16–36.

Jeffersonian critique of federal deficits and debt was dominated by the notion of political corruption. By the time of Andrew Jackson's presidency, the moral and political objections had been joined to a coherent set of economic arguments: "(1) interest on the public debt was a burden on the working classes; (2) interest payments involved a redistribution of income in favor of the well-to-do; and (3) the capital freed from unproductive employment through debt reduction would find its way into productive uses."[100]

There were additional glosses on these claims about fiscal policy. Martin Van Buren, who took office when state debts had reached unprecedented levels, was concerned about the political mischief that foreign-held debt might promote. James Polk believed that a nation "wholly exempt from indebtedness" would have "a still more commanding position among the nations of the earth."[101] James Buchanan was anxious that the public credit not be squandered during peacetime so that it would be readily available in case of war.[102]

This consensus on the need to balance spending and revenue did not, however, limit the conflicts over specific policies. On the revenue side, customs duties continued to provide most of the federal government's income, but sharp political divisions emerged over the use of tariffs for protection. Less intense disputes arose over the pricing and sale of public lands. Spending policy controversies were monopolized by partisan disagreements over internal improvements. The constitutionality of federally funded internal improvements was debated endlessly, and the issue took on added urgency when the federal government faced the seemingly enviable prospect of budget surpluses. During the several decades leading up to the Civil War, the arguments over tariffs and internal improvements were closely intertwined. A tariff-for-revenue-only policy was limited by the size of the federal budget, but the more abundant revenues provided by protective tariffs could be used to justify additional spending for internal improvements.[103]

The balanced-budget rule did not resolve every important question about the size and role of the federal government, but it did impose certain priorities on budget policy. In particular, most of the government's revenue was earmarked for interest payments and debt retirement. A meaningful debate

100. Kimmel, *Federal Budget and Fiscal Policy, 1789–1958*, 19.
101. Richardson, *A Compilation of the Messages and Papers of the Presidents*, 6:2500.
102. Kimmel, *Federal Budget and Fiscal Policy, 1789–1958*, 25.
103. Kimmel, *Federal Budget and Fiscal Policy, 1789–1958*, 35.

over protective tariffs and internal improvements was possible only when these commitments had been met and a budgetary margin became available.

Extinguishing the Debt

Between 1815 and 1835, nearly the entire federal debt was retired, with the official debt principal dropping to $38,000 in 1835 and 1836.[104] In less than half a century, the federal government had managed to finance more than $400 million in debt-related expenditures—$257 million in principal repayments and $158 million in interest.[105] After the War of 1812, the program of debt reduction, pursued with great consistency during different administrations, was accomplished by maintaining customs duties above prewar levels, supplementing revenues through the sale of public lands, and imposing tight controls on non-interest spending. In 1817, Congress established a revised sinking-fund system, with $10 million in pledged revenues annually, and this very high level of dedicated revenues inevitably acted as a ceiling on additional spending.

As shown in Table 2.5, the budget was almost always in surplus, despite the inherent difficulty of estimating revenues from customs duties. The 1820 and 1821 deficits, for example, occurred because of unexpected declines in custom duties caused by economic dislocations in the United States. In response to the 1821 deficit, a select congressional committee recommended that strict retrenchments in expenditures be undertaken to prevent future deficits and to ensure consistent reductions in the public debt.[106] Thereafter, expenditures were tightly limited. Despite the growth in revenue levels after 1825, spending remained almost flat. During the early 1830s, surpluses averaged 40 percent of total receipts.

Revenue Policy

During the 1820s and early 1830s, the issue of protective tariffs created a constitutional crisis, as southern states, led by South Carolina, saw their economic interests and political influence threatened by a protectionist majority. The battle over tariff policy was fought in a series of major legislative battles—the extensions in 1824 and 1828 and rollbacks in 1832 and 1833— over the types of manufactures and commodities for which protection was

---

104. *Historical Statistics of the United States, Colonial Times to 1970, Part 2*, 1118.
105. Kimmel, *Federal Budget and Fiscal Policy, 1789–1958*, 22–23.
106. Bolles, *The Financial History of the United States from 1789 to 1860*, 530–31.

Table 2.5 Federal Budget Totals, 1816–1835 (in millions of dollars)

Fiscal Year	Total Revenues	Total Outlays	Deficit (−) /Surplus
1816	$ 47.7	$ 30.6	$ 17.1
1817	33.1	21.8	11.3
1818	21.6	19.8	1.8
1819	24.6	21.5	3.1
1820	17.9	18.3	−0.4
Average	$ 29.0	$ 22.4	$ 6.6
1821	$ 14.6	$ 15.8	$− 1.2
1822	20.2	15.0	5.2
1823	20.5	14.7	5.8
1824	19.4	20.3	−0.9
1825	21.8	15.9	6.0
Average	$ 19.3	$ 16.3	$ 3.0
1826	$ 25.3	$ 17.0	$ 8.2
1827	23.0	16.1	6.8
1828	24.8	16.4	8.4
1829	24.8	15.2	9.6
1830	24.8	15.1	9.7
Average	$ 24.5	$ 16.0	$ 8.5
1831	$ 28.5	$ 15.2	$ 13.3
1832	31.9	17.3	14.6
1833	33.9	23.0	10.9
1834	21.8	18.6	3.2
1835	35.4	17.6	17.9
Average	$ 30.3	$ 18.3	$ 12.0

SOURCE: *Historical Statistics of the United States, Colonial Times to 1970, Part 2* (Washington, D.C.: U.S. Bureau of the Census, 1975), 1104.

sought and the degree of protection, in terms of scheduled duties, to be provided. These battles, however, were only tangentially about revenue levels, since Congress's "framing of the successive schedules . . . was hardly a fiscal process."[107] In the debate over the 1824 tariff, President James Monroe's messages treated "revenue needs and protection . . . separately and without interconnection. . . . [M]ost congressmen had no idea what the effect of the proposed bill might be on revenues."[108]

The revenue productivity of the tariff, then, was heavily influenced by economic factors. With no great economic disturbances occurring between

107. Dewey, *Financial History of the United States*, 173.
108. Forsythe, *Taxation and Political Change in the Young Nation, 1781–1833*, 76–77.

Table 2.6 Federal Revenues, 1816–1835 (in millions of dollars)

Fiscal Years	Total	Customs	Public Lands	Internal and Other
		Average Annual Amount		
1816–20	$ 29.0	$ 23.0	$ 2.2	$ 3.8
1821–25	19.3	17.5	1.2	0.6
1826–30	24.5	22.2	1.5	0.8
1831–35	30.3	23.5	5.9	0.9

SOURCE: *Annual Report of the Secretary of the Treasury on the State of the Finances for Fiscal Year Ended June 30, 1945* (Washington, D.C.: Government Printing Office, 1946), 444, 445, 500.

1822 and 1835, there were few sharp drop-offs in expected receipts. As shown in Table 2.6, aggregate revenue levels were unusually high in the years following the War of 1812. After a sharp decline caused by an economic slump in the early 1820s, tariffs recovered as did overall revenue levels. During the early 1830s, receipts from the sale of public lands increased significantly, helping to offset the elimination of internal tax revenues.

By the time of the Jackson presidency, revenue levels were approximately double what they had been under Jefferson, although tax policy was essentially unchanged. Tariffs were, by far, the most productive source of revenues. Internal taxes were insignificant. So long as commercial activity with other nations continued to expand, the federal government could pursue limited protectionist goals without endangering revenue levels, and it could avoid imposing highly unpopular internal taxes.

Spending Policy

To produce the large surpluses necessary for debt redemption, total expenditures had to be tightly controlled, but there was a growing margin for new spending as interest obligations fell in conjunction with declining debt (Table 2.7). There was a severe retrenchment in outlays during the early 1820s, but most of this reduction was in spending by the War and Navy Departments. The defense portion of the budget then began to grow, followed, in the early 1830s, by spending for veterans' pensions and for other domestic programs.

The most controversial spending programs of this period involved internal improvements. Presidents Madison, Monroe, and, especially, Jackson opposed direct federal funding for roads, canals, and other internal improvements as an unconstitutional intrusion on the reserved powers of the states. Under

Table 2.7 Federal Outlays, 1816–1835 (in millions of dollars)

Fiscal Years	Total	Interest	War and Navy	Veterans' Pensions	Other
1816–20	$ 22.4	$ 6.0	$ 11.4	$ 1.4	$ 3.6
1821–25	16.3	4.9	6.3	1.4	3.7
1826–30	16.0	3.0	8.1	1.1	3.8
1831–35	18.4	0.5	9.6	2.5	5.8

SOURCE: *Historical Statistics of the United States, Colonial Times to 1970, Part 2* (Washington, D.C.: U.S. Bureau of the Census, 1975), 1115.

John Quincy Adams, whose administration supported these types of programs, spending for internal improvements was increased, but its budgetary impact remained limited.[109] The disputes over internal improvements and their potential budgetary consequences took on considerably greater importance as the prospects improved for large, uncommitted surpluses. Jackson favored a scheme for distributing surplus funds to the states, and Congress authorized an apportionment of budgeted surpluses among the states beginning in 1837. Before this legislation could be fully implemented, the economy collapsed, and the surpluses disappeared.

The Second Bank of the United States

The antipathy that had caused the demise of the First Bank of the United States was revived with even greater vehemence by Andrew Jackson against its successor. For Jackson as for Jefferson, federal debt was a corrupting influence in American life, and the Bank was an especially dangerous institution, serving the interests of the wealthy and propertied classes at the expense of workers and farmers. It was also an independent institution that resisted Jackson's efforts to control its operations.

Jackson's battle against the Bank began with his decision to withdraw federal deposits. When Jackson's first three Treasury secretaries opposed this policy, he replaced each until a compliant officer was found.[110] The advice of other cabinet members was similarly disregarded. The Bank's charter, due to expire in 1836, was renewed by Congress in 1832, but Jackson vetoed the extension. The Second Bank had performed important functions

---

109. Kimmel, *Federal Budget and Fiscal Policy, 1789–1958*, 30.
110. See Bolles, *The Financial History of the United States from 1789 to 1860*, 336–37.

for the federal government and national economy, not the least of which was establishing a sound, uniform national currency. A congressional committee report issued in 1830 concluded that "no country in the world has a circulating medium of greater uniformity than the United States; and that no country of any thing like the same geographical extent has a currency at all comparable to that of the United States on the score of uniformity."[111] With the Bank's demise, the number of state banks rose sharply, and the amount of unregulated paper currency exploded. With this infusion of cheap credit, speculative ventures soared, with much of this activity involving purchases of public lands. Soon the federal government found itself in the midst of financial turmoil. Efforts to reduce speculation by requiring specie payments for public land sales were unsuccessful, and the government's deposits in state banks were threatened. Under Jackson's successor, Martin Van Buren, comprehensive financial reforms were stalled, and the economic dislocations worsened. The "Panic of 1837" and depression that followed were unusually severe, perhaps the worst of the nineteenth century, and the nation did not begin to recover until 1843.[112] By that time, the federal debt had climbed to well over $30 million.

Resurrecting the Debt

The brief period during which the federal government was free of any debt failed to ensure economic prosperity. Nevertheless, the post-Jackson administrations endeavored to reestablish the fiscal rules of the 1820s and early 1830s. Between 1844 and 1846, the debt was reduced by more than one-half, but the Mexican War that began in May 1846 resulted in a series of deficits only slightly smaller than those of the War of 1812. The wartime debt then was substantially decreased until 1858, when another financial panic caused an unusually large peacetime deficit. The budget policy issues during this period mirrored those of the Jackson era—protective tariffs on the revenue side and internal improvements on the spending side. But there was considerable volatility in both revenue and spending levels quite apart from wartime spending (Table 2.8). During the 1850s, revenue levels were relatively high, but outlay growth was even steeper. As a result, the large surpluses for the earlier part of the decade were matched by equally large deficits for the latter part.

---

111. *Annals of Congress*, 21st Cong., 1st sess., appendix, 118.
112. See Buchanan and Wagner, *Democracy in Deficit*, 13.

Table 2.8 Federal Budget Totals, 1836–1860 (in millions of dollars)

Fiscal Year	Total Revenues	Total Outlays	Deficit (−) /Surplus
1836	$ 50.8	$ 30.9	$ 20.0
1837	25.0	37.2	−12.3
1838	26.3	33.9	−7.6
1839	31.5	26.9	4.6
1840	19.5	24.3	−4.8
Average	$ 30.6	$ 30.6	$ −0.02
1841	$ 16.9	$ 26.6	$ −9.7
1842	20.0	25.2	−5.2
1843	8.3	11.9	−3.6
1844	29.3	22.3	7.0
1845	30.0	22.9	7.0
Average	$ 20.9	$ 21.8	$ −0.9
1846	$ 29.7	$ 27.8	$ 1.9
1847	26.5	57.3	−30.8
1848	35.7	45.4	−9.6
1849	31.2	45.1	−13.8
1850	43.6	39.5	4.1
Average	$ 33.3	$ 43.0	$ −9.6
1851	$ 52.6	$ 47.7	$ 4.9
1852	49.8	44.2	5.7
1853	61.6	48.2	13.4
1854	73.8	58.0	15.8
1855	65.4	59.7	5.6
Average	$ 60.6	$ 51.6	$ 9.1
1856	$ 74.1	$ 69.9	$ 4.5
1857	69.0	67.8	1.2
1858	46.7	74.2	−27.5
1859	53.5	69.1	−15.6
1860	56.1	63.1	−7.1
Average	$ 59.9	$ 68.8	$ −8.9

SOURCE: *Historical Statistics of the United States, Colonial Times to 1970, Part 2* (Washington, D.C.: U.S. Bureau of the Census, 1975), 1104.

As shown in Table 2.9, the heavy dependence of the federal government on customs duties continued until the Civil War, although there were recurring legislative battles over protective tariffs and free trade and over the type of collection system that would minimize fraud and evasion. After the major tariff reductions enacted in the early 1830s, demands for additional revenues

Table 2.9 Federal Revenues, 1836–1860 (in millions of dollars)

	Average Annual Amount			
Fiscal Years	Total	Customs	Public Lands	Internal and Other
1836–40	$ 30.6	$ 17.5	$ 9.0	$ 4.1
1841–45	20.9	18.7	1.5	0.7
1846–50	33.3	30.0	2.4	0.9
1851–55	60.6	54.5	5.2	0.9
1856–60	59.8	54.5	4.0	1.3

SOURCE: *Annual Report of the Secretary of the Treasury on the State of the Finances for Fiscal Year Ended June 30, 1945* (Washington, D.C.: Government Printing Office, 1946), 444, 445, 500.

and growing protectionist pressures led to passage of a highly protective tariff in 1842. By 1846, the movement toward free trade had regained momentum, and the several tariff measures enacted thereafter were oriented primarily toward revenue needs. Heavy reliance on customs duties, however, meant that federal revenues were often unpredictable, necessitating frequent adjustments and revisions in tariff schedules. The only other source of appreciable revenues was the sale of public lands, and here, too, year-to-year fluctuations were commonplace. With essentially no internal taxes at all for the 1840s and 1850s, even during the Mexican War, federal revenue levels had limited elasticity in terms of policy adjustments.

The population and territory of the United States became much larger during the 1840s and 1850s, and the size and cost of government went up accordingly. The number of federal civilian employees more than tripled between 1831 and 1861, although almost all of this increase was in the Post Office or other service agencies.[113] Domestic expenditures for the construction of public buildings and facilities to house these agencies rose sharply during the 1850s, and federal spending was substantially affected by the cost of liquidating Mexican claims under the peace treaty of 1848.[114]

Interest costs between 1836 and 1860 were negligible, while veterans' pensions accounted for a small and diminishing share of the federal budget (Table 2.10). Expenditures for the Army and Navy Departments remained relatively high after the Mexican War, absorbing more than 40 percent of the budget during the 1850s. But beyond these spending categories, spending

113. *Historical Statistics of the United States, Colonial Times to 1970, Part 2*, 1103.
114. Dewey, *Financial History of the United States*, 268.

Table 2.10 Federal Outlays, 1836–1860 (in millions of dollars)

Fiscal Years	Average Annual Amount				
	Total	Interest	War and Navy	Veterans' Pensions	Other
1836–40	$ 30.6	$ 0.1	$ 17.1	$ 2.7	$ 10.7
1841–45	21.8	0.9	12.0	1.8	7.1
1846–50	43.0	2.3	28.1	1.6	11.0
1851–55	51.6	3.3	21.9	1.8	24.6
1856–60	68.8	2.2	33.7	1.2	31.7

SOURCE: *Historical Statistics of the United States, Colonial Times to 1970, Part 2* (Washington, D.C.: U.S. Bureau of the Census, 1975), 1114–15.

for domestic purposes was beginning to have an appreciable impact on spending growth. Between 1800 and 1830, federal outlays rose by less than $5 million. Over the next three decades, the increase was nearly $50 million, with much of this growth absorbed by domestic programs. The long-term conflicts over federal internal improvements were still unsettled, but resistance to federal domestic spending was weakening. Also, the enthusiasm for spending retrenchments waned as debt was reduced and surpluses appeared. Instead of a sustained policy of spending control during the 1850s, appropriations limits were routinely evaded, contingency funds were exploited, and transfer authorities were abused.[115] Despite complaints from its investigating committees, "Congress hesitated to begin the greatly needed work of reform . . . [and] the cry of retrenchment was neither strong nor effective. The spirit of reform that existed in Congress was faint and fitful, and spent itself chiefly in lamentation."[116]

Deficits, Debt, and Small Government

Paeans to classical notions of fiscal responsibility are not entirely consistent with federal fiscal practices in the several decades before the Civil War. There was little systematic coordination in budgeting, particularly when Congress discouraged executive branch leadership. The controls on expenditures were, for much of this period, rudimentary. The discipline in federal budget policy that was achieved owed much of its strength to the constraints

115. Bolles, *The Financial History of the United States from 1789 to 1860*, 584.
116. Bolles, *The Financial History of the United States from 1789 to 1860*, 584, 586.

imposed by interest costs and debt retirement. When these constraints occasionally eased, spending pressures proved harder to suppress.

The fiscal picture becomes even more complicated when the states are taken into account. The federal government financed internal improvements not only through budget outlays but also through "in-kind" subsidies in the form of donated lands. While money estimates of these subsidies are problematical, the amount of land donated for capital projects and education was considerable.[117] In addition, the Jeffersonian and Jacksonian notions of fiscal responsibility regarding deficits and debt did not apply to the states.

Through the 1820s, state debt levels were quite low and concentrated in just a few states.[118] Over the next three decades, heavy borrowing occurred in most states, and debt levels climbed rapidly.[119] By 1841, collective state debts were more than $190 million. In 1860, the total was nearly $260 million. This borrowing supported traditional internal improvements to promote commerce and industry, such as railroads, roads, canals, bridges, and reservoirs, but a number of states also borrowed to subsidize state banks and to subsidize commercial enterprises.[120]

The high levels of state borrowing proved disastrous in a number of cases, with several states actually repudiating the debts they had contracted. In 1843, the situation had become so serious that a proposal was introduced in Congress to have the federal government assume state debts incurred for public works "to strengthen the bonds of union, multiply the avenues of commerce, and augment the defences against foreign aggression."[121] This initiative was unsuccessful, but the rationale was not easily dismissed. In refusing to use its taxing and spending powers to fund essential public works, the federal government had shifted the responsibility to the states. Moreover, Jackson's decision to eliminate the Bank of the United States, and the refusal of his successors to resurrect it, removed credit and currency controls that might otherwise have moderated if not entirely prevented state borrowing excesses. These factors in combination proved extremely damaging to the fiscal health of many states and led most of them to adopt constitutional limits on their borrowing.[122] In

---

117. For estimates of the amount, see William Letwin, ed., *A Documentary History of American Economic Policy Since 1789* (New York: Norton, 1972), xix.

118. B. U. Ratchford, *American State Debts* (Durham: Duke University Press, 1941), 79.

119. Ratchford, *American State Debts*, 79, 127.

120. Ratchford, *American State Debts*, 88.

121. Quoted in Dewey, *Financial History of the United States*, 245.

122. See Savage, *Balanced Budgets and American Politics*, 117.

1790, Hamilton had estimated the outstanding federal and state debts at less than $90 million. In 1860, after two wars, a major depression, and several less severe financial difficulties, the federal debt was less than $65 million, while the states, whose wartime debts had been assumed under Hamilton's plan, had accumulated $257 million in debt.

The financial history of the pre–Civil War era demonstrates the political dimension of classical fiscal theory. The federal government was expected to balance its budget and retire its debt, but the states were not held to the same standard. This distinction between the federal and state governments made no sense if debt finance was viewed as primarily an economic policy concern, but the distinction was in fact about the power and responsibility of the federal government. For Hamilton, the aggressive exercise of the federal powers to spend, tax, and borrow would allow the federal government to "nationalize" economic policy. The Jeffersonian movement opposed this political objective, regardless of its economic merits.

Finally, there was no formal budget process during this period, particularly in terms of coordinating spending and revenue levels. Hamilton's efforts to develop an executive budget were rebuffed by Congress, which had no comprehensive budget of its own. Appropriations bills were used to direct and control executive departments, not to establish spending policy, and tariff bills were governed by protectionist demands as well as revenue requirements. This fragmentation was not particularly troublesome when the economy was growing and trade was expanding, but it was ill-suited to wars and financial emergencies.

The fiscal record from 1789 to 1860 is more complex than many contemporary accounts might indicate. Federal budgets were relatively small and usually balanced, because the political majority for most of this period wanted to protect the powers and prerogatives of the states and to restrict the size and authority of the federal government. Fiscal responsibility, at least at the federal level, was not a heroic exercise, but the means to a political end.

☆ ☆ ☆

BUDGETING FOR GOVERNMENT GROWTH

(1860–1915)

Military historians consider the Civil War to be the first "modern war."[1] Its magnitude and duration necessitated an enormous mobilization of economic resources and led to a major upward shift in government spending. From 1850 to 1860, federal spending averaged less than $60 million annually; the total federal debt in 1860 was under $65 million. Five years later, spending was $1.3 billion, and the debt had climbed to more than $2.7 billion. Civil War spending averaged 15 percent of gross national product (GNP), three times the level of the War of 1812 and almost as high as that of World War I.[2]

The Civil War also marked a turning point in American political development. Over the next half-century, the "combined impact of *crisis, class conflict,* and *complexity* was concentrated on a national scale for the first time in American history."[3] By the end of this period, the United States had emerged "as a world power in the industrial age."[4] The scope of budget policy was

---

1. See James M. Morris, *America's Armed Forces: A History,* 2d ed. (Upper Saddle River, N.J.: Prentice-Hall, 1996), 129–31.

2. The GNP measures for this period are problematical. This estimate is from W. Elliott Brownlee, *Federal Taxation in America* (Cambridge: Cambridge University Press, 1996), 23.

3. Stephen Skowronek, *Building a New American State: The Expansion of National Administrative Capacities, 1877–1920* (Cambridge: Cambridge University Press, 1982), 10.

4. Skowronek, *Building a New American State,* 11.

substantially enlarged, as the federal government promoted economic development and industrialization through spending subsidies and high tariffs. Spending for rivers and harbors, one of the leading forms of internal improvements, totaled less than $4 million from 1850 to 1860.[5] From 1880 to 1890, the total was more than $100 million.[6] The politics of taxation reflected sharpening regional and class divisions, with the Republican party fighting to preserve its high-tariff regime against growing popular support for a federal income tax.

During this period, the federal government also assumed an expensive if narrowly targeted social welfare responsibility, in the form of a Civil War pension system that "became one of a handful of major distributive policies that helped to fuel and sustain late-nineteenth-century U.S. patronage democracy."[7] By the early 1890s, veterans' pensions accounted for approximately 40 percent of total federal spending. In 1910, an estimated 18 percent of all U.S. residents aged sixty-five and older were pension beneficiaries, including not only men but also women who qualified for survivors' benefits.[8]

The modern-day perception that nineteenth-century budgeting was highly disciplined ignores the serious fiscal problems that emerged during and after the Civil War. Wartime financial controls were poorly conceived, and the deficiencies in federal credit operations were strikingly similar to those of the Revolutionary War and the War of 1812. Because of the types and amounts of debt incurred during the Civil War, postwar debt management proved arduous and complicated. In the decades after the Civil War, coordination between budget policy and monetary policy was almost nonexistent, which contributed to the frequency and severity of financial panics.

A more concerted effort to centralize and coordinate budget decision making in Congress was only marginally successful. Spending discipline in Congress began to deteriorate in the 1880s and was further undermined by lax controls over executive agencies. By the 1890s, Congress's "spending heyday" was being decried as a "national scandal."[9] Between 1895 and 1915,

---

5. Savage, *Balanced Budgets and American Politics*, 131.
6. Savage, *Balanced Budgets and American Politics*, 131.
7. Theda Skocpol, *Protecting Soldiers and Mothers: The Political Origins of Social Policy in the United States* (Cambridge: Harvard University Press, 1992), 130.
8. Skocpol, *Protecting Soldiers and Mothers*, 132.
9. Joseph P. Harris, *Congressional Control of Administration* (Washington, D.C.: Brookings Institution, 1969), 54.

spending continued to grow, and the budget was frequently in deficit. The accounting and financial controls in place during this period "did practically nothing that was effective to promote economy and efficiency in government."[10] Furthermore, with Congress maintaining exclusive control over spending, "there were few opportunities for the President to take the initiative with economizing measures."[11]

With heightened demands for domestic spending, consistent adherence to the balanced-budget rule proved difficult at the federal level. For state and local governments, which were responsible for the bulk of domestic spending, debt finance was routine.[12] By the time World War I began, total government debt had risen to more than $5.6 billion, with approximately 80 percent of this total held by local and, to a lesser extent, state governments.[13]

Structural weaknesses in budgeting and budget processes were common to all levels of government in the post–Civil War era, giving rise to an influential budget reform movement that began at the local level but soon expanded its domain to include national budgeting. The result, as embodied in the 1921 Budget and Accounting Act, was a new budget process featuring a presidential budget. This important change reflected the widespread belief that Congress could not, on its own, provide the centralized spending control on which political and financial accountability depended.

Civil War Financing

Although the federal government's finances were in dismal condition well before the Civil War began, the erosion of its credit became truly serious over the course of the war. In January 1861, the Buchanan administration's Treasury Secretary, General John A. Dix, informed the House Ways and Means Committee that no funds were available to redeem outstanding debt. "Within the last few days the amount of over due treasury notes presented for redemption has exceeded the power of the Treasurer to place drafts in payment on the assistant treasurer at New York, where the holders desired the remittances to be made, and an accumulation of warrants to the amount

10. Smithies, *The Budgetary Process in the United States*, 66.
11. Smithies, *The Budgetary Process in the United States*, 66.
12. The first comprehensive report on governmental finance in the United States was issued in 1902. See Ballard C. Campbell, *The Growth of American Government: Government from the Cleveland Era to the Present* (Bloomington: Indiana University Press, 1995), 18.
13. *Historical Statistics of the United States, Colonial Times to 1970, Part 2*, 1116–34.

of about $350,000 has occurred, on this account, in the Treasurer's hands, which he has been unable to pay."[14] Congress authorized new borrowing, but the Treasury could not sell new issues of securities, even at very high rates of interest. Between June 1860 and March 1861, four loan authorizations totaling $66 million were enacted by Congress, but only about half this amount was actually subscribed.[15] Federal credit was so poor that Congress considered asking several of the more prosperous states to endorse federal securities to make them more attractive to lenders.[16]

The Lincoln administration took office on March 4, 1861, and its first Secretary of the Treasury, Salmon P. Chase, immediately attempted to use these unsubscribed loan authorizations to replenish the Treasury. Long-term borrowing, however, remained difficult, and the attack on Fort Sumter in April increased financial pressure on the administration. Chase first employed short-term debt to make up the borrowing shortfalls, but as the war's costs mounted, the Treasury turned to large issues of unsecured paper currency.[17] The latter produced massive price inflation during the Civil War, and the heavy reliance on short-term borrowing proved costly as well.[18] The effects of these policies continued to be felt long after the war's conclusion. In fact, the government's credit "was not fully restored until fourteen years after the war had ended."[19]

The Chase Program

When the thirty-seventh Congress convened on July 4, 1861, Secretary Chase submitted his proposals for wartime financing. War-related appropriations for fiscal year (FY) 1862 were estimated at approximately $220 million; all other spending was estimated at an additional $100 million.[20] Chase

14. U.S. House, *Letter on the Condition of the Treasury*, 36th Cong., 2d sess., 1861, H. Mis. Doc. 20. When Congress had convened the preceding December, no funds had been available to pay its members.

15. Robert T. Patterson, *Federal Debt-Management Policies, 1865–1879* (Durham: Duke University Press, 1954), 16.

16. Albert S. Bolles, *The Financial History of the United States from 1861 to 1885* (New York: D. Appleton and Company, 1886), 5.

17. For the differences between short-term notes and paper currency, see Bolles, *The Financial History of the United States from 1861 to 1885*, 8.

18. Patterson, *Federal Debt-Management Policies, 1865–1879*, 10.

19. Patterson, *Federal Debt-Management Policies, 1865–1879*, 10–11.

20. Bolles, *The Financial History of the United States from 1861 to 1885*, 11. From 1789 to 1842, the fiscal year for the federal government was January 1–December 31. It was then changed to July 1–June 30. Since FY 1977, the schedule has been October 1–September 30.

recommended that $80 million of the $320 million in total spending be financed by taxation and the remainder by borrowing.[21] Two weeks later, Congress approved a $250 million loan authorization. Another $50 million was authorized the following month.

Chase's proposals for taxation included "such modifications of the existing tariff as would produce the principal part of the needed revenue, and such resort to direct taxes, or internal duties or excises, as circumstances might require in order to make good whatever deficiency might be found to exist."[22] "Needed revenue" was defined as the amount "for the prompt discharge of all ordinary demands, for the punctual payment of the interest on loans, and for the creation of a gradually increasing fund for the redemption of the principal."[23] Taxation to finance wartime expenditures was seen as unnecessary, given the administration's hope that the war would be over quickly, and it was feared that increased taxes might threaten popular support for the war. The war instead proved to be lengthy and unusually costly, and the unexpectedly large deficits that were incurred made sound borrowing more and more difficult.

The actual deficit for FY 1862 was nearly twice the initial estimate (Table 3.1). Over the next three years, taxes were increased repeatedly, but spending underestimates continued to be a serious problem. Early in the war, appropriations were "a guess, for no one could foretell what amount would be required for anything."[24] The situation improved only slightly over time. In FY 1865, the last year of the war, spending was still four times greater than revenues, and the deficit was more than $960 million.

Taxation and the Legal-Tender Acts

The taxes enacted during the Civil War included, for the first time in the nation's history, a tax on individual incomes. The income tax measure passed in 1861 levied a 3 percent tax on incomes above $800. Tax bills later in the war lowered the amount of exempted income and also applied graduated rates. In 1865, there was a 5 percent rate applied to income between $600 and $5,000 and a 10 percent rate on income above $5,000. It took some time for the federal government to develop an effective administrative system for collecting this tax, but by the final stages of the war an estimated 10 percent

21. Bolles, *The Financial History of the United States from 1861 to 1885*, 6.
22. Bolles, *The Financial History of the United States from 1861 to 1885*, 6.
23. Bolles, *The Financial History of the United States from 1861 to 1885*, 6.
24. Bolles, *The Financial History of the United States from 1861 to 1885*, 227.

Table 3.1 Civil War Spending, Revenues, Deficits, and Debt (in millions of dollars)

Fiscal Year	Total Spending	Total Revenues	Deficit	Gross Debt
1861	$ 66.5	$ 41.5	$ 25.0	$ 90.6
1862	474.8	52.0	422.8	524.2
1863	714.7	112.7	602.0	1,119.8
1864	865.3	264.6	600.7	1,815.8
1865	1,297.6	333.7	963.8	2,677.9

SOURCE: *Historical Statistics of the United States, Colonial Times to 1970, Part 2* (Washington, D.C.: U.S. Bureau of the Census, 1975), 1104.

of Union households were paying income taxes, and the revenues obtained were more than one-fifth of total receipts in 1865.[25]

Congress also relied heavily on traditional tariffs and excises. The 1861 Morrill Tariff Act imposed an average rate of 20 percent on dutiable imports. Additional tariff measures enacted during the war raised tariff rates and extended duties to more types of goods. Scheduled tariff rates under the Tariff Act of 1864 were close to 50 percent of the total value of dutiable imports.[26] Excise taxes were applied to all types of consumer goods and manufactured products, yielding substantial new revenues. In 1863, excises on alcohol, tobacco, and manufactures were under $27 million. In 1865, the total was more than $105 million. As shown in Table 3.2, the composition and level of revenue changed as internal taxes were applied. Even with tariff receipts rising, income and internal taxes accounted for more than one-third of total revenues in 1863 and nearly two-thirds two years later.

Because taxes were repeatedly overestimated and spending greatly underestimated, these revenue increases failed to curb heavy borrowing. The initial estimates prepared by the Treasury Department set the ratio of borrowing to taxes at 3 to 1. The actual ratio of borrowing to taxes was more than 8 to 1 in FY 1862 and improved only marginally in 1863. With borrowing requirements so high and the government's credit already impaired, the Treasury Department could not sell long-term bonds as rapidly as funding needs arose and could not sell these bonds at all except at a steep discount. During the first months of the war, Secretary Chase accepted the necessity for paying a rate of interest "somewhat higher than that allowed in ordinary

25. Brownlee, *Federal Taxation in America*, 26–27.
26. Brownlee, *Federal Taxation in America*, 24.

Table 3.2 Composition of Federal Revenues, 1861–1865 (in millions of dollars)

Fiscal Year	Total Revenues	Percentage of Total		
		Customs	Internal Revenue	Other
1861	$ 41.5	95.4%	0.0%	4.6%
1862	52.0	94.4	0.0	5.6
1863	112.7	61.3	33.4	5.3
1864	264.6	38.7	41.5	19.9
1865	333.7	25.3	62.8	11.8

SOURCE: *Historical Statistics of the United States, Colonial Times to 1970, Part 2* (Washington, D.C.: U.S. Bureau of the Census, 1975), 1106.

times."[27] He abandoned this policy as interest costs mounted and resorted to paper currency whose immediate costs were negligible.

The First Legal-Tender Act was signed into law on February 25, 1862. It authorized the issuance of $150 million in paper currency denominations of not less than five dollars that would serve as "lawful money and a legal tender in payment of all debts, public and private, within the United States, except duties on imports and interest [on bonds and notes]."[28] Five months later, the Second Legal-Tender Act was passed, providing an additional $150 million; a third enactment, of $150 million, was passed in March 1863.

Congressional debate on the first of these measures lasted several weeks. The constitutionality of unsecured paper currency troubled many members of Congress, who pointed to the absence of any express provision in the Constitution permitting federal "bills of credit." The main practical objection was the inflation risk of issuing large amounts of unsecured paper money, as opponents repeatedly drew unflattering parallels to the Revolutionary War and the War of 1812. There were, in fact, very few supporters of paper money as a matter of principle, but majorities of the House and Senate were finally persuaded that the government had no other option.

27. Chase explained, "It is beneficial to the whole people that a loan distributed among themselves should be made so advantageous to the takers as to inspire satisfaction and hopes of profit rather than annoyance and fears of loss; and, if the rate of interest proposed be somewhat higher than allowed in ordinary times, it will not be grudged to the subscribers when it is remembered that the interest on the loan will go into the channels of home circulation, and is to reward those who come forward in the hour of peril to place their means at the disposal of their country." *Report of the Secretary of the Treasury, July 4, 1861*, 37th Cong., 1st sess., 1861, S. Ex. Doc. 2, 12–13.

28. *Statutes at Large*, Vol. 12, *1859–1863* (Boston: Little, Brown and Company, 1863), 345.

The need for these legal-tender authorizations grew out of a complicated set of circumstances. When the Treasury Department sold bonds to northern banks during summer and fall 1861, it required payments in specie. At the end of the year, credit markets were disrupted by fears that the Union might be forced to fight a second war. A U.S. warship had seized two Confederate officials from a British ship (the "Trent Affair"), and the British government had threatened to retaliate unless the prisoners were released and an apology issued. The resulting turmoil in credit markets caused the banks to suspend specie payments, and the Treasury Department then reported that its earlier estimate of borrowing requirements had been too optimistic. Spending was running more than $200 million higher than had been anticipated in July, while revenues were some $25 million less. The federal government needed large infusions of cash quickly, but banks and other lenders could not meet this need, and the situation was made even worse by the failure of the Treasury to "present a definite plan of finance based upon adequate taxation."[29] Although it would have taken time to implement an expanded tax program, such a step "would have strengthened the credit of the government and so enabled it to borrow more freely and on better terms."[30] The Lincoln administration feared, however, that either a "heavy federal income tax or high internal duties" would undermine popular support for the war.[31]

With the banks unable to support specie-based lending to the government, the Treasury in turn was forced to suspend its own specie requirements for borrowing and for redeeming expiring debt. When this suspension occurred, the legal-tender authorization was seized on as the only available means for financing the war. The chief sponsor of the legal-tender authorization, Elbridge G. Spaulding of the House Ways and Means Committee, explained Congress's dilemma: "[T]he Treasury note bill . . . is a measure of *necessity* and not one of *choice*. . . . We will be out of means to pay the daily expenses in *about thirty days*, and the Committee do not see any other way to get along till we can get the tax bills ready, except to issue temporarily Treasury notes. . . . We must have at least $100,000,000 during the next three months, or the Government must stop payment."[32]

---

29. Wesley Clair Mitchell, *A History of the Greenbacks, with Special Reference to the Economic Consequences of Their Issue, 1862–65* (Chicago: University of Chicago Press, 1903), 37.
30. Mitchell, *A History of the Greenbacks,* 72.
31. Mitchell, *A History of the Greenbacks,* 72.
32. E. G. Spaulding, *History of the Legal Tender Paper Money Issued During the Great Rebellion* (1869; reprint, Westport, Conn.: Greenwood Press, 1971), 17–18.

Despite the $300 million in paper money issued during 1862, the government was running out of money to pay its troops by the end of the year. An authorization of $100 million was approved in March 1863 to provide immediate funds for the Army and Navy Departments. President Abraham Lincoln wrote to Congress of his "sincere regret that it has been found necessary to authorize so large an additional issue of United States notes," since paper money had "become already so redundant as to increase prices beyond real values . . . to the injury of the whole country."[33] Lincoln also had urged Congress to establish a national banking system that would strengthen the monetary system and make it easier for the government to borrow in the future. In 1863, Congress passed the National Banking Act and approved the administration's proposals for heavier taxation.[34] These steps gradually improved the government's ability to borrow, as did the more favorable military situation.

The Treasury Department experienced funding problems until the very last months of the Civil War but was able, after 1863, to rely more and more on sustainable, long-term borrowing. The legal-tender acts had produced serious inflation, which greatly increased the actual costs of the war, and it was apparent, at least in retrospect, that increased taxation had been postponed much too long. Nevertheless, it was impossible to foresee in 1861 or 1862 just how long and how costly the war would prove to be, and it was difficult for the federal government to assign high priority to financial administration when national survival was at risk.

When the Civil War ended in 1865, the debt continued to climb for several months. Finally, in September 1865, the Treasury reported that revenues were exceeding spending, and its forecast for FY 1867 showed a $111 million surplus that could be applied to debt reduction.[35] The accumulated debt reached its peak of $2.7 billion during August 1865.[36] The size of the debt was one problem. The various types of debt, ranging from unsecured legal-tenders to long-term bonds, posed another. The federal government had to refund its debt and restore a sound currency. Neither of these tasks was accomplished easily or quickly.

---

33. *Congressional Globe*, 37th Cong., 3d sess., 1863, 33, pt. 1: 392.

34. The banking system established in 1863 did not become fully operational until after the Civil War. The legislation did, however, limit postwar paper currencies to federal government-issued notes and certificates and national banknotes.

35. Patterson, *Federal Debt-Management Policies, 1865–1879*, 49.

36. Patterson, *Federal Debt-Management Policies, 1865–1879*, 50.

Debt Retirement and Postwar Budget Policy

The quarter century after the Civil War was governed by one budget policy imperative—rapid extinction of the wartime debt. The course of budget policy was, at least on the surface, unambiguous. Federal spending declined, with budget expenditures exclusive of debt repayment dropping from $521 million in 1866 to under $320 million in 1890.[37] Budgets were in surplus each year from 1866 to 1893, with average annual surpluses during the 1880s of nearly $100 million. The total federal debt was reduced from $2.8 billion in 1866 to $961 million in 1893, as these surpluses were used to purchase and retire debt.

Hugh McCulloch, Secretary of the Treasury from 1865 to 1869 and again from 1884 to 1885, revived the rhetoric of the Jeffersonian era in explaining the urgency of extinguishing the Civil War debt as quickly as possible: "Its influences are anti-republican. It adds to the power of the Executive by increasing federal patronage. It must be distasteful to the people because it fills the country with informers and tax gatherers. It is dangerous to the public virtue, because it involves the collection and disbursement of vast sums of money, and renders rigid national economy almost impracticable."[38] The views of McCulloch's successors at Treasury were perhaps less strongly stated, but their insistence on debt reduction was no less intense. Within Congress, there was overwhelming support for replicating the debt policies implemented after the Revolutionary War and the War of 1812. A sinking-fund requirement had, in fact, been passed by Congress in 1862, which was modeled on Hamilton's redemption funds of 1790 and 1795.[39] Interest payments and debt retirement took precedence over all other appropriations, although strict adherence to statutory debt-retirement schedules sometimes proved impractical.[40] The primacy of debt retirement notwithstanding, budget policy was moving in a different direction from that of the prewar period. The balanced-budget principle was still widely endorsed, but it no longer imposed an automatic limit on the size and scope of the federal government.[41] With tariff policy largely dic-

---

37. *Historical Statistics of the United States, Colonial Times to 1970, Part 2*, 1104.

38. *Report of the Secretary of the Treasury on the State of the Finances for the Year 1865* (Washington, D.C.: Government Printing Office, 1865), 16.

39. See Patterson, *Federal Debt-Management Policies, 1865–1879*, 136–37.

40. Patterson, *Federal Debt-Management Policies, 1865–1879*, 138–42.

41. Savage describes this as "distorting a symbol." *Balanced Budgets and American Politics*, 121–60.

tated by protectionism, the revenue side of the budget did not restrain spending but rather encouraged it.

Appropriations Reforms

Studies of pre–World War I budget policy have highlighted the importance of centralized appropriations controls in providing the heavy post–Civil War surpluses, and the breakdown in these controls in the 1880s is usually cited as a major cause of the deficit problems that soon followed.[42] In 1865, the House established its Committee on Appropriations, with exclusive jurisdiction over annual spending bills, and the Senate created a counterpart committee two years later. Previously, the Ways and Means and Finance Committees had been responsible for revenue legislation and appropriations, but neither of these committees seriously challenged the contention that its workload had grown too large. During House debate, the chairman of Ways and Means, Thaddeus Stevens, expressed some reservations about the "propriety" of separating "the duties of finance from those of appropriations . . . [since] the two subjects seem to be very properly connected."[43] Samuel Cox, whose committee had proposed the separation, insisted that the loss of coordination would be more than offset by the heightened scrutiny of spending programs: "I need not dilate upon the importance of having hereafter one committee investigate with wisest heed all matters concerned with economy. The tendency of the time is to extravagance in private and in public. We require of this new committee their whole labor in the restraint of extravagant and illegal appropriations."[44] The House easily passed the reorganization, as Stevens declared himself satisfied "that this matter has not been prompted by any action of the present committee."[45]

While structural changes in the appropriations process were important, their significance in terms of budget reform can easily be exaggerated. After the Civil War, standing committees proliferated in the House and Senate, and jurisdictional changes were not uncommon.[46] Banking and credit oversight, which involved equally pressing financial issues, was transferred from

42. See Charles H. Stewart III, *Budget Reform Politics: The Design of the Appropriations Process in the House of Representatives, 1865–1921* (Cambridge: Cambridge University Press, 1989), 133–71.
43. *Congressional Globe,* 38th Cong., 2d sess., 1865, 35, pt. 2: 1315.
44. *Congressional Globe,* 38th Cong., 2d sess., 1865, 35, pt. 2: 1312.
45. *Congressional Globe,* 38th Cong., 2d sess., 1865, 35, pt. 2: 1315.
46. See Christopher J. Deering and Steven S. Smith, *Committees in Congress,* 3d ed. (Washington, D.C.: Congressional Quarterly, 1997), 26–27.

Ways and Means to yet another new committee when the appropriations
process was restructured. While the Appropriations Committees had been
established to strengthen spending control, the jurisdictional split among
spending, revenue, and credit divided budgetary responsibilities and made
coherent decision making more difficult.

Congress faced numerous fiscal problems after the Civil War, of which
spending control was the most straightforward. Interest on the debt absorbed
a large portion of total spending—an average of nearly 40 percent of budgeted expenditures each year from 1866 to 1880. It was not until the 1880s
that this interest burden eased appreciably. Postwar military spending and
veterans' pension commitments also accounted for large budget shares—
approximately 40 percent of expenditures in the early 1880s.[47] The Appropriations Committees had a relatively narrow spending margin with which
to work, given these more or less fixed obligations. Within this margin, their
responsibilities as "guardians of the Treasury" had important implications
for the spending preferences of other members of Congress, but the overall
budget policy effects were limited.

Debt Policy

In addition, congressional disputes over debt management and currency
policies often overshadowed appropriations decision making. Immediately
after the war, Congress authorized the Secretary of the Treasury to retire the
existing legal-tender issues, or greenbacks, and to convert short-term debt
into long-term bonds. The restoration of "hard money" and debt conversion
was hampered, however, by frequent congressional policy reversals. In 1866,
limits were placed on the Treasury's authority to convert greenbacks into
bonds, and Congress completely revoked the authority two years later. In
1869, Congress passed the Public Credit Act, pledging specie redemption of
all debt, including legal-tender notes, and committing itself to provide for
legal-tender redemption "at the earliest practicable period."[48] No such provision was actually made, however, and Congress continued to be stymied by
competing pressures for currency inflation and currency contraction.

The panic of 1873, brought on by an inflated currency and speculative credit
markets, actually increased congressional support for currency inflation.[49]

---

47. *Historical Statistics of the United States, Colonial Times to 1970*, Part 2, 1114.
48. *Statutes at Large*, Vol. 16, 1869–1971 (Boston: Little, Brown and Company, 1871), 1.
49. See Patterson, *Federal Debt-Management Policies, 1865–1879*, 186–87.

The Republican-controlled Congress, in "a last desperate chance to find favor with a depression-ridden population," approved an infamous "Inflation Bill" that was vetoed by President Ulysses S. Grant.[50] The party's fears were confirmed by the 1874 election, when the Democrats captured almost half of the Republican seats in the House and took control of the chamber for the first time since 1859. After the election, the lame-duck Republican Congress reconvened and sent to the president the Resumption Act of 1875. This measure, which Grant promptly signed, was almost exactly opposite to the one he had vetoed, since it mandated that a specie-based currency be restored.

The currency debate, however, was far from over. In 1877, House Democrats moved to repeal the Resumption Act and expand the currency by requiring the monetization of silver. The repeal effort was unsuccessful, but the debate over silver continued for more than two decades. Because silver had, in effect, "supplanted greenbacks as *the* means for promoting cheaper-money policies," Congress kept returning to the issue of silver coinage.[51] For Democrats representing agrarian debtor groups in the South and Midwest, free-silver policies promised substantial debt relief; many Republicans from silver-producing states in the West were attracted by the potential economic benefits to their states from increased demand for silver.[52] Congressional efforts to enact free-silver laws were thwarted by presidential opposition, and the effective end of the silver impasse came in 1900, when gold was made the "sole legal tender monetary metal."[53]

The restoration of federal credit involved complex and often unpredictable interactions between debt management and monetary policy. Congress and its committees remained active in setting broad policies and in monitoring detailed Treasury Department operations. On these matters, there was considerably less centralization of control and consistency in policy direction than was evidenced in appropriations decision making; coordination between debt management and appropriations spending appears to have been nonexistent. The budget surpluses and debt reduction that followed the Civil War were but one aspect of an otherwise highly politicized and costly legislative approach to financial policy.

50. Patterson, *Federal Debt-Management Policies, 1865–1879*, 189.

51. Richard H. Timberlake, *Monetary Policy in the United States: An Intellectual and Institutional History* (Chicago: University of Chicago Press, 1993), 166.

52. Timberlake, *Monetary Policy in the United States*, 166–67.

53. Timberlake, *Monetary Policy in the United States*, 167.

Tax Policy and Tariffs

Postwar tax policy was not dictated by revenue requirements but rather by economic protectionism. Tariff rates had been raised to very high levels during the war because of the urgent need for revenues. The inevitable disruptions of trade that occurred had limited the revenue productivity of these higher tariffs, but tariff receipts still climbed well above their prewar levels. Once peacetime commercial relations had been restored, increased trade would have provided ample revenues at lower tariff levels, particularly if moderate levels of direct taxation had been maintained. Instead, high tariffs were continued, while most direct taxes were repealed. While congressional Democrats generally supported a tariff "for revenue only," the heavily Republican Congresses of the immediate postwar period wanted to ensure long-term protection for American manufacturing and industrial interests. Tariff schedules and rates were adjusted on occasion, but the "fundamental structure" of the Civil War tariff system remained in place, as "the ratio between duties and the value of dutiable goods rarely dropped below 40 percent and was frequently close to 50 percent."[54] Protection was especially strong for manufactured items, such as "metals and metal products, including iron and steel, cotton textiles, and certain woolen goods," with tariff rates on many of these reaching 100 percent.[55]

From 1866 to 1870, tariff receipts averaged almost $180 million per year, almost 50 percent higher than the annual interest charges on the debt for this period and more than three times the annual average for the 1850s.[56] Given their protectionist agenda, congressional Republicans moved quickly to eliminate competing revenue sources. In 1866, the special wartime tax on manufacturers was repealed. Over the next several years, excise taxes other than alcohol and tobacco were reduced or canceled. In 1867, the exemption level for the income tax was raised and the tax rate was lowered, and further cuts were made in 1870. The income tax was then allowed to expire, along with the wartime federal inheritance tax. Between 1866 and 1874, tax receipts from these sources dropped by almost $200 million.[57]

The wholesale application of wartime excise taxes had produced serious economic distortions, and the burden on consumers became more severe

---

54. Brownlee, *Federal Taxation in America*, 29. The 1864 rate schedules, for example, remained largely intact for almost twenty years.
55. Brownlee, *Federal Taxation in America*, 29.
56. *Historical Statistics of the United States, Colonial Times to 1970, Part 2*, 1106.
57. *Historical Statistics of the United States, Colonial Times to 1970, Part 2*, 1091, 1108.

Table 3.3 Composition of Federal Revenues, 1866–1890 (in millions of dollars)

		Annual Average		
		Percentage of Total		
Fiscal Years	Total Revenues	Customs	Alcohol and Tobacco	Other
1866–70	$ 447.3	40.0%	14.6%	45.4%
1871–75	336.8	55.3	27.6	17.1
1876–80	288.1	50.9	36.8	12.3
1881–85	367.0	55.0	34.0	11.0
1886–90	375.4	57.7	33.5	8.8

SOURCE: *Historical Statistics of the United States, Colonial Times to 1970, Part 2* (Washington, D.C.: U.S. Bureau of the Census, 1975), 1106, 1108.

with the price deflation after the war. Thus, the tax relief sought by economic interests enjoyed popular support.[58] And although the income tax affected only a small minority of the population, it had failed to gain widespread acceptance as a permanent source of revenue. In addition, opposition to the income tax was intense in the handful of wealthy states that provided most of the income tax revenue.[59] The primary objective of postwar tax policy, however, was to reestablish the tariff as the one indispensable source of federal revenues. The transition in revenue policy was rapid. In 1865, tariff revenues were one-fourth of total receipts. That year, liquor and tobacco taxes supplied about 10 percent of total receipts. By the 1870s, the share for tariffs had risen above 50 percent, where it remained for two decades (Table 3.3). Meanwhile, the liquor and tobacco tax shares more than tripled. By the 1880s, these internal taxes and the tariff were supplying roughly 90 percent of total budget receipts.

Redefining Balanced Budgets

The pace of debt reduction was extremely rapid from 1866 to 1873. The panic of 1873 then reduced budget surpluses and, hence, debt repayment for several years. By the end of the decade, however, surpluses were again beginning to build and soon were outstripping the supply of government debt

---

58. Bolles, *The Financial History of the United States from 1861 to 1885,* 399–405.

59. The seven New England states along with California provided 70 percent of the income tax revenues. New York alone accounted for approximately one-third of the total collected. John F. Witte, *The Politics and Development of the Federal Income Tax* (Madison: University of Wisconsin Press, 1985), 70.

scheduled for redemption. The Treasury was then forced to pay a heavy pre-mium to purchase unmatured debt on the open market, but these purchases still could not exhaust its large and growing surpluses.

Budget policy in the 1880s could accommodate two sharply contrasting types of balanced budgets. Budgets could be balanced by expanding pro-grammatic spending to fill the margins left by declining interest payments and practicable debt reduction, or revenue levels could be lowered to elimi-nate these margins. The level of available revenues was therefore directly tied to the partisan divisions over how budgets should be balanced. In 1876, the Democratic party's platform sharply attacked protective tariffs. "We denounce the present tariff levied upon nearly four thousand articles as a masterpiece of injustice, inequality, and false pretense, which yields a dwin-dling and not a yearly rising revenue, [and] has impoverished many industries to subsidize a few. . . . We demand that all custom-house taxation shall be only for revenue."[60] The 1880 and 1884 platforms likewise endorsed a tariff "for revenue only," and the 1888 platform went on to connect tax reform and spending control: "All unnecessary taxation is unjust taxation. . . . Every Democratic rule of governmental action is violated when through unneces-sary taxation a vast sum of money . . . is drawn from the people and the channels of trade, and accumulated as a demoralizing surplus in the National Treasury. . . . The Democratic remedy is to enforce frugality in public expense and abolish needless taxation."[61]

The Republican party's support for protective tariffs was unapologetic. The 1884 platform specifically rejected a revenue-determined tariff: "We . . . demand that the imposition of duties on foreign imports shall be made, not 'for revenue only,' but that in raising the requisite revenues for the govern-ment, such duties shall be so levied as to afford security to our diversified industries and protection to the rights and wages of the laborer."[62] Four years later, the party endorsed a spending program that would solve the problem of excess revenue:

> [W]e demand appropriations for the early rebuilding of our Navy; for the construction of coast fortifications and modern ordnance, and other approved modern means of defense . . . ; for the payment

60. *Guide to U. S. Elections*, 2d ed. (Washington, D.C.: Congressional Quarterly, 1985), 56.
61. *Guide to U. S. Elections*, 61.
62. *Guide to U. S. Elections*, 59.

of just pensions to our soldiers; for the necessary works of national importance in the improvement of . . . internal, coastwise, and foreign commerce; for the encouragement of the shipping interests of the Atlantic, Gulf, and Pacific states, as well as for the payment of the maturing public debt.[63]

The tensions over spending policy were aggravated by the House's adoption in 1875 of the Holman rule, which "allowed an appropriations bill to change existing law if such action was germane and retrenched expenses, and thus authorized the Appropriations Committee to invade virtually at will the jurisdictions of other committees."[64] In 1877, the House reversed course and began to curb the independence and "excessive economy-mindedness" of its Appropriations Committee by removing from its jurisdiction the rivers and harbors bill.[65] Three years later, the agriculture appropriations bill was taken from the committee. In 1885, six of the remaining twelve appropriations bills were removed and, as in the earlier cases, transferred to their respective authorizing committees. These actions "removed nearly one-half of the total federal budget, and many of that budget's most controversial items, from the purview of the Appropriations Committee . . . as effective an emasculation of a committee's influence as could be imagined."[66]

Growing spending pressures affected a wide range of programs, including pensions, internal improvements, and postal services. In 1872, the House had been informed that the substantial costs of Civil War pensions would "hereafter steadily decrease, unless our legislation should be unwarrantably extravagant."[67] Over the next several years, Congress resisted the temptation to alter pension policy, and pension costs did, in fact, decline. But then Congress enacted the 1879 Pensions Arrears Act, which proved to be enormously expensive. In its haste to satisfy veterans' demands for more generous Civil War pension benefits, the House bypassed its Committee on Invalid Pensions and passed a liberalized pension measure with "no report of the probable expenditure."[68] The Senate's brief debate on the bill included a "modest

63. *Platforms of the Two Great Political Parties, 1856–1928, Inclusive* (Washington, D.C.: Government Printing Office, 1936), 75.
64. Ippolito, *Congressional Spending*, 41–42. See also Stewart, *Budget Reform Politics*, 84–89.
65. Fenno, *The Power of the Purse*, 43.
66. Fenno, *The Power of the Purse*, 43.
67. *Congressional Globe*, 42d Cong., 2d sess., 1872, 45, pt. 1: 538.
68. Bolles, *The Financial History of the United States from 1861 to 1885*, 544.

guess of eighteen or twenty millions [that] vanished on the very eve of paying the arrears, and the hundreds of millions that have followed have not filled the chasm of expenditure created by Congress without a serious recorded thought."[69]

Internal improvements legislation followed a similar course. The rivers and harbors appropriations bill was under $4 million in 1870; the Congress elected in 1880 raised this appropriation to nearly $19 million.[70] When Republican President Chester A. Arthur vetoed the 1882 rivers and harbors appropriation "on the grounds of its unconstitutionality and unwarranted diversion of public funds," the Republican-controlled Congress overrode his veto within twenty-four hours.[71] In addition, the federal government provided substantial sums for other internal improvements, particularly railroad development. Cash grants for construction of the transcontinental railroad were supplemented by land grants to the railroads estimated at 100 million acres.[72] During the 1870s and 1880s, Congress greatly enlarged the size of federal agencies, notably the Post Office. The number of civilian employees more than tripled, to nearly 160,000, with the Post Office alone growing by 60,000 positions. During this period, federal expenditures to meet deficiencies in postal service operations totaled approximately $100 million.[73]

Presidential intervention in budget policy matters was sporadic and unsystematic. Congress was opposed to anything resembling an executive budget, which effectively barred the president from countering "the haphazard construction of appropriations bills by separate committees not concerned in planning for the revenue."[74] The frequency of divided party control among the presidency, Senate, and House further reduced the ability of presidents to coordinate policy. It was difficult to combat new spending in the face of large surpluses. These surpluses, in turn, were tied to high tariffs. With Congress unwilling to relax tariff protections, the efforts of several administrations to retrench expenditures were largely unsuccessful. The impasse between Congress and the executive was especially pronounced during Grover

69. Bolles, *The Financial History of the United States from 1861 to 1885*, 544–45.

70. Alexander Dana Noyes, *Forty Years of American Finance: A Short Financial History of the Government and People of the United States Since the Civil War, 1865–1907* (New York: G. P. Putnam's Sons, 1898), 89.

71. Noyes, *Forty Years of American Finance*, 89–90.

72. Savage, *Balanced Budgets and American Politics*, 172.

73. *Historical Statistics of the United States, 1789–1945* (Washington, D.C.: U.S. Bureau of the Census, 1949), 299–301.

74. Noyes, *Forty Years of American Finance*, 133.

Cleveland's first term. Cleveland was committed to lower spending and challenged Congress through unprecedented use of the veto power. Cleveland was also opposed to high tariffs, but Congress blocked his reform proposals. In the end, neither tariff policy nor spending policy was greatly altered, although Cleveland's pension-bill vetoes probably contributed to his reelection defeat in 1888. In four years, Cleveland issued more than three hundred vetoes, nearly three times as many as all previous presidents combined.[75] Approximately 80 percent of Cleveland's vetoes were against pension bills.

Moreover, not all presidents shared Cleveland's opposition to federal spending.[76] Rutherford B. Hayes believed that federal funding should be used for public improvements "of national importance" wherever "local and private enterprise are inadequate."[77] In particular, Hayes favored federal grants to help build a nationwide system of free public schools. Benjamin Harrison echoed Hayes, pointing to "a present exigency that calls for still more liberal and direct appropriations in aid of common-school education in the states."[78] Although Harrison warned that "wastefulness, profligacy, or favoritism in public expenditures is criminal," he urged Congress to increase spending for pensions, the military, and even rivers and harbors improvements.[79]

These ambivalences and inconsistencies characterized post–Civil War spending policy. Total federal expenditures hardly grew at all over the extended period of balanced budgets, which seems to confirm that "economy remained a leading goal of public policy."[80] There was, however, a postwar deflation that suppressed aggregate spending growth.[81] More important, domestic programmatic spending began to rise as military and interest expenditures diminished (Table 3.4). Between 1875 and 1880, spending for pensions roughly doubled, and a similar increase occurred during the latter half of the 1880s. Spending for various civil functions, including postal deficiencies and Indian affairs, dropped between 1875 and 1880 but then rose sharply over the next decade.

75. Fisher, *Presidential Spending Power*, 26.

76. Kimmel, *Federal Budget and Fiscal Policy, 1789–1958*, 78–81.

77. *Letters and Messages of Rutherford B. Hayes* (Washington, D.C.: Government Printing Office, 1881), 306.

78. Kimmel, *Federal Budget and Fiscal Policy, 1789–1958*, 81.

79. Richardson, *A Compilation of the Messages and Papers of the Presidents*, 12:5447.

80. Kimmel, *Federal Budget and Fiscal Policy, 1789–1958*, 75.

81. On this and other complications in measuring spending growth, see Stewart, *Budget Reform Politics*, 35–41.

Table 3.4 Federal Spending Trends, 1870–1890 (in millions of dollars)

Fiscal Year	Veterans' Pensions	Civil and Other	War and Navy Departments*	Interest	Total
1870	$ 28.3	$ 72.6	$ 79.4	$ 129.2	$ 309.7
1875	29.5	79.5	62.6	103.1	274.6
1880	56.8	63.5	51.7	95.8	267.6
1885	56.1	94.0	58.7	51.4	260.2
1890	106.9	108.4	66.6	36.1	318.0
Change	+ $78.6	+ $35.8	−$12.8	−$93.1	+ $8.3

* Includes rivers and harbors spending.

SOURCE: *Historical Statistics of the United States, Colonial Times to 1970, Part 2* (Washington, D.C.: U.S. Bureau of the Census, 1975), 1114.

Deficits and Policy Change

The "problem" of surplus budgets disappeared during the early 1890s. From 1894, when the first post–Civil War deficit was incurred, through 1915, there were fourteen deficit budgets. The 1898 and 1899 deficits, totaling more than $125 million, were brought on by the Spanish-American War. The remainder, which totaled nearly $420 million, occurred during peacetime.

The congressional budget process has received a great deal of criticism for this deficit record. A widespread perception at the time, and one shared in many recent studies, was that the fragmentation of the appropriations process and the corresponding rise of electorally beneficial spending decisions caused federal expenditures to grow at unacceptably high rates. The evidence, as examined here, is mixed with respect to this argument. What appears more persuasive is that Congress was finding it more and more difficult to coordinate revenue and spending and that this structural weakness helped to build support for a national budget system. While presidential budget reform was not enacted until after World War I, its genesis is found in the budget policy vicissitudes of the preceding decades.

Spending Policy

Between 1890 and 1915, federal expenditures more than doubled, from $318 million to $760 million. The latter was ten times higher than the peak spending level reached before the Civil War and was fairly close to what had been spent in the middle years of the war itself. More to the point, since spending was virtually flat from 1870 to 1890, this abrupt upward trend over the next quarter century certainly suggests a breakdown in spending control.

Program Expansions. Numerous domestic policy expansions contributed to budgetary growth. The 1890 Dependent Pensions Act, for example, was enormously costly. It provided a service-disability pension for any Civil War veteran suffering from a physical or mental impairment, regardless of whether the disability had been incurred during wartime.[82] The Grand Army of the Republic, the leading veterans' organization, hailed this measure as "the most liberal pension measure ever passed by any legislative body in the world . . . [that] will place upon the rolls all of the survivors of the war whose conditions of health are not practically perfect."[83] By 1893, the number of pension beneficiaries had soared to over one million, while pension costs were absorbing more than 40 percent of the federal budget.[84] In 1907, 1908, and 1912, pension policy was further liberalized, although the budgetary impact of these changes was moderated by the natural attrition of aging beneficiaries.

The Republican party was largely responsible for creating this generous and extensive pension system. Pension benefits were used to build electoral support and to protect high tariffs, but this strategy had been evident well before the 1890s. The 1879 Pensions Arrears Act had more than doubled annual pension spending, and Congress made sure that more generous benefits would continue by rejecting administrative reforms designed to standardize eligibility and control costs. Starting in 1890, Congress expanded the Civil War pension system beyond its war-related restrictions on eligibility to cover postwar disabilities and, finally, old-age benefits. Over an extended period, therefore, "the federal government . . . became the source of generous and honorable social provision for a major portion of the American citizenry."[85]

Alongside these pre–New Deal experiments in social welfare policy, regulatory and service agencies were widening the scope of federal government functions and swelling the size and cost of the civilian bureaucracy. Federal civilian employment was about 150,000 in 1890. Twenty-five years later, it was approaching 400,000. The Post Office alone employed more than 200,000 people in 1915, which was twice the size of the entire federal bureaucracy in

82. Skocpol, *Protecting Soldiers and Mothers*, 128.
83. Quoted in Skocpol, *Protecting Soldiers and Mothers*, 128.
84. Skocpol, *Protecting Soldiers and Mothers*, 128–29.
85. Skocpol, *Protecting Soldiers and Mothers*, 101.

1880. Between 1890 and 1915, funding for the civil departments of the federal government rose from under $100 million to more than $200 million. As with pension policy, however, much of the foundation for spending increases had been established during the 1870s and 1880s. Appropriations for the Department of Agriculture more than doubled between 1890 and 1900, but much of this growth took place in bureaus and programs that had previously been added to the department's jurisdiction.[86] And while government employment grew much more rapidly than the population between 1890 and 1915, equally large differentials between these growth rates had taken place over the preceding decades.[87]

The domestic policy changes fueling government growth were complemented by transformations in the missions and capabilities of the American military. The U.S. Navy's "dark ages" lasted for almost two decades, as its 700-ship Civil War fleet was reduced to a handful of aging vessels with poorly trained crews and ineffective leadership.[88] By the early 1880s, however, a strategic rationale was being developed for a large and modern Navy that could protect U.S. commercial and trading interests throughout the world. In 1883, Congress authorized the construction of four steam-powered steel ships, and an enormous shipbuilding program, featuring first-class battleships, was soon underway. By the time World War I began, the United States had an impressive fleet and a highly professional officer cadre. It also had a Navy Department budget that accounted for nearly one-fifth of federal spending.

Because the Army had been responsible for the Reconstruction occupation of the Southern states that lasted until 1877 and for fighting the Indian wars in the West until 1890, its funding never dropped as low as the Navy's. Nevertheless, the post–Civil War Army suffered from many of the same deficiencies in training, equipment, and leadership. The creation of a modern Army was hampered by rivalries with state militias and by entrenched "fears of a large standing army as a danger to liberty and of an elite officer class as antidemocratic."[89] It was not until the turn of the century that the "politics of army reform changed dramatically. . . . [As] new army professionals gained

86. Stewart, *Budget Reform Politics*, 138–39.

87. Between 1865 and 1890, the population of the United States increased by 80 percent, while federal civilian employment approximately tripled. From 1890 to 1915, population growth was just under 60 percent, while civilian employment rose by 250 percent.

88. Morris, *America's Armed Forces*, 150.

89. Morris, *America's Armed Forces*, 148.

an institutional power base . . . against the forces of localism, amateurism, and the pork barrel."[90] By 1915, the Army's budget had reached $200 million, four times higher than the War Department's total spending before the Spanish-American War.

The federal budget's growth between 1890 and 1915 was perhaps more robust than it might have been had centralized spending controls in Congress remained in place. The policy bases for growth, however, did not emerge overnight. Instead, federal domestic and military policy was gradually being reshaped over an extended period to meet emerging social, economic, and international political realities. There was an inevitable lag between new policy commitments and their budgetary effects, especially the cumulative, aggregate effects across policy areas.

Worth noting as well was the remarkably successful financing of the Spanish-American War. While the war was relatively short, it was expensive. Total federal expenditures in 1898 and 1899 were close to $1.5 billion, but the deficits for these years were only 12 percent of expenditures. The corresponding deficit percentages for earlier wars were much higher—57 percent for the War of 1812, 39 percent for the war with Mexico, and 65 percent for the Civil War.[91] Because the demand for credit during the Spanish-American War was controlled, financing was accomplished without the disruptions that had occurred during previous years. Funds were obtained quickly, at low rates of interest, and "the [wartime] credit of the country was so used that it grew stronger rather than weaker" for the first time in the nation's history.[92]

Composition and Growth. In 1888, the Republican party regained control of Congress and the White House, and in a very short time the surpluses of the Cleveland presidency had disappeared. The fifty-first Congress, which served from 1889 to 1891, set a new standard in legislative activity, enacting many more public and private bills than any of its predecessors.[93] It also gained notoriety as the "Billion Dollar Congress" for its spending largesse. Between 1888 and 1891, budget expenditures grew by almost $100 million,

90. Skowronek, *Building a New American State*, 213.

91. Kimmel, *Federal Budget and Fiscal Policy, 1789–1958*, 316.

92. Carl C. Plehn, "Finances of the United States in the Spanish War," *University Chronicle* 1 (October 1898): 419.

93. In the fifty-first Congress, 19,630 measures were introduced. Congress enacted 2,251 measures, including 611 public bills and 1,640 private bills. This total was more than 400 bills greater than any preceding Congress and was not eclipsed for another decade. Erik W. Austin, *Political Facts of the United States Since 1789* (New York: Columbia University Press, 1986), 47–48.

Table 3.5 Federal Spending, 1870–1915 (as a percentage of GNP)

Fiscal Year	Total	War and Navy Departments	Interest	Veterans' Pensions	Civil and Other
1870[a]	4.2%	1.1%	1.7%	0.4%	1.0%
1875[a]	3.7	0.8	1.4	0.4	1.1
1880[b]	2.4	0.5	0.9	0.5	0.6
1885[b]	2.3	0.5	0.5	0.5	0.8
1890	2.4	0.5	0.3	0.8	0.8
1895	2.6	0.6	0.2	1.0	0.7
1900	2.8	1.0	0.2	0.8	0.8
1905	2.3	1.0	0.1	0.6	0.6
1910	2.0	0.9	0.1	0.5	0.6
1915	1.9	0.9	0.1	0.4	0.5

[a] Percentages based on average annual GNP figures for 1869–78.
[b] Percentages based on average annual GNP figures for 1879–88.

SOURCE: *Historical Statistics of the United States, Colonial Times to 1970, Parts 1 and 2* (Washington, D.C.: U.S. Bureau of the Census, 1975), 224, 1114–15.

to $365 million. Since spending levels had increased hardly at all over the preceding decade, the fifty-first Congress was setting a very different course. Criticism of its record and of later Congresses plagued with budget deficits was harsh, and the prevailing view was that Congress lacked the institutional structure and will to control spending.

Though there undoubtedly was a good deal of waste and extravagance in specific appropriations, total spending levels were fairly stable during the post-1890 period. Using the conventional measure of the size of government—spending versus GNP—the federal budget grew marginally between 1890 and 1900 but then dropped sharply (Table 3.5). In 1915, federal spending was less than 2 percent of GNP, well below the levels of the 1870s or 1880s.

Furthermore, the decline in the relative size of government was concentrated in domestic programs—veterans' pensions and the operations of the civil departments. The composition of the federal budget was shifting toward the military, even as its overall growth lagged behind that of the economy. In 1890, expenditures for the Army and Navy accounted for one-fifth of the budget, while domestic spending was approximately two-thirds. By 1915, the military and domestic shares were equal. Even with interest entirely removed from these calculations, spending as a percentage of GNP was much lower in 1915 than it had been during the balanced-budget era after the Civil War.

While the data are limited, comparisons with state and local spending underscore the distinctiveness of this federal trend. The federal government published its first comprehensive report on government finances in 1902.[94] Combined state and local spending that year was 5.1 percent of GNP, with direct local expenditures (4.2 percent) contributing by far the greater share of this total. From 1902 to 1913, federal spending decreased from 2.6 percent to 2.4 percent of GNP; local and state expenditures, by comparison, increased to 5.7 percent. For a number of important domestic functions— education, roads, health and public welfare services—federal spending was minuscule compared with local and state funding.

Still, a new spending philosophy was taking shape around the turn of the century. Although the traditional rhetoric about balanced budgets continued to define fiscal policy debates at the federal level, a more activist federal role in economic and social policy matters was giving rise to more nuanced views about spending. Theodore Roosevelt urged the federal government to promote "the welfare of each citizen, and therefore the welfare of the aggregate of citizens which makes the nation" through "wise legislation and honest and intelligent administration."[95] William Howard Taft declared that "the scope of a modern government in what it can and ought to accomplish for its people has widened far beyond the principles laid down by the old 'laissez faire' school of political writers."[96] For Woodrow Wilson, the case for federal activism was even stronger.

With the scope of government becoming wider, the criteria for evaluating spending were changing. Economy in government could no longer be measured strictly by low costs or reduced expenditures. Instead, economy was defined as the efficient implementation of spending programs with demonstrated merit. A 1909 Treasury Secretary's report warned, "It would be a great mistake . . . to let this epoch of economy discredit itself and come to an untimely end by reason of losing the sense of difference between reductions of appropriations that we are better without and reductions of the appropriations that we are better with."[97] It was likewise thought necessary

94. In 1913, total local government expenditures were $1.96 billion, and total outstanding debt was $4.035 billion. State government spending totaled less than $400 million, and state debt less than $400 million as well. *Historical Statistics of the United States, Colonial Times to 1970, Part 2,* 1130–32.

95. Richardson, *A Compilation of the Messages and Papers of the Presidents,* 15:6645.

96. Richardson, *A Compilation of the Messages and Papers of the Presidents,* 17:7370.

97. *Annual Report of the Secretary of the Treasury on the State of the Finances for the Fiscal Year Ended June 30, 1909* (Washington, D.C.: Government Printing Office, 1909), 3.

to distinguish between capital outlays and operating expenditures, for purposes of accurate budget accounting and even for borrowing. As President
Wilson pointed out, peacetime borrowing was permissible "when permanent things are to be accomplished which many generations will certainly
benefit by and which it seems hardly fair that a single generation should pay
for."[98]

The great difficulty was in reconciling this new spending philosophy
with the old balanced-budget requirement. Revenues would have to be
elastic to support higher spending, but tariffs were proving less and less
dependable as a revenue source and were susceptible to attack on grounds of
equity or fairness. Revenue policy, then, would have to change, as would the
budget process, to provide a systematic, comprehensive review of proliferating spending programs.

Revenue Policy

The federal government's heavy dependence on tariffs for protection and
revenue was extremely controversial, regardless of whether budgets were balanced. Tariffs were highly regressive, as were other consumption taxes levied
by the federal government, and the distribution of economic benefits and
costs from a high-tariff regime reinforced the already deep sectional cleav-
ages in American politics. Until the 1890s, however, the Republican party was
able to fend off any substantial challenge to "the most prominent and persistent category of nineteenth-century American economic policymaking."[99]

In 1890, the Republican party enacted the McKinley Tariff Act, which
raised average tariff rates for most goods but notably removed duties on
sugar, the second largest revenue-producing item in the tariff schedule. The
loss in revenue from the exclusion for sugar was much greater than expected.
Between 1890 and 1892, customs revenues fell by more than $50 million;
total receipts dropped by nearly 12 percent. There was a modest recovery
the following year, but the panic of 1893 depressed revenues once again. In
1894, customs receipts were almost $100 million below 1890 levels, and the
budget was in deficit for the first time since 1865.

The Democratic party gained a majority in the House in the 1890
midterm election. Two years later, it captured the White House and Senate.

---

98. Richardson, *A Compilation of the Messages and Papers of the Presidents*, 18:8112.

99. Morton Keller, *Regulating a New Economy: Public Policy and Economic Change in America,
1900–1933* (Cambridge: Harvard University Press, 1990), 193.

Nearly four decades had passed since the Democratic party had last controlled the government, and it capitalized on this opportunity to lower tariffs and to impose a tax on incomes. Divisions within the party, however, greatly limited the scope of tax reform.

The 1894 Wilson-Gorman Tariff Act reduced tariff rates only marginally and reinstituted the duty on sugar. The latter was one of the more than four hundred tariff compromises made to gain Senate approval.[100] The income tax added to the tariff bill applied to corporations and individuals and covered "dividends, interest, rents, sales of real estate and property, and gifts, as well as wages and salaries."[101] The exemption level, however, was an extremely high $4,000, limiting the income tax's coverage to less than one-half of 1 percent of the population.[102] Furthermore, the tax rate was a flat 2 percent, compared with the graduated rate of up to 10 percent that had been in effect in 1865 and 1866.

The acrimonious congressional debate on the income tax featured routine charges and countercharges about class warfare and socialism, enlivened by occasional discourses on the French Revolution, communism, and devilism.[103] Almost entirely ignored amid all this rhetoric was the claim that the income tax, unlike the tariff, could be easily adjusted to meet new revenue needs, without negatively affecting business. One income tax supporter lauded its fairness and flexibility: "If the tax is increased by the necessities of the Government for larger revenue, it does not affect . . . business interests, because only incomes are to be taxed. There will be no discharge of employés; there will be no change of prices as a result of the change of law; there will be no increasing of the costs of raw material, or of the return of the manufactured product, but all will depend upon success in business and the demand for revenue."[104]

There was no opportunity to test this argument, or any other, since the Supreme Court soon invalidated the entire income tax section of the Wilson-Gorman Act. In 1895, the Court held that federal taxes on the interest from state and municipal bonds and on income from property were direct taxes

100. Ronald F. King, *Money, Time, and Politics: Investment Tax Subsidies and American Democracy* (New Haven: Yale University Press, 1993), 97.

101. Witte, *The Politics and Development of the Federal Income Tax*, 73. Exemptions from the tax were extremely limited.

102. Witte, *The Politics and Development of the Federal Income Tax*, 72–73.

103. See King, *Money, Time, and Politics*, 95–98.

104. *Congressional Record*, 53d Cong., 2d sess., 1894, 26, pt. 1: 277.

and accordingly had to be apportioned among the states on the basis of population.[105] Then, in an unusual second hearing, the Court held that these provisions were so central to the scheme of taxation Congress had approved that all of the income taxes levied were "wholly inoperative and void."[106] The Court took pains to disclaim any policy judgment in its ruling: "We are not here concerned with the question whether an income tax be or be not desirable, nor whether such a tax would enable the government to diminish taxes on consumption and duties on imports, and to enter upon what may be believed to be a reform of its fiscal and commercial system."[107] Regardless, the Court's decision blocked any such reform, and in 1896 the Republican party regained control of the executive branch and Congress, foreclosing any more experiments in income taxation.

The 1898 Dingley Tariff Act raised tariff rates once more. With the depression coming to an end and trade increasing, these higher duties boosted customs receipts, but the immediate gains were much less than expected. Over time, the composition of imports had shifted from manufactured goods to raw materials. As a result, the share of imports subject to customs duties had shrunk, as had the ratio of duties to all imports. Under the Dingley Tariff Act, the average rates on dutiable goods were the highest of the entire postwar era, but the revenue yield from tariffs was not commensurate. The share of federal revenues supplied by tariffs remained below the levels of the 1870s and 1880s; when tariff rates were reduced—by the Payne-Aldrich Tariff Act in 1909 and then by the Underwood Tariff Act in 1913—the share dropped still further.

Because of their limited elasticity, neither the tariff nor consumption taxes were generally well-suited to sharp, erratic increases in spending. During the Spanish-American War, deficits were moderated by a significant increase in revenues, primarily through internal taxes on liquor, tobacco, and stamps. But in 1904 and 1905, when large expenditures for construction of the Panama Canal commenced, budget receipts remained flat, and budget deficits totaled more than $65 million. An economic panic that began in 1907 caused revenues to drop by 10 percent in just one year and to remain at depressed levels until 1910. At the same time, budgets could not be reduced because of ongoing military commitments. The combined deficits from 1908 to 1910 were more than $160 million.

105. *Pollock v. Farmers' Loan and Trust Co.*, 157 U.S. 429 (1895).
106. *Pollock v. Farmers' Loan and Trust Co.*, 158 U.S. 601 (1895), p. 637.
107. *Pollock v. Farmers' Loan and Trust Co.*, 158 U.S. 601 (1895), p. 634.

The asymmetry between spending commitments and revenues was not terribly serious over an extended period. Between 1890 and 1915, the United States suffered a war and two financial panics and the federal government mounted an enormously expensive public works project, but cumulative surpluses and cumulative deficits were nearly equal. The public debt increased by less than $70 million during the entire period. Year-to-year fluctuations between spending and revenue levels, however, were unpredictable and often severe.

The need for a predictable revenue source made it difficult to dismiss the growing sentiment for a more equitable form of taxation. A number of progressive Republicans had joined congressional Democrats in calling for income taxation, and Presidents Roosevelt and Taft endorsed reforms that would distribute at least a portion of the federal tax burden on the basis of the ability to pay. In 1909, a bipartisan coalition in the Senate attached an income tax amendment to what finally emerged as the Payne-Aldrich Tariff Act. With the House Republican leadership strenuously opposed to the tax, the Taft administration offered a compromise that was ultimately accepted. The proposed new taxes on individual and corporate income were split. The former was put in the form of a constitutional amendment to allow the federal government to tax individual incomes from any source without apportionment among the states, thereby removing the obstacle the Supreme Court had erected in invalidating the 1894 income tax. By statute, Congress imposed a 1 percent tax on corporate profits but designated it "as an excise on the privilege of doing business as a corporation."[108] The Supreme Court later accepted this rationale, and, in 1910, the tax generated more than $20 million.

In 1912, the Democratic party captured control of the White House and Congress. With ratification of the Sixteenth Amendment in February 1913, the incoming Wilson administration called for reduced tariffs and for passage of a federal income tax to offset the revenue loss. Congress approved the Underwood Tariff of 1913, which removed duties on certain classes of goods and lowered the average tariff rates on those that remained dutiable. The debate on the individual income tax was chiefly concerned with exemption levels and rates, but important precedents were established regarding exclusions, deductions, and "conditions and expenses affecting the creation of income."[109] The exemption level was set at $4,000 (for a married couple),

---

108. Joseph A. Pechman, *Federal Tax Policy*, 5th ed. (Washington, D.C.: Brookings Institution, 1987), 135.

109. Witte, *The Politics and Development of the Federal Income Tax*, 79.

with graduated rates from 1 percent on the first $20,000 of taxable income to 7 percent on taxable income above $500,000. The high exemption level greatly limited the application of the tax. From 1913 to 1915, the number of returns filed averaged only about 350,000; as a percentage of the labor force, less than 2 percent filed returns for these years. While the average was to expand greatly during World War I, the income tax's "elite impact" continued until World War II.[110] Congress also enacted a corporation income tax but did not appreciably alter the structural features that had been in place under the corporation excise tax.

Budget Reform

Federal budget reform was enacted after World War I, but its rationale and parameters had been established much earlier. As the demands on the federal government began to grow in the 1880s and 1890s, serious inadequacies were uncovered in federal financial administration and, more generally, in federal policy administration. Budget reform was a major part of the drive to modernize and strengthen the administrative capabilities of government. It was also extremely controversial, since it threatened traditional congressional prerogatives. The need for a national budget might be conceded, but there was a fundamental disagreement over "what form it should take and who should control it—Congress or the president?"[111] On these questions, Congress and the executive branch remained divided.

Financial Administration

In the latter part of the nineteenth century, governments at all levels were plagued by administrative shortcomings. Corruption was a serious problem in many states, as party machines exploited governments for patronage, contracts, and other forms of political favoritism. Less spectacular, but perhaps more critical, were systemic deficiencies with respect to information, personnel, and management structure. Governments had not developed the basic administrative resources necessary to plan, implement, and monitor the increasingly diverse and complex functions for which they were responsible.

110. Witte, *The Politics and Development of the Federal Income Tax*, 78–79.
111. Jonathan Kahn, *Budgeting Democracy: State Building and Citizenship in America, 1890–1928* (Ithaca: Cornell University Press, 1997), 162.

The private sector, by comparison, was moving rapidly toward a corporate model of professionally managed, investor-owned businesses with effective, efficient administrative control systems. Furthermore, the emergence of large, integrated industrial enterprises presented a regulatory challenge for government. Their enormous economic power presented a political challenge, "with categorically new demands for national control . . . [and] administrative expansion."[112]

Soon after the Civil War, Congress began to investigate federal administrative practices and business methods, "first to address problems of debt and retrenchment in the aftermath of war, and later to address the concerns of citizens and organizations doing business with the government."[113] These early investigations were highly particularistic, since investigative committees were concerned with how individual departments and bureaus could reduce their huge backlogs of claims and accounts, but the cumulation of evidence and findings eventually led to broader appraisals of the accounting and auditing methods that should be applied across agencies and departments.

In 1893, Congress established the Dockery-Cockrell Commission, a joint committee supported by professional staff, to examine executive departments and to make recommendations for improving the efficiency and economy of their operations. The commission's work included the first comprehensive compilation of the legal authorizations, organizations, and personnel of executive departments; this "'anatomy of federal administration' not only helped to crystallize awareness of the nature and scope of the administrative apparatus of government but also provided the first intimations of a means to control it."[114] The 1894 Dockery Act, another product of the commission's inquiry, reorganized the Department of the Treasury to improve its handling of public accounts. The Treasury, together with congressional committees, had been "primarily concerned with the legality of expenditures rather than with an understandable record of what was bought with the money spent."[115] While this preoccupation did not end with the Treasury's reorganization, the standardization of auditing and accounting systems that it initiated was an important prerequisite for systematic expenditure review.

112. Skowronek, *Building a New American State*, 35.
113. Kahn, *Budgeting Democracy*, 139.
114. Kahn, *Budgeting Democracy*, 145.
115. Smithies, *The Budgetary Process in the United States*, 63.

These tentative steps toward administrative restructuring were designed to assist Congress in its oversight responsibilities; the case for executive-oriented administrative reforms was promoted by Progressive reformers, largely outside Congress, who advocated administrative centralization at the local and state as well as national levels. The administrative philosophy of the Progressive movement made little headway at the federal level until Theodore Roosevelt succeeded to the presidency in 1901. Roosevelt was committed to a chief executive model of presidential leadership, and he quickly "seized the initiative from Congress and embarked on a program of administrative reform to assert presidential control over the executive branch."[116] Roosevelt's party controlled the House and Senate throughout his tenure as president, but Congress still fought to guard its prerogatives against what many viewed as overly aggressive presidential leadership.

A major impediment to Roosevelt's hierarchical vision of executive authority was the entrenched relationship between congressional committees and agencies in the executive branch. Roosevelt attempted to weaken this relationship by blocking unfiltered communication between agency heads and congressional committees where possible and by instituting stronger hierarchical controls within departmental administrative structures. In 1902, Roosevelt issued an executive order that required subordinate officials to work through department heads whenever they wished to influence legislation or other matters pending in Congress.[117] Four years later, similar restrictions were imposed on the independent regulatory agencies. In addition, Roosevelt appointed a series of commissions to investigate administrative organization and practices within the departments. The most important of these, the 1905 Keep Commission, produced a comprehensive program for restructuring and reform within the executive branch.

In some cases, Roosevelt was able to implement his commissions' recommendations by executive order. More sweeping proposals required congressional approval, but Congress was becoming increasingly disenchanted with Roosevelt's methods and substantive program. The Keep Commission's guidance was firmly rejected; Congress even refused to authorize the printing of its final report.[118] In 1909, Congress eliminated independent presidential commissions altogether by mandating specific congressional authorization before any future commissions could be funded.

---

116. Kahn, *Budgeting Democracy*, 147.
117. Kahn, *Budgeting Democracy*, 147–48.
118. Skowronek, *Building a New American State*, 185.

Congress's hostility toward executive authority made fiscal management, particularly spending oversight, much more difficult. Regardless of the specificity of legislative appropriations, congressional controls over budget execution were inadequate. Many agencies deliberately overspent appropriations during the fiscal year, leaving Congress no choice but to fund these "coercive deficiencies." Congressional attempts to curb deficiencies began in 1870, with a statutory prohibition against any agency actions that would obligate funds in excess of specific appropriations.[119] Restrictions of this type were not very effective, and in 1905 Congress reacted to an embarrassing increase in deficiency requests by requiring that appropriations be apportioned on a scheduled basis, monthly or otherwise, "to prevent undue expenditures in one portion of the year that may require deficiency or additional appropriations to complete the service of the fiscal year."[120] Department heads, however, were authorized to alter these apportionments and routinely issued waivers and modifications. In 1906, Congress was forced to tighten the apportionment requirements by restricting waivers to specified emergencies or unforeseen contingencies. What Congress refused to consider was making the president and his department heads directly responsible for budget execution.

Spending oversight was further compromised by the fragmented appropriations process. With multiple committees acting independently on appropriations bills, systematic review of spending programs was virtually impossible. Attempts to bolster legislative oversight through expenditure committees proved futile, since "committee members had neither the technical expertise nor the interest to do the job well."[121] Even more troubling as peacetime deficits recurred was the lack of responsibility for spending totals. While significant improvements had been made in the basic record-keeping for financial administration, the federal government still lacked coordinated budgeting and a comprehensive budget process.

Budget Controls and the Taft Commission

During the nineteenth century, several presidents took an active role in revising the budget estimates submitted to Congress by departments and agencies.[122] Such interventions were sporadic, however, and direct ties between

---

119. U.S. Senate, Committee on the Budget, *The Congressional Budget Process: An Explanation* (Washington, D.C.: Government Printing Office, 1996), 7.

120. *Statutes at Large, Vol. 33, 1903–1905* (Washington, D.C.: Government Printing Office, 1905), 1258.

121. Ippolito, *Congressional Spending*, 40.

122. Fisher, *Presidential Spending Power*, 9–10.

executive agencies and congressional committees became the norm. By the end of the Roosevelt presidency, however, a countervailing case for institutionalized presidential leadership in fiscal matters was beginning to take shape.

Roosevelt's response to the burgeoning deficits in 1907 and 1908 was to order the Army and Navy Departments to reduce their budget requests for FY 1910. His Secretary of the Treasury, George Cortelyou, proposed that Congress create a joint committee on budget revision, which would be authorized to revise appropriations already approved by Congress to ensure that spending totals matched available revenues.[123] Cortelyou's recommendation was ignored, but over the next few years alternative congressional and executive budget process reforms began to emerge.

In 1909, Congress directed the Secretary of the Treasury to prepare plans for dealing with projected deficits, including appropriations reductions, new taxes, or loans.[124] With Congress seemingly receptive to executive budget planning, President Taft and his cabinet launched a detailed review of agency budget requests. Taft reported to Congress that this review had reduced agency budget requests substantially and vowed to prevent agencies from proposing additional spending to Congress. Executive Order 1142 conferred on department heads authority to review and approve all agency requests for additional appropriations or other legislation, as well as their responses to congressional demands for information.[125]

Taft's Secretary of the Treasury, Franklin MacVeagh, was a tireless proponent of major institutional reforms, including omnibus appropriations bills, formal coordination between spending and revenue legislation, and even a joint executive-legislative budget board.[126] The House and Senate took some tentative steps along the lines MacVeagh was suggesting. In 1909, a Committee on Public Expenditures was appointed by Senate leaders in the hope that appropriations bills passed by the House could be consolidated into one measure. The Senate refused, however, to grant appropriations jurisdiction to the new committee, and it eventually dissolved.[127] In 1910, the House debated whether to return exclusive control over spending to its Appropriations Committee or to create a new committee with responsibility for coordinating spending and revenue bills. Neither change

123. Stewart, *Budget Reform Politics*, 178.
124. Fisher, *Presidential Spending Power*, 28–29.
125. Fisher, *Presidential Spending Power*, 29.
126. Stewart, *Budget Reform Politics*, 179.
127. Stewart, *Budget Reform Politics*, 180.

was made, and the House continued to debate these matters for another decade.

During the first two years of Taft's presidency, the Republican leadership in Congress was amenable to a limited presidential role in coordinating budget policy, notably when deficits threatened, and was prepared to consult with administration officials on fiscal policy. The movement toward formal reform also moved forward, when in 1910 Congress provided funding for President Taft's proposed Commission on Economy and Efficiency. Taft's hope was that this commission could develop a national budget system, with defined responsibilities for the chief executive and for Congress. The commission's investigatory work began during September 1910, under the direction of Frederick Cleveland, the nation's leading expert on municipal budget reform. By the time the full commission was appointed the following March, however, Democrats had captured control of the House, and the prospects for executive budget reform abruptly dimmed.

Congressional Democrats were generally hostile toward executive centralization, and they were able to join with enough recalcitrant Republicans to reverse some of Taft's most important initiatives. Legislative restrictions narrowed the authority of executive officials over civil service employees, and Congress began to restore direct ties with executive agencies.[128] Executive budgeting, the urgent priority of Taft's Commission on Economy and Efficiency, presented to Democrats yet another egregious example of presidential prerogative and executive centralization. Congress ignored the Taft Commission's recommendations for a national budget system. It also rejected Taft's assertion that the president had the constitutional authority to prepare a budget for congressional consideration.

In 1912, Taft announced that he would submit to Congress a "model" executive budget, along with the traditional Book of Estimates budget format.[129] Congress then attached a rider to an appropriations bill that declared the legislature alone would determine what budgetary information it would require and receive; no executive budget had been authorized, nor should one be submitted. Taft ordered his department heads to ignore Congress's warning and, in 1913, presented to Congress the first executive budget program. True to form, Congress dismissed Taft's budget entirely. The House even refused to have it printed.[130]

128. See Skowronek, *Building a New American State*, 186–94.
129. Skowronek, *Building a New American State*, 192–93.
130. Stewart, *Budget Reform Politics*, 188.

Within Congress, internal reform proposals suffered a similar fate. The House rejected its Appropriations Committee's efforts to regain exclusive control over appropriations legislation, and neither the House nor Senate was willing to experiment with budget committees to set spending and revenue totals and to allocate spending among committees.[131] Even though Taft's successor, Woodrow Wilson, had endorsed budget reform, attempts to enlist his support for congressional reorganization proved futile. During most of his tenure, Wilson remained indifferent toward executive reform initiatives.

Its immediate failure notwithstanding, the Taft Commission was extremely influential in reshaping federal financial administration. After World War I, Congress adopted the commission's recommendations for a presidential budget and reorganized its own budget process. The commission's 1912 report helped to convince legislators that budget reform could strengthen, rather than threaten, the separation of powers.

The Federal Reserve

While Congress failed to act on budget reform before the war, passage of the 1913 Federal Reserve Act resolved continuing concerns over federal credit and financial management. The creation of a new central banking system, with authority to regulate the money supply and the banking sector, resolved important debt management problems. In particular, the perverse connection between government debt and the money supply—whereby the Treasury's actions to retire debt automatically contracted the money supply—was finally broken.[132]

The Federal Reserve System also provided Congress with an acceptable way to separate control over fiscal policy and monetary policy. The Department of the Treasury had limited authority over the former, given the absence of executive budgeting, and its attempts to deal with the latter almost always aroused congressional opposition. The Treasury's efforts to act as a central bank during the panic of 1907 were greatly hampered by Congress's unwillingness to grant the needed powers to the Secretary of the Treasury. As a quasi-governmental, politically neutral institution, the Federal Reserve System did not arouse the same congressional fears about executive power. Congress was therefore willing to provide the Federal Reserve with regulatory authority that had been denied to the Treasury Department.

131. See Stewart, *Budget Reform Politics*, 191–97.
132. See Stabile and Cantor, *The Public Debt of the United States*, 74–75.

Nevertheless, the reluctance of Congress, particularly its Democratic majority, to embrace centralized control on fiscal matters affected the final design of the Federal Reserve. Instead of one central bank, Congress established a system of twelve regional banks with semiautonomous authority to manage borrowing rates and credit in response to regional economic considerations. The board of supervisors for the system had only limited powers in terms of a nationwide monetary policy. Those who wrote the final version of the Federal Reserve Act even "claimed it was not . . . a central bank . . . [but] a system of autonomous regional reserve banks."[133] While some standardization in monetary policy strategy and implementation was achieved over the next two decades, it was the Banking Act of 1935 that finally concentrated authority over monetary policy in the Federal Reserve Board of Governors.

Balanced Budgets and Budget Control

The balanced-budget rule, with its corollary requirements for debt retirement, was viewed by Jeffersonians as a prescription for limited government. The post–Civil War period, however, demonstrated that this prescription did not work automatically. The Republican party that dominated national politics for much of this latter period embraced the balanced-budget rule, but Republicans were also wedded to the protectionist tariffs that produced surplus revenue levels. To protect high tariffs, Republicans promoted additional spending, first for aggressive debt retirement and later for internal improvements and pensions.

The centralization of the appropriations process after the Civil War and the decentralization that began in the late 1870s was tied to this shift in spending policy. Congress created powerful appropriations committees to control spending and retire wartime debt. As debt obligations and interest commitments declined, surplus revenues were available to fund new spending. When its appropriations committees proved unsympathetic to these spending demands, Congress transferred their authority to committees with a less parsimonious approach. In opposing the executive budget reforms promoted by Roosevelt and Taft, Congress was defending a legislative power of the purse that promoted spending.

The balanced-budget rule's limitations in terms of spending control extended to broader issues of financial management. Civil War financing

---

133. Timberlake, *Monetary Policy in the United States*, 231.

was poorly executed, as Congress repeatedly delayed the tax increases necessary to complement federal borrowing. Postwar debt management policies failed to stabilize currency values or to facilitate efficient Treasury operations. Frequent monetary policy reversals by Congress undermined economic recovery after the war and contributed to the several economic panics that followed.

The budgetary record of the post–Civil War period was, at best, mixed. Congress could not maintain centralized control over spending, particularly as domestic spending demands proliferated. Congress also failed to coordinate revenue, spending, and debt management policies. Despite the rapid reduction of the Civil War debt, fiscal discipline was limited and sporadic.

The evolution of federal budget policy after the Civil War provides an important corollary to the balanced-budget rule. In order for that rule to limit the size and scope of government, revenue levels must be kept low. The high-tariff regime that the Republican party managed to preserve for nearly a half century, however, provided not only abundant revenues but also political benefits. Economic interests that the Republican party represented were rewarded on the tax side with protection against foreign competition and, on the spending side, with economic subsidies and internal improvements. In addition, surplus revenues allowed the party to broaden its popular support through increasingly generous pension programs.

The Republican party's commitment to ambitious fiscal policies was part of its larger embrace of federal authority. Like their predecessors, Hamilton's Federalists and the Whigs, post–Civil War Republicans believed that the federal government could promote economic development and national prosperity. Contrary to the Jeffersonian model championed by the Democratic party, Republicans were not concerned with using the balanced-budget rule to limit the federal government's powers to buttress the states.

THE TRANSITION TO MODERN GOVERNMENT

(1915–1940)

The quarter century between the beginning of World War I and that of World War II marked a watershed in the history of federal budget policy. It was during World War I that the United States first implemented modern wartime finance, along with extensive economic controls that foreshadowed the comprehensive economic management that emerged over the course of the New Deal. A national budget system, with the president's budget as its centerpiece, was inaugurated by the Budget and Accounting Act of 1921. At about the same time, the House and Senate reorganized their internal budgetary processes.

During the 1920s, these budget reforms operated according to the traditional Republican version of the balanced-budget rule. Revenues, including receipts from tariffs, were kept well above pre–World War I levels to ensure surpluses for debt reduction. In addition, spending for the military and for veterans' programs remained high, and Republicans continued to provide funding for economic development in the form of public works and aid to agriculture. There was virtually no support, however, for civilian social welfare initiatives.

The balanced-budget orthodoxy of the 1920s was not directed toward reducing the size or authority of the federal government. Rather, it allowed the dominant Republican majority to serve its business and economic constituencies by reducing corporate and individual tax burdens and, at the same time, continuing federal support for a targeted range of spending programs that bolstered national economic development. Thus, the presidential and congressional budgets of the 1920s were anchored to traditional Republican understandings about the role and objectives of federal financial policy.

With the Great Depression, the policy framework for budget decision making was transformed. Fiscal policy management, in the form of deficits and economic stimulus, displaced the balanced-budget rule. Under the Roosevelt administration, the spending side of the budget incorporated federal social welfare programs for the poor and the elderly, and tax policy acquired redistributive purposes. Credit programs and entitlements employed backdoor spending mechanisms that, over time, greatly reduced budget controllability. By the time World War II began, conflicts over the size, shape, and economic implications of the budget had moved to "the heart of the political process."[1]

The policy changes of the 1930s also permanently changed the fiscal relationships between the federal government and the states. Before World War I, governmental finance in the United States was, at least during peacetime, largely the province of state and local governments, whose spending and borrowing greatly outweighed those of the federal government. By the late 1930s, rapidly growing federal budgets and federal borrowing had erased these disparities, and the federal government was assuming more and more responsibility for funding state and local programs. Furthermore, the growing acceptance of activist fiscal policy reinforced the primacy of federal budgeting, since state and local governments lacked the resources and tools for national economic stabilization.[2]

An ironic twist in the history of this period was the fact that budget reform after World War I was clearly intended to restore spending discipline and the balanced-budget rule. Instead, the Great Depression made balanced budgets impractical and limited government unacceptable. Thus, presidential budgeting became the vehicle for fiscal policy leadership and governmental expansion.

1. Aaron Wildavsky and Naomi Caiden, *The New Politics of the Budgetary Process*, 3d ed. (New York: Longman, 1997), 6.
2. See Jesse Burkhead, *Government Budgeting* (New York: John Wiley and Sons, 1956), 75–76.

Financing World War I

Like the Civil War, World War I introduced a new scale to federal finance. In the years leading up to World War I, federal spending was approximately $700 million annually, and the public debt was under 2.5 percent of GNP. During the war, spending reached $18.5 billion, and deficits climbed above $13 billion (Table 4.1). By the end of the war, the debt-GNP ratio was more than 30 percent. For the next several years, annual interest costs on the federal debt averaged approximately $1 billion, some 30 percent higher than total spending before the war.

Unlike the Civil War, these immense costs were managed without serious financial disruptions. To mobilize the vast resources needed to fight the war, the federal government greatly extended its regulation and control of the domestic economy, particularly the industrial, transportation, and agricultural sectors.[3] In addition, a "public finance regime" was created in the Treasury Department "for learning about financial policy and its social implications, for shaping the definition of financial issues and administration programs, and for mobilizing support for those programs."[4] As a result, World War I was the first major conflict in which the federal government successfully implemented a coherent financing program.[5] The Federal Reserve System used its monetary controls to support government borrowing. The Treasury Department integrated short-term financing and long-term borrowing. And the federal government demonstrated the enormous potential of its power to tax incomes.

Wartime Spending and Taxation

World War I began on August 4, 1914, but the United States did not declare war on Germany until April 6, 1917. During this period, preparations for

---

3. See Charles Gilbert, *American Financing of World War I* (Westport, Conn.: Greenwood Press, 1970), 216–19. According to Gilbert, "Equally as important as the changed international position of the United States was the extension of Federal influence over domestic economic life. Many policies adopted much later by other administrations in both war and nonwar situations can be found in their embryonic stages during World War I" (217).

4. Brownlee, *Federal Taxation in America*, 57.

5. Secretary of the Treasury William Gibbs McAdoo later recounted that the financial history of the Civil War provided him and other policymakers with "a pretty clear idea of what not to do." McAdoo was determined to avoid the Civil War's "hodge-podge of unrelated expedients" and to enlist the public in a coordinated program of taxation and borrowing. William G. McAdoo, *Crowded Years* (Boston: Houghton Mifflin, 1931), 323.

Table 4.1 Federal Budget Totals, 1915–1920 (in millions of dollars)

Fiscal Year	Total Revenues	Total Outlays	Deficit (−) /Surplus	Total Public Debt
1915	$ 683	$ 746	$ −63	$ 1,191
1916	761	713	48	1,225
1917	1,101	1,954	−853	2,976
1918	3,645	12,677	−9,032	12,455
1919	5,130	18,493	−13,363	25,485
1920	6,649	6,358	291	24,299

SOURCE: *Historical Statistics of the United States, Colonial Times to 1970, Part 2* (Washington, D.C.: U.S. Bureau of the Census, 1975), 1104.

war developed very slowly. For fiscal years 1913–16, military outlays changed only marginally, and total spending was almost flat. In 1916, Congress authorized small increases in the Army's active-duty force and in the Navy's shipbuilding program, but the United States delayed putting its military on a wartime footing until well after the 1916 election. Thus, it was not until early 1917 that a wartime tax program began to take shape.

The first war-related tax bill was the Emergency Revenue Act of 1914. The outbreak of war in Europe disrupted trade with the United States, leading to a precipitous decline in U.S. customs duties. Congress raised liquor taxes and imposed special excises to offset a revenue shortfall estimated at $30 million.[6] The revenue problem turned out to be more serious than anticipated, resulting in a FY 1915 deficit of more than $60 million. But as trading resumed, the budget outlook greatly improved, and a surplus of almost $50 million was achieved in FY 1916. Since the federal government's traditional revenue sources—customs duties and excise taxes—were more than adequate to support its normal spending commitments, there was no compelling need to resort to income taxation.[7] In FY 1916, individual and corporation income taxes totaled $125 million or about 15 percent of total receipts. Four years later, the total was almost $4 billion, and income taxation had become the major source of federal revenue.[8]

6. The 1914 tax legislation was modeled on the excise tax program used to finance the Spanish-American War.

7. The tax increases under the Emergency Revenue Act of 1914 were to terminate at the end of 1915. Congress later extended the expiration date through December 31, 1916.

8. These figures include taxes on individual and corporation income and taxes on excess profits. *Annual Report of the Secretary of the Treasury on the State of the Finances for the Fiscal Year Ended June 30, 1945* (Washington, D.C.: Government Printing Office, 1946), 446.

Income Taxation. The restructuring of tax policy was driven by revenue demands that escalated rapidly. In reporting the FY 1917 budget estimates to Congress, the Treasury Department indicated that higher appropriations for the Army and Navy could result in a deficit as high as $100 million.[9] Treasury officials recommended that income taxes be raised so as to avoid going "constantly into debt for current expenditures . . . [and] eventually impairing credit."[10] By the time Congress began its deliberations, the deficit estimate had climbed to more than $260 million, and on September 8, 1916, Congress approved a much larger tax increase than the Treasury had proposed.

The Revenue Act of 1916 inaugurated an expanded system of income taxation. The normal, or base, tax rate on individual incomes was doubled from 1 to 2 percent, and surtax rates were raised, creating a top marginal rate of 15 percent on taxable income above $2 million. Taxes on corporations were boosted through a higher base rate and an excess profits tax on armament manufacturers.[11] A permanent federal estate tax was levied as well, at rates ranging from 1 to 10 percent, on estates valued above $50,000.

Revenue gains from the 1916 tax bill exceeded expectations. Total budget receipts were $1.1 billion in FY 1917, an increase of $340 million over the previous year, with nearly three-fourths of the gain supplied by higher taxes on incomes and profits. As American involvement in the war drew closer, however, much larger revenues were needed, and the shift toward income taxation grew more pronounced.

On March 3, 1917, Congress created a special fund for military appropriations to be supported through expanded estate and excess profits taxes. One month later, Congress declared war, and the Wilson administration requested an immediate appropriation of $3.5 billion for the military and an authorization of $3 billion for loans to the allies.[12] President Wilson declared that "so far as practicable the burden of the war shall be borne by taxation of the present generation rather than by loans."[13] Congress was asked to repeal the March tax bill and to substitute for it a $1.6 billion package of higher taxes, including a broader tax base and steeper rates for individual and corporation taxation.

9. Gilbert, *American Financing of World War I*, 77.
10. Quoted in Gilbert, *American Financing of World War I*, 77.
11. Similar taxes on producers of armaments had been levied by Great Britain, Germany, France, and several other belligerents. Witte, *The Politics and Development of the Federal Income Tax*, 81.
12. Gilbert, *American Financing of World War I*, 83.
13. Quoted in Gilbert, *American Financing of World War I*, 84.

The War Revenue Act of 1917, approved by Congress on October 3, levied an estimated $2.5 billion in additional taxes, of which $1.85 billion was expected from incomes and profits taxation.[14] The coverage of the individual income tax was broadened through greatly reduced exemption levels, and an exceptionally steep marginal rate structure was applied to taxable income. The top marginal rate of 15 percent under the 1916 tax law was boosted to 67 percent in 1917. The normal tax rate for corporations was tripled, to 6 percent, while excess profits taxation was imposed on a much more broadly defined category of businesses. Once again, the revenue yield from higher taxes was impressive. Budget receipts rose by $2.5 billion between FY 1917 and FY 1918, and income and excess profits taxes accounted for 80 percent of this growth.[15] Over this brief span, however, spending grew by almost $11 billion. In spring 1918, the Wilson administration called for another tax increase to reduce what it viewed as dangerously high deficits.

This time, Congress failed to act quickly. The War Revenue Act of 1918 was not passed until February 3, 1919, three months after the war had ended. Its main provisions were, like earlier wartime measures, geared toward incomes and excess profits. The normal rate on individual income was raised to 6 percent for 1918, with a reduced rate of 4 percent to take effect in 1919. The surtax went up as well, creating a top marginal rate of 77 percent for 1918 and a 73 percent rate for 1919. Corporate taxation was augmented through higher normal rates and excess profits rates, along with a new "war profits" tax for the 1918 tax year. The peak revenue level of the World War I period was registered in FY 1920, with income and excess profits taxes of almost $4 billion and total budget receipts of $6.7 billion.[16] By then, spending had dropped sharply, and the budget was in surplus by more than $290 million.

Revenue Levels. When World War I began, Treasury officials hoped that taxes could finance as much as one-half of wartime spending. Treasury Secretary William G. McAdoo soon lowered this to one-third, explaining that "if you take the whole of a man's surplus income through taxes, you cannot expect him to buy bonds, nor can you expect industry to expand and prosper."[17] McAdoo's goal was not met each year, but over the course of the war

14. For a comparison of the original Treasury proposal and the enacted tax bill, see Gilbert, *American Financing of World War I*, 85, 95.

15. *Annual Report of the Secretary of the Treasury for Fiscal Year 1945*, 446.

16. *Annual Report of the Secretary of the Treasury for Fiscal Year 1945*, 446.

17. Quoted in Gilbert, *American Financing of World War I*, 91.

budget receipts did cover nearly 30 percent of total spending.[18] In addition, the United States relied more heavily on taxation than did other World War I combatants, even though its costs, once it entered the war, were considerably higher.[19] The most productive tax levied during the war was the excess profits tax. From 1917 to 1920, total taxes paid by corporations were more than $9 billion, and more than two-thirds of this total was from excess profits levies.[20] By comparison, taxes on individual incomes—both normal and surtax—were under $4.3 billion.[21]

The full revenue potential of the individual income tax was not exploited during World War I, because exemption levels remained relatively high. Only 5.5 million taxable returns were filed in 1920, out of a labor force of over 40 million.[22] Furthermore, low marginal rates for most taxpayers limited their tax liabilities. In income years 1917–19, less than 1 percent of returns accounted, on average, for 70 percent of the income taxes paid.[23] Nevertheless, World War I legitimated the political authority of the federal government with respect to income taxation. Any uncertainties about the political significance of the Sixteenth Amendment were settled in a few short years, as both the level and composition of federal revenues changed to a remarkable degree (Table 4.2). The federal government now had a flexible revenue source with enormous capacity, and it had learned important lessons about how to raise vast sums very quickly.

Borrowing and Loans

The Treasury Department's financing program for World War I did have some serious flaws. To minimize borrowing costs, Treasury officials insisted that the Federal Reserve support government borrowing at below-market rates of interest, making it difficult for the Federal Reserve to counter wartime price inflation.[24] Inflationary pressures were further exacerbated by the Treasury's inability to raise the level of public savings through wartime loan campaigns, and the Treasury Department's use of tax incentives to pro-

---

18. This percentage is based on fiscal years 1917–19.

19. Brownlee, *Federal Taxation in America*, 51.

20. These figures are for calendar years. *Historical Statistics of the United States, Colonial Times to 1970, Part 2*, 1109.

21. *Historical Statistics of the United States, Colonial Times to 1970, Part 2*, 1110.

22. Witte, *The Politics and Development of the Federal Income Tax*, 86.

23. Witte, *The Politics and Development of the Federal Income Tax*, 86.

24. Robert C. West, *Banking Reform and the Federal Reserve, 1863–1923* (Ithaca: Cornell University Press, 1977), 186–88.

Table 4.2 Composition of Federal Revenues, 1915–1920 (in millions of dollars)

| | | | Percentage of Total | | |
| | | | Internal Revenue | | |
Fiscal Year	Total Revenues	Customs	Incomes and Profits	Other	Misc.
1915	$ 698	30%	11%	48%	10%
1916	783	27	16	50	7
1917	1,124	20	32	40	8
1918	3,665	5	63	24	8
1919	5,152	4	59	25	13
1920	6,695	5	59	22	14

SOURCE: *Annual Report of the Secretary of the Treasury on the State of the Finances for the Fiscal Year Ended June 30, 1945* (Washington, D.C.: Government Printing Office, 1946), 446.

mote government borrowing was often at odds with its overall tax program.[25] Beyond these specific shortcomings, policymakers had only a rudimentary grasp of monetary and fiscal policy effects; miscalculations regarding debt finance during and after the war suggest that "neither the Fed nor anyone else understood the dynamics of inflation and recession."[26]

These problems notwithstanding, World War I represented an enormous improvement in debt finance. The Treasury coordinated short-term and long-term borrowing much more effectively than it had in past wars. Borrowing authorizations were fully subscribed in a timely manner. Federal credit remained strong from beginning to end, despite an unprecedented volume of borrowing.

Short-Term Borrowing. The Treasury Department was authorized under the March 1917 Revenue Act to issue up to $300 million in certificates of indebtedness. These debt obligations had a short maturity (less than one year) and were to be used to fund Treasury operations in anticipation of new tax revenues to be received at the end of the fiscal year. This authority was exercised immediately, as the Treasury borrowed $50 million from Federal Reserve banks. The participating banks purchased ninety-day certificates, paying 2 percent interest, with the stipulation that these certificates counted toward their required reserves. The Treasury, in turn, received cash payments for the certificates.

25. Gilbert, *American Financing of World War I*, 118–20.
26. Donald F. Kettl, *Leadership at the Fed* (New Haven: Yale University Press, 1986), 27.

Over the next two years, Congress included similar authorizations in tax bills and loan acts. In both cases, the purpose was to provide the Treasury with ready access to cash in advance of the moneys it would receive when taxes were paid and bonds were purchased. Authorization levels were raised as additional short-term borrowing became necessary, and the Treasury was granted greater discretion over interest rates. A crediting system was also initiated that eliminated cumbersome cash payments, allowing the Treasury instead to draw on its accounts in participating banks. In all, the Treasury issued forty-eight series of certificates totaling almost $22 billion between March 1917 and July 1919.[27] This relationship between the Treasury and the Federal Reserve was an important legacy of World War I, since it created the market for short-term government debt on which the open-market operations of the Federal Reserve have since been based.[28]

Long-Term Borrowing. Authorizations for the issuance of long-term debt were provided in four Liberty Loan Acts passed during the war and a Victory War Act passed in 1919. The First Liberty Loan Act was approved by Congress on April 24, 1917, and granted the Treasury Department authorization for up to $5 billion in bonds, with a maximum interest rate of 3.5 percent, a federal income tax exemption for interest earned on the bonds (except for estate tax liabilities), and a convertibility feature that allowed purchasers to exchange bonds for future issues. The Treasury Department announced the first loan campaign on May 9 and established loan committees throughout the country to encourage widespread public participation. The hope was that highly publicized patriotic appeals would build public support for the war effort and allow the government to borrow at the lowest possible cost.

The First Liberty Loan was extremely successful, with the Treasury receiving $3 billion in subscriptions for the $2 billion in its initial offering. As increasingly large borrowings became necessary, however, the Treasury was forced to adjust its strategy. Interest rates were raised during the several loan campaigns, with the Victory Loan offering in 1919 reaching 4.75 percent, and various forms of tax exemption were attached to each issue. To allow more small investors to participate, very small denomination bonds were offered, using war savings certificates, war savings stamps, and thrift stamps that could be purchased in post offices and banks.

27. Gilbert, *American Financing of World War I*, 147.
28. West, *Banking Reform and the Federal Reserve*, 192.

Most Treasury borrowing was secured through high-denomination bonds, but the nationwide marketing campaign for a public savings program managed to raise $1.6 billion from small investors.[29] The Federal Reserve provided some assistance in this campaign, but its major contribution was to ensure that the banking system supported large-scale Treasury borrowing, both in direct purchases by banks and by bank financing for purchases by private investors.[30] Each of the five Treasury loan offerings from 1917 to 1919 was substantially oversubscribed.

Wartime Finance and Debt

The net increase in debt over the wartime period was more than $24 billion. Approximately 20 percent of this debt was held by Federal Reserve and commercial banks, and most of the remainder by nonbank investors.[31] In comparison with other major belligerents, the United States borrowed at lower rates of interest and suffered less price inflation.[32] Price inflation was also considerably less in World War I than it had been during the Civil War.[33] World War I had established the salient features of modern wartime finance. The tax system was expanded. The Federal Reserve and banking system were adapted to facilitate government borrowing. Marketing tools were created to build public participation in loan campaigns. As a consequence, massive spending and borrowing were managed without severe economic disruption. In World War II, each of these financing mechanisms would be refined and extended.

Presidential and Congressional Budget Reform

The financial repercussions of World War I greatly strengthened the case for budget reform. In 1919, Congress drafted legislation authorizing a presidential budget, and the final version of the landmark Budget and Accounting Act was passed two years later. In 1920, the House revised its rules to restore the spending powers of its Appropriations Committee, and the Senate followed the House's lead in 1922. Each of these initiatives centralized

---

29. Stabile and Cantor, *The Public Debt of the United States*, 79.

30. On the statutory changes and Federal Reserve policies that facilitated this support, see Gilbert, *American Financing of World War I*, 184–97.

31. Gilbert, *American Financing of World War I*, 229.

32. Gilbert, *American Financing of World War I*, 223–31.

33. Gilbert, *American Financing of World War I*, 231.

controls over spending, but more comprehensive budget process reforms were perceived as unnecessary. Congress would only accept what it termed a "limited" executive budget, and its internal reforms were limited as well.

The Democratic Party Impasse

A variety of budget reform options were brought before Congress during the Wilson presidency, with the House much more actively involved than the Senate. The Democratic majority that controlled the House from 1911 to 1919 supported a legislative budget rather than the presidential budget system proposed by the Taft Commission, but party members could not agree on a specific format. In 1913, the House Democratic caucus authorized a special committee "to consider the wisdom of adopting a National budget in handling the regular appropriations."[34] This special committee recommended that the House adopt an annual budget, including total revenues and total spending, with the latter allocated among the spending bills handled by House committees. Jurisdiction over the annual budget would rest with a new budget committee, whose membership would include the senior leadership of the House's tax and spending committees.[35]

The Democratic caucus rejected this proposal and, in 1915, commissioned another study committee. The budget committee plan resurfaced, but efforts to secure the Wilson administration's backing were unsuccessful, and the deadlock continued. The Democratic party's 1916 platform then called for a more modest reorganization of the appropriations process: "We . . . favor a return by the House of Representatives to its former practice of initiating and preparing all appropriation bills through a single committee . . . in order that responsibility may be centered, expenditures standardized and made uniform, and waste and duplication in the public service as much as possible avoided."[36] President Wilson echoed this recommendation in his annual message to Congress the following year.[37] John Fitzgerald, chairman of the House Appropriations Committee, naturally favored this change but insisted that it be accompanied by congressional enactment of a comprehensive executive budget system.[38] Fitzgerald also recommended that Congress institute

---

34. Quoted in Stewart, *Budget Reform Politics*, 193.

35. The concept of a budget committee had first surfaced in a 1910 proposal for a Committee on Estimates and Expenditures. See Stewart, *Budget Reform Politics*, 191–92.

36. *Congressional Record*, 66th Cong., 2d sess., 1920, 59, pt. 8: 8113.

37. Fisher, *Presidential Spending Power*, 32.

38. Fisher, *Presidential Spending Power*, 31.

a two-thirds majority requirement for any appropriation exceeding presidential spending estimates.[39] House Democrats were unwilling to recentralize spending controls in the Appropriations Committee, much less to couple a more powerful Appropriations Committee to an executive budget process, and the reform debate in Congress effectively ended when the United States entered the war.

Republican Reform Initiatives

In the 1918 midterm elections, Republicans regained control of Congress. When the sixty-sixth Congress convened in 1919, party leaders in the House and Senate promptly appointed select committees to formulate executive budget plans. An executive budgeting statute was passed by both chambers in 1920 but vetoed by President Wilson. A slightly revised version was enacted in 1921. While Congress had no serious reservations about the need for an executive budget, albeit a narrowly defined one, the issue of congressional reform proved to be highly controversial. In the end, Congress adopted appropriations process changes but almost immediately took steps to curb their impact.

Executive Initiation. The House Select Committee on the Budget took the lead in drafting plans for a national budget, holding extensive hearings during September and October 1919 and reporting its recommendations for an executive budget shortly thereafter. The committee's report carefully differentiated between "an Executive budget" and "Executive initiation . . . [where] the President's responsibility ends when he has prepared the budget and transmitted it to Congress."[40] Any new authority to be conferred on the president should not in any way "give the Executive any greater power . . . over the consideration of appropriations by Congress."[41] The president would be responsible for reviewing, revising, and coordinating the funding estimates for executive departments, but Congress would retain full discretion over the estimates it received. Both in committee and on the floor, Congress would determine by its own rules how appropriations bills would be acted on. There would be no mandatory up-or-down vote on the president's budget,

---

39. Fisher, *Presidential Spending Power,* 31. This provision was modeled after the "no legislative increase" controls that several states had considered for their constitutional budget reforms. See Burkhead, *Government Budgeting,* 24–25.

40. U.S. House, Select Committee on the Budget, *National Budget System* (Washington, D.C.: Government Printing Office, 1919), 7.

41. U.S. House, Select Committee on the Budget, *National Budget System,* 7.

or any bar against legislative increases, or any floor privileges allowing Cabinet members to defend their budgets in the House and Senate.[42]

The main features of the committee's bill were a "limited executive budget" and an auditing agency, independent of the executive branch, to provide Congress with improved controls over budget execution. Under the proposed budgeting system, the president would have sole authority to submit budget estimates to Congress. A new Bureau of the Budget would serve as the president's personal staff agency for revising and correlating spending estimates and for balancing spending against available revenues, but auditing responsibilities would be transferred from the Treasury Department to a new Accounting Department, headed by a Comptroller General. This officer, and the Assistant Comptroller General, would be appointed by the president, subject to Senate confirmation, but would thereafter be answerable to Congress, with removal only for cause and then only by concurrent resolution of the House and Senate. A concurrent resolution required agreement by the House and Senate but, unlike a joint resolution, did not require presidential approval. This attempt to exclude the president from a decision to remove the Comptroller General proved to be a stumbling block when the final version of the budget reform bill was sent to President Wilson. The House approved the committee's proposals by a vote of 285 to 3 on October 21, 1919.

Because the Senate was preoccupied with the Treaty of Versailles, hearings on the House-passed bill did not open until December. At that time, President Wilson finally endorsed an executive budget process. The Senate Select Committee concluded its hearings in January and reported out a draft bill similar to the House version. The major differences affected the Bureau of the Budget and the Accounting Department. The Senate bill, adopted by a unanimous vote, moved the Bureau of the Budget to the Department of the Treasury and made the Treasury Secretary its director. It also conferred on the independent auditing agency, now the General Accounting Office, broader authority over accounting methods and financial activities in executive departments.

The conference bill, which was reported out at the end of May and easily passed, placed the Bureau of the Budget in the Treasury Department but provided for a separate director to serve the president. The conference measure also incorporated the Senate's version of a General Accounting Office. On June 4, President Wilson vetoed the bill, focusing his objections on the

---

42. On this last issue, see Burkhead, *Government Budgeting*, 27.

removal procedure for the Comptroller General. Wilson's veto message stated that "the accepted construction of the Constitution [has been] that the power to appoint officers of this kind carries with it . . . the power to remove."[43] Wilson argued that Congress lacked the constitutional authority "to limit the appointing power and its incident, the power of removal derived from the Constitution."[44] The House failed to override Wilson's veto, and the congressional session ended before action could be taken on a new bill.

The sixty-seventh Congress that opened in 1921 had larger Republican majorities and a Republican president. Agreement was quickly reached on the final version of the Budget and Accounting Act, with President Warren G. Harding signing it into law on June 10. What Harding's first budget message hailed as "the greatest reformation in governmental practices since the beginning of the Republic" was a remarkably brief statute.[45] The president was authorized to transmit each year to Congress "[e]stimates of the expenditures and appropriations necessary in his judgment for the support of the Government."[46] These estimates would include all "departments and establishments" but would exclude Congress and the courts. In addition to spending estimates, the president was instructed to provide Congress with "estimates of the receipts . . . under (1) laws existing at the time the Budget is transmitted and also (2) under the revenue proposals, if any, contained in the Budget."[47] In the event that estimated receipts and spending differed, the president's budget was to include recommendations for funding the deficit or disposing of the surplus. Finally, "departments and establishments" were barred from submitting directly to Congress any spending requests or revenue proposals "unless at the request of either House of Congress."[48]

Under the 1921 Budget and Accounting Act, the duties and powers of the Bureau of the Budget and of the General Accounting Office were unchanged from the bill that President Wilson had vetoed. The tenure and removal provisions for the Comptroller General, however, were altered. The 1921 Budget Act provided for a fifteen-year, nonrenewable term, with a joint reso-

43. *Congressional Record*, 66th Cong., 2d sess., 1920, 59, pt. 8: 8609.
44. *Congressional Record*, 66th Cong., 2d sess., 1920, 59, pt. 8: 8609.
45. *Congressional Record*, 67th Cong., 2d sess., 1921, 62, pt. 1: 37.
46. *United States Statutes at Large, Vol. 42, 1921–1923* (Washington, D.C.: Government Printing Office, 1923), 20.
47. *United States Statutes at Large, Vol. 42, 1921–1923*, 20.
48. *United States Statutes at Large, Vol. 42, 1921–1923*, 21.

lution requiring the president's signature necessary for removing the Comptroller General before the expiration of that term. Nevertheless, the General Accounting Office remained a congressional staff agency, as both the House and Senate had originally intended.

Appropriations Process Reorganization. The House Select Committee that drafted the original national budget plan agreed that the exclusive spending jurisdiction of the Appropriations Committee should be restored but waited until congressional action on the budget statute was completed before bringing this issue before the House.[49] In contrast to its overwhelming support for the presidential budget, the House was sharply divided over changes in the appropriations process. One Agriculture Committee member complained that giving "35 members . . . jurisdiction over appropriations" was not merely "autocracy as against democracy, pure and simple" but autocracy of "a more malignant form than ever."[50] Another opponent recalled the "40 years' fight . . . to obtain the present system" of appropriations from the "power and tyranny" of the old appropriations committee: "Mr. Speaker . . . when you put all the power of appropriating money in the hands of one committee of this House, the rest of you may just as well pack up your trunks and go back home and stay there, for they will not have any use for you then. . . . If you do as is proposed here, you will turn back the House 40 years and fix upon us a system that you will regret to the longest day you spend here."[51]

James W. Good, chairman of both the Appropriations Committee and the Select Budget Committee, conceded that the Appropriations Committee was unpopular but declared "when it becomes popular I for one shall question the quality of its work."[52] Good claimed that "real economy in appropriations and Government expenditure" would never be achieved so long as legislative committees were allowed to pursue their distinctive goals:

> It is, indeed, true that a legislative committee is appointed to guard the interests of a particular department committed to its care . . . to defend that department and to assist in every worthy ambition for the growth and development of that department, even to the extent

49. The chairman of the committee, James W. Good, explained that "it was thought unwise for this Congress to attempt to adopt rules for the next Congress by an act of Congress, and so we determined to take two steps." *Congressional Record*, 66th Cong., 2d sess., 1920, 59, pt. 8: 8116.

50. *Congressional Record*, 66th Cong., 2d sess., 1920, 59, pt. 8: 8109.

51. *Congressional Record*, 66th Cong., 2d sess., 1920, 59, pt. 8: 8105.

52. *Congressional Record*, 66th Cong., 2d sess., 1920, 59, pt. 8: 8116.

of taking up new projects that involve additional expenditures at a time when there should be rigid economy and a retrenchment. . . . This is not true of the Committee on Appropriations. It has no particular department to defend, no particular project to advance. It stands as the impartial arbiter of all the legislative committees . . . and the appropriations for each will be measured by the necessities and national importance of the service appropriated for.[53]

The decisive vote on whether to change House rules regarding appropriations came on the privileged resolution, or special rule, calling for immediate consideration by the House. The rule was adopted by a 158 to 154 margin, with deep divisions between the parties and among committees.[54] When the substantive rules change was voted on, the majority increased to 200 to 117. The new House Rule XXI prohibited legislative committees from proposing, directly or indirectly, any appropriations measure. "No bill or joint resolution carrying appropriations shall be reported by any committee not having jurisdiction to report appropriations, nor shall an amendment proposing an appropriation be in order during the consideration of a bill or joint resolution reported by a committee not having that jurisdiction."[55]

The House soon signaled, however, that the Appropriations Committee's victory was not complete. Appropriations Committee leaders had assumed that all thirteen of the regular "appropriations bills will be presented to the House as part of one great budget bill."[56] Only an omnibus measure, they argued, would permit both the Appropriations Committee and the House to take "all the departments into consideration at one and the same time . . . [in] a budget that will really amount to something."[57] Instead, the House continued to act on spending bills separately, at different times, and with the expectation that Appropriations subcommittees would be accorded "a substantial degree of autonomy because of the intense specialization required."[58] With the Appropriations Committee deferring to its subcommittees and with each

53. *Congressional Record*, 66th Cong., 2d sess., 1920, 59, pt. 8: 8117.

54. Republicans voted 104 to 57 for the rule, while Democrats opposed it by a vote of 54 to 97. Members of the Appropriations Committee supported the rule by a 15 to 0 vote, while members of the seven legislative committees whose jurisdictions were affected voted 67 to 38 against the rule. Fenno, *The Power of the Purse: Appropriations Politics in Congress*, 45.

55. *Congressional Record*, 66th Cong., 2d sess., 1920, 59, pt. 8: 8109.

56. *Congressional Record*, 66th Cong., 2d sess., 1920, 59, pt. 8: 8113.

57. *Congressional Record*, 66th Cong., 2d sess., 1920, 59, pt. 8: 8113.

58. Fisher, *Presidential Spending Power*, 37.

subcommittee reporting independently of the others, the House avoided a single vote on total spending.

An additional concession to spending interests was made by House Democrats at their postelection caucus in 1920. The party decided to fill its new seats on the expanded Appropriations Committee with members of legislative committees whose spending jurisdictions had just been abolished.[59] Moreover, the caucus agreed to waive its restrictions on multiple assignments and to allow those selected for the Appropriations Committee to maintain their legislative committee assignments.[60]

When the Senate changed its appropriations process in 1922, the representation of legislative committees was formalized. Like the House, the Senate's standing rules were amended to confer exclusive jurisdiction over "all general appropriations bills" to its Appropriations Committee.[61] The new Senate rules provided, however, that when a spending bill previously handled by a legislative committee was brought to the Appropriations Committee, three members of that legislative committee would sit ex officio during its consideration. One of these legislative committee members would serve as well on any appropriations conference committee that might be necessary.[62] This unusual arrangement, which persisted for more than fifty years, was defended on the grounds that it added to the "knowledge and information" available to the Appropriations Committee.[63] Critics argued that the real reason was to keep the legislative committees from opposing appropriations reforms in their entirety.

Republican Balanced Budgets

The 1920 presidential election completed the Republican party's return to power. Over the next decade, the party maintained control of the White House and Congress and pursued what Harding termed "America's present need" for "normalcy."[64] The Republican version of normalcy featured a

59. Stewart, *Budget Reform Politics*, 109.

60. Stewart, *Budget Reform Politics*, 109.

61. *Congressional Record*, 67th Cong., 2d sess., 1922, 62, pt. 4: 3430.

62. At least one committee representative was required on any appropriations conference with the House. *Congressional Record*, 67th Cong., 2d sess., 1922, 62, pt. 4: 3431.

63. *Congressional Record*, 67th Cong., 2d sess., 1922, 62, pt. 4: 3419. The Senate finally abolished this requirement when it adopted new standing rules for the ninety-fifth Congress in 1977.

64. See Frederick E. Schortheimer, *Rededicating America: Life and Recent Speeches of Warren G. Harding* (Indianapolis: Bobbs-Merrill, 1920), 223.

conservative approach to budget policy. Republican leaders were committed to curtailing income taxation and reviving the tariff, while practicing "rigid and yet sane economy" in spending.[65] Their paramount goal was to revive the distinctive balanced-budget orthodoxy of the late nineteenth century, but Republicans also called for improved financial accounting by state, county, and local governments.[66]

The Republican party's commitment to reducing federal debt produced a steady stream of surpluses that averaged more than $750 million per year from 1920 to 1930 (Table 4.3). In fiscal years 1926–28, annual spending was under $3 billion, but each year's budget surplus was nearly $1 billion. By 1930, the World War I debt had been reduced by one-third, and the debt-GNP ratio had dropped by 40 percent.[67] To ensure that large surpluses would be available for debt retirement, Congress was forced to maintain income taxation at levels that would have been unimaginable before the war. Likewise, the executive branch and Congress had to limit new spending. Budgeting for surpluses imposed strong constraints on revenue policy and spending policy, and these constraints held firm until the Great Depression.

Revenue Policy

The starting point for postwar revenue policy was widespread agreement that wartime tax rates could not be enforced during peacetime. David F. Houston, who served as Secretary of the Treasury in the final months of the Wilson administration, conceded that "a progressive income tax schedule rising to rates in excess of 70 percent . . . cannot be successfully collected."[68] Taxpayers were already finding ways to avoid or evade their tax liabilities, and Houston was convinced that high rates would inevitably encourage more and more taxpayers to follow their example. Regardless of the symbolic appeal that steep progressivity had for progressives in both parties, its long-term impact on revenue productivity was a serious practical concern.

Andrew W. Mellon was appointed Secretary of the Treasury by President Harding in 1921 and served until 1932. His long tenure was characterized by

65. The quoted phrase is from Harding's 1921 inaugural address. *Congressional Record*, 67th Cong., 1st sess., 1921, 61, pt. 1: 5.

66. See Kimmel, *Federal Budget and Fiscal Policy, 1789–1958*, 81–90.

67. On the factors reducing the debt-GNP ratio, see E. Cary Brown, "Episodes in the Public Debt History of the United States," in *Public Debt Management: Theory and History*, ed. R. Dornbusch and M. Draghi (Cambridge: Cambridge University Press, 1990), 237–39.

68. Quoted in Witte, *The Politics and Development of the Federal Income Tax*, 88.

Table 4.3 Federal Budget Totals, 1920–1930 (in millions of dollars)

Fiscal Year	Total Revenues	Total Outlays	Deficit (−) /Surplus	Total Public Debt
1920	$ 6,649	$ 6,358	$ 291	$ 24,299
1921	5,571	5,062	509	23,977
1922	4,026	3,289	736	22,963
1923	3,853	3,140	713	22,350
1924	3,871	2,908	963	21,251
1925	3,641	2,924	717	20,516
1926	3,795	2,930	865	19,643
1927	4,013	2,857	1,155	18,512
1928	3,900	2,961	939	17,604
1929	3,862	3,127	734	16,931
1930	4,058	3,320	738	16,185

SOURCE: *Historical Statistics of the United States, Colonial Times to 1970, Part 2* (Washington, D.C.: U.S. Bureau of the Census, 1975), 1104.

extraordinary influence over fiscal policy and taxation. Mellon believed that high tax rates would adversely affect revenues, but he was equally concerned with their economic impact. According to Mellon, high rates undermined the incentives to work and to invest on which continued economic growth depended. The tax-reduction bills that Mellon engineered through Congress were designed to minimize these disincentives while ensuring the government adequate revenues.

Individual Income Taxation. The restructuring of tax policy after the war comprised lower rates and higher exemption levels for individual taxpayers. The steep marginal rate structure of World War I was modified, but the actual distribution of tax burdens among income groups remained highly progressive. The top marginal rate on taxable income, for example, was 73 percent in 1920 and 25 percent in 1930, but the income bracket at which this rate applied was lowered from $1 million to $100,000. For lower-income taxpayers, personal exemptions nearly doubled, earned-income credits were established, and first-bracket rates were sharply reduced.[69] The effect of these changes was to eliminate tax liabilities for many taxpayers. The number of taxable returns dropped by more than 3 million between 1920 and 1930, but the percentage of net income paid in taxes remained fairly high,

69. *Historical Statistics of the United States, Colonial Times to 1970, Part 2*, 1095.

and the proportion of income tax revenues from the higher marginal brackets increased despite the reduced rates.[70]

The tax code did become more complex, as Congress added special provisions for taxing capital gains, exclusions for employer contributions to pensions, and new interest deductibility rules. Attempts to repeal the estate tax did not succeed, but rates were lowered, and the federal tax credit for state inheritance tax payments was liberalized. Although Republicans defined "normalcy" as prewar income taxation, their tax-cutting program was more restrained. The income tax remained a major revenue source, and the tax burden was concentrated on an even smaller fraction of the population. Conservative Republicans were unenthusiastic about income taxation and progressivity, but they repeatedly subordinated their ideological preferences to the dictates of fiscal policy. Such concessions would no doubt have been more difficult to secure if progressive taxation had been tied to a redistributive philosophy, but balanced-budget principles were another matter entirely. Indeed, faith in these principles was so strong that it ultimately led Republicans to the disastrous course of raising taxes when the Great Depression began.

Corporation Taxation. The heaviest wartime tax on corporations, the excess profits tax, was scaled back in 1919 and repealed entirely in 1921. The elimination of excess profits taxation was accompanied, however, by an increase in the normal income tax rate on corporations from 10 to 12.5 percent. The normal tax rate was raised to 13.5 percent during 1926–27 but then dropped to 12 percent for the 1930–31 income years. Over this entire period, the exemption level for computing taxable income remained very low—$2,000 from 1918 to 1927 and $3,000 from 1928 to 1931; the only important tax preference affecting corporations was a liberalized oil and gas depletion allowance added to the Revenue Act of 1926.[71]

The Republican tax cuts after the war greatly reduced the tax burden on corporations. During the war, combined income and profits taxation had risen as high as 37 percent of net income.[72] From 1922 to 1930, corporation

70. The proportion of individual income tax revenues produced by the normal tax decreased substantially during the 1920s, while the proportion accounted for by surtaxes correspondingly increased. From 1920 to 1923, the normal tax provided approximately 45 percent of income tax revenues. From 1928 to 1930, the yield was slightly more than 20 percent.

71. See Witte, *The Politics and Development of the Federal Income Tax*, 94.

72. King, *Money, Time and Politics*, 103.

income taxes as a percentage of net income were less than one-third this level. But even these reduced levels were much higher than prewar tax burdens, which had amounted to less than 1 percent of net income and which had provided, at their peak, less than $60 million in revenues.[73]

Corporations clearly benefited from the tax-reduction environment of the 1920s, but Congress's support for business was tempered by its concern over potential revenue losses. Even as large surpluses accumulated during the mid-1920s, the structure of corporation taxation remained intact. When corporate profits and tax revenues unexpectedly plummeted in 1930, Congress attempted to counter the revenue shortfall by raising the tax rate. As with individual income taxation, this strategy failed completely.

Tariffs, Excises, and Revenues. The impact of Prohibition on federal revenues was powerful. Alcohol excise taxes produced $1.2 billion in revenues from 1917 to 1919.[74] In 1930, the federal tax on alcohol yielded less than $12 million. Congress also responded to business entreaties by repealing many wartime excises. Manufacturer excises totaled $270 million in 1920 and under $3 million in 1930. The only exception to the excise tax cuts of the postwar decade was tobacco, whose revenue yield increased by 50 percent.

To offset these revenue losses and to revive protectionism, Republicans more than doubled tariff rates under the Fordney-McCumber Tariff Act of 1922. Customs duties averaged $330 million annually from 1920 to 1922.[75] With the higher tariff schedules in place, revenues climbed to $560 million in 1923 and averaged more than $575 million per year through 1930. When customs duties then began to fall, Congress raised tariff rates even higher in the Smoot-Hawley Tariff Act of 1930. Instead of the higher revenues Congress expected, these tariff increases contributed to a downturn in international trade that depressed revenue levels even further.

Revenue policy in the 1920s was heavily oriented toward income taxation, with well over half of total revenues for the period provided by taxes on individuals and corporations. Tariffs and excises, which had supported the federal government for much of the nineteenth century, had become secondary revenue sources. Important political benefits were still conferred and withdrawn as Congress dealt with tariff and excise tax legislation, but World War I had permanently altered the revenue structure of the federal government.

---

73. *Historical Statistics of the United States, Colonial Times to 1970, Part 2,* 1109.
74. *Historical Statistics of the United States, Colonial Times to 1970, Part 2,* 1106–7.
75. *Historical Statistics of the United States, Colonial Times to 1970, Part 2,* 1106.

Spending Policy

The budget policy consensus of the 1920s assigned considerable importance to spending control. Debt reduction obviously required that spending be kept well below revenues, but the spending philosophy of the 1920s had more ambitious goals. Policymakers believed that economic prosperity depended on limiting spending to a narrow set of federal responsibilities—national defense, internal improvements, and basic civil services. This restrictive spending policy was viewed as a bulwark against excessive taxation.

The new budget process embodied this orientation. The Bureau of the Budget quickly established itself as the president's fiscal guardian, consistently trimming budget requests from departments and agencies and strictly enforcing presidential decisions. Congress endorsed the Bureau's role and reinforced its retrenchment orientation. Even when large surpluses were assured, congressional appropriators refused to restore funds that had been eliminated during the Bureau's review of departmental requests.[76] Between 1920 and 1930, total federal spending declined by more than $3 billion, and the spending-GNP ratio fell by nearly 50 percent.

Administrative Centralization. The Bureau's direct relationship to the president was underscored by an early executive order, stating that "under the supervision of the Director and subject to review and determination by the President [the Bureau] shall assemble, revise, reduce, or increase the estimates of the departments."[77] The order further specified that the Director "acts for the President, and his calls upon the Chiefs of Bureaus and other Administrative Officers for purposes of consultation or information take precedence over the Cabinet head of a Department."[78] In practice, the Bureau was responsible for bringing all departmental budgets within an expenditure limit initially set by the president. That expenditure limit, in turn, was typically determined by tax-reduction and debt-reduction objectives.

Much of what the Bureau accomplished in its first few years of operation involved administrative systems and procedures. The accounting systems used by departments were standardized, as were government purchasing and contracting rules. Budget offices were established within departments to

76. Kahn, *Budgeting Democracy*, 203.

77. Executive Order 3578. The executive orders and budget circulars for this early period are reprinted in W. F. Willoughby, *The National Budget System* (Baltimore: Johns Hopkins University Press, 1927), 301–21.

78. Willoughby, *The National Budget System*, 201–21.

provide the technical expertise and information needed for Bureau reviews. Coordinating agencies and boards were set up to lend coherence to executive branch administration.

More important were the steps taken to centralize policy control within the executive branch. To preserve the integrity of the executive budget, departments were required to defend the president's estimates before Congress. President Harding warned that "advocacy of an estimate before the congressional committee in excess of the Executive recommendation will be looked upon as sufficient reason to give consideration towards severance of employment."[79] The Bureau of the Budget reinforced this basic principle by ordering executive departments to secure formal approval for any requests or recommendations to Congress on matters related to the budget, particularly legislative proposals that would affect future spending. The purpose of this new "central clearance" was to ensure that departmental advocacy was in conformity with the president's programs and views.[80] The Bureau also extended its authority over budget execution, directing the departments to prevent deficiencies by establishing reserves and improving apportionment controls.

The budget process in the executive branch made it more difficult for departments to evade presidential control with respect to spending and legislative policy. Because the retrenchment orientation was so pronounced during the 1920s, very little took place with respect to policy innovation. Nevertheless, the structural changes that supported a coherent budget program provided the president with considerable leverage over policy innovation once these restraints on spending were lifted.

Composition and Growth. The spending philosophy of the postwar decade was undeniably conservative. For Republican leaders of this era, economy in government "was more than a laudable fiscal objective. It was an end in itself— a virtue of unexcelled purity."[81] By 1922, all vestiges of wartime expenditures had disappeared from the budget, and outlays then stayed fairly stable. These fixed budgets were well above prewar spending, even with interest costs excluded, but much of the additional spending was absorbed by the military and by veterans' benefits. There was limited growth in most domestic

79. Quoted in Kahn, *Budgeting Democracy*, 202.

80. See Burkhead, *Government Budgeting*, 288–92. On the expansion of central clearance from fiscal to programmatic reviews, see Richard E. Neustadt, "Presidency and Legislation: The Growth of Central Clearance," *American Political Science Review* 48 (September 1954): 641–71.

81. Kimmel, *Federal Budget and Fiscal Policy, 1789–1958*, 98.

Table 4.4 Composition of Federal Outlays, 1920–1930 (in billions of dollars)

Fiscal Year	Total	National Security and International Affairs	Veterans' Services and Benefits	Interest	Other
		Percentage of Total			
1920	$ 6.4	70%	5%	16%	9%
1921	5.1	53	13	20	15
1922	3.3	29	21	30	20
1923	3.1	22	24	34	20
1924	2.9	23	23	33	21
1925	2.9	21	26	31	23
1926	2.9	21	27	29	24
1927	2.8	21	28	28	24
1928	2.9	23	27	25	25
1929	3.1	23	26	23	28
1930	3.3	23	25	21	32

Source: *Historical Statistics of the United States, Colonial Times to 1970, Part 2* (Washington, D.C.: U.S. Bureau of the Census, 1975), 1115.

programs, and the federal government's social welfare responsibilities were almost nonexistent.

As shown in Table 4.4, military spending and veterans' benefits accounted for nearly half of total outlays after spending levels had stabilized. Military spending remained high, because the United States maintained a much larger peacetime force than it had after previous wars. Active-duty force levels during the 1920s were well above 250,000, roughly double what they had been from 1900 to 1915 and five times higher than the post–Civil War force. The increased spending for veterans resulted from traditional pension and compensation payments and also from several new programs.[82] In 1918, Congress had established readjustment benefits for World War I veterans, including vocational training and rehabilitation and supportive medical services. World War I veterans were also covered by insurance against death or disability, with costs for this program reaching almost $140 million in 1930.[83]

82. Pension benefits and compensation differed, in that the latter was payable only for service-related disabilities. For these and other veterans' program descriptions, see *Historical Statistics of the United States, Colonial Times to 1970, Part 2*, 1138–40.

83. *Historical Statistics of the United States, Colonial Times to 1970, Part 2*, 1147.

The remainder of the budget covered interest payments on the debt and "all other" (domestic) spending. Since the budget share for interest remained close to 30 percent through 1927, there was little margin for new or expanded domestic program spending. Total outlays for domestic programs did not increase at all from 1922 to 1927, and the increases that did take place over the next several years were primarily for public works spending and federal agricultural aid.

Only a minuscule portion of the domestic budget share was directed toward social welfare programs for civilians. The programs then in existence were narrowly targeted and indirect. In 1917, the federal government had instituted a grant-in-aid program to assist the states with vocational education, and a grant program for vocational rehabilitation was adopted after the war. In 1921, the Sheppard-Towner Act had authorized federal grants-in-aid to the states for health services to combat infant and maternal mortality. Funding for these programs was limited. Less than $1.2 million in federal funds was disbursed to the states for the infant and maternal health program in 1929, and the program was terminated that year.[84] Total federal social welfare expenditures for civilian programs were estimated at $.09 per capita in 1913 and $.25 in 1928.[85] Of the $100 million in federal grants to state and local governments in 1930, highway funds accounted for more than three-fourths of the total.[86]

State and Local Spending

The budgetary record of the federal government during the 1920s was not matched by state and local governments. From 1922 to 1927, the federal debt dropped by almost $4.5 billion, while state and local government indebtedness rose by $4.7 billion.[87] Federal spending over this period fell by $500 million; state and local spending increased by $2.2 billion. At the end of the decade, nearly three-fourths of all government spending in the United States was state and local.

The types of expenditures were very different as well. The federal budget was heavily weighted toward defense, veterans' benefits, and interest

84. *Annual Report of the Secretary of the Treasury on the State of the Finances for the Fiscal Year Ended June 30, 1930* (Washington, D.C.: Government Printing Office, 1931), 622.

85. Edward D. Berkowitz and Kim McQuaid, *Creating the Welfare State: The Political Economy of Twentieth-Century Reform*, rev. ed. (Lawrence: University Press of Kansas, 1992), 75–76.

86. *Historical Statistics of the United States, Colonial Times to 1970, Part 2*, 1125.

87. *Historical Statistics of the United States, Colonial Times to 1970, Part 2*, 1130, 1132.

payments on the debt. For state and local governments, the dominant categories were education, capital construction (especially highways), and government services such as fire, police, and sanitation. Virtually all expenditures for categorical public assistance and other public welfare were state and local, and these governments also provided most of the funding for hospital and health services. Combined expenditures for these purposes were under 7 percent of total state and local outlays in 1922, but climbed to more than 10 percent over the next decade.

The limited programmatic demands on the federal government made it possible to keep budgets small and balanced. Moreover, because federal budgets were relatively small, their impact on the national economy was minimal. When it became clear that state and local governments could not deal with the social or economic dislocations of the Great Depression, however, the size, composition, and fiscal policy goals of the federal budget changed dramatically and irreversibly.

From Hoover to Roosevelt

President Herbert C. Hoover responded to the Great Depression with cautious, conventional changes in budget policy. Even as economic and social problems deepened, Hoover and his advisors remained committed to balanced, limited budgets. His successor, Franklin D. Roosevelt, professed the same commitment when he took office in 1933 but quickly discovered that budgets could be neither balanced nor limited if the federal government wanted to combat the unemployment and poverty brought on by the depression. Under Roosevelt's New Deal, fiscal policy management displaced the balanced-budget rule, domestic spending programs proliferated, and the federal government moved decisively into the modern era of policy activism.

Fiscal Policy

The United States had suffered three recessions in the years leading up to the Great Depression. The first of these occurred just after World War I and was severe, with GNP dropping by nearly 25 percent between 1920 and 1921, but the economy began to recover the following year. Recessions in 1924 and 1927 were less serious and equally short-lived. During each of these episodes, federal spending was tightly controlled, and budget surpluses were large. When another economic downturn began in 1929, the Hoover administration and Congress believed that, once again, the economy would recover quickly and largely on its own. In the meantime, they agreed, the federal government should follow its customary practice of reducing spending, while encouraging businesses to promote recovery and state and local governments to provide any needed relief.[88]

Instead of recovering, the economy collapsed. Between 1929 and 1933, GNP fell by 50 percent, and the unemployment rate soared from 3 to 25 percent. On taking office in 1933, the Roosevelt administration responded to this economic emergency with immediate public relief programs and then with additional spending to promote economic recovery. Between 1930 and 1940, the ratio of spending to GNP tripled. The budget was in deficit each year beginning in 1931, with the cumulative peacetime deficits of nearly $25 billion exceeding those of World War I (Table 4.5). By the end of Roosevelt's second term, the budget embodied a new understanding of the "continuous responsibility of the government for the maintenance of economic stability [and] the central role of fiscal policy in carrying out that responsibility."[89]

From 1929 to 1933. Six weeks after the October 1929 stock market crash, President Hoover submitted his FY 1931 budget to Congress. Because a large surplus was projected, Hoover recommended, and Congress approved, a small, temporary tax cut for individuals and corporations.[90] The budget was expected to remain in surplus, taking into account both the tax reduction and $500 million in scheduled debt retirement. Hoover concluded that "[o]ur finances are in sound condition. . . . Our estimated expenditures for this and the next year are well within our expected receipts."[91]

One year later, the Treasury Department reported that the anticipated surplus had disappeared. The Treasury report noted that the 1930 "income tax reduction [had] offered relief to both individuals and corporations during a period of unfavorable business developments," but the need for additional revenues to bring the budget back into balance meant that the tax cut could not be continued.[92] The Treasury assumed these higher rates would yield additional revenues. Instead, income tax collections dropped by $550 million

88. See Herbert Stein, *The Fiscal Revolution in America* (Chicago: University of Chicago Press, 1969), 14.

89. Stein, *The Fiscal Revolution in America,* 128.

90. The reduction affected 1929 income taxes payable in 1930, with individual and corporation normal tax rates lowered by one percentage point. The estimated revenue loss was $80 million. *Annual Report of the Secretary of the Treasury for Fiscal Year 1930,* 2.

91. *Congressional Record,* 71st Cong., 2d sess., 1929, 72, pt. 1: 100.

92. *Annual Report of the Secretary of the Treasury for Fiscal Year 1930,* 38.

Table 4.5 Federal Budget Totals, 1930–1940 (in millions of dollars)

Fiscal Year	Total Revenues	Total Outlays	Deficit (−) /Surplus
1930	$ 4,058	$ 3,320	$ 738
1931	3,116	3,577	−462
1932	1,924	4,659	−2,735
1933	1,997	4,598	−2,602
1934	2,955	6,541	−3,586
1935	3,609	6,412	−2,803
1936	3,923	8,228	−4,304
1937	5,387	7,580	−2,193
1938	6,751	6,840	−89
1939	6,295	9,141	−2,846
1940	6,548	9,468	−2,920

SOURCE: *Historical Tables, Budget of the United States Government, Fiscal Year 2002* (Washington, D.C.: Government Printing Office, 2001), 21.

from 1930 to 1931.[93] Total budget receipts fell by more than $800 million, and the FY 1931 deficit swelled to $460 million.

Nevertheless, the Hoover administration determined that a further increase in tax rates was needed to protect the "financial stability of the United States Government."[94] The budget presented to Congress in December 1931 contained a 20 percent increase in individual and corporation income taxes, along with higher excises and other receipts "calculated to balance the . . . budget exactly—without provision for the sinking fund debt reduction."[95] Hoover's concerns about the need to protect federal credit and build public confidence were legitimate, given the turmoil in domestic and international financial markets, but his budgetary prescriptions proved counterproductive. Congress agreed to raise taxes, but the higher rates it imposed did not increase revenues. Total receipts plunged by almost $2 billion from 1930 to 1933, with income tax collections dropping from $2.4 billion to under $750 million.[96]

93. Individual income tax collections fell from $1.146 billion to $834 million. The corporation tax revenue was $1.263 million in 1930 and $1.026 million in 1931.

94. Hoover's State of the Union message explained that increased taxes "should not cover the whole of these [current] deficits. . . . [But] the amount of taxation should be fixed so as to balance the Budget for 1933 except for the statutory debt retirement." *Public Papers of the Presidents of the United States: Herbert Hoover, 1931* (Washington, D.C.: Government Printing Office, 1976), 587–88.

95. Stein, *The Fiscal Revolution in America*, 32.

96. *Annual Report of the Secretary of the Treasury on the State of the Finances for the Fiscal Year Ended June 30, 1935* (Washington, D.C.: Government Printing Office, 1936), 323.

This deteriorating fiscal situation had a paralyzing effect on spending policy. The Hoover administration sponsored small increases in federal construction and public works spending and persuaded Congress to create a Reconstruction Finance Corporation to make loans to banks and businesses, but the responsibility for emergency relief was left in the hands of state and local governments. Fearful of additional spending, Hoover vetoed an emergency veterans' bonus bill in 1931, although Congress overrode the veto. During Hoover's presidency, "depression-induced expenditures" were only $1.2 billion, less than one-tenth of total federal spending.[97] His final budget warned that "a large excess of expenditures . . . can not be continued without disaster to the Federal budget."[98]

From 1933 to 1941. In his 1932 campaign for the presidency, Franklin Roosevelt attacked Hoover's failure to balance the budget, and the Democratic party platform pledged to restore balance through "an immediate and drastic reduction . . . of not less than twenty-five percent" in federal spending and "a system of taxation levied on the principle of the ability to pay."[99] Once Roosevelt took office, however, immediate steps were taken to expand federal emergency spending for employment and relief. The projected deficits were greater than Roosevelt and his advisers thought desirable, but they hoped these deficits would at least be temporary.

Roosevelt's efforts to revive the economy went far beyond budget policy. Monetary reforms, bank insurance, antitrust enforcement, and economic regulation were an exponential advance in federal economic policy activism. Moreover, while Roosevelt's monetary policy and banking initiatives allowed the Treasury and Federal Reserve to manage deficit financing more easily, his initial commitment to spending stimulus was less than wholehearted. In 1933 and 1934, the administration reduced what it designated as ordinary spending, while accelerating emergency program expenditures. Roosevelt claimed that the emergency programs were not as costly as they appeared, since loans would be "repaid to the Treasury" and other spending would be funded through new "taxes to pay the interest and the installments on that part of the debt."[100] In fact, federal spending for relief and recovery could

97. M. Slade Kendrick, *A Century and a Half of Federal Expenditures* (New York: National Bureau of Economic Research, 1955), 32.

98. *Congressional Record*, 72d Cong., 2d sess., 1932, 76, pt. 1: 84.

99. *Guide to U.S. Elections*, 2d ed. (Washington, D.C.: Congressional Quarterly, 1985), 91.

100. *The Public Papers and Addresses of Franklin D. Roosevelt* (New York: Random House, 1938), 2:296.

not be accurately estimated or easily controlled. The deficits that were incurred were not planned at a specific level but "were a reflection of the fiscal impact of a wide variety of policies that had as their common goal the financing of relief and recovery needs."[101]

Further complications resulted from questionable budget accounting practices. The treatment of federal lending programs was not always consistent during this period, which meant that reported spending and deficit levels were problematical. An even more serious confusion in the opposite direction was presented by the substantial Social Security trust fund surpluses that began to accumulate in 1937. These budget accounting problems were finally corrected with the consolidated cash budget format that was instituted at the end of World War II.

Nevertheless, Roosevelt's second term was a turning point in the implementation of deficit finance. The economy had reached its lowest point in 1933, and over the next three years GNP increased by 50 percent. Unemployment remained high, but the recovering economy was boosting revenues, and the need for emergency spending seemed less pressing. In his budget message to Congress on January 8, 1937, Roosevelt promised an end to the cycle of budget deficits. "The programs inaugurated during the last four years to combat the depression and to initiate many needed reforms have cost large sums of money, but the benefits obtained from them are far outweighing all their costs. We shall soon . . . [have] a balanced Budget that will also include provision for reduction of the public debt."[102] During the next year, however, the economy entered an unexpected recession, revenue growth stalled, and prospects for balancing the budget dimmed. A major stock market decline in October 1937 triggered fears of a new depression, but Roosevelt was reluctant to abandon his hopes for a balanced budget. In November, Roosevelt reported that a deficit for FY 1938 might prove unavoidable but assured Congress that "the proposed Federal budget for the coming [1939] fiscal year . . . can be brought within a definite balance."[103]

The FY 1939 budget sent to Congress on January 3, 1938, was less optimistic. Acknowledging that the economic downturn was proving to be more severe than he had expected, Roosevelt warned that additional spending might soon become "necessary to save thousands of American families from

---

101. Kimmel, *Federal Budget and Fiscal Policy, 1789–1958*, 182–83.
102. *Congressional Record*, 75th Cong., 1st sess., 1937, 81, pt. 1: 116.
103. *The Public Papers and Addresses of Franklin D. Roosevelt, 1937* (New York: Macmillan, 1941), 493.

dire need."[104] In April, Roosevelt called on Congress to appropriate more than $3 billion in budget authority and loan authority to fund employment and relief programs.[105] The administration announced that the Treasury and Federal Reserve would take immediate steps to expand the supply of credit and to reinforce this spending stimulus. In early June, Congress followed Roosevelt's lead and passed the multibillion-dollar Work Relief and Public Works Appropriation Act.

The rationale for deficit financing was advanced even more forcefully in the New Deal's final peacetime budgets. Roosevelt's annual message to Congress in 1939 called for additional spending "to get enough capital and labor at work to give us a total turnover of business, a total national income of at least eighty billion dollars a year."[106] The FY 1941 budget message pointedly defended this new approach to fiscal policy:

> In the early thirties—prior to 1933—fiscal policy was exceedingly simply in theory and disastrous in practice. It consisted in trying to keep expenditures as low as possible in the face of shrinking national income . . . [and] came near to bankrupting both our people and our Government.
>
> Following 1933 the fiscal policy of the Government was more realistically adapted to the needs of the people. . . . The deliberate use of Government funds and of Government credit to energize private enterprise . . . had a profound effect both on Government and on private incomes.[107]

There had been, Roosevelt concluded, "conscious or unconscious deception" about government debt; in the future, government debt, like individual or corporate debt, should no longer be "judged in a vacuum; it must be considered in light of earnings, assets, and credit standing."[108] Based on these considerations, Roosevelt argued, his administration's record on deficits and debt was fully justified: "When the increase in the national debt is viewed against the background of what was accomplished by the growth of useful

104. *Congressional Record*, 75th Cong., 3d sess., 1938, 83, pt. 1: 62.

105. Kimmel, *Federal Budget and Fiscal Policy, 1789–1958*, 185.

106. *The Public Papers and Addresses of Franklin D. Roosevelt, 1939* (New York: Macmillan, 1941), 8.

107. *Congressional Record*, 76th Cong., 3d sess., 1940, 86, pt. 1: 47.

108. *Congressional Record*, 76th Cong., 3d sess., 1940, 86, pt. 1: 50.

physical assets, and of effective national earning power, and by the strengthening of the Nation's credit and morale, there is no economic ground for
anxiety, so far as the national debt is concerned, as to the Nation's future."[109]

Roosevelt's rationale for stimulative fiscal policy was not universally
accepted, even within the Democratic party. Congress did not approve a
number of major spending initiatives Roosevelt proposed in the latter part of
his second term, and congressional criticism of peacetime budget deficits
continued right up to World War II. Nevertheless, the Great Depression
had discredited long-standing beliefs about what the federal government
could do, and should do, to bring about economic recovery. Passivity was
unacceptable, since depressions were not self-correcting. Raising taxes to
balance the budget was unwise and impractical; raising expenditures, regardless of deficits, allowed the federal government to provide interim relief and
to foster long-term recovery.

Building on the practical lessons of depression-era politics, the Roosevelt
administration also strengthened fiscal policy advisory systems. In 1938,
Roosevelt established a Monetary and Fiscal Advisory Board. In 1939, the
Bureau of the Budget was transferred to the Executive Office of the President, and its staff and responsibilities were expanded. Shortly thereafter,
the Bureau's fiscal policy role was formalized. Professional economists were
recruited to help develop a more sophisticated understanding of fiscal policy
effects, and the influence of Keynesian economics began to spread, at least
within the executive branch.

Spending Policy

When the Hoover presidency began, federal spending was 3 percent of GNP,
and the budget was in surplus. Over the next decade, the budget climbed to
10 percent of GNP, and deficits soared. This escalation in domestic spending
was driven by emergency programs to combat the Great Depression and
permanent income security programs for the aged, unemployed, and poor.
Most of the former and all of the latter were New Deal initiatives, and they
collectively redefined the federal government's domestic policy responsibilities. Roosevelt claimed that bigger budgets simply "mirrored the changing
attitudes of the people toward the growing needs which they expect their
Government to meet."[110] The "relatively minor role" of the federal govern-

109. *Congressional Record*, 76th Cong., 3d sess., 1940, 86, pt. 1: 50.
110. *Congressional Record*, 76th Cong., 3d sess., 1940, 86, pt. 1: 47.

ment during the 1920s had permitted a "relatively low and constant level of expenditures."[111] As needs and expectations had changed, the federal government's domestic budgets had expanded accordingly.

The Hoover Program. The fiscal policy goals and spending philosophy of the Hoover administration precluded the wholesale expansion of both ordinary and emergency spending programs. Instead, the budgets submitted by President Hoover attempted to reduce spending to pre-depression levels. Under the Hoover administration's budget program, the responsibility for depression relief was left in the hands of state and local governments, and federal efforts to relieve unemployment were narrow and targeted.

In December 1930, President Hoover acknowledged that the country was in a depression, but his fiscal 1932 budget message to Congress cautioned that "[t]his is not a time when we can afford to embark upon any new or enlarged venture of government."[112] The budget Hoover submitted called for spending cuts rather than increases, and even larger reductions were recommended as the depression worsened. The FY 1934 request for $3.3 billion in expenditures was $800 million less than Hoover had recommended in his first budget. Since the FY 1934 spending total included more than $350 million in debt retirement, there was no margin to accommodate emergency spending even if the administration had been willing to call for such spending. The "official" spending totals for Hoover's presidency were increased after he left office through a technical reclassification involving Reconstruction Finance Corporation (RFC) lending. The RFC was the only spending innovation of Hoover's presidency. Under the 1932 Reconstruction Finance Corporation Act and the subsequent Emergency Relief and Construction Act, the RFC was authorized to lend several billion dollars to private banks and railroads and to state governments for relief programs and public works projects.

According to its legislative charter, the RFC was permitted to finance its lending by borrowing directly from the Treasury. Since loan repayments were expected to cover the RFC's Treasury debt, the RFC was not included in Hoover's spending requests or in the administration's periodic reports of actual spending. When the Roosevelt administration took office, however, most of the RFC's loans had not been repaid, and the decision was made to classify these defaulted loans as spending. For fiscal years 1932–33, reclassified

111. *Congressional Record*, 76th Cong., 3d sess., 1940, 86, pt. 1: 47.
112. *Congressional Record*, 71st Cong., 3d sess., 1930, 74, pt. 1: 134.

RFC expenditures boosted actual spending totals by nearly $1.4 billion.[113] In FY 1934, the multibillion-dollar difference between the original Hoover budget and spending reported by the Treasury was the result of reclassified RFC spending and of emergency programs initiated by the Roosevelt administration.[114]

With the exception of this RFC anomaly, the Hoover administration's spending budgets were tightly controlled. Most spending categories grew minimally, if at all, between 1929 and 1933, and the composition of the expenditure side of the budget was nearly indistinguishable from that of the 1920s. In the final year of his presidency, Hoover continued his attack against spending, rejecting demands for federal direct relief and work relief and opposing the prepayment of veterans' bonuses.

The Roosevelt Program. Roosevelt, however, moved quickly to expand emergency spending in the form of direct relief, work relief, and public works. The Federal Emergency Relief Act, signed into law May 12, 1933, authorized $500 million in grants to the states for relief and work relief programs. The National Industrial Recovery Act, passed several weeks later, included a multibillion-dollar authorization for public works and construction projects. The first major price support program to stabilize farm income was established in 1933, with the Agricultural Adjustment Act, and federal loans and credit subsidies for farmers were instituted under the 1933 Farm Credit Act. While these and other new spending proposals were being advanced, Roosevelt called on Congress to cut ordinary, or nonemergency, spending for federal pay and administrative expenses and for veterans' pensions. The Economy Act of 1933 contained an estimated $500 million in annual savings in such spending.[115]

The distinction between ordinary and emergency spending was a prominent feature of the New Deal's early budgets. From 1933 to 1937, "ordinary" spending by executive departments and agencies was flat, but expenditures for relief and relief work, public works, and aid to agriculture increased from

113. See *Annual Report of the Secretary of the Treasury for Fiscal Year 1935*, 318–19. The only Reconstruction Finance Corporation (RFC) transaction included in Hoover's budget was $500 million for the federal government's purchase of capital stock.

114. For FY 1934, total emergency spending was more than $4 billion, with RFC expenditures of approximately $1 billion. Before 1934, there was no separate designation for emergency expenditures. See *Annual Report of the Secretary of the Treasury for Fiscal Year 1935*, 317–19.

115. Kimmel, *Federal Budget and Fiscal Policy, 1789–1958*, 176.

$1 billion to $4.4 billion.[116] According to Roosevelt, it was not "inconsistent for a government to cut down its regular expenses and at the same time to borrow and to spend billions for an emergency . . . because a large portion of the emergency money has been paid out in the form of sound loans which will be repaid . . . and to cover the rest we have imposed taxes to pay the interest and the installments on that part of the debt."[117] In a further attempt to deflect criticism of new spending and higher deficits, the administration's budget requests sometimes excluded spending for emergency programs. The FY 1935 budget, for example, did not include $2 billion Roosevelt had requested for relief and recovery programs or an additional $525 million in scheduled debt retirement.[118] Under Roosevelt, unlike Hoover, actual spending was a more reliable guide to deliberate spending policy than were official budget estimates, since New Deal programs were often funded through supplemental and deficiency requests sent to Congress after action on the "ordinary" budget was completed.

Although there was a profound difference between the Roosevelt and Hoover administrations in federal economic regulation, the unprecedented scope of the New Deal's regulatory innovations was not necessarily reflected in budgetary commitments. The divergence in spending philosophy, however, was evidenced in the scale and the variety of spending programs inaugurated by Roosevelt. His administration freely utilized direct relief and employment for individuals, credit assistance to small businesses, direct loans and subsidies to farmers and homeowners, and grants to the states. Direct spending and subsidized credit were used to revive and strengthen entire sectors of the economy, most notably agriculture, housing, and transportation. Massive public works commitments spurred regional economic development through flood control, power production, rural electrification, and irrigation and reclamation projects. From 1935 to 1940, these relief and recovery spending initiatives averaged more than $4 billion annually, levels that dwarfed depression-related expenditures during the entire Hoover presidency.

Moreover, the Roosevelt administration's domestic spending agenda was not confined to emergency measures. Instead, planning for long-term federal commitments complemented many temporary recovery efforts. The

---

116. *Annual Report of the Secretary of the Treasury on the State of the Finances for the Fiscal Year Ended June 30, 1940* (Washington, D.C.: Government Printing Office, 1941), 22–36.

117. Quoted in Stein, *The Fiscal Revolution in America*, 46.

118. *Congressional Record*, 73d Cong., 2d sess., 1934, 78, pt. 1: 31.

agriculture policy structure created during the 1930s, with price supports, loan programs, and production controls for major commodities, lasted for well over half a century.[119] Federal transportation planning and funding have been fixtures of domestic budgets since the New Deal, and direct loan and loan guarantee programs have been extensively used to provide federal support for housing, business and commerce, and education.[120] And ever since the New Deal's Federal Emergency Relief Act of 1933, grants-in-aid have figured prominently in federal-state relations. In the domestic policy arena, the Roosevelt administration "extended federal commitments to new policy areas while transforming modest federal domestic commitments into substantial and continuous ones . . . [and] legitimated federal support to distressed sectors of the economy and underdeveloped regions of the country."[121]

A parallel transition took place in social welfare policy. In 1933, the federal government began to provide direct relief and work relief through its own agencies, such as the Works Progress Administration (later the Work Projects Administration), Civil Works Administration, Federal Emergency Relief Administration, and Civilian Conservation Corps, while channeling substantial assistance through state agencies. The following year, Roosevelt appointed the Committee on Economic Security to develop a comprehensive, permanent program that would address the needs of the unemployed and the elderly and lend some coherence to the provision of public assistance by the states. In 1935, Congress passed the landmark Social Security Act, which combined a federal old-age insurance program with federal-state unemployment insurance and public assistance programs (Table 4.6). The approach and structure of the 1935 Social Security Act represent the base on which social welfare policy in the United States has since rested.[122]

The federal old-age insurance (OAI), or Social Security, program was designed to provide automatic benefits to retired workers. Financing was based on a payroll tax on employers and employees, with a designated trust

---

119. See Dennis S. Ippolito, *Uncertain Legacies: Federal Budget Policy from Roosevelt through Reagan* (Charlottesville: University Press of Virginia, 1990), 195–98. Comprehensive changes in subsidies and production controls were finally made in the 1996 Freedom to Farm Act, which dismantled the New Deal regulatory structure.

120. For the development and use of federal credit programs, see Dennis S. Ippolito, *Hidden Spending: The Politics of Federal Credit Programs* (Chapel Hill: University of North Carolina Press, 1984), 26–41.

121. Ippolito, *Uncertain Legacies*, 194.

122. Pre-1935 federal social welfare programs were essentially for veterans and for mothers. See Skocpol, *Protecting Soldiers and Mothers*.

Table 4.6 Major Components of the 1935 Social Security Act (P.L. 74-271)

I. Old-Age Insurance (OAI)

Recipient Population	Retired workers, 65 or older, in covered employment
Financing	Federal payroll tax, trust fund ("old-age reserve account")
Administration	Federal
Eligibility	Automatic (age eligibility)
Benefit Level	Based on preretirement earnings ($85 maximum per month)

II. Unemployment Insurance

Recipient Population	Unemployed workers in covered employment
Financing	State payroll tax on employers (credited against federal payroll tax
Administration	State (under federally approved plan)
Eligibility	Determined by state
Benefit Level	Determined by state

III. Old-Age Assistance (OAA)

Recipient Population	Indigent aged, 65 or older ("aged needy individuals")
Financing	Federal matching grants, 50 percent of benefit (maximum federal grant of $15 per month per recipient)
Administration	State (under federally approved plan)
Eligibility	Determined by state (under federal guidelines)
Benefit Level	Determined by state

IV. Aid to the Blind (AB)

Recipient Population	Indigent blind adults ("needy individuals who are blind")
Financing	Federal matching grants, 50 percent of benefit (maximum federal grant of $15 per month per recipient)
Administration	State (under federally approved plan)
Eligibility	Determined by state (under federal guidelines)
Benefit Level	Determined by state

V. Aid to Dependent Children (ADC)

Recipient Population	Indigent children ("needy dependent children")
Financing	Federal matching grants, one-third of benefit (maximum federal grant of $6 per month for the first child, $4 each additional child)
Administration	State (under federally approved plan)
Eligibility	Determined by state (under federal guidelines)
Benefit Level	Determined by state

SOURCE: *Statutes at Large, Vol. 49, 1935–1936* (Washington, D.C.: Government Printing Office, 1936), 620–48.

fund receiving these taxes and paying out benefits. The unemployment compensation program was likewise based on insurance principles, with payroll taxes into a trust fund used to fund benefits when needed. Since the federal government wanted to encourage states to establish their own programs, the federal tax on employees could be offset by payments into state unemployment compensation plans.[123] Within a few years, all of the states had taken advantage of this opportunity, creating unemployment benefit coverage for workers, primarily those in industrial occupations.

Under the Social Security Act, public assistance programs were to be administered by the states with the federal government providing matching grants for targeted programs.[124] The old-age assistance (OAA) program's recipient population was the indigent aged. Aid to the indigent blind (AB) provided similar federal funding levels, while lesser matching grants were authorized for state programs serving children for whom adequate support was lacking because of the death, incapacity, or absence of a parent. The federal guidelines governing each of these programs were minimal, which allowed the states considerable discretion over eligibility standards and benefit levels.

The social welfare system that Congress created in 1935 was limited in scope. While the Committee on Economic Security had endorsed national health insurance in its report, President Roosevelt did not include it in his 1935 proposal, nor did he recommend it when the Social Security system was expanded in 1939. Conservative opposition to the federalization of welfare ensured that the states retained substantial control over the administration of public assistance programs, and widespread concerns about cost kept initial benefit levels low for the Social Security and public assistance programs. The Social Security trust fund was further buttressed by having payroll taxes collected for five years before the first benefits were to be distributed.[125]

The constitutionality of the old-age insurance and unemployment compensation programs was upheld by a sharply divided Supreme Court in 1937,

123. Wisconsin's was the first state program, enacted in 1934. When the 1935 Social Security Act was passed, only eight states had unemployment compensation programs. See Edwin Amenta, *Bold Relief: Institutional Politics and the Origins of Modern American Social Policy* (Princeton: Princeton University Press, 1998), 100.

124. Title V of the Social Security Act authorized federal grants-in-aid for maternal and child health services, services for crippled children, and child welfare services. Authorization was also provided for public health work, administered by the Public Health Service.

125. On the decision to change reserve requirements and pay benefits more quickly, see Berkowitz and McQuaid, *Creating the Welfare State*, 130–36.

but political opposition to social welfare expansion remained formidable.[126] In 1937, the administration was able to secure federal retirement and unemployment coverage for railroad workers. The 1939 Social Security Act Amendments authorized benefits for dependents and survivors of covered workers under the Social Security program, liberalized eligibility standards and benefit formulas, and moved up the starting date for distributing benefits from 1942 to 1940. The 1939 legislation also raised the federal matching grants for public assistance programs. Congress was not receptive, however, to proposals for extending Social Security coverage to disabled workers or for adding health insurance to the Social Security system.

Nevertheless, the peacetime budgets that the Roosevelt administration pushed through Congress were not only much higher than those of any prior administration but were much more heavily oriented toward domestic program spending. From 1933 to 1940, federal spending totaled more than $60 billion (Table 4.7). Approximately one-half of this spending was for depression-related programs. By the end of the decade, federal emergency and public works expenditures had risen to well above $4 billion annually, and the federal government was directly employing more than 3 million workers.[127] Social welfare spending for permanent programs, by comparison, was considerably less, since Social Security had yet to distribute appreciable benefits.[128] Between 1936 and 1940, however, federal public assistance grants under the 1935 Social Security Act were beginning to have an impact on total spending, rising from under $30 million to more than $350 million.[129]

Under the New Deal, traditional restrictions on federal domestic spending were lifted. Economic stimulus in the form of deficit spending became acceptable. Direct federal relief and work relief were used on a massive scale for the first time in the nation's history. In addition to its emergency programs, the Roosevelt administration extended the federal government's permanent responsibilities to include a broad range of domestic programs, including social welfare for the aged and poor.

---

126. The Supreme Court's decisions were handed down in three cases on May 24, 1937. *Carmichael v. Southern Coal and Coke Co.*, 301 U.S. 495 (1937); *Helvering v. Davis*, 301 U.S. 619 (1937); and *Steward Machine Co. v. Davis*, 301 U.S. 548 (1937). The votes were 5 to 4 in the *Carmichael* and *Steward Machine* cases. In *Helvering*, the margin was 7 to 2.

127. See Amenta, *Bold Relief*, 144.

128. Social Security (OAI) benefit payments in 1940 were only $16 million.

129. *Annual Report of the Secretary of the Treasury for Fiscal Year 1940*, 28.

Table 4.7 Total Expenditures from General and Special Accounts, 1933–1940 (in millions of dollars)

Depression-Related:	$29,650
Relief and Work Relief	(15,507)
Aid to Agriculture	(7,643)
Public Works	(6,500)
Social Welfare:	$8,355
Grants to States	(1,143)
Social Security	(——)
Veterans' Pensions and Benefits	(7,212)
Other:	$22,823
National Defense (War and Navy Departments)	(7,497)
Executive Departments and Agencies	(3,188)
Transfers to Trust Accounts, Miscellaneous	(3,193)
Interest on the Public Debt	(6,790)
Debt Retirement	(2,155)
Total	$60,828

SOURCE: *Annual Report of the Secretary of the Treasury on the State of the Finances for the Fiscal Year Ended June 30, 1940* (Washington, D.C.: Government Printing Office, 1941), 25.

Tax Policy

The Hoover administration's approach to tax policy was dominated by revenue considerations. The Republican tax cuts of the 1920s, the last of which occurred in 1929, were made possible by the confluence of large postwar surpluses, the belief that low tax rates were more productive than higher ones (at least over time), and an ideological commitment to low taxes and small government. When those surpluses were threatened by the onset of the Great Depression, Hoover and most Republicans readily agreed that taxes had to be raised and balanced budgets restored. The 1929 tax cut was rescinded the following year, and when revenue projections continued to lag, excise and income taxes were raised.

The 1932 Revenue Act, shaped in large part by Hoover's Treasury Department, eliminated the exemption for small corporations and substantially increased corporation and individual income tax rates. The top marginal rate for individuals jumped from 25 to 63 percent, the highest rate since 1921, and the corporate tax rate of 13.75 percent was actually higher than the World War I level.[130] In the face of a fiscal emergency, then, Republican

130. See Pechman, *Federal Tax Policy*, 313, 321.

leaders were willing to accept not only much higher taxes but also a much more progressive allocation of tax burdens. They strongly opposed, however, coupling this tax program to a redistributive spending program.

The tax philosophy of the Roosevelt era did not ignore revenue considerations, but beginning in 1935 tax policy became part of a national debate over economic equity and the distribution of wealth. President Roosevelt went beyond attacking tax avoidance by the wealthy to arguing for redistributive taxation, albeit not always consistently and, in the end, with mixed results in terms of substantive tax policy. Still, the New Deal managed to alter the politics of income taxation in ways that no other administration has equaled.

During Roosevelt's first two years in office, these reformist impulses were not in evidence. Several relatively minor tax increases were passed by Congress, but tax policy was largely unchanged. The National Recovery Tax Act of 1933 reinstated a minimal corporation excess profits tax and placed a new 5 percent levy on corporate dividends. Much more important in terms of additional revenue was the Agricultural Adjustment Act of 1933, which imposed a processing tax on farm products that generated more than $950 million before being invalidated by the Supreme Court in 1936. The Revenue Act of 1934 contained a number of structural reforms designed to reduce tax avoidance and evasion, but the administration blocked more sweeping changes in the tax treatment of corporations.[131] Revenues were also affected by the end of Prohibition, which led to a resurgence in alcohol taxes. In 1935, alcohol excise taxes were more than $400 million, and total excises that year were approximately equal to combined individual and corporation income tax receipts.

On June 19, 1935, the president sent a special tax message to Congress that abruptly raised the stakes over income taxation. Decrying what he termed "an unjust concentration of wealth and economic power," Roosevelt called for the federal government to use its taxing powers to encourage "a wider distribution of wealth."[132] Among Roosevelt's recommendations were a federal inheritance tax, higher tax rates for wealthy individuals, and graduated corporation tax rates. Congress did not accept the proposed inheritance tax but did agree to increase estate and gift taxes. The 1935 "Wealth Tax" also raised the top marginal rate for individual taxpayers to 79 percent (for taxable

131. See Witte, *The Politics and Development of the Federal Income Tax*, 98–100.
132. *Congressional Record*, 74th Cong., 1st sess., 1935, 79, pt. 9: 9657.

income above $5 million) and instituted a graduated corporation income tax with a minimum rate of 15 percent. Corporation taxation was further strengthened with a tax on intercorporate dividends that reduced the opportunity for tax avoidance.

While the Social Security Act of 1935 was largely divorced from the debate over tax policy, the payroll tax it imposed has had a lasting effect on structural tax policy. Payroll taxes have become the second largest source of federal revenue, and their growth has diminished the overall progressivity of federal tax liabilities. The New Deal's tax policy legacy has been compromised, ironically, by one of its most important spending initiatives.

Roosevelt's influence on tax policy began to wane during his second term. In 1936 and 1937, the administration launched a series of attacks against tax avoidance by corporations and by wealthy individuals. Congress enacted a highly controversial tax on undistributed profits in 1936, although the measure was considerably less sweeping than the administration's proposal, and corporation income tax liabilities were further increased through rate changes and structural reforms. The 1937 tax reforms were aimed at wealthy individuals who were using holding companies, family trusts and partnerships, and other devices to shelter income from taxation. Highly publicized hearings conducted by a Joint Committee on Tax Evasion and Avoidance provided detailed evidence of serious abuses on the part of wealthy families, and Congress quickly approved Roosevelt's proposals.

Businesses and high-income taxpayers, however, were stepping up their opposition to the New Deal's tax program, and the recession that began in the latter part of 1937 added weight to their arguments that heavy tax burdens were stifling economic recovery. Congressional conservatives capitalized on this situation by moving to reverse some of Roosevelt's most important initiatives. The tax on undistributed profits was lowered in 1937 and repealed in 1939. Loss carryovers, which permitted businesses to deduct current losses against future income, were reintroduced by the 1939 Revenue Act after having been eliminated in the National Industrial Recovery Act of 1933. Capital gains taxation for individuals and corporations was reduced, and tax rates for small businesses were lowered. While Congress could not entirely undo the structural reforms of 1935 and 1936, progressivity and equity had lost much of their force in the debate over tax policy.

Nevertheless, the New Deal's impact on tax policy was not merely symbolic. Serious efforts were made to strengthen progressivity in individual

Table 4.8 Composition of Federal Revenues, 1934–1940 (in millions of dollars)

Fiscal Year	Total Revenues	Percentage of Total				
		Individual Income Taxes	Corporation Income Taxes	Social Insurance	Excise Taxes	Other
1934	$ 2,955	14.2%	12.3%	1.0%	45.8%	26.7%
1935	3,609	14.6	14.7	0.9	39.9	30.0
1936	3,923	17.2	18.3	1.3	41.6	21.6
1937	5,387	20.3	19.3	10.8	34.8	14.9
1938	6,751	19.1	19.1	22.8	27.6	11.5
1939	6,295	16.3	17.9	25.3	29.7	10.7
1940	6,548	13.6	18.3	27.3	30.2	10.7

SOURCE: *Historical Tables, Budget of the United States Government, Fiscal Year 2002* (Washington, D.C.: Government Printing Office, 2001), 29, 31.

and corporation income taxation, but the revenue levels in place during the 1930s necessarily limited the redistributive efforts of federal taxes. Individual income taxes represented only 1.3 percent of personal income in 1940, about the same level as in 1930.[133] There was an increase in corporation income taxes as a percentage of net product over this same period, but the level in 1940 was still only 5.5 percent.[134] During the peacetime years of the Roosevelt presidency, the share of federal revenues provided by income taxation increased only slightly (Table 4.8). In 1940, that share was less than one-third, while regressive taxes—excise and social insurance payroll taxes—accounted for almost 60 percent. With the enormous revenue demands of World War II, however, income taxation became considerably more important, and progressivity principles acquired much greater salience.

Expanding the Scope of Budget Policy

Until the 1930s, the goals of federal budget policy were modest. During the 1920s, the Republican majority restrained domestic spending, reduced revenues to keep income taxes from impairing incentives to work and invest, and ensured that surpluses were applied to debt reduction. In the face of several 1920s recessions, the prescription was higher taxes, lower spending, and

133. Ippolito, *Uncertain Legacies*, 32.
134. Ippolito, *Uncertain Legacies*, 32.

more stringent fiscal discipline. The executive budget adopted after World War I, and the accompanying recentralization of the congressional budget process, served to reinforce this conservative approach to fiscal policy.

While Roosevelt frequently professed his belief in the desirability of limited, balanced budgets, the cumulative result of New Deal measures was to legitimize fiscal stimulus through increased spending. Roosevelt's program of relief and recovery spending initiatives was a direct response to the emergency needs created by the Great Depression, but Roosevelt eventually defended this program in terms of a more "realistic" understanding of deficits and debt. Federal spending and federal credit were necessary to spur employment and economic growth, and budgets neither could nor should be balanced until economic recovery had been achieved.

The New Deal also broadened the scope of spending and tax policy. The Social Security Act of 1935 signaled the birth of a permanent social welfare state, but the New Deal was responsible as well for an entirely new scale of federal domestic activism—massive public works programs, regional economic development, subsidies and other assistance to the agricultural, transportation, and housing sectors of the economy. What had been modest and sporadic federal domestic initiatives in the past were transformed into substantial, permanent, and more encompassing commitments under the Roosevelt administration. The New Deal created, in sum, the programmatic base of modern domestic politics.

On the tax side, Roosevelt's impact was equally profound. Progressivity and equity became central prescriptive criteria for income taxation. Tax policy also developed into an instrument for redistributing income, as the funding requirements for social welfare programs grew. With respect to fiscal policy, spending, and taxation, the period between the world wars encompassed two different versions of budget policy, and the New Deal's commitment to activist policy brought the federal government decisively into a new era.

WAR AND DEFENSE BUDGETS

(1940–1970)

The fiscal and political conditions that had simplified previous postwar retrenchments were largely absent after World War II. The debt incurred during the war was so large that rapid retirement was impractical. New public expectations about the federal government's domestic responsibilities had been created by the New Deal, and the United States was soon confronted with the need to support a large and costly Cold War military establishment for an indefinite period.

Nevertheless, fiscal controls were surprisingly effective for nearly two decades. Conflicts between defense and domestic needs were not highly politicized, spending levels were stabilized within a narrow range, and high levels of taxation were kept in place. As a result, deficits were sporadic and usually small. This fiscal discipline was accomplished, moreover, without major budget process reforms. Congress experimented with legislative budgets and omnibus appropriations in the late 1940s, but these initiatives were quickly abandoned. Instead, Congress relied heavily on the president for budget policy leadership, particularly in reconciling national security needs with competing budgetary demands. Once Cold War defense budgets were in place, Congress typically deferred to the president on spending totals and fiscal policy. Then, with defense and discretionary domestic programs dominating the spending side of the budget, Congress depended on its powerful Appropriations Committees to make marginal adjustments within spending totals set by the president.

This division of institutional responsibilities between Congress and the executive branch produced stable budget policies, so long as presidents were willing to make politically difficult decisions. President Harry S Truman vetoed postwar tax cuts and then raised taxes and cut domestic spending to pay for the Korean War. President Dwight D. Eisenhower kept high revenue levels in place and enforced ceilings on defense during his tenure. Truman and Eisenhower were both concerned with the negative economic consequences of uncontrolled spending and unbalanced budgets, and they elevated these economic concerns above short-term political considerations.

The commitment to balanced budgets during the Truman and Eisenhower presidencies was not absolute. The need for fiscal policy stabilization of the economy was generally acknowledged, which meant that deficits were acceptable during economic slowdowns. In addition to the automatic stabilization provided by declining income tax revenues and increasing unemployment and transfer payments during recessions, both administrations reluctantly supported additional stimulus in the form of limited tax cuts or spending increases.

The balanced-budget rule for this period was, in effect, a moderate form of Keynesian fiscal policy—budget deficits to promote employment and growth during recessions and budget surpluses to counter high inflation. At the same time, the expectation was that budgets would be balanced under normal conditions, with permanent increases in spending paid for by higher taxes. This balanced-budget approach was greatly facilitated by the high degree of controllability in peacetime spending. Since the budget was largely made up of defense and domestic programs governed by annual appropriations (i.e., discretionary spending), the president and Congress could limit year-to-year increases in spending. Under these conditions, spending controls were reasonably comprehensive and spending totals reasonably predictable.

This budget policy approach began to unravel, however, during the 1960s. The efforts of the Johnson administration to finance the Vietnam War while expanding domestic spending and deferring tax increases destabilized budget policy. The political and financial strains of the Vietnam War weakened presidential leadership on budget policy and also fractured the Cold War strategic consensus on defense. Finally, the wholesale expansion of social welfare entitlements during the Johnson presidency created spending-control problems that intensified during the 1970s.

Financing World War II

The costs of World War II were enormous, with federal expenditures rising from less than $10 billion in 1940 to more than $90 billion in 1945. During the peak spending period from 1943 to 1945, outlays exceeded 40 percent of GDP, and deficits averaged almost 25 percent of GDP (Table 5.1). Publicly-held debt at the end of the war was nearly 110 percent of GDP, almost four times higher than the gross debt after World War I, but the financing of World War II was accomplished with comparatively modest fiscal and economic dislocations. Federal credit remained strong throughout World War II, interest costs were relatively low, and both wartime and postwar inflation, while troublesome, were less severe than in earlier and comparatively less expensive wars.[1]

The Roosevelt administration's budgets for "a nation at war in a world at war" could not keep pace with the explosive growth of defense spending.[2] "Total war expenditures are now running at a rate of 2 billion dollars a month," the 1943 budget reported, "and may surpass 5 billion dollars a month during the fiscal year 1943."[3] One year later, the defense projection was $8 billion per month, with "96 cents of every dollar expended by the Federal Government . . . used to pay war costs and interest on the public debt, and only 4 cents for all the so-called nonwar purposes."[4] The Treasury Department's official goal of financing two-thirds of wartime expenditures through taxation was never achieved, but the tax system was radically and permanently changed.[5] In particular, the individual income tax became a mass tax, with low exemption levels, steeply graduated marginal rates, and extremely high revenue yields. This mass tax system helped to finance World War II and then supported the massive defense budgets that were needed during the Cold War.

Wartime Spending and Taxation

The path to World War II mobilization was far from smooth. Roosevelt's efforts to accelerate military preparedness in the years leading up to the war

1. Henry C. Murphy, *The National Debt in War and Transition* (New York: McGraw-Hill, 1950), 287.
2. *Congressional Record*, 77th Cong., 2d sess., 1942, 88, pt. 1: 36.
3. *Congressional Record*, 77th Cong., 2d sess., 1942, 88, pt. 1: 37.
4. *Congressional Record*, 78th Cong., 1st sess., 1943, 89, pt. 1: 98, 101.
5. See Paul Studenski and Herman E. Kroos, *Financial History of the United States*, 2d ed. (New York: McGraw-Hill, 1953), 438.

Table 5.1 Federal Budget Totals, 1940–1946 (as a percentage of GDP)

Fiscal Year	Total Revenues	Total Outlays	Total Deficit	Total Publicly-Held Debt
1940	6.8%	9.8%	3.0%	44.2%
1941	7.6	12.0	4.3	42.3
1942	10.1	24.4	14.2	47.0
1943	13.3	43.6	30.3	70.9
1944	20.9	43.7	22.8	88.4
1945	20.4	41.9	21.5	106.3
1946	17.6	24.8	7.2	108.6

SOURCE: *Historical Tables, Budget of the United States Government, Fiscal Year 2002* (Washington, D.C.: Government Printing Office, 2001), 23, 116.

were hampered by congressional opposition. For FY 1940, the defense budget was under one-fifth of total spending and only 1.7 percent of GDP.[6] Active-duty force levels, which had dropped to 250,000 by 1935, were still less than 460,000 in 1940.[7] The 1940 Selective Service Act provided only a twelve-month authorization for the draft, and an eighteen-month extension the following year passed the House by a single vote. The initial defense supplementals for fiscal years 1940 and 1941 totaled under $600 million.[8] In spring 1940, with German armies advancing across Europe, the pace of the American buildup intensified. Although Congress and the administration soon found it necessary to cooperate on defense budget increases, there were clashes over the tax program to fund these increases. The Roosevelt administration repeatedly pushed for steeply progressive individual income taxation and strict excess profits taxation, while Congress favored a more broadly based income tax and a narrower application of excess profits rules.

Income Taxation. The first war-related tax measure was enacted on June 25, 1940. While its revenue goals were modest, this legislation established a pattern that later tax bills followed. During the late 1930s, only about 10 percent of the labor force filed tax returns, and approximately half of these returns were nontaxable. The Revenue Act of 1940 broadened the coverage of the income tax by reducing exemption levels and imposing more stringent

6. *Historical Tables, Budget of the United States Government, Fiscal Year 2002* (Washington, D.C.: Government Printing Office, 2001), 44.
7. *Historical Statistics of the United States, Colonial Times to 1970, Part 2,* 1141.
8. Ippolito, *Uncertain Legacies,* 97.

filing requirements. Effective tax rates for most income brackets were raised through a 10 percent surcharge on income, and Congress also approved a separate administration-sponsored bill that instituted an excess profits tax, with graduated rates of up to 50 percent.

The Treasury Department returned to Congress with a much more extensive list of tax increases the following year. Testifying before the House Ways and Means Committee, Secretary of the Treasury Henry Morgenthau pledged to "raise at least two-thirds of the costs of defense from taxes."[9] While members of Congress initially applauded Morgenthau's approach to wartime finance, they became less enthusiastic as revenue requirements began to escalate.[10] Congress did, however, agree to reduce exemption levels for the individual income tax, thereby extending the filing requirements to an additional 5 million people in 1941.[11] Marginal rates for individuals and corporations were also raised, as were excess profits and gift and estate taxes. In 1942, the administration presented Congress with an even larger tax package, including much steeper marginal rates for individuals, but congressional resistance to higher taxes was mounting. The Revenue Act of 1942 ignored the administration's call for heightened progressivity. Instead, Congress adopted a variety of proposals, including reduced exemptions and higher first-bracket rates, which actually shifted tax burdens to lower-income groups. The administration was more successful in persuading Congress to raise rates for corporation income and excess profits taxes and to strengthen enforcement of the tax laws. A good portion of the 1942 act was devoted to technical corrections in what was becoming an enormously complicated and administratively unwieldy tax system.

Roosevelt was dissatisfied with Congress's handiwork in 1942, but his influence over tax policy soon became even more tenuous. To remedy income tax collection problems, the administration introduced a proposal for permanent tax withholding in 1943. The Current Tax Payment Act that Congress approved tied tax withholding to a generous forgiveness of past tax liabilities, a compromise that Roosevelt was forced to accept. Congress then rejected a Treasury plan for a major individual income tax increase, approving instead a much smaller revenue bill that relied chiefly on excise taxes. While the excess profits tax rate was raised to 95 percent, Congress added a

9. See Studenski and Kroos, *Financial History of the United States*, 438.
10. On these problems, see Witte, *The Politics and Development of the Federal Income Tax*, 112–14.
11. Witte, *The Politics and Development of the Federal Income Tax*, 113.

variety of exceptions and deductions that greatly reduced the projected gain in corporate tax revenues. On February 22, 1944, Roosevelt vetoed the bill, and Congress responded by overriding his veto.[12] The impasse over higher taxes continued until the end of the war. Congress did enact, in 1944, changes in tax administration and enforcement, including simplified filing requirements for workers, graduated withholding, and standard deductions.[13] The purpose of this legislation was not to impose higher taxes but to make it easier for the tens of millions of new taxpayers to comply with a rapidly expanding tax code.[14]

Revenue Levels. The differences between World War I and World War II income taxation were substantial. Personal exemptions were lower in World War II and filing requirements more stringent (Table 5.2). Approximately 75 percent of the labor force filed taxable returns by the end of World War II, compared with about 15 percent during World War I.[15] The rates for World War II were also much higher for all income brackets, and the brackets themselves were narrower. Steeply progressive rates therefore applied to a substantial segment of the taxpaying public. A similar pattern distinguished World War II corporation taxation—coverage was broader, particularly with respect to excess profits taxation, and rates were higher.

As a result, revenue levels during World War II were extremely high, climbing above 20 percent of GDP in 1944 and 1945 (Table 5.3). The growth of income taxation, both individual and corporation, accounted for almost all of the change in revenue levels over the course of the war. Excise taxes, which had played a prominent role in financing previous wars, were much less important during World War II. This shift signified a lasting change in taxation. By 1945, there was in place "an enormously powerful new revenue-raising machine . . . a broad-based individual income tax, capable of nearly universal application."[16]

Borrowing and Loans

Despite the unprecedented extension of income taxation during World War II, the Roosevelt administration missed its revenue goals by a wide margin. In 1942 and 1943, revenues were approximately one-third of spending. During

---

12. Witte, *The Politics and Development of the Federal Income Tax,* 121. This was the first revenue bill veto in U.S. history. The vote to override was 299 to 95 in the House and 72 to 14 in the Senate.

13. See Witte, *The Politics and Development of the Federal Income Tax,* 122–23.

14. Witte, *The Politics and Development of the Federal Income Tax,* 122–23.

15. Ippolito, *Uncertain Legacies,* 33.

16. Herbert Stein, *Presidential Economics* (New York: Simon and Schuster, 1984), 68.

Table 5.2 World War II Individual Income Tax Provisions

	Income Year			
	1940	1941	1942–43	1944–45
Personal Exemptions (Married Couple)	$ 2,000	$ 1,500	$ 1,200	$ 1,000
Requirements for Filing (Gross Income, Married Couple)	$ 2,000	$ 1,500	$ 1,200	$ 500[a]
Tax Rates (Taxable Income)				
First Bracket (up to)	$ 4,000	$ 2,000	$ 2,000	$ 2,000
Rate	4.4%[b]	10%[b]	19%[b]	23%
Top Bracket (over)	$5,000,000	$5,000,000	$ 200,000	$ 200,000[c]
Rate	81.1%	81%	88%	94%

[a] For each spouse.
[b] Earned income credit equal to 10 percent of earned net income as a deduction.
[c] Subject to maximum effective rate of 90 percent.

SOURCE: *Historical Statistics of the United States, Colonial Times to 1970, Part 2* (Washington, D.C.: U.S. Bureau of the Census, 1975), 1093, 1095.

the final two years of the war, this percentage increased but never reached 50 percent, much less the administration's original two-thirds target. Substantial borrowing was therefore necessary throughout the war, and Secretary of the Treasury Morgenthau crafted a voluntary borrowing program in 1941 that, with periodic adjustments and revisions, proved remarkably successful.

The Treasury Department had inaugurated a savings bond program in 1935 that provided a way for the public to help finance the New Deal's employment and social welfare programs. Encouraging even broader public participation in the wartime financing effort, Morgenthau argued, would help to curb price inflation, by drawing off excess purchasing power, while raising the large sums likely to be necessary to support the military.[17] Morgenthau was also convinced that savings bond campaigns were a "powerful propaganda instrument" that would help unify the nation during a critical period.[18]

Opposition to Morgenthau's plan came chiefly from proponents of "compulsory lending" or "forced borrowing."[19] This approach, developed by

17. Murphy, *The National Debt in War and Transition*, 37; also Studenski and Kroos, *Financial History of the United States*, 440.
18. Murphy, *The National Debt in War and Transition*, 37.
19. See Jarvis M. Morse, *Paying for a World War: The United States Funding of World War II* (Washington, D.C.: U.S. Savings Bonds Division, Department of the Treasury, 1971), 93.

Table 5.3 Composition of Federal Revenues, 1940–1945 (as a percentage of GDP)

Fiscal Year	Individual Income Taxes	Corporation Income Taxes	Social Insurance	Excise Taxes	Other	Total
1940	0.9%	1.2%	1.8%	2.0%	0.7%	6.8%
1941	1.2	1.9	1.7	2.2	0.7	7.6
1942	2.3	3.3	1.7	2.4	0.6	10.1
1943	3.6	5.3	1.7	2.3	0.4	13.3
1944	9.4	7.1	1.7	2.3	0.5	20.9
1945	8.3	7.2	1.6	2.8	0.5	20.4

SOURCE: *Historical Tables, Budget of the United States Government, Fiscal Year 2002* (Washington, D.C.: Government Printing Office, 2001), 33.

John Maynard Keynes, relied on heavy taxation of all income groups, with a portion of the taxes paid by lower- and middle-income earners treated as interest-bearing loans, to be repaid after the war. Forced borrowing, it was claimed, would be more effective than voluntary borrowing in controlling inflation and in supporting the scale of borrowing the war was likely to require. Forced borrowing would also achieve income redistribution by increasing the effective progressivity of income taxation.

Early in 1941, Roosevelt approved a new Series E "Defense Savings Bond," to be sold in several denominations from $25 to $1,000, with a fixed redemption schedule of ten years. Additional series, with different interest rates, maturities, and payment schedules, were soon introduced, along with "Defense Stamps," small denomination purchases from post offices that could be combined and exchanged for bonds.[20] The following April, the Treasury Department introduced a system for purchasing savings bonds through payroll deduction. The variety of securities issues available to the public and to investors, the payroll deduction option, and the promotional efforts of the Treasury Department broadened public support for Morgenthau's voluntary borrowing plan, which quickly demonstrated its enormous capacity for financing the war.

The first of the wartime loan campaigns was launched in November 1942, with an announced goal of $9 billion. In less than one month, this campaign raised nearly $13 billion. Although there was some disappointment with the level of sales to individuals in this initial campaign, subsequent

20. See *A History of the United States Savings Bond Program* (Washington, D.C.: U.S. Savings Bonds Division, Department of the Treasury, 1984), 8.

loan drives were able to raise public participation. Publicity efforts became more elaborate as the war progressed, with the War Advertising Council's radio spots and movie theater advertisements, school campaigns, and city-wide drives. Within the Treasury, separate organizations were established to promote sales to different types of individual investors.

The seven war loan drives and the Victory campaign at the end of the war raised more than $150 billion.[21] Each campaign was oversubscribed, and individual sales targets were usually exceeded. What Morgenthau had hoped to accomplish—reliable borrowing of large sums at reasonable cost from diverse investors—was largely achieved. Voluntary borrowing proved less effective at controlling inflationary pressures than had been hoped, but the Treasury's anti-inflation program had been compromised by Congress's unwillingness to raise income taxes after 1943. The FY 1945 budget, for example, described the administration's tax program as "a minimum," and Roosevelt complained that "the failure thus far to enact an adequate fiscal program has aggravated the difficulties of maintaining economic stabilization."[22] Congress, however, remained unyielding.

Anti-inflation efforts were also compromised by the Treasury's domination of the Federal Reserve. While the Federal Reserve's independence from political control had ostensibly been affirmed in the Banking Act of 1935, President Roosevelt had expected and received cooperation from the Federal Reserve in financing New Deal deficits at low cost. When World War II began, this cooperation became more explicit. The Federal Reserve agreed to support Treasury borrowing at specified low interest rates (the "peg") whenever necessary and in any amount.[23] While this agreement kept borrowing costs low, it greatly impaired the Federal Reserve's control of the money supply and, hence, of monetary policy. The Treasury Department continued to pressure the Federal Reserve after the war was over, again to keep the costs of refinancing wartime debt as low as possible. When the Korean War broke out, the Truman administration increased this pressure. This time, however, the Federal Reserve challenged the president and, after an unusually acrimonious and open conflict, an "accord" was reached that established the Federal Reserve's independence from the Treasury and from other political constituencies as well.[24]

21. Murphy, *The National Debt in War and Transition*, 135–55.
22. *Congressional Record*, 78th Cong., 2d sess., 1944, 90, pt. 1: 145.
23. See Kettl, *Leadership at the Fed*, 59–66.
24. Kettl, *Leadership at the Fed*, 75–81.

The Fall and Rise of Defense

After both the Civil War and World War I, spending retrenchments had been rigorously enforced, so that substantial tax cuts and debt reduction could be achieved simultaneously. In addition, budget process reforms had been enacted, primarily to strengthen the spending controls on which this fiscal strategy depended. After World War II, there was considerable support in Congress for following these earlier precedents, but there was neither the unified control of government nor the underlying political consensus about the role of the federal government that had made previous retrenchments possible. Instead, President Truman and Congress fought often and bitterly over postwar tax policy. In his budget message to Congress on January 21, 1946, Truman concluded, "The responsibilities of the Government . . . have increased greatly in the past decade. . . . We cannot shrink the Government to prewar dimensions unless we slough off these new responsibilities—and we cannot do that without paying an excessive price in terms of our national welfare."[25] The fiscal realities of the Cold War soon introduced a new dimension to the debates over federal budget policy, and, with the Korean War, defense budgets began climbing to levels that made a return to "small government" impossible.

Revenue Policy

The period between the end of World War II and the outbreak of war in Korea left undisturbed the mass tax system that had been built during the early 1940s. Total receipts as a percentage of GDP dropped from 20.4 percent in 1945 to 14.4 percent in 1950, but the latter was still more than double prewar levels. In addition, most of the decline in revenue levels resulted from terminating excess profits taxation. Individual income taxes remained at relatively high levels—nearly 6 percent of GDP in 1950 compared with less than 1 percent ten years earlier.

Opposition to major tax cuts was signaled early in the Truman presidency. Just after World War II ended, the Truman administration and Congress agreed to a repeal of the excess profits tax and to a very slight reduction in marginal tax rates—from 23 to 19 percent for the lowest taxable income bracket and from 94 to 86.45 percent for the highest. Personal exemption levels remained unchanged as did income brackets. Still, several months

---

25. *Congressional Record*, 79th Cong., 2d sess., 1946, 92, pt. 1: 155.

later Truman complained that the approximately $6 billion in cuts under the Revenue Act of 1945 were "substantially in excess of the reductions proposed by the Secretary of the Treasury to congressional tax committees."[26] In fact, congressional add-ons to the Treasury proposal had been minor, but Truman declared that he would make "no recommendation for tax reduction" in 1946 and that any future reductions would "depend on the budgetary situation and the economic situation."[27] The official rationale for Truman's stance was that "inflationary pressures still appear dangerously powerful and ill-advised tax reductions would operate to strengthen them still further."[28] But tax cuts would also have made it difficult to resurrect the New Deal domestic agenda that had been interrupted by World War II.

The Republican party gained control of Congress in the 1946 midterm elections, picking up fifty-five House seats and twelve Senate seats. Taxes had been an important campaign issue for Republicans, and they used their sweeping victory to press for large, across-the-board reductions in income taxes. Republican leaders in Congress revived the post–World War I theories of Andrew Mellon, arguing that tax cuts were necessary to sustain economic growth. Republicans were also eager, however, to reduce the budgetary margin available for domestic programs. Harold Knutson, chairman of the House Ways and Means Committee, encouraged his colleagues to "cut off much of the government's income by reducing taxes and compelling the government to retrench."[29] Knutson's committee reported out a bill with graduated reductions in tax rates, ranging from 30 percent for low-income taxpayers to 10 percent for the top marginal bracket. The House approved the Ways and Means proposal, and the Senate made only minor changes in the reduction schedule. Bowing to Democratic complaints that such a large tax cut would fuel inflationary pressures and swell the deficit, the Senate agreed to postpone the effective date of tax relief for six months, to July 1, 1947. The Senate rejected, however, Democratic attempts to grant relief primarily through higher exemption allowances. After a brief conference, the House and Senate sent the 1947 tax-cut legislation to the president on June 3.

Truman vetoed the measure, attacking it as inflationary and inequitable.[30] After the House narrowly sustained Truman's veto, Republicans proposed a

26. *Congressional Record*, 79th Cong., 2d sess., 1946, 92, pt. 1: 149.
27. *Congressional Record*, 79th Cong., 2d sess., 1946, 92, pt. 1: 149.
28. *Congressional Record*, 79th Cong., 2d sess., 1946, 92, pt. 1: 150.
29. Quoted in Witte, *The Politics and Development of the Federal Income Tax*, 132.
30. Witte, *The Politics and Development of the Federal Income Tax*, 134.

virtually identical tax-cut measure, this time with an effective date of January 1, 1948. Congress easily approved this measure, and, after Truman's veto, the House voted to override. Following intense lobbying on the president's behalf, the Senate supported his veto, albeit by a narrow two-vote margin.

Republicans resurrected their tax initiative when Congress reconvened in 1948. Their case was strengthened by the large surplus that had been recorded in FY 1947 and by the even larger one projected for FY 1948. Truman sought to blunt the election-year tax-cutting drive, proposing a $40 individual tax credit, "particularly helpful to those in the low-income group," to be paid for by a $3.2 billion increase in corporation taxes.[31] Republicans responded with a broad tax-cut package that attracted strong support from congressional Democrats. Marginal rate reductions were combined with a variety of targeted reductions—increased exemption allowances (from $500 to $600) to benefit low-income taxpayers, extra exemption allowances to aid the elderly and the blind, and income-splitting options for joint returns to help married couples. When Congress sent Truman this bill, he cast another veto, but this one was overridden.

These battles between the Republican-controlled Congress and President Truman reflected the growing importance of income taxation in economic and budget policy debates. Tax policy was, as always, a crucial factor in balancing the budget, but it had become an important instrument for promoting growth and for controlling prices. And with World War II having imposed significant tax burdens on all income classes, despite steeply progressive marginal rates, any proposed change in taxation raised questions about equity. After the war, for example, 93.8 percent of all income tax returns and 44.4 percent of income tax revenues were from taxpayers with adjusted gross incomes under $5,000.[32] Less than 2 percent of returns, but more than 40 percent of revenues, came from adjusted gross incomes of more than $10,000. Thus, proposed changes in exemption levels or in marginal rates were argued in terms of distributional impact as well as revenue effects. The liberal-conservative split on tax equity was especially difficult to resolve, since both sides also believed that tax policy would ultimately shape domestic program decisions.

This last consideration was evident in 1949, when Truman proposed a $4 billion increase in corporation and individual income taxes, along with

---

31. *Congress and the Nation, 1945–1964* (Washington, D.C.: Congressional Quarterly, 1965), 399.

32. *Congress and the Nation, 1945–1964,* 398.

higher estate and gift taxes. Although Congress had returned to Democratic control with Truman's surprising reelection in 1948, there was strong congressional opposition to the president's proposal. The economy had entered a recession, so there were fiscal policy objections to higher taxes, but Truman's budget also made provision "for inaugurating essential economic and social programs which should no longer be delayed," including aid to education, federal housing programs, expanded Social Security coverage, and a "comprehensive national health program . . . centering in a national system of medical-care insurance."[33] While conservatives in both parties were prepared to follow Truman's lead in boosting defense budgets, his domestic policy initiatives were another matter entirely. Truman's bid to reverse the 1948 tax reduction was dropped, after which Congress agreed to pass some technical corrections that the Treasury Department had requested. In his January 1950 budget message, Truman bowed to congressional pressure, requesting only minor "adjustments" in tax levels, despite a projected deficit of more than $5 billion.[34]

The interwar period was, in effect, a standoff on tax policy. Truman succeeded in maintaining relatively high revenue levels against conservative pressures to shrink the federal government's tax base. Within that base, he was able for a time to transfer resources from defense to domestic programs, but when the defense buildup commenced in 1949, Truman could not expand the base to accommodate new domestic program initiatives.

Once the Korean War began, the Truman administration moved aggressively to raise taxes. In August 1950, the Treasury Department proposed increases in individual and corporation income tax rates, and Congress quickly approved these proposals. In a special session called after the November midterm elections, Congress also agreed to reinstate the excess profits tax. The estimated revenue gain from these measures was $8.8 billion.[35] As wartime spending rapidly escalated, Truman insisted that additional taxes be imposed. The administration was committed to financing the war without deficits, particularly since higher taxes would help to curb inflationary pressures. The Revenue Act of 1951 did not raise taxes to the levels Truman called for, nor did it follow the administration's recommendations for structural tax reforms. The legislation did include, however, significant increases in individual and corporation tax rates, an expansion of the excess profits tax

33. *Congressional Record*, 81st Cong., 1st sess., 1949, 95, pt. 1: 134, 142.
34. *Congressional Record*, 81st Cong., 2d sess., 1950, 96, pt. 1: 207.
35. *Congress and the Nation, 1945–1964*, 397.

base, and higher excise taxes. The net gain for the 1951 tax bill was estimated at $5.7 billion.[36]

These tax increases raised revenue levels from 14.4 percent of GDP in 1950 to 19 percent two years later. While wartime deficits still occurred, revenue levels that were only marginally lower than those during World War II kept Korean War budgets close to net balance.[37] Truman's position on tax policy and balanced budgets remained consistent, even as spending policy shifted to defense.

Reversing Spending Policy

The demobilization that followed World War II was extremely swift—defense spending dropped from more than $80 billion in FY 1945 to under $10 billion three years later, and active-duty forces were cut by more than 10 million. The defense-GDP share of 3.6 percent in 1948 would stand for nearly forty years as the nadir of the modern era. This defense cutback allowed the Truman administration to bring the budget into balance, while transferring a portion of the "savings" to domestic programs. Between 1940 and 1945, total nondefense spending—excluding net interest payments—fell. Over the next three years, spending for nondefense programs rose sharply (Table 5.4). The nondefense-GDP share, which had fallen by more than 50 percent during the war, had returned to its prewar level by 1949. A substantial portion of this growth was accounted for by education, health, and other benefit programs for veterans. In FY 1948, outlays for these programs accounted for one-fifth of total federal spending—roughly double the share for all other social welfare programs.

In early 1947, the United States adopted a containment strategy for dealing with the Soviet Union. The Truman Doctrine, set forth in an address to Congress on March 12, 1947, pledged the United States to provide economic and military aid to nations threatened by Communist aggression. Two months later, Congress approved the first installment of aid, a $400 million authorization for Greece and Turkey. On June 5, Secretary of State George C. Marshall presented the administration's plan for rebuilding Europe. The European Recovery Program, or Marshall Plan, envisioned U.S. financing for a comprehensive plan to rebuild European economies. On April 3, 1948, President Truman signed into law the Marshall Plan authorization.

---

36. *Congress and the Nation, 1945–1964*, 397.
37. The net deficits for 1950–54 averaged approximately 0.3 percent of GDP annually.

Table 5.4 Composition of Federal Outlays, 1940–1950 (as a percentage of GDP)

Fiscal Year	Defense	Nondefense	Net Interest	Total
1940	1.7%	7.2%	0.9%	9.8%
1941	5.6	5.5	0.8	12.0
1942	17.8	5.9	0.7	24.4
1943	37.0	5.8	0.8	43.6
1944	37.9	4.7	1.1	43.7
1945	37.5	3.0	1.4	41.9
1946	19.2	3.8	1.8	24.8
1947	5.5	7.4	1.8	14.7
1948	3.6	6.4	1.7	11.6
1949	4.8	7.7	1.7	14.3
1950	5.0	8.7	1.8	15.6

SOURCE: *Historical Tables, Budget of the United States Government, Fiscal Year 2002* (Washington, D.C.: Government Printing Office, 2001), 44–45.

With these and related initiatives, military and economic aid outlays increased rapidly—from under $2 billion in 1946 to nearly $6 billion in 1947. The military requirements and implications of containment policy, however, did not emerge for quite some time. Both the Truman administration and Congress hoped that comparatively low military budgets, bolstered by strategic air power and a monopoly of atomic weapons, would suffice. Truman was determined to stabilize military spending, imposing a ceiling of one-third of total expenditures on the defense budget share.[38] Congress, which repeatedly became entangled in interservice quarrels over funding, had no enthusiasm for resolving these disputes through larger defense budgets. Truman's FY 1948 budget submission, for example, was well below the weapons procurement requests of the services. The Air Force's seventy-group plan was reduced to fifty-eight, the Navy's bid for new aircraft carrier forces was rejected, and much of the Army's plan for new equipment and weapons was disallowed. The House Appropriations Committee then proceeded to cut the Navy's budget estimate by 10 percent and the Army-Air Force estimate by a slightly smaller amount. Under pressure from the Senate, much of this funding was restored, but final appropriations were still below the administration's proposals.

With the Berlin blockade and other Soviet challenges in early 1948, a slow reversal of this defense decline began. The president's initial budget

38. *Congress and the Nation, 1945–1964*, 237.

request of $11 billion was followed by a supplemental appropriation of $3.5 billion. This time, Congress was much more sympathetic to the services' pleas for even greater help, but Truman threatened to impound congressional add-ons to his budget.[39] When the services submitted requests totaling $30 billion for FY 1950, Truman announced that a $15 billion ceiling would be enforced and ordered cutbacks in projected force levels to maintain that ceiling.

According to Truman, his administration's objective was a "position of relative military readiness" that could be continued for "the foreseeable future at approximately the level recommended in this [FY 1950] budget."[40] Despite the 1949 Communist takeover in China and the Soviet Union's successful atomic bomb test that same year, Truman's defense program continued to emphasize "a balanced structure which can be maintained over a period of years without an undue use of national resources."[41] Indeed, the administration's fiscal 1951 defense request was $1.2 billion below the previous year's figure.

While congressional leaders repeatedly criticized Truman over Air Force funding, they did not dispute the need to limit defense budgets. According to the Joint Chiefs of Staff, "semireadiness" required $30 billion in annual defense expenditures, while complete readiness would cost as much as $60 billion.[42] The chairman of the House Appropriations Subcommittee on Defense, George Mahon, explained to his colleagues that the FY 1950 appropriations for defense were less than one-half the semireadiness estimate. However, he contended that "nothing would please a potential enemy better than to have us bankrupt our country and destroy our economy by maintaining over a period of years complete readiness."[43] On the Senate side, Mahon's view was echoed in an Appropriations Committee report that warned against "enervating overpreparation for defense against . . . a cunning and patient enemy who fully realizes the debilitating influences of a war-geared economy over a long period of time."[44] The Senate then approved a $1.1 billion cut in the House-passed bill. After the House finally succeeded in restoring its level of Air Force funding, Truman announced he would refuse to spend the "increased authorization" Congress had passed.[45]

39. *Congress and the Nation, 1945–1964*, 251.
40. *Congressional Record*, 81st Cong., 1st sess., 1949, 95, pt. 1: 138.
41. *Congressional Record*, 81st Cong., 2d sess., 1950, 96, pt. 1: 214.
42. Ippolito, *Uncertain Legacies*, 100.
43. *Congressional Record*, 81st Cong., 1st sess., 1949, 95, pt. 4: 4428.
44. *Congress and the Nation, 1945–1964*, 254.
45. *Congress and the Nation, 1945–1964*, 254.

It was becoming increasingly difficult for both Truman and Congress, however, to ignore the mounting criticisms of allegedly "adequate" defense budgets and the lack of clear direction in national military strategy. On January 31, 1950, Truman responded to the "probable fission bomb capability and possible thermonuclear bomb capability of the Soviet Union" by directing the Atomic Energy Commission "to continue its work on all forms of atomic weapons, including the so-called hydrogen or super-bomb."[46] Truman also ordered a complete review of U.S. national security policy and defense capabilities.[47] The report that followed this review, "NSC-68," pointed out critical weaknesses in U.S. conventional and strategic forces and recommended a massive rearmament effort. The costs of the U.S. defense program set forth in NSC-68 were, according to later calculations, more than three times the FY 1951 budget submitted by President Truman.[48]

On June 25, 1950, less than three months after Truman received the NSC-68 policy review, North Korea invaded South Korea. On June 27, President Truman ordered U.S. naval and air forces to assist South Korea, and the United States became embroiled in a conflict that lasted more than three years and resulted in almost 150,000 American casualties. The increase in defense spending during the Korean conflict was rapid, with supplementals enacted during FY 1951 nearly doubling the size of the defense budget to $23.6 billion. By FY 1953, defense outlays had climbed to well above $50 billion and accounted for 70 percent of total federal spending.[49] In constant dollars, the FY 1953 defense budget was more than one-half the peak level during World War II.[50]

The direct costs of the Korean War, however, were well below these levels. The defense buildup that began in 1950 was also a response to the wide-ranging military deficiencies described in NSC-68. U.S. conventional and strategic forces had to be expanded and modernized. Department of Defense procurement outlays, which had dropped to $1.5 billion in 1950, were increased to $17 billion in 1953, and military construction and atomic energy spending was raised by nearly $3 billion. The hydrogen bomb program was

46. *Congress and the Nation, 1945–1964*, 262.
47. Letter of the President to the Secretary of State, January 31, 1950. *Foreign Relations of the United States, 1950* (Washington, D.C.: Government Printing Office, 1977), 1:141–42.
48. Iwan W. Morgan, *Eisenhower Versus "The Spenders": The Eisenhower Administration, the Democrats, and the Budget, 1953–1960* (New York: St. Martin's Press, 1990), 27. According to Morgan, this was estimated at $50 billion.
49. *Historical Tables, Budget of the United States Government, Fiscal Year 2002*, 110.
50. *Historical Tables, Budget of the United States Government, Fiscal Year 2002*, 109.

accelerated, as were numerous other weapons research and development programs. In September 1950, Truman announced the decision to send additional U.S. ground forces to Europe as part of a major buildup in North Atlantic Treaty Organization (NATO) forces. On February 15, 1951, Secretary of Defense Marshall briefed Congress on plans for a forty-division NATO force, with six U.S. divisions, but cautioned that even more American troops might be needed in the case of an emergency.[51]

There was criticism of the president's aggressive Cold War strategy, especially among Senate Republicans. But Truman's position prevailed in the Senate's "Great Debate" in early 1951, and Congress approved a series of funding increases to support a broad-based expansion of strategic and conventional forces. In the budget he sent to Congress on January 21, 1952, Truman noted that "the unprovoked attack upon the Republic of Korea [eighteen months earlier] made it clear that the Kremlin would not hesitate to resort to war in order to gain its ends."[52] While there had been "significant progress in rebuilding our defenses," Truman warned that "peak production rates for all of our major military items" would not be reached until the end of the FY 1953 budget cycle.[53] It then might be possible "to reduce budget expenditures," but only on the condition that "new international tensions do not develop, and if no further aggressions are attempted."[54] On January 9, 1953, shortly before leaving office, Truman reported that defense spending would continue to rise for at least another year before declining to the "35 to 40 billion dollars annually" required "to keep our Armed Forces in a state of readiness."[55]

The Cold War defense program the Truman administration inaugurated was far removed from the priorities that had guided spending policy through the late 1940s. Between 1950 and 1953, the defense-GDP ratio nearly tripled—to more than 14 percent—and the defense budget share rose to more than twice the ceiling Truman had hoped to impose. Moreover, Truman was forced to sacrifice much of his domestic agenda when he reversed his defense program. Total nondefense outlays dropped by more than $5.5 billion from 1950 to 1953, with a reduction in real dollar spending of more than 30 percent.[56]

51. *Congress and the Nation, 1945–1964*, 265.
52. *Congressional Record*, 82d Cong., 2d sess., 1952, 98, pt. 1: 331.
53. *Congressional Record*, 82d Cong., 2d sess., 1952, 98, pt. 1: 331.
54. *Congressional Record*, 82d Cong., 2d sess., 1952, 98, pt. 1: 331.
55. *Congressional Record*, 83d Cong., 1st sess., 1953, 99, pt. 1: 298.
56. *Historical Tables, Budget of the United States Government, Fiscal Year 2002*, 110.

Executive and Congressional Budget Processes

Truman had established, in effect, a framework for presidential defense budgeting that lasted until Vietnam. The United States would maintain a large, permanent military establishment with global war capabilities. The defense spending levels to support these capabilities would represent the central priority in federal budget policy, with the president responsible for balancing this priority against other long-term considerations—fiscal policy objectives, nondefense spending needs, and economic capacity.

The emergence of "top-down" defense budgeting in the executive branch effectively ended a brief experiment in legislative budget process reform. The Legislative Reorganization Act of 1946 included provisions for a Joint Committee on the Legislative Budget, consisting of members of the House and Senate Appropriations, Ways and Means, and Finance Committees. This committee was to report out annual concurrent resolutions, with spending and revenue totals, which would allow Congress to establish its own fiscal policy. The Committee on the Reorganization of Congress, which sponsored the legislative budget, was intent on reducing presidential influence over budget policy. Its 1946 report concluded: "The executive has mingled appropriations, brought forward and backward unexpended and anticipated balances, incurred coercive deficiencies, and otherwise escaped the rigors of congressional control."[57]

The legislative budget remedy, however, never worked as intended. The House and Senate could not agree on a fiscal plan in 1947. The legislative budget in 1948 contained a $2.5 billion cut in the president's budget, but Congress promptly violated its own spending ceiling by $6 billion.[58] Congress then extended the deadline for adopting the next year's legislative budget but failed to adopt a final version. With the onset of the Korean War, the legislative budget concept was abandoned.

Equally unsuccessful was the attempt by Clarence Cannon, chairman of the House Appropriations Committee, to combine all annual spending in an omnibus appropriations bill.[59] In 1949, Cannon reorganized the membership and staff of the Appropriations Committee so that subcommittees could work simultaneously on their separate bills, and, in 1950, he set reporting deadlines for the subcommittees. Cannon then supervised the drafting of an

57. *Congressional Record*, 79th Cong., 2d sess., 1946, 92, pt. 8: 10047.
58. See Ippolito, *Congressional Spending*, 48.
59. Ippolito, *Congressional Spending*, 49–50.

omnibus bill that was reported to the House and approved on May 10. The
Senate Appropriations Committee had agreed to coordinate its hearings with
the House and to follow a similar format, but final action on the omnibus bill
was not completed until nearly two months after the fiscal year began. In
addition, the controversial spending cuts that Congress initially approved
were overwhelmed by a series of deficiency and supplemental appropriations. In 1951, the chairmen of the House Appropriations subcommittees
forced Cannon to abandon the omnibus approach, and subsequent attempts
to revive it were not successful.

The failure of these budget reforms, however, posed no real problem for
effective budget control. Truman was strongly committed to curbing inflationary pressures, as his tax-cut vetoes and Korean War tax increases demonstrated. With defense budgets dominating spending policy, and with no real
congressional pressure to expand domestic funding, the only spending ceilings that really mattered were the annual defense funding bills. The strategic
consensus that Truman shaped in the early 1950s precluded massive defense
cuts, and that same consensus accorded the president considerable deference
in bringing national security needs within acceptable spending limits.

The Eisenhower Program

Gen. Dwight D. Eisenhower resigned as NATO Supreme Commander on
April 2, 1952, captured the Republican party's presidential nomination in
July, and pledged during his campaign to bring the Korean War to an end
and to pursue "security with solvency" thereafter.[60] The Korean Armistice
was signed on July 27, 1953, and by the end of the year the United States had
begun to withdraw its forces from Korea. During his first months in office,
President Eisenhower outlined a post-Korea defense program predicated on
fiscal sustainability—"one which we can bear for a long—and indefinite—
period of time."[61] Eisenhower directed the Department of Defense to cut
Truman's FY 1954 budget estimates by approximately 10 percent and, on
May 7, 1953, submitted a revised budget to Congress. Then, in a national
radio address on May 19, Eisenhower explained that future defense planning
would emphasize "cost, order, and efficiency."[62] There was, he declared, "no

---

60. *Congress and the Nation, 1945–1964*, 270.
61. *Congress and the Nation, 1945–1964*, 275.
62. *Congress and the Nation, 1945–1964*, 275.

given number of ships, no given number of divisions, no given number of air wings . . . , no given number of billions of dollars, that will automatically guarantee security."[63] For the remainder of his presidency, Eisenhower insisted on defense budget ceilings that would stabilize spending levels and keep budgets balanced.

The Korea Transition

The financing of the Korean War was unusual. First, heavy taxation during the war meant there was no appreciable change in debt levels and interest obligations. Indeed, the economic burden of the debt actually declined during the early 1950s. Publicly-held debt was under 60 percent of GDP in 1955 compared with 80 percent five years earlier. Net interest obligations were, in current dollars, virtually unchanged during and immediately after the war.

Second, the decline in spending after Korea was negligible, because Cold War defense budgets remained high. After World War II, federal spending had dropped by nearly $40 billion in one year and by an additional $25 billion over the next two years. After Korea, the trend was different. Total spending fell by about 10 percent between 1953 and 1955. By 1957, total spending had climbed above the 1953 wartime peak, and the defense share of the budget was still approximately 60 percent.

For the Eisenhower administration, which was committed to balanced budgets, these postwar spending requirements precluded major tax cuts. The "peacetime" Eisenhower presidency, as a result, was characterized by high revenue levels, by gradual and modest tradeoffs between defense and domestic programs, and by conservative fiscal policies. Despite having to deal with a Democratic-controlled Congress for all but the first two years of his tenure, Eisenhower maintained unusually firm control over budget policy.

Revenue Policy

The first tax bill of the Eisenhower era was not what Eisenhower's fellow Republicans had expected, and their disappointment would persist for a long time. Individual income tax increases from the war were scheduled to terminate on December 31, 1953, and Republican members of the House Ways and Means Committee proposed to move this schedule forward by six months. Eisenhower's Treasury Department not only argued against early

63. *Congress and the Nation, 1945-1964*, 275.

repeal but also asked Congress to extend the wartime excess profits tax, which was scheduled for automatic termination. With support from Democrats, this extension finally passed a sharply divided House and was ratified by the Senate.[64]

Eisenhower's Secretary of the Treasury, George Humphrey, tried to mollify congressional Republicans by promising tax cuts once the administration's program to reduce spending was implemented. Spending levels, however, never dropped sufficiently to allow large-scale tax cuts. Competing theories of income taxation—economic efficiency and growth versus progressivity and equity—were largely ignored during the 1950s. Instead, the Eisenhower administration focused on the revenue levels needed to fund post-Korea budgets. Since these budgets remained high, tax policy adjustments were constrained as well.

In 1954, for example, the president's budget message declared, "Our whole system of taxation needs revision and overhauling. . . . [It] should be completely revised."[65] Drawing on a year-long study conducted by the Treasury Department in collaboration with congressional leaders and staff, Eisenhower endorsed more than two dozen major proposals for making "the income tax system fairer to individuals and less burdensome on production and continued economic growth."[66] The overall tax reduction from these proposals, however, was under $1.5 billion.[67] Eisenhower made clear that only "further reductions in Government expenditures will make possible additional reductions in the deficit and tax rates."[68] Moreover, he recommended that scheduled reductions in wartime corporation income tax rates and excise taxes be postponed to offset any revenue losses that might result from revising the tax code.

The Internal Revenue Code of 1954, which incorporated most of the changes the Treasury Department had proposed, included substantive as well as administrative reforms. A variety of structural modifications in both individual and organization income taxation were enacted, including new exclusions and deductions, that spread tax reductions widely but thinly. However, the legislation did not change exemption levels nor did it appre-

---

64. On these early clashes between Eisenhower and congressional Republicans, see Morgan, *Eisenhower Versus "The Spenders,"* 56–60.

65. *Congressional Record,* 83d Cong., 2d sess., 1954, 100, pt. 1: 569.

66. *Congressional Record,* 83d Cong., 2d sess., 1954, 100, pt. 1: 572.

67. See Morgan, *Eisenhower Versus "The Spenders,"* 58.

68. *Congressional Record,* 83d Cong., 2d sess., 1954, 100, pt. 1: 572.

ciably affect marginal rates. The 1951 revenue act had raised the marginal rates for all income brackets and had scheduled partial reductions in rates beginning in 1954. The 1954 tax bill left in place these changes and maintained the relatively low personal exemptions that had been in effect since the early 1940s.[69] House Democrats attempted to inject equity arguments into the debate over the 1954 tax bill, calling for higher personal exemptions, but they were unsuccessful; Eisenhower was unwilling to accept any tax revisions that involved a substantial revenue loss.[70]

Most of the tax reductions that occurred during Eisenhower's first two years in office resulted from automatic expirations of wartime taxes rather than from policy changes. In 1954, the administration agreed, with great reluctance, to excise tax reductions that had passed Congress with strong bipartisan support, but Eisenhower continued to reject major tax cuts even as a recession took hold early in the year. In a concession to countercyclical fiscal theory, the administration accelerated spending on existing programs and endorsed liberalization of monetary and credit policy, but it rejected permanent tax cuts and new spending commitments.

In January 1955, with the recession over and Democrats in control of Congress, Eisenhower's budget message stated that taxes remained too high and were "a serious obstacle to the long-term dynamic growth of the economy which is so necessary for the future."[71] The president proposed a tax cut "to relieve individual tax burdens and to increase incentives for effort and investment," but he wanted to wait for at least another year for the "savings in expenditures and economic growth that [would] make such reductions possible."[72] When the Democratic leadership called for an immediate cut in individual income taxes, Eisenhower denounced the proposal. In May, he announced to his cabinet that no tax cut would be considered until the budget was in surplus.[73]

Contrary to expectations, the 1956 budget registered a substantial surplus, and Eisenhower's FY 1957 budget projected another surplus, but tax cuts remained off the agenda. In fact, Eisenhower raised his standard for a "justifiable" tax cut; he insisted that future tax cuts be integrated into "a

69. See Ippolito, *Uncertain Legacies*, 103–4.

70. The estimated revenue loss for the higher exemption level was $2.5 billion. See Morgan, *Eisenhower Versus "The Spenders,"* 67–68.

71. *Congressional Record*, 84th Cong., 1st sess., 1955, 101, pt. 1: 389.

72. *Congressional Record*, 84th Cong., 1st sess., 1955, 101, pt. 1: 389.

73. Morgan, *Eisenhower Versus "The Spenders,"* 71.

budget which makes provisions for some reductions, even though modest, in our national debt."[74] For an election year, this aversion to tax cuts was certainly unusual, and Eisenhower became even more averse during his second term. Countercyclical tax cuts were rejected by the administration during the 1957–58 recession, a position that probably contributed to heavy Republican losses in the 1958 midterm elections.

During the final years of his presidency, Eisenhower eschewed major tax initiatives. Minor cuts were made in corporate and excise tax rates, but Social Security taxes were raised in 1959 (and additional increases in the Social Security tax rate scheduled through 1969), and gasoline taxes were increased to bring the Highway Trust Fund into balance. In his fiscal 1961 budget message, Eisenhower forecast a $4.3 billion surplus but called for debt reduction, not tax cuts. He proposed to leave to the next administration and Congress "the choice they should rightly have in deciding between reductions in the public debt and lightening of the tax burden, or both."[75]

Fiscal discipline during the Eisenhower presidency was extremely strong. Despite his personal belief that high taxes were unfair and economically burdensome, Eisenhower was unwilling to accept the scale or types of tax cuts embraced by most of his fellow Republicans. As a result, peacetime revenue levels were much higher under Eisenhower than they had been under Truman and nearly double those during the New Deal. The composition of revenues, moreover, remained heavily weighted toward the types of taxes that the Republican party had opposed most strenuously. From 1955 to 1961, individual income taxes and corporation income taxes produced approximately 70 percent of total revenues, only slightly lower than wartime levels. The GDP share of the individual income tax during this period averaged more than 7.5 percent annually, close to average levels for World War II and the Korean War (Table 5.5). For corporation income taxes, the GDP decline from wartime levels was greater, but it was the automatic expiration of wartime excess profits taxes that produced this drop-off. For both individuals and corporations, tax rates remained high, and the tax base remained broad. Adjusted gross income, for example, was 79.2 percent of personal income in 1950 and 78.9 percent ten years later.[76]

---

74. *Congressional Record*, 84th Cong., 2d sess., 1956, 102, pt. 1: 565.

75. *Budget of the United States Government, Fiscal Year 1961* (Washington, D.C.: Government Printing Office, 1960), M8.

76. Ippolito, *Uncertain Legacies*, 39.

Table 5.5 Composition of Federal Revenues, 1955–1961 (as a percentage of GDP)

Fiscal Year	Individual Income Taxes	Corporation Income Taxes	Social Insurance	Excise Taxes	Other	Total
1955	7.3%	4.5%	2.0%	2.3%	0.5%	16.6%
1956	7.5	4.9	2.2	2.3	0.5	17.4
1957	7.9	4.7	2.2	2.3	0.6	17.7
1958	7.5	4.4	2.4	2.3	0.6	17.3
1959	7.5	3.5	2.4	2.1	0.6	16.1
1960	7.8	4.1	2.8	2.3	0.8	17.8
1961	7.8	3.9	3.1	2.2	0.7	17.7

SOURCE: *Historical Tables, Budget of the United States Government, Fiscal Year 2002* (Washington, D.C.: Government Printing Office, 2001), 33.

Preservation of a high-tax system obviously owed a great deal to balanced-budget conservatism, but Eisenhower's conception of "fiscal integrity" went beyond short-term calculations. Initially, he stated his willingness to finance tax cuts out of budget surpluses, but when these surpluses occurred, he opted instead for debt reduction. Eisenhower probably was convinced that defense spending commitments would have to remain high indefinitely and that it would be unwise to mortgage, in effect, the revenue levels needed to sustain that spending. A similar caution may help to explain his resistance to countercyclical tax cuts, even when that stance was politically costly.

Spending Policy

Defense. The main justification for the scale and pace of Truman's rearmament program was a looming year of "maximum peril," when the Soviet Union would have the atomic weaponry and conventional capabilities to threaten the United States and its allies directly.[77] Truman's national security planners had, before Korea, set 1954 as the "dangerous period," but the date was moved up after war broke out. In December 1950, the Joint Chiefs of Staff refocused their planning efforts on 1952.[78] In 1952, Truman reported "substantial progress in building military strength for use in the event of an all-out emergency" but added that the budget called for "somewhat higher goals than we had planned a year ago."[79] Several years earlier, the administration

77. Paul Y. Hammond, "NSC-68: Prologue to Rearmament," in *Strategy, Politics, and Defense Budgets*, eds. W. R. Schilling et al. (New York: Columbia University Press, 1962), 306.
78. *Congress and the Nation, 1945–1964*, 260.
79. *Congressional Record*, 82d Cong., 2d sess., 1952, 98, pt. 1: 333.

had rejected a 70-group Air Force as too large and costly, but its 1952 defense program included a 143-group Air Force, along with twenty-one Army divisions, and a 408-ship Navy with sixteen carrier groups.[80] Active-duty forces for the services were nearly 3.5 million, more than double the pre-Korea level.

Eisenhower explicitly rejected this "maximum peril" planning focus. Defense planning, he stated, should not "be based on . . . a D-day of desperate danger, somewhere in the near future, to which all plans can be geared."[81] His administration's "new concept for planning and financing our national security program" would instead provide procurement and personnel plans that "can be maintained over the extended period of uneasy peace."[82] Eisenhower's strategic calculus was complex. It embraced a view of the Soviets as intent on forcing "America and the free world [to bear] an unbearable security burden leading to economic disaster."[83] National Security Council debates during the early years of Eisenhower's presidency revealed a strong concern with this dual threat—"the external threat of Soviet power; the internal threat of weakening our economy and changing our way of life."[84]

Economic and budgetary considerations were long-standing elements in defense policy debates, but Eisenhower did not want to ignore the social implications of "an armed peace."[85] At a meeting of his National Security Council on October 7, 1953, the president reportedly expressed his doubts that "we could get this so-called adequate defense over a sustained period without drastically changing our whole way of life."[86] When others argued that defense spending could be increased "without radically changing" American society, Eisenhower countered that "the American people [might] make these sacrifices voluntarily for a year or two or three but . . . [not] for the indefinite future."[87]

The budget ceilings or "directed verdicts" that Eisenhower imposed on defense were a way to reconcile defense needs with these economic and social considerations and to permit "constructive forward steps in our domestic

---

80. *Congressional Record*, 82d Cong., 2d sess., 1952, 98, pt. 1: 333.
81. *Congressional Record*, 83d Cong., 1st sess., 1953, 99, pt. 4: 5180.
82. *Congressional Record*, 83d Cong., 2d sess., 1954, 100, pt. 1: 577.
83. *Congressional Record*, 83d Cong., 1st sess., 1953, 99, pt. 4: 5180.
84. See *Foreign Relations of the United States, 1952–1954*, vol. 2: *National Security Affairs* (Washington, D.C.: Government Printing Office, 1984), 514–34.
85. *Congressional Record*, 83d Cong., 2d sess., 1954, 100, pt. 1: 577.
86. *Foreign Relations of the United States, 1952–1954*, vol. 2: *National Security Affairs*, 520.
87. *Foreign Relations of the United States, 1952–1954*, vol. 2: *National Security Affairs*, 520.

responsibilities and programs."[88] Some conservative Republicans had hoped to reverse the domestic agenda of the New Deal, but Eisenhower's first budget endorsed an expanded Social Security system and proposed new, if limited, federal initiatives in education, housing, healthcare, and environmental protection. Over the next several years, inflation-adjusted nondefense spending grew at a fairly steady pace, even though Eisenhower and the congressional Democratic leadership repeatedly clashed over specific spending bills.

The cuts that Eisenhower ordered in Truman's defense estimates were designed to reduce outlays to approximately $35 billion by FY 1956.[89] This ceiling could not be achieved, but the defense spending-GNP ratio was lowered by about one-third. Under Eisenhower, 10 percent of GNP served as a de facto limit on peacetime defense spending, which precluded the conventional force levels Truman had envisioned, especially for the Army.[90] Eisenhower's "New Look" deterrent strategy depended on nuclear weapons and strategic airpower rather than conventional forces. In a speech on January 12, 1954, Secretary of State John Foster Dulles outlined this new strategy, which became known as massive retaliation. In the case of Communist aggression, the United States would reserve the option "to retaliate, instantly, by means and at places of our choosing."[91] Later that year, a National Security Council planning paper (NSC 162/2) instructed military leaders to begin to reduce conventional force levels with the understanding that, if necessary, the tactical or strategic use of nuclear weapons would be authorized by the president.[92]

The doctrine of massive retaliation generated intense criticism at home and abroad, but did allow the United States to exploit its strategic weapons superiority. Neither the United States nor its NATO allies thought it feasible to build the level of conventional forces that could "defend the NATO area against a full-scale Soviet block attack," so it was essential that "atomic weapons in substantial quantities . . . be available for the support of . . .

88. *Congressional Record*, 83d Cong., 2d sess., 1954, 100, pt. 1: 567.

89. *Foreign Relations of the United States, 1952–1954*, vol. 2: *National Security Affairs*, 311–16.

90. For an explanation of planning requirements for conventional force deterrence, see Richard K. Betts, *Military Readiness: Concepts, Choices, Consequences* (Washington, D.C.: Brookings Institution, 1995), 20.

91. Address by Secretary Dulles before the Council on Foreign Relations, New York, New York, on January 2, 1954. *Department of State Bulletin* (Washington, D.C.) 30, 761 (1954): 108.

92. *Congress and the Nation, 1945–1964*, 277–78.

programmed forces."[93] The conventional force retrenchments that Eisenhower ordered were sharply attacked by congressional Democrats, who repeatedly attempted to boost funding for the Air Force and Army. Many Republican conservatives were upset as well, although their objection was that defense spending had not been cut nearly enough. In the spring of 1953, Senator Robert A. Taft, the Republican majority leader, attacked Eisenhower for "taking us down the same road Truman traveled."[94] Taft demanded a "complete reconsideration" of defense policy and less costly defense budgets. During the FY 1954 budget cycle, the Republican-controlled eighty-third Congress cut the president's defense estimates, although a large backlog of unspent appropriations from prior years largely canceled the impact of this action on spending levels. In later years, with Korean War spending no longer a factor, Republicans rallied behind the president's defense program, but Democrats demanded even higher budgets.[95] Senator John F. Kennedy, one of Eisenhower's persistent critics, charged the administration with placing "fiscal security ahead of national security," a theme he highlighted during his 1960 presidential campaign.[96]

This Democratic critique took on added weight in 1957, when the Soviet Union successfully launched the first earth satellite. The rocket boosters used in the *Sputnik* launch and a second 1,100-pound satellite launch several weeks later indicated the Soviets had much more sophisticated scientific and technological capabilities than had been assumed. Because large rocket boosters were the key to intercontinental ballistic missile development, concerns about the U.S.-Soviet strategic balance quickly intensified. During this period, several defense policy study groups also weighed in with recommendations for strengthening strategic and conventional forces and for boosting defense budgets immediately.[97] The National Security Council, for example, received a confidential analysis prepared by a committee of scientists and business leaders appointed by the president that reportedly urged a one-third increase in defense spending by 1960.[98]

Eisenhower admitted to Congress "that we are probably somewhat behind the Soviets in some areas of long-range ballistic missile development" and

93. *Foreign Relations of the United States, 1952–1954*, vol. 5: *Western European Security* (Washington, D.C.: Government Printing Office, 1983), 511–12.
94. See Morgan, *Eisenhower Versus "The Spenders,"* 53.
95. Morgan, *Eisenhower Versus "The Spenders,"* 35.
96. Quoted in Morgan, *Eisenhower Versus "The Spenders,"* 35.
97. Ippolito, *Uncertain Legacies*, 107.
98. *Congress and the Nation, 1945–1964*, 298.

agreed to seek additional funding to ensure "we will have the missiles in the needed quantity and in time to sustain and strengthen the deterrent power of our increasingly efficient bombers."[99] The administration's fiscal 1959 budget requests, however, contained only marginal increases in the $38 billion ceiling the president had established. A $1.3 billion defense supplemental was sent to Congress, along with a $39.6 billion defense appropriations request. To accommodate sharply increased funding for ballistic missile and other strategic weapons systems within acceptable fiscal limits, Eisenhower proposed offsetting cuts in active-duty and reserve force levels and in conventional weapons procurement programs. Congress added back some $800 million to maintain force levels, but there was no sustained effort to fund additional conventional force capabilities.

In 1959 and 1960, the administration continued to impose tight ceilings on the military, and prominent Democrats stepped up their attack on the size and composition of the defense budget. Under Eisenhower, budgets had already shifted decisively toward the Air Force, and manpower reductions in the Army had been disproportionately high. With defense budgets tilting even more sharply toward strategic weapons, Democrats charged that conventional force support was dangerously inadequate. Moreover, the administration's stepped-up strategic program was also challenged as insufficient by "missile gap" proponents, who claimed that the Soviets had already achieved, or would soon attain, strategic superiority. John F. Kennedy's 1960 presidential campaign highlighted these claims, and the Democratic platform pledged to erase the strategic gaps and to revive "essential programs now slowed down, terminated, suspended, or neglected for lack of budgetary support."[100]

Most analysts later agreed that the "missile gap" charges had been unfounded.[101] Moreover, the Democratic commitment to higher defense budgets proved to be modest and temporary, once the Kennedy administration took office. By any standard, however, defense budget control under Eisenhower was strong and consistent. The defense-GNP share was kept within targeted levels, real spending was stabilized, and tax policy was subordinated to overall spending requirements.

Domestic Programs. The defense ceilings of the Eisenhower era provided a margin for increased domestic expenditures, but the growth in domestic budgets was limited and selective. The administration's domestic initiatives

99. *Congress and the Nation, 1945–1964,* 298.

100. Kirk H. Porter and Donald B. Johnson, eds., *National Party Platforms, 1840–1968* (Urbana: University of Illinois Press, 1970), 575.

101. See Ippolito, *Uncertain Legacies,* 110–11.

featured capital investment projects, such as the interstate highway system. Social Security coverage was extended under Eisenhower, and public assistance grants to the states were increased, but no new social welfare programs were enacted. The social welfare commitments of the New Deal were, by and large, institutionalized during the 1950s. Truman's Fair Deal initiatives, most notably national healthcare, were blocked.

For discretionary domestic programs, the authorization and appropriations processes allowed both the administration and Congress to check spending that lacked bipartisan support. There were frequent clashes between Eisenhower and congressional Democrats over agriculture policy, housing programs, and water and power projects, and it took several years to resolve differences over how to finance the interstate highway system. In many domestic program categories, disagreements over policy and concerns about cost kept spending tightly controlled.[102] Highway funding was one of the few domestic categories that grew rapidly during the late 1950s, but even in this case cost concerns were taken seriously. Revenues for the interstate system were restricted to a trust fund, financed by fuel taxes and user fees. The Highway Revenue Act of 1956 specified that the trust fund could not operate at a deficit, which meant that taxes would have to be increased in line with additional spending.

The relative growth of domestic programs during the Eisenhower era was therefore constrained by balanced-budget requirements and by the large budget share for defense. The outlays-GDP ratio for domestic programs was slightly lower in 1960 than it had been ten years earlier, as most, but not all, of the domestic retrenchment that had occurred during Korea was restored under postwar budgets. Social welfare payments for individuals were 5 percent of GDP in 1950 compared with 4.7 percent in 1960. All other domestic program outlays were approximately 2.5 percent of GDP in 1950 and 2.4 percent in 1960.[103]

The Kennedy-Johnson Fiscal Rules

The Democratic victory in the 1960 presidential election had a far-reaching impact on budget policy. Shortly after taking office, President Kennedy

102. See Ippolito, *Uncertain Legacies*, 204–8.

103. Includes "physical resources" and "other functions" excluding international affairs. *Historical Tables, Budget of the United States Government, Fiscal Year 2002*, 45–46, 110–11.

asked Congress to boost defense spending. He then began to push for new domestic programs. In addition, the central importance Truman and Eisenhower had assigned to balanced budgets was called into question by the Kennedy administration's 1963 proposal for planned deficits to spur economic growth. Kennedy's budget planners hoped that more aggressive fiscal stimulus would strengthen the economy and lead to higher revenues. Once the budget returned to balance, they expected defense transfers to help finance domestic initiatives. Whether this approach could have worked over the long term is uncertain. What is clear is that the Vietnam War produced a destabilizing fiscal strategy. Under Lyndon Johnson, both wartime and domestic spending needs were accommodated, while tax increases were postponed. In addition, Johnson's Great Society agenda put in place the social welfare programs that eventually made budget control even more difficult.

Tax Cuts and Deficits

In 1961, President Kennedy called for tax law changes but did not recommend a tax cut. Following Eisenhower's lead, Kennedy recommended that Congress extend the corporation income and excise tax rates that were due to expire, claiming that "we cannot afford the loss of these revenues at this time."[104] Bowing to business demands for liberalized depreciation allowances, Kennedy proposed an investment tax credit for new plants and equipment and then called on Congress to strengthen tax enforcement and to repeal tax preferences to offset any revenue loss.

Congress passed, without great controversy, the Tax Rate Extension Act of 1961, which maintained corporation income and excise tax rates for another year, but action was postponed on tax law revisions. In 1962, Congress passed a similar extension and, in the Revenue Act of 1962, approved a reduced investment tax credit, absent the restrictions and revenue offsets Kennedy had requested. By midyear, however, economic growth had begun to slow, and the administration announced that a comprehensive proposal for tax reform and tax cuts would be presented in 1963.

The case for lower taxes, according to Kennedy, hinged on incentives and purchasing power. He explained that "our present tax system exerts too heavy a drag on growth . . . it siphons out of the private economy too large a share of personal and business purchasing power . . . [and] reduces the financial

104. *Congress and the Nation, 1945–1964*, 427.

incentives for personal effort, investment, and risktaking."[105] Kennedy's argument that tax burdens affected economic growth was hardly new; his departure from conventional fiscal policy was the call for major tax cuts when budget deficits were already quite large. The Kennedy administration's tax-cut program, however, distinguished between "chronic deficits arising out of a slow rate of economic growth, and temporary deficits stemming from a tax program designed to promote a fuller use of our resources and more rapid economic growth."[106]

When Kennedy sent his special tax message to Congress on January 24, 1963, the projected deficits for fiscal years 1963–64 were almost $20 billion. Despite these deficits, the administration proposed substantial tax cuts—a 20 percent reduction in individual income tax liabilities, along with corporation income tax cuts and permanent reductions in long-term capital gains taxation. The centerpiece of the Kennedy tax program was a comprehensive reduction of marginal rates on individual income, with the bottom rate bracket lowered from 20 to 14 percent and the top bracket from 91 to 65 percent. The administration also proposed structural reforms to broaden the tax base for high-income taxpayers. Nevertheless, all income classes were to receive net tax reductions. The projected revenue loss for the entire tax package was more than $10 billion.[107]

There was widespread congressional support for a tax cut, but the prospect of larger deficits was unsettling for many. In particular, conservatives in both parties argued for domestic spending cuts to offset at least some of the revenue loss projected in Kennedy's budget. The House Ways and Means Committee defeated Republican efforts to make a portion of the scheduled tax cuts contingent on spending reductions, but the final committee bill contained "sense of Congress" language that called for greater spending control and lower deficits. The House passed the Ways and Means proposal in September, but renewed concerns about revenue losses and deficits delayed action in the Senate until after Kennedy's assassination. The Johnson administration then agreed to include substantial spending reductions in its FY 1965 budget, and congressional action on the tax bill was completed on February 26, 1964.

The Revenue Act of 1964 represented the most significant change in tax policy since World War II. Congress rejected some of the tax reforms in the

---

105. *Congress and the Nation, 1945–1964*, 434.
106. *Budget of the United States Government, Fiscal Year 1964*, 10–11.
107. *Congress and the Nation, 1945–1964*, 435.

original Kennedy administration proposal and scaled back the upper-bracket rate reductions, but the size of the final tax cut was substantial—an estimated $11.5 billion over two years, with more than $9 billion in tax savings for individuals. The revised rate schedule, phased in over two years, lowered the rate for individuals in the bottom taxable income bracket from 20 to 14 percent, while the top rate went from 91 to 70 percent. For the majority of taxpayers in the nearly two dozen intermediate brackets, marginal rate reductions represented a drop in tax liabilities of almost 20 percent.[108] Corporation tax changes were less sweeping. The normal tax rate was lowered from 30 to 22 percent, while surtax rates were raised. For larger corporations subject to the combined rate, the effective change was a four percentage point reduction, to 48 percent, over two years.

The goal of the Kennedy-Johnson tax program was to stimulate economic growth, and the 1964 tax cut was followed by an exceptionally strong economic expansion.[109] The deficit effects, moreover, were much smaller than anticipated. Total revenue levels rose in 1964 and 1965, and the anticipated short-term decline in individual income tax receipts did not occur. Actual deficits for 1963 and 1964 totaled $10.7 billion, approximately one-half of the administration's initial estimates. In FY 1965, higher revenues and lower spending reduced the deficit to under $1.5 billion.

During the first half of the 1960s, the spending side of the budget was still dominated by discretionary programs, and outlay growth remained tightly controlled. As a result, revenues and outlays were reasonably close to balance, and spending-GDP ratios were not very different from those during the Eisenhower administration (Table 5.6). Spending levels, however, then began to rise. Lyndon Johnson's landslide reelection in 1964 and the huge Democratic majorities in House and Senate elections led to the enactment of an extraordinary domestic agenda during the eighty-ninth Congress. Johnson initially hoped that his Great Society domestic programs could be financed through defense cutbacks, but these hopes evaporated during 1965. As the combined costs of domestic initiatives and the Vietnam War began to mount, Johnson acknowledged that additional revenues were required, but he repeatedly delayed moving forward with a tax program that might endanger support for Great Society programs or for the war. In January 1966,

---

108. Ippolito, *Uncertain Legacies*, 42.

109. For an assessment of how these tax cuts affected economic growth, see Stein, *Presidential Economics*, 110–13.

Table 5.6 Federal Budget Totals, 1955–1965 (as a percentage of GDP)

Fiscal Year	Total Revenues	Total Outlays	Deficit (−) /Surplus
1955	16.6%	17.3%	−0.8%
1956	17.4	16.5	0.9
1957	17.7	17.0	0.8
1958	17.3	17.9	−0.6
1959	16.1	18.7	−2.6
1960	17.8	17.8	0.1
1961	17.7	18.4	−0.6
1962	17.5	18.8	−1.3
1963	17.8	18.6	−0.8
1964	17.6	18.5	−0.9
1965	17.0	17.2	−0.2

SOURCE: *Historical Tables, Budget of the United States Government, Fiscal Year 2002* (Washington, D.C.: Government Printing Office, 2001), 23.

Johnson stated that a general tax increase was "not clearly required at this time," instead calling on Congress to delay scheduled excise tax reductions and to speed up individual and corporation tax payments.[110]

The Tax Adjustment Act of 1966 accelerated tax payments by requiring graduated withholding for individuals and current-year tax remittances by corporations. It also contained the excise tax extensions Johnson had requested. Later in the year, with signs of inflation becoming more serious, Johnson asked for temporary suspensions of the investment tax credit and of accelerated depreciation for building construction. Congress once again complied, although these tax benefits were restored the following year.

In his State of the Union message on January 10, 1967, Johnson finally endorsed a general tax increase, recommending to Congress a 6 percent surcharge on individual and corporation tax payments. Seven months later, the administration sent to Congress its detailed proposal for a 10 percent surcharge, effective during the 1967 tax year on a prorated basis, for both individual and corporation tax payments. The president's accompanying message to Congress tried to blur the connection between higher taxes and rising spending, emphasizing instead the need to contain inflationary pres-

110. *Congress and the Nation, 1965–1968* (Washington, D.C.: Congressional Quarterly, 1969), 153.

sures.[111] Key members of Congress, however, insisted that the administration agree to domestic spending cuts as a precondition for any tax increase. For two years, Johnson had worked hard to avoid this kind of tradeoff, and he bitterly attacked Congress for "courting danger by this continued procrastination . . . [for holding] up the tax bill until you can blackmail someone into getting your own personal viewpoint over on reductions."[112]

The House Ways and Means Committee, however, refused to act on taxes until Johnson compromised on spending. After months of delay and acrimony, Johnson got his tax increase, including the 10 percent surcharge on individual and corporation income taxes. Johnson was forced to accept, as part of the Revenue and Expenditure Control Act of 1968, a spending cut and outlay ceiling for FY 1969, a $10 billion reduction in his budget authority requests, and a cutback of 245,000 in federal civilian employment positions.[113] The new tax surcharge raised FY 1969 receipts to the highest level since World War II, and the accompanying spending ceiling sharply reduced discretionary domestic outlays. The FY 1969 budget was balanced, but prior-year deficits had contributed to high inflation rates and inflationary pressures remained strong. Equally important, Johnson's refusal to choose between the war and his Great Society, and his reluctance to pay for this with a general tax increase, undercut long-term fiscal discipline.

When the Korean War began, the Truman administration had raised taxes, cut domestic spending, and imposed price controls. Each of these decisions was politically difficult, and the domestic retrenchments erased much of what Truman had struggled to accomplish after World War II. Nevertheless, fiscally restrictive actions were taken to achieve wartime economic stabilization. In the case of Vietnam, restrictive policies were not imposed for several years and then only on a temporary basis. Unlike Truman, Johnson tried to avoid the politically difficult tradeoffs on which wartime budget control depended.

Defense Transfers and Domestic Spending

An important change in the composition and controllability of the budget also took place during the 1960s. The Kennedy administration initially

111. *Congress and the Nation, 1965–1968,* 158.
112. *Congress and the Nation, 1965–1968,* 170, 172.
113. *Congress and the Nation, 1965–1968,* 173.

increased defense spending but then began to orient its budget planning toward domestic programs. Under Johnson, defense budget shares were substantially lower than they had been under Eisenhower, even during the Vietnam War. As the composition of federal spending shifted toward domestic programs, spending and deficit-control problems became more severe.

When the Kennedy administration took office, a new deterrent strategy of "Flexible Response" replaced "Massive Retaliation." Kennedy believed that conventional and limited-war forces had been neglected under Eisenhower. Balanced forces, he argued in 1961, were needed to provide realistic "options" other than "humiliation or all-out nuclear action" in countering Soviet military threats.[114] Among the immediate objectives Kennedy's defense planners identified for improved non-nuclear capabilities were additional forces, new weapons development and procurement, and greater airlift mobility. In addition, the administration called for stepped-up strategic modernization, particularly stronger and less vulnerable nuclear second-strike forces.

Kennedy had attacked Republican defense budgets as inadequate, and he moved quickly to increase the size of the defense budget and to implement Flexible Response priorities. On March 8, 1961, the president requested $2.7 billion in additional funding for the Polaris submarine program and for expanded limited-war forces. Congress was also asked to rescind $750 million that had already been appropriated for strategic bomber and other weapons development. During the next several months, a series of crises in U.S.-Soviet relations led Kennedy to propose, and Congress to ratify, the largest defense budget increases since the Korean War. Over the longer term, however, differences between Eisenhower's defense budgets and the Kennedy-Johnson defense program evaporated.

During spring and summer 1961, Congress completed action on a FY 1961 defense supplemental and on authorization and appropriations measures that boosted FY 1962 defense funding by nearly $6 billion above Eisenhower's final budget. Some of this additional funding reflected strategic adjustments in U.S. defense policy, but a large portion was tied to specific Soviet actions in Europe. The Soviet Union had denounced the United States for its involvement in the failed invasion by Cuban rebel forces at the Bay of Pigs on April 17, and Premier Nikita Khrushchev challenged the United States on a variety of other Cold War issues at the Vienna Summit held in early June. Most important, Khrushchev announced his intention to conclude a

114. *Congress and the Nation, 1945–1964,* 311.

peace treaty with East Germany and to make Berlin a demilitarized "free city" with access controlled by the East German government. One month later, Khrushchev ordered an increase in Soviet military spending and turned up the pressure on Berlin. On July 25, in a nationally broadcast speech, Kennedy declared that, if necessary, force would be used to protect allied rights in Berlin. The president stated that he would ask Congress to bolster U.S. military capabilities immediately, with an additional $3.5 billion in funding and an increase of more than 200,000 in active-duty force levels. For the United States to "meet a world-wide threat, on a basis which stretches far beyond the present Berlin crisis," Kennedy wanted emergency authority to call up reservists and extend active-duty service tours.[115]

The confrontation over Berlin continued well into 1962, and the Cuban missile crisis during October brought the United States and the Soviet Union to the brink of actual war. Under these conditions, defense budget increases could hardly be avoided. The budgets for FY 1963 and FY 1964 contained additional funding for a broad range of forces and programs. Kennedy's fiscal 1963 budget acknowledged that substantially higher funds were needed "than would have been required to carry forward the program as it stood a year ago."[116] In the fiscal 1964 budget, which was sent to Congress just three months after the Cuban missile crisis was resolved, Kennedy declared that "there is no discount price for defense."[117] The United States would have to be prepared "at all times to face the perils of global nuclear war, limited conventional conflict, and covert guerrilla activities."[118]

One year later, the Johnson administration's FY 1965 budget signaled that the defense emergency was over. Johnson asserted that the budgetary increases of the past several years had created "the most formidable defense establishment the world has ever known."[119] The U.S. strategic arsenal was so "vastly superior to the Soviet nuclear force" that funding could be reduced by more than $3 billion below the budget authority level for FY 1962.[120] A new doctrine of strategic parity being promoted by the civilian leadership in the Department of Defense was used to justify this reversal in

115. *Congress and the Nation, 1945–1964*, 311.

116. *Budget of the United States Government, Fiscal Year 1963* (Washington, D.C.: Government Printing Office, 1962), 11.

117. *Budget of the United States Government, Fiscal Year 1964*, 17.

118. *Budget of the United States Government, Fiscal Year 1964*, 17.

119. *Budget of the United States Government, Fiscal Year 1965* (Washington, D.C.: Government Printing Office, 1964), 8.

120. *Budget of the United States Government, Fiscal Year 1965*, 74.

funding priorities, but the fact that no increases were recommended for the conventional forces or the mobility forces prominently featured in previous years indicated that defense cuts were being implemented to transfer budgetary resources to domestic programs. When the escalation in Vietnam during 1965 threatened this budget policy shift, the administration tried to downplay the costs of its Vietnam commitment. Its original FY 1966 defense budget was $51.6 billion, $600 million below the previous year's budget. Johnson also called for an increase of nearly $3 billion in domestic spending, so that the nation could begin "to grasp the opportunities of the Great Society."[121] After these proposals were sent to Congress, Johnson submitted a $700 million FY 1965 supplemental request for the "Southeast Asian Emergency Fund," and a second Vietnam supplemental for $1.7 billion for 1966 was submitted shortly thereafter.

In 1965, there was little opposition in Congress to Johnson's Vietnam policy, although some Republican members of Congress charged that the administration was understating the fiscal requirements of the war to protect its domestic legislative program. Republicans on the House Appropriations Subcommittee on Defense argued that Johnson's defense requests provided "inadequate funding" for the war and that defense policy reflected "an approach falling far short of what we believe must be done" in critical areas.[122] Congressional Democrats refused to join the attacks on "phony" budgets, but there was widespread concern that defense budgets were too low to accommodate both emergency war costs and continuing non-Vietnam defense requirements.

By the time the FY 1967 budget was sent to Congress, the U.S. troop commitment in Vietnam was close to 200,000, and war costs were rising well beyond initial estimates.[123] The administration's defense budget request of under $60 billion was again attacked by Republicans as misleading, and the military committees in both houses began to press the administration more strenuously on providing adequate funding for defense. The FY 1967 authorization and appropriations bills added funding for military programs that had not been included in the defense budget, and the civilian leadership of the Defense Department, notably Secretary Robert S. McNamara, was

---

121. *Budget of the United States Government, Fiscal Year 1966* (Washington, D.C.: Government Printing Office, 1965), 7.

122. *Congress and the Nation, 1965–1968*, 835.

123. Troop levels had climbed to nearly 400,000 by the end of 1966. Two years later, U.S. forces in South Vietnam numbered more than 535,000.

denounced by members of both parties for neglecting defense needs. In reporting out its FY 1967 defense procurement authorization, the House Armed Services Committee charged McNamara with having rejected the Joint Chiefs of Staff's "sound military recommendations" and then having misled Congress about his actions.[124]

Conflicts between Congress and McNamara over the war, weapons systems, and defense policy intensified during 1966 and 1967. In an attempt to defuse criticism of his defense program, Johnson included $3 billion in non-Vietnam defense increases to his FY 1968 budget. Johnson was also concerned with the deteriorating relationship between Congress and the Department of Defense and, in November 1967, forced McNamara out as Secretary of Defense. Any hopes that long-standing controversies over defense funding might be resolved, however, were shattered in 1968. The Tet offensive by the North Vietnamese in late January and February catalyzed opposition to the war and dramatically shifted congressional attitudes toward military spending. A spending ceiling added to the Federal Revenue and Expenditure Control Act of 1968 forced the Appropriations Committees to cut the FY 1969 defense budget, but congressional military advocates fully expected this reduction to be temporary. The chairman of the Senate Armed Services Committee, Richard B. Russell, warned his colleagues that they could not avoid "substantially increasing the size of our defense budget in the near future."[125] With Richard M. Nixon's victory in the 1968 presidential election, Russell's warning was underscored. The 1968 Republican platform had charged the Johnson administration with having "frittered away superior military capabilities, enabling the Soviets to narrow their defense gap, in some areas to outstrip us, and to move to cancel our lead entirely by the early Seventies."[126] The Republican party, it pledged, would "restore the pre-eminence of U.S. military strength."[127]

The turmoil and divisiveness of the Vietnam War, however, had destroyed public and congressional support for larger defense budgets. The Nixon administration confronted a Congress determined to reduce defense spending while the war was still being fought and to expand domestic program budgets immediately. What occurred in terms of defense transfer pressures

124. *Congress and the Nation, 1965–1968*, 841.
125. *Congress and the Nation, 1965–1968*, 830.
126. *Congressional Quarterly Almanac, 1968* (Washington, D.C.: Congressional Quarterly, 1968), 998.
127. *Congressional Quarterly Almanac, 1968*, 998.

at the midpoint of the Vietnam War was markedly different from previous postwar budget policy shifts. In the case of Vietnam, the antidefense animus in Congress was unmistakable. More important, the budget policy context was quite dissimilar. During both World War II and Korea, defense budget growth had greatly curtailed domestic spending. The domestic budget share in 1945 was under 10 percent, compared with more than 70 percent before the war. During Korea, the domestic share was cut by more than half, falling to approximately 25 percent in 1954. In both of these situations, domestic GDP shares fell sharply, and constant-dollar spending was reduced.

In the case of Vietnam, the spending pattern was different, even during the initial wartime buildup. Between 1965 and 1968, constant-dollar defense spending increased by more than 40 percent, but domestic program outlays also rose. Social welfare entitlements, for example, matched the real growth in defense between 1965 and 1968. Moreover, when real defense spending then began to drop, social welfare and other nondefense outlays continued to climb. By 1970, the defense budget share and GDP ratio were actually lower than they had been before the war (Table 5.7). During the final years of the Vietnam conflict, this shift to domestic spending priorities became even more pronounced. By the time that the Vietnam Peace Agreement was signed on January 27, 1973, the defense budget share had fallen to 30 percent.

It had been possible after World War II and Korea to boost domestic spending and to balance budgets, because wartime defense commitments had been so high. With Vietnam, there were similar, indeed even more pronounced, pressures for a postwar "peace dividend," but the defense budgets of the Vietnam era were simply too small to accommodate these pressures. Instead, the growth in nondefense spending substantially outpaced defense cuts, and, by the mid-1970s, deficits were higher than they had been during the war.[128]

The Erosion of Budget Control

The domestic policy initiatives of the New Deal and the defense requirements of the Cold War created a substantially larger federal government after World War II. During the late 1940s and the 1950s, federal outlay-GDP levels averaged approximately 16.5 percent annually, roughly five

---

128. In 1975 and 1976, deficits averaged nearly 4 percent of GDP. The largest Vietnam deficit was 2.9 percent in 1968.

Table 5.7 Defense Spending Trends, 1960–1970

Fiscal Year	Percentage of Total Outlays	Percentage of GDP	Constant (FY 1996) Dollars (in Billions)
1960	52.2%	9.3%	$ 273.0
1961	50.8	9.3	274.2
1962	49.0	9.2	287.3
1963	48.0	8.9	281.5
1964	46.2	8.5	286.5
1965	42.8	7.4	264.5
1966	43.2	7.7	292.3
1967	45.4	8.8	346.9
1968	46.0	9.4	379.1
1969	44.9	8.7	361.0
1970	41.8	8.1	338.5

SOURCE: *Historical Tables, Budget of the United States Government, Fiscal Year 2002* (Washington, D.C.: Government Printing Office, 2001), 111–12.

times greater than pre–New Deal spending. This dramatic expansion in the size of the federal budget, however, did not cause serious deficit problems. The Truman and Eisenhower administrations pursued conservative fiscal policies, and the dominant types of spending—discretionary domestic programs and, especially, defense—were controlled without great difficulty by the president and Congress. The large budget shares for defense limited the margins available for domestic programs. Defense needs also provided a compelling justification for high revenue levels.

The policy consensus on which budget control was based, however, began to unravel during the Kennedy and Johnson presidencies. Truman and Eisenhower had been greatly concerned with the inflationary effects of budget deficits, and their embrace of Keynesian fiscal policies was tempered by this concern. Kennedy's economic advisers were convinced that more aggressive fiscal policies, particularly planned deficits, would promote higher economic growth and employment. Once "full employment" and high growth were in place, budgets would automatically move toward balance.

While this approach to deficits did not displace the balanced-budget rule entirely, it did represent a practical weakening of that rule. Where Truman and Eisenhower were willing to accept deficits during clear-cut downturns in the economy, the Kennedy economic program argued for deficits under conditions of slow growth and less-than-full employment. By redefining the purposes and measurement of budget surpluses and deficits, the "new economics" of the Kennedy-Johnson years greatly relaxed the balanced-budget rule.

Kennedy and Johnson were also committed to expanding domestic spending. For a brief period, defense cutbacks provided additional funds for domestic programs, but the Vietnam War brought an end to this transfer strategy. President Johnson was determined, however, to pursue his ambitious domestic agenda regardless of wartime defense requirements. He was equally determined to avoid a tax increase that might imperil support for either his domestic program or the war. As a result, both defense and domestic spending increased during the late 1960s, while revenue levels lagged behind.

The Vietnam War had a profound effect on the politics of the budgetary process as well. The bipartisan consensus on defense spending was broken, and congressional conflicts over the size and composition of the budget intensified. By the time Johnson left office, congressional deference to the president on defense policy had greatly diminished, as had Congress's willingness to follow the president's lead on spending, tax, and fiscal policies. By the late 1960s, budget policy was highly politicized, and institutional responsibilities were neither fixed nor straightforward. This confluence of weakened fiscal rules, heightened domestic spending pressures, and diminished presidential influence created serious and long-lasting problems in budget control.

SOCIAL WELFARE BUDGETS AND DEFICITS

(1970–1990)

During the 1970s, social welfare entitlements and other mandatory spending displaced defense as the largest component of federal spending.[1] Between 1970 and 1980, the defense budget share plummeted to under 25 percent, while mandatory spending rose above 50 percent. Mandatory spending-GDP levels climbed as well, averaging nearly 10 percent annually during the 1970s and more than 12 percent during the 1980s. Over this period, spending growth was unusually high, largely as a result of social welfare costs, and deficit-control problems became more severe.

This period was also marked by escalating conflicts between the executive branch and Congress over control of budget policy. The Nixon administration and Congress clashed repeatedly over defense and domestic spending, and Congress adopted, in 1974, budget process reforms that allowed it to challenge the president's budget program. The 1974 Congressional Budget and Impoundment Control Act provided for annual legislative budgets, incorporating fiscal policy and spending priorities, along with procedures to ensure executive compliance with congressional spending decisions.

---

1. Mandatory programmatic spending includes Social Security, Medicare, and other entitlements (including the food stamp program, which is funded by pro forma appropriations). Included

This new budget process highlighted policy differences between the president and Congress, and the magnitude of these differences made it difficult to control spending and deficits. The usual postwar pattern of spending retrenchments and balanced budgets was not repeated after Vietnam. Instead, spending continued to rise, and deficits averaged almost 3 percent of GDP between 1975 and 1980.

During the Reagan presidency, deficits climbed even higher. From 1981 to 1989, average annual deficits were more than $165 billion, and the publicly-held debt nearly tripled, to $2.2 trillion. Despite mounting concerns over chronic deficits and soaring debt, the Reagan administration and Congress could not agree on policy changes to bring the budget closer to balance. One dimension of the stalemate involved Reagan's defense buildup and tax-cut program. A second dimension, equally important, was congressional opposition to social welfare retrenchments. Reagan's attempts to reverse the social welfare expansions initiated by the Great Society were unsuccessful. Instead, social welfare spending continued to grow during Reagan's tenure.

The intractability of the deficit problem during the 1980s was rooted in basic disagreements over the size and shape of the federal budget. While Reagan and congressional Democrats repeatedly declared their commitment to balanced budgets, there was no consensus on the policy sacrifices needed to achieve balance. For Reagan and his Republican followers, the only acceptable path to a balanced budget comprised revenue levels below 20 percent of GDP, low marginal rates of income taxation, and spending budgets that reversed the 1970s decline in defense. For Reagan's Democratic opponents, these policy prescriptions meant abandoning many of the domestic program commitments their party had struggled to implement for decades, in particular the social welfare expansions of the 1960s and 1970s. This historical context was a critical element in the budget policy impasse of the Reagan era. In fighting to determine the future size and shape of government, all sides were drawing on different lessons from the past.

---

as well are net outlays (usually negative) of the federal government's deposit insurance program. Mandatory spending totals are adjusted, in the official budget tables, for undistributed offsetting receipts. These include the employer share of federal employee retirement funds, federal asset sales, and certain rents and royalties from oil leases on the outer continental shelf. Finally, programmatic spending and net interest are usually totaled together as representing the mandatory share of the budget. See *Historical Tables, Budget of the United States Government, Fiscal Year 2002*, 9, 123–26.

Redefining Social Welfare Policy

The social welfare base established under the New Deal grew slowly for approximately three decades. Then in the mid-1960s, the Johnson administration expanded this base with additional programs for the elderly and poor and wholesale liberalizations of existing benefits. The budgetary impact of these social welfare extensions was muted in the early stages of the Vietnam War buildup but then began to accelerate. During a relatively brief period, social welfare spending emerged as the dominant component of federal budget policy.

The New Deal Base

The 1935 Social Security Act had established federal social welfare responsibilities for the elderly and the poor.[2] Over the next three decades, Social Security coverage was extended to additional occupational groups, and benefits were periodically raised (Table 6.1). Many of these changes occurred during the 1950s, making Social Security a more comprehensive insurance program for workers and the elderly. By the early 1960s, Social Security was by far the largest federal entitlement program, accounting for approximately one-half of all payments for individuals.[3] Nevertheless, its budgetary impact remained fairly modest. Social Security outlays were under 15 percent of total spending, and Social Security payroll taxes produced about the same percentage of federal revenues. In addition, the large increases in Social Security benefit payments between 1950 and 1965 were partially offset by reductions in other entitlements, so that the growth in total social welfare spending did not greatly exceed the rate of growth in the rest of the budget.

Over this period, public assistance programs were also augmented. Eligibility was eased for the Aid to Dependent Children (ADC) cash benefit program, as part of the Social Security Act Amendments in 1950 and 1956. The Public Welfare Amendments in 1962 then replaced the ADC program with Aid to Families with Dependent Children (AFDC), making both parents and children in indigent households eligible for assistance. The federal government enacted a new public assistance program for the disabled poor

2. A separate and, for several decades, comparatively larger program was created for retired railroad workers in 1937. The original Railroad Retirement Act was passed in 1934 but ruled unconstitutional by the Supreme Court the following year.

3. *Historical Tables, Budget of the United States Government, Fiscal Year 2002,* 187.

Table 6.1 Social Security Program Coverage and Benefits, 1935–1965

Employment Coverage

1935	Workers in commerce and industry
1950	Farm and domestic workers
	Self-employed (nonfarm, nonprofessional)
1954	Self-employed farmers
	Self-employed professionals (except physicians and lawyers), Optional for ministers
1956	Lawyers and dentists
	All professionals except physicians and federal employees
1965	Physicians

Benefit Eligibility

1935	Workers aged 65
1939	Dependents and survivors (OASI)
1956	Women aged 62–64 (reduced benefits)
	Disabled workers—OASDI (age 50–64)
1958	Dependents of disabled workers (age 50–64)
1960	Disabled workers (under 50 years of age)
1961	Men aged 62–64 (reduced benefits)

Average Monthly Benefits (Worker)

1939	$22.60
1950	$43.86
1952	$49.25
1954	$59.14
1958	$66.35
1964	$77.57

Taxable Earnings and Tax Rate
(Employee/Employer, respectively)

1935	$3,000 (1.0 percent)
1950	$3,000 (1.5 percent)
1951	$3,600 (1.5 percent)
1954	$3,600 (2.0 percent)
1955	$4,200 (2.0 percent)
1957	$4,200 (2.25 percent)
1959	$4,800 (2.5 percent)
1960	$4,800 (3.0 percent)
1962	$4,800 (3.125 percent)
1963	$4,800 (3.625 percent)

SOURCE: Compiled by author.

in 1950. Aid to the Permanently and Totally Disabled (APTD) provided matching grants to the states for cash assistance to indigent disabled persons over the age of eighteen. In 1950, Congress authorized federal grants to the states for medical services to welfare recipients, and reimbursement formulas for each of the federally assisted welfare programs were subsequently increased. The 1960 Social Security Act Amendments instituted a new program, medical assistance to the aged (MAA), to help the states provide medical services for the "medically needy" elderly (persons sixty-five years of age or older who did not qualify for public assistance). Numerous proposals were introduced in Congress for a comprehensive, national program of healthcare assistance to the poor, but none of these advanced very far. Instead, Congress approved more limited extensions of individual programs that accorded the states considerable discretion over medical-care provisions for the poor.

Federal support for food and housing assistance followed a similar pattern. Low-income families had been provided with food stamps under a New Deal program that lasted from 1939 until 1943. During the 1950s, surplus commodities acquired by the federal government under its price-support agriculture programs were donated to state agencies and charitable organizations serving the poor. In 1961, the Kennedy administration sponsored a pilot food stamp program in eight test areas, and, in 1964, a permanent program was established that allowed low-income individuals to purchase food stamps for cash and to use these stamps to buy food worth more than the stamps had cost. The subsidy cost of these food purchases was funded entirely by the federal government, with the states partially responsible for their administrative costs in implementing the program. State participation in the food stamp program, however, was optional, as was participation in the various surplus commodities distribution programs.

The Housing Act of 1937 had provided for federal subsidies for the construction of public housing for low-income families. This program lapsed during the war but was revived and expanded as part of the Housing Act of 1949, which authorized federal urban renewal assistance along with subsidies for low-income public housing. These initiatives were continued during the 1950s, but the Eisenhower administration successfully fought to limit the scale and cost of federal involvement. In 1961, an omnibus housing bill was enacted that greatly increased public housing construction funds and made housing credit more available to low-income families. Federal support for low-income housing in urban and rural areas was augmented in 1962 and 1964, and special assistance was provided for the elderly and the handicapped.

The various public assistance programs in place by the early 1960s had substantially broadened federal aid to the poor. Between 1945 and 1964, for example, the ADC/AFDC beneficiary population climbed from 700,000 to 4.3 million; by 1964, other federal-state welfare programs served more than 7.3 million elderly, poor, and disabled individuals.[4] The federal share of total costs for these programs was 60 percent in 1964, compared to well under 50 percent in 1945.

Nevertheless, there were glaring discrepancies in the types and amounts of benefits available in different states. A number of states did not participate in one or more of the joint assistance programs, with twelve states making no provisions for medical-care payments for ADC recipients.[5] Among participating states, average monthly benefits were several times higher in some states than in others, and residency and other eligibility criteria differed greatly as well. These differences in program structure from state to state were, for social welfare advocates, just one of the major shortcomings in an underfunded, inadequate, and inchoate social welfare system. The welfare reform agenda for the Johnson administration, therefore, comprised national program initiatives and substantially greater federal funding.

The Great Society Expansion

Social welfare reforms that had been stalled in Congress for many years were finally enacted under Lyndon Johnson, but the changes in social welfare policy during his administration were more sweeping than even the most ambitious of earlier reform plans. Among the numerous domestic initiatives of Johnson's presidency were several major bills that redefined the federal government's role in healthcare, education, food and housing assistance, and job training and employment (Table 6.2). The Johnson administration also sponsored Social Security increases that raised inflation-adjusted benefits well above previous levels.

In addition, the philosophy of social welfare changed during the Johnson era. Administrative policies and court decisions strengthened legal access to public assistance benefits and reduced the stigma traditionally associated with welfare.[6] It was during this period that the concept of entitlements acquired a legal rights dimension that went far beyond the technical, budgetary definition

---

4. *Congress and the Nation, 1945–1964*, 1274.
5. *Congress and the Nation, 1945–1964*, 1275.
6. On changes in the politics of welfare, see James T. Patterson, *America's Struggle Against Poverty, 1900–1994* (Cambridge: Harvard University Press, 1994), 157–70.

Table 6.2 Major Social Welfare Legislation, 1964–1968

1964

Economic Opportunity Act of 1964 (P.L. 88-452): authorized funds for the operation of the Office of Economic Opportunity (OEO) for employment, training, and education programs.

Food Stamp Act of 1964 (P.L. 88-525): established a national food stamp program for low-income households.

1965

Elementary and Secondary Education Act of 1965 (P.L. 89-10): authorized federal aid for local school districts, particularly those with low-income families.

Social Security Amendments of 1965 (P.L. 89-97): created the Medicare program, which provides health insurance for those aged 65 and older; also established the Medicaid program, which provides health insurance for certain low-income families with dependent children as well as for aged, blind, or permanently and totally disabled individuals. This act also provided a 7 percent benefit increase for Social Security recipients.

Higher Education Act of 1965 (P.L. 89-329): provided grants and guaranteed, interest-subsidized loans for higher education for those in financial need.

1966

Child Nutrition Act (P.L. 89-642): appropriated annual funds for a School Breakfast Program (permanently authorized in 1975).

Demonstration Cities and Metropolitan Development Act (P.L. 89-754): authorized funds for rebuilding and community improvement projects in urban areas.

1968

Social Security Amendments of 1967 (P.L. 90-248): provided a 13 percent benefit increase for Social Security recipients. This act also allowed disabled widows and widowers to receive reduced Social Security benefits at age 50.

Housing and Urban Development Act of 1968 (P.L. 90-448): established new federal insurance and subsidy programs.

SOURCE: Compiled by author.

of the term.[7] While public assistance programs never enjoyed the overwhelming legitimacy and political support accorded Social Security, they still "expanded to dimensions that would have been unimaginable in 1960."[8]

Social Security and Medicare. Omnibus Social Security bills in 1965 and 1967 raised cash benefits and filled some of the remaining gaps in coverage for the retirement and disability programs (OASDI). Enactment of the

7. Patterson, *America's Struggle Against Poverty, 1900–1994*, 183–84.
8. Patterson, *America's Struggle Against Poverty, 1900–1994*, 164.

Medicare program, Title XVIII of the 1965 Social Security Act Amendments, also ended the long-term debate over healthcare coverage for the elderly. Acting quickly and more ambitiously than the Johnson administration had expected, Congress approved both a basic plan to cover hospital and nursing home costs and a supplementary program to pay for physicians' and other healthcare services. The 1965 legislation was considered to be "the most important welfare measure since passage of the original Social Security Act in 1935."[9] Its long-term budgetary impact has borne out that assessment.

The Medicare hospital insurance plan that Congress passed in 1965 was similar to bills it had rejected as recently as 1964. Johnson reintroduced his hospital insurance plan as the first legislative priority for the heavily Democratic eighty-ninth Congress, and, on March 24, 1965, the House Ways and Means Committee reported out a two-part Medicare bill—a compulsory hospital insurance program modeled on the administration's proposal and a voluntary, but exclusively federal, supplemental insurance program to cover fees for physicians, surgeons, and other healthcare providers. The hospital insurance (Part A) component was based, like Social Security, on payroll taxes collected and distributed through a trust fund. Part B supplemental coverage was tied to premiums (initially $3 per month) and federal matching funds drawn from general revenues. The House, acting under a closed rule, passed the Ways and Means bill by a 313 to 115 vote on April 8. The Senate completed action on a similar two-part program, with somewhat more generous coverage, on July 9. The conference report was filed shortly thereafter and approved by large margins in both chambers. On July 30, President Johnson signed the bill during a ceremony in Independence, Missouri, that honored President Harry Truman, who had launched the federal health insurance effort nearly two decades earlier.

Congress and the administration also capitalized on the favorable legislative climate in early 1965 to raise Social Security benefit levels. A 7 percent across-the-board increase was approved for monthly retirement and disability payments in 1965, with additional increases scheduled through 1971. Maximum benefit payments were substantially raised, with the limit on benefits payable to a family going up nearly 50 percent over six years. Eligibility restrictions were eased, as benefits were authorized for persons seventy-two years of age and older who did not qualify under the covered employment

9. *Congress and the Nation, 1965–1968,* 751.

test. Disability coverage restrictions were loosened, and new protections were introduced for divorced and remarried spouses of eligible workers. The 1967 Social Security Act Amendments provided an across-the-board increase of 13 percent in monthly benefits for retirees and for disabled individuals and made each of the special benefits programs from 1965 more generous. The first-year cost of the OASDI provisions was estimated at more than $4 billion, an increase of about 20 percent in Social Security spending.[10]

With Social Security benefit increases outpacing inflation, the poverty rate among the elderly began to drop sharply. Between 1960 and 1970, the percentage of persons sixty-five and older below the official poverty line declined from 35 percent to under 25 percent.[11] To finance these higher benefits, however, stepped-up increases in the Social Security wage base and tax rate were necessary. The 1965 and 1967 Social Security bills increased the taxable base from $4,800 to $7,800, and the tax rate for employees and employers was set at 4.8 percent for 1969–70, with further increases to 5.9 percent by 1987.[12] The Social Security portion of total tax revenues went up accordingly. By 1970, social insurance taxes had replaced corporation income taxes as the second largest source of federal revenues.

Increases in Social Security cash benefits were deliberate, but Medicare costs proved more difficult to contain. The Medicare program became fully effective at the beginning of 1966. By the end of the year, 19.5 million persons were covered under the compulsory hospital insurance plan (Part A), and 17.5 million were enrolled in the supplemental insurance program.[13] In FY 1967, total Medicare outlays were $3.2 billion. Two years later, the total was $6.3 billion.[14] These unexpectedly high initial costs caused problems for the Johnson administration. Hospital charges rose sharply in 1966 and 1967, as did medical-care costs generally, raising concerns that Medicare was fueling healthcare cost inflation. In addition, projections of long-term Medicare spending were mounting. The administration asked Congress for new authority over Medicare payment methods and cost controls, but no action was taken. Congress also rejected, as too expensive, the administration's proposal to extend Medicare coverage to the disabled.

10. *Congress and the Nation, 1965–1968*, 774.
11. Michael J. Boskin, *Too Many Promises: The Uncertain Future of Social Security* (Homewood, Ill.: Dow Jones-Irwin, 1986), 26–27.
12. *Congress and the Nation, 1965–1968*, 747.
13. *Congress and the Nation, 1965–1968*, 765.
14. *Historical Tables, Budget of the United States Government, Fiscal Year 2002*, 202.

Public Assistance. Fiscal problems notwithstanding, Medicare quickly acquired the strong public support that the Social Security program had enjoyed for many years. The public assistance initiatives of the Johnson years, however, were buffeted by controversies over philosophy as well as costs. The most heated political battles involved the antipoverty effort launched in 1964. The administration had persuaded Congress to create an Office of Economic Opportunity (OEO), within the Executive Office of the President, to direct and coordinate the new and expanded employment, training, and education programs that constituted the antipoverty agenda. The Economic Opportunity Act of 1964 also authorized $950 million for the first year of OEO operations. Although the OEO's financial practices and program administration generated strong criticism from state and local government officials and from congressional conservatives, the administration managed to increase appropriations for its antipoverty initiatives to nearly $2 billion by 1968. There was, however, no consensus on the long-term direction or effectiveness of antipoverty policy, which left many of these programs vulnerable to budget cuts when Johnson left office.

Much more significant, in terms of long-term budgetary impact, were the enhancements to traditional types of public assistance during Johnson's tenure. As part of the 1965 Social Security Act Amendments, Congress established the Medicaid program of federally subsidized healthcare for the poor. Under Medicaid, federal matching funds were authorized for state programs providing medical-care assistance to AFDC recipients and to the indigent blind and disabled. The coverage of the indigent aged, which had been authorized under the Medical Assistance to the Aged (MAA) program in 1960, was continued, with the new requirement that any state participating in the MAA program make coverage available for other groups with comparable financial needs. States were directed to employ flexible income tests in determining eligibility to ensure equitable coverage. Federal reimbursement formulas, which applied to a broad range of medical services, were more generous than under the original MAA program, with federal matching rates of more than 80 percent for low-income states. The Medicaid program was expected to benefit approximately 8 million persons initially, but state participation and program costs turned out to be higher than anticipated.[15] In 1967, Congress tightened eligibility to lower costs, but Medicaid spending continued to rise steeply. FY 1969 spending had been originally

---

15. *Congress and the Nation, 1965–1968,* 748.

projected at $1.7 billion, but actual Medicaid costs were $2.3 billion, approximately double what they had been just two years earlier.[16] By 1970, Medicaid spending accounted for more than one-fourth of all means-tested entitlement outlays.

Food assistance was also made available to a growing beneficiary population. Federal funding for food stamps was increased, as was federal support for child nutrition and school breakfast and lunch programs. Between 1965 and 1970, the number of participants in the food stamp program increased by nearly 4 million, with 4.3 million average monthly participants during FY 1970.[17] Neither national coverage nor national eligibility and benefit standards were in place during this period, however, as Congress refused to reduce the flexibility enjoyed by the states. When national requirements were imposed during the 1970s, food stamp participation soared, along with federal outlays.

The housing assistance initiatives of the Johnson years included direct aid to the poor in the form of rent supplements and mortgage subsidies, and the administration also encouraged private development of rental housing for low-income groups through insured loans and grants. The Great Society's housing agenda also included substantial funding for model cities and urban renewal. The 1966 Demonstration Cities and Metropolitan Development Act authorized a three-year, $1.2 billion plan to rebuild deteriorating urban areas. Both the rent supplement and model cities programs were reauthorized in 1968, with $5.3 billion in funding to provide 1.7 million units of new or rehabilitated housing for low-income families.[18] The 1968 Housing and Urban Development Act then added a number of new federal insurance and subsidy programs. Many of the program authorizations that the Johnson administration sponsored were not fully funded during the 1960s but were supported much more generously over the next decade.

An enlarged federal role was evident as well in education policy. The landmark education bills of the Johnson presidency—the Elementary and Secondary Education Act of 1965 and the Higher Education Act of 1965—authorized federal support for educational resources and programs, but their common emphasis was federal assistance to needy students. Title I of the Elementary and Secondary Education Act authorized direct federal aid to

16. *Historical Tables, Budget of the United States Government, Fiscal Year 2002*, 202.

17. James C. Ohls and Harold Beebout, *The Food Stamp Program* (Washington, D.C.: Urban Institute Press, 1993), 189.

18. *Congress and the Nation, 1965–1968*, 215.

local school districts under a funding formula that targeted aid to districts with large numbers of children from low-income families. Federal funds could be used for any purpose "designed to meet the special educational needs of educationally deprived children."[19] In 1966, the compensatory component of federal education aid was strengthened, with substantially higher allotments to poorer districts. The higher education authorization included "educational opportunity grants," or scholarships, for students with "exceptional financial need."[20] For students from middle-income families, Title IV of the Higher Education Act established a program of guaranteed, interest-subsidized loans. As was the case for housing assistance, funding for the new education assistance programs grew slowly at first, but the program authorizations Johnson established eventually had a substantial budgetary impact.

Congressional ambivalence over welfare policy was most pronounced when cash assistance was at issue. Over the years, the federal matching shares for cash assistance to the aged, blind, and disabled, and to needy children had been raised, and income eligibility had been eased. This trend continued with the 1965 Social Security Act Amendments, which increased the federal share for all of the federal-state public assistance programs. Two years later, Congress attempted to cut back on the AFDC program. States were required to offer work training for adult recipients and to place recipients in private or, if necessary, public employment. Recipients who were unwilling to comply with training and work benefits were to be denied benefits, and state-by-state caps on AFDC participation were instituted beginning in 1968. These restrictions actually had very little effect on overall AFDC participation, but AFDC and other cash assistance funding continued to be constrained by Congress's concerns over the philosophy and costs of welfare policy.

The Entitlement Agenda

The Johnson presidency initiated the most important changes in federal social welfare policies and commitments since the New Deal. For the elderly, the most far-reaching change was the Medicare program, particularly given the two-part Medicare coverage established at the outset. Both parts of the Medicare program turned out to be much more expensive than expected. In addition to healthcare coverage, the Social Security legislation of the Johnson

19. *Congress and the Nation, 1965–1968*, 710.
20. *Congress and the Nation, 1965–1968*, 716.

years provided for significant increases in the real value of cash benefits. The combined result of subsidized healthcare and higher cash benefits was a dramatic improvement in the financial well-being of the elderly population and the transformation of Social Security into an increasingly costly, but enormously popular, entitlement. For the poor, the impact of the Great Society programs was more problematical, since the administration did not "federalize" welfare policy. Congress blocked efforts to establish national standards for public assistance eligibility and benefits, and congressional support for the AFDC program was especially unstable. Nevertheless, state controls over public assistance eligibility criteria were limited by court decisions, federal agency directives, and statutory mandates. In addition, AFDC participation became much more attractive, even in states with low cash benefits, as beneficiaries qualified for new Medicaid coverage and food and housing assistance. From 1965 to 1969, AFDC rolls increased by more than 40 percent, to 6.1 million recipients.[21]

Lyndon Johnson had launched, in effect, a major redefinition of the federal government's social welfare responsibilities, and, over the next decade, the politics of social welfare policy was dominated by efforts to expand the Great Society's entitlement agenda. As these efforts proceeded, the fiscal consequences of the Johnson presidency began to emerge more fully. By the end of the 1970s, the budget share for social welfare was double that for defense, revenue levels were unusually high, and budget deficits had become chronic.

The Road to "Tax and Spend"

The 1970s produced major upheavals in the budget process, as Congress and the executive branch competed for control over spending policy. In terms of policy change, the most abrupt trend during this period was the decline in defense spending. Between 1970 and 1980, the defense budget share was cut nearly in half, and defense-GDP levels dropped below 5 percent for the first time since the late 1940s. At the same time, the growth in domestic spending, especially for social welfare entitlements, more than offset the defense cuts. By the end of the Carter presidency, domestic programs—discretionary and social welfare—were 15 percent of GDP, and total spending had climbed to well over 20 percent.

21. See Patterson, *America's Struggle Against Poverty, 1900–1994*, 171.

Another striking feature of budget policy change in the 1970s was the paucity of major new domestic programs. Ironically, the success that congressional Democrats had in expanding existing domestic programs during the Nixon-Ford years made it impossible to enact national health insurance, welfare reform, and other Democratic priorities once the party regained the presidency. Despite the vetoes, impoundments, and spending ceilings of the Nixon presidency, domestic outlays had risen significantly, and their growth accelerated during the Ford administration. By the time the Carter administration took office, the fiscal margin to expand the social welfare system had disappeared.

Divided Control: The Nixon-Ford Years

Richard Nixon was the first president in more than a century to enter office with the opposition party controlling both houses of Congress. He also had to deal with an intensely divisive war and an unstable economy. The prospects for a bipartisan approach to budget policy were, under these conditions, nonexistent, and Nixon's first term featured repeated clashes with Congress over spending priorities and deficit control. Nixon routinely vetoed domestic appropriations bills, while Congress slashed the administration's defense budget requests. When Congress provided funding for programs the administration opposed, Nixon sometimes refused to spend the funds. These impoundments, not surprisingly, created a backlash in Congress, but the administration remained adamant. Finally, tax reform and welfare reform were stymied by a liberal-conservative crossfire in Congress, and spending ceilings were violated by both sides.

Nixon's landslide reelection in 1972 had almost no impact on the partisan composition of Congress, so that the budget policy battles of his first term were resumed in 1973. As Nixon stepped up his attacks on congressional spending policy, Congress established a Joint Study Committee on Budget Control to propose reforms in congressional budgeting. Numerous proposals were also put forward to restrict the president's use of impoundments. Initially, the budget reform debate in Congress was confined to Nixon's prescriptions for tighter controls over spending. The Watergate investigations that were launched in 1973, however, soon reduced Nixon's leverage over budget reform and over budget policy more generally. By 1974, the Nixon administration had abandoned its drive for spending ceilings and domestic program cuts, and Congress was recasting the parameters and goals of budget reform. When Gerald Ford succeeded Nixon, a new, "independent" congressional budget process was in place. The 1974 midterm elections then gave the Democrats huge majorities in the House and Senate, and the shift toward Democratic spending priorities became even more decisive.

The Spending Conflicts. The ideological and partisan splits on spending policy during the Nixon-Ford years were especially pronounced on appropriations bills for defense and discretionary domestic programs. The strategic consensus that had protected Cold War defense budgets eroded during Vietnam, and political demands for a "peace dividend" intensified during the latter stages of the war. Both Nixon and Ford tried to fend off domestic transfer pressures—congressional efforts to cut defense budgets and to pass on the "savings" to domestic programs. Many of the more than one hundred presidential vetoes from 1969 to 1977, along with dozens of impoundments ordered by Nixon, were aimed at congressional add-ons to domestic authorizations and appropriations.[22] In 1970, Nixon vetoed five domestic spending bills, two of which were passed over his veto. Three budget-related vetoes were cast in 1971, all of which were sustained. In the FY 1973 budget submitted to Congress in January 1972, Nixon decried "the dangerous course of trying to match domestic spending increases with cuts in vitally needed defense programs" and warned Congress against adding "to my recommendations for domestic spending as it did last year."[23] When Congress refused to back down, Nixon vetoed sixteen bills. The $30 billion Labor-Health, Education and Welfare (HEW) appropriations bill was vetoed twice, and several large domestic authorizations were pocket vetoed.[24] The veto strategy continued in 1973, with five spending bills successfully blocked. President Ford vetoed fourteen appropriations and authorization measures for "excess spending," but Congress successfully overrode eight of those.

For its part, Congress ignored most Republican proposals to trim domestic programs and virtually all recommendations for program terminations. Congress also opposed the bulk of the Nixon-Ford requests to convert categorical grants-in-aid to block grants that would give the states greater control over how funds were spent. The few block grants that were approved, together with the revenue-sharing plan in the State and Local Fiscal Assistance Act of 1972, provided for additional domestic spending. The domestic policy

22. The total vetoes include pocket as well as regular vetoes. See Ippolito, *Uncertain Legacies*, 214–15.

23. *Budget of the United States Government, Fiscal Year 1973* (Washington, D.C.: Government Printing Office, 1972), 15.

24. *Congress and the Nation, 1969–1972* (Washington, D.C.: Congressional Quarterly, 1973), 75.

Table 6.3 Discretionary Program Outlays, 1969–1977 (in billions of FY 1996 dollars)

Fiscal Year	Defense	Domestic	International	Total
1969	$ 362.0	$ 131.4	$ 17.9	$ 511.3
1970	339.5	138.2	16.2	493.9
1971	309.0	147.6	14.2	470.8
1972	283.1	156.2	16.2	455.5
1973	256.7	161.4	16.2	434.3
1974	249.1	160.0	19.7	428.8
1975	243.8	176.1	23.7	443.5
1976	232.2	204.1	19.9	456.2
1977	230.8	219.7	19.5	469.9

SOURCE: *Historical Tables, Budget of the United States Government, Fiscal Year 2002* (Washington, D.C.: Government Printing Office, 2001), 124.

centralization that had begun under the Great Society continued under Nixon and Ford, and, as presidential influence waned after 1973, Congress was able to support this centralization with much greater funding.

These annual appropriations struggles between the Democratic-controlled Congress and Republican administrations had, in the end, a decisive result. From FY 1969 to 1977, discretionary spending was substantially reallocated. Real spending for defense was cut by more than one-third, while domestic outlays increased by more than two-thirds (Table 6.3). By 1977, defense and domestic discretionary outlays were nearly equal, at just under 5 percent of GDP. This was the lowest GDP share for defense in almost thirty years, while the domestic discretionary spending level was much higher than it had been even during the Great Society.

A more complicated ideological split occurred over public assistance programs. In 1969, the Nixon administration surprised both its congressional allies and opponents by sponsoring a guaranteed minimum income program for poor and working poor families.[25] While some Johnson administration policy planners had argued for a guaranteed income alternative to the patchwork system of public assistance, Johnson had been unwilling to endorse such a controversial change in welfare policy. Nixon's Family Assistance Plan was designed to replace the AFDC program, which the president called "unfair to the welfare recipient, unfair to the working poor, and unfair to the taxpayer," with federal cash benefits and food stamps for families that

25. See Leslie Lenkowsky, *Politics, Economics, and Welfare Reform* (Washington, D.C.: American Enterprise Institute, 1986).

traditionally had qualified for public assistance and with cash assistance supplements for families of the working poor.[26] This approach proved unacceptable, however, to congressional liberals, who called for even more sweeping alternatives, and to conservatives, who were concerned over costs. The House passed the original Family Assistance Plan in 1970 and a revised version in 1971, but the Senate could never overcome a liberal-conservative split centered in its Finance Committee.

The administration and Congress were able to agree, however, on major revisions in non-AFDC programs. In 1972, a Supplemental Security Income (SSI) program was enacted that replaced the federal-state assistance programs for the blind, disabled, and aged poor with uniform national eligibility criteria, administrative requirements, and benefit levels. States were allowed to supplement federal payments and were required to fund specified benefit increases, but recipients were guaranteed a "floor" benefit level regardless of where they lived. The food stamp program also was federalized. In 1971, uniform national benefit levels and benefit schedules were established, and mandatory food stamp participation, with national eligibility standards, was extended to all states two years later. Annual cost-of-living adjustments (COLAs) were applied to income eligibility and benefit levels in 1971, and semiannual benefit adjustments were instituted in 1973. After SSI benefits were increased in 1973, indexing was provided for future benefits. Indexing was also applied to Medicaid income eligibility standards as part of the 1973 Social Security Amendments.

Other public assistance programs, including housing, compensatory education aid, and targeted food programs, were more contentious. The Nixon and Ford administrations repeatedly, if unsuccessfully, called for tighter eligibility standards for these programs, and their block grant proposals would have given the states more authority over benefit levels. Congress eventually managed to broaden eligibility for housing and education aid, but the spending impact of these changes was negligible. Outlays for all means-tested entitlements did rise from 0.9 percent of GDP in FY 1969 to 1.7 percent in FY 1977, but most of this growth was concentrated in the newly federalized programs and in Medicaid.[27]

For Social Security and Medicare, partisan differences were minor, and the Nixon administration presided over quite remarkable increases in cash

26. *Congress and the Nation, 1969–1972*, 623.
27. Ippolito, *Uncertain Legacies*, 172–74.

benefits. In 1969, Nixon called for an immediate 10 percent increase in Social Security benefits and proposed that automatic cost-of-living adjustments in future benefits be adopted as well. Nixon coupled the latter to indexing in the Social Security taxable wage base, arguing that these changes would stabilize and depoliticize the Social Security system.[28] Congress then boosted across-the-board Social Security benefits by 15 percent but did not approve the indexing proposals. In the absence of indexing, benefits were raised by an additional 10 percent in 1971 and 20 percent in 1972, with the 1972 Social Security program changes incorporating the indexing provisions that Nixon had requested three years earlier. The following year, Congress approved an 11 percent benefit increase to take effect in 1974 and revised the cost-of-living adjustment schedule to make future increases more timely.

With the indexing of railroad retirement benefits in 1974, annual, or in some cases semiannual, cost-of-living adjustments were in place for each of the federal government's retirement programs.[29] The effect of legislated and automatic benefit increases was substantial. Between 1969 and 1977, Social Security and Medicare outlays climbed from 3.5 percent to 5.3 percent of GDP.[30] Other federal retirement and disability expenditures went up at similar rates, bringing the total for non-means-tested retirement and healthcare entitlements to almost 6.5 percent of GDP by the mid-1970s.

Despite enormous increases in entitlement spending during the Nixon and Ford presidencies, not all programs fared equally well. With the impasse over welfare reform, cash assistance for the poor was beginning to lag behind Medicaid and food stamp assistance. Within the social welfare budget as a whole, moreover, the largest and fastest-growing entitlements were the retirement and healthcare benefits for the elderly. As a result, the gap in federal support for the poor and for the elderly was beginning to widen.

The magnitude of Social Security increases, and the greater than anticipated growth in Medicare spending, was also beginning to strain the financial stability of the system's trust funds. Although payroll taxes had been repeatedly raised, trust fund reserves were being rapidly depleted. The 1975 report of the Social Security Board of Trustees warned that without modifications in benefits and increases in taxes, Social Security costs would exceed trust

28. *Congress and the Nation*, 1969–1972, 611.

29. See R. Kent Weaver, *Automatic Government: The Politics of Indexation* (Washington, D.C.: Brookings Institution, 1988), 42–43.

30. Congressional Budget Office, *The Budget and Economic Outlook: Fiscal Years 2002–2011* (Washington, D.C.: CBO, 2001), 151.

fund incomes for the next seventy-five years.[31] The projected shortfalls, moreover, were substantial—averaging more than 5 percent of taxable payroll annually. Congress was reluctant even to consider benefit adjustments, however, ignoring completely President Ford's proposal to place a 5 percent ceiling on cost-of-living increases. Congress also took no action to correct an acknowledged flaw in the Social Security benefit formula. The Social Security Board of Trustees report in 1975 had recommended that the benefit formula be "decoupled" from both wages and prices, since the existing formula had resulted in "unintended and excessively costly benefit payments."[32] This change was finally made in 1977, but its effective date was then postponed until 1979, which meant that overcompensation for inflation was left in place when inflation rates were extremely high.

During the Nixon-Ford era, Congress won most of the important battles over spending policy, but these victories carried a heavy cost. Despite the defense cuts that Congress engineered, spending and deficit levels were extremely high. With indexing having been applied to so many programs, the budget's year-to-year controllability had been greatly reduced, and the growing weight of politically popular entitlements such as Social Security and Medicare made it even more difficult to restrain spending growth.

Revenue Policy. The political disputes over spending policy carried over to the revenue side of the budget. In 1969, Congress approved a temporary extension of the Vietnam surtax and then went on to pass a major new tax law. The 1969 Tax Reform Act, which drew on recommendations of the Johnson and Nixon Treasury Departments, shifted tax burdens to higher-income groups by raising standard deductions and personal exemptions and by repealing tax preferences for individuals and corporations. These structural reforms were part of an effort to raise revenue levels by a substantial margin. For fiscal years 1969 and 1970, revenues averaged more than 19 percent of GDP, the highest levels since World War II and Korea, and the Nixon administration's FY 1971 budget message proposed additional tax increases to balance future spending and revenues.

Congress rejected most of Nixon's recommendations, and the reform impulse of 1969 soon disappeared in the face of economic and budgetary problems. On August 15, 1971, Nixon announced a comprehensive economic

---

31. *Congress and the Nation, 1973–1976* (Washington, D.C.: Congressional Quarterly, 1977), 424–25.

32. *Congress and the Nation, 1973–1976,* 424–25.

recovery program that included wage and price controls, an end to the gold standard, and a large tax cut. The Revenue Act of 1971, cleared by Congress on December 9, had an estimated three-year cost of more than $25 billion, with even larger reductions expected after 1973. The reductions in individual income tax liabilities included accelerating scheduled increases in personal exemptions and standard deductions, while investment tax credits and more liberal depreciation allowances were provided for businesses.

After his reelection, Nixon attempted to revive structural tax reform, but Congress rejected recommendations to broaden the tax base by curbing large tax preferences. In 1974, Congress moved in the opposite direction, instituting more favorable tax treatment of pension plans and retirement accounts.[33] The revenue impact of tax preferences (or "tax expenditures") was becoming much greater during this period, but Congress was usually more sympathetic to tax reductions than to tax reform.[34]

Congress proved even less amenable to presidential direction of tax policy under Gerald Ford. Shortly after taking office, Ford proposed an income tax surcharge as the centerpiece of his program to reduce deficits and counter inflation. Congress rejected the surcharge and ignored the other revenue-raising initiatives Ford had recommended. In 1975, Ford agreed to a tax cut to spur economic recovery but argued that reductions should be limited and temporary. Congress passed a tax cut that was much larger than Ford had called for and that contained new tax preferences whose revenue effects were permanent. Congress also used this tax legislation as a vehicle to boost spending by nearly $2 billion, granting bonus payments to Social Security, railroad retirement, and SSI recipients and extending emergency unemployment benefits.[35]

After signing the 1975 tax cut, Ford attempted to regain the initiative on tax policy, presenting Congress with a comprehensive reform package and calling for spending reductions to offset any future tax cuts. When Congress finally cleared the Tax Reform Act of 1976, it bore little resemblance to Ford's proposals. New tax preferences outweighed structural reform provisions, and the bill's estimated revenue loss for the 1977 tax year was almost $16 billion.[36]

---

33. See Witte, *The Politics and Development of the Federal Income Tax*, 182.

34. From 1967 to 1973, the estimated revenue loss from tax preferences was less than 25 percent of revenues. From 1975 to 1977, the revenue cost rose to more than 30 percent. Stanley S. Surrey and Paul R. McDaniel, *Tax Expenditures* (Cambridge: Harvard University Press, 1985), 35.

35. *Congress and the Nation, 1973–1976*, 94–96.

36. *Congress and the Nation, 1973–1976*, 105.

Tax policy during this period was highly unstable. Despite large and growing budget deficits, Congress was reluctant to raise revenue levels. With the exception of the Tax Reform Act of 1969, the tax bills that were enacted under Nixon and Ford were either temporary or permanent tax reductions. The types of tax cuts that Congress approved, moreover, did not greatly improve tax equity.[37] The proliferation of tax preferences—exclusions, deductions, and credits—narrowed the tax base, and large numbers of taxpayers found themselves paying steeper marginal rates, as inflation pushed them into higher income tax brackets. Many low-income taxpayers, whose income tax liabilities had been reduced, were faced with rising payroll taxes that offset these gains. Between 1969 and 1977, the percentage of total revenues from individual income taxes remained steady at around 45 percent, but payroll taxes jumped from 20 to 30 percent.[38] With payroll taxes having escalated so rapidly, progressivity in overall tax burdens was, by some measures, considerably reduced from what it had been a decade earlier.[39]

Congressional Budgeting. The partisan disadvantages facing the Ford administration in Congress were reinforced by the new congressional budget process unveiled in 1975. The effort to reform congressional budgeting had begun two years earlier, and the initial focus had been on tightening controls over spending. The initial reform proposal, developed by the Joint Study Committee on Budget Control, had featured firm and enforceable spending ceilings.[40] Congressional budgets, in the view of the Joint Study Committee, should complement, not displace, the president's budget.

The Congressional Budget and Impoundment Control Act that President Nixon signed into law on June 12, 1974, was a more complex and ambitious undertaking, and it reflected the demands of House and Senate liberals that the budget process not be biased in favor of spending controls. Instead, the House and Senate adopted a more flexible and policy-neutral set of reforms that allowed Congress to establish its own fiscal policy and program priorities. The annual congressional budget resolutions mandated by the 1974

37. C. Eugene Steuerle, *The Tax Decade* (Washington, D.C.: Urban Institute Press, 1992), 22–26.

38. *Historical Tables, Budget of the United States Government, Fiscal Year 2002,* 31.

39. Ippolito, *Uncertain Legacies,* 47.

40. The Joint Study Committee proposed, for example, that the president's budget would serve as the spending ceiling for Congress, if the House and Senate failed to adopt a concurrent budget resolution by May 1. The Committee did not recommend impoundment controls, assuming that they would be unnecessary with improved spending controls. See Ippolito, *Congressional Spending,* 60–61.

Budget Act included budget aggregates (total spending, total revenues, deficit or surplus levels, and public debt levels) and spending allocations for broad programmatic groupings (functional categories), mirroring the breakdowns in the president's budget. In addition to ending the president's monopoly over fiscal policy planning, the Budget Act abolished unilateral presidential impoundments. Title X allowed Congress to block even temporary delays in spending appropriated funds; any presidential attempt to cancel spending permanently was automatically barred in the absence of rescission legislation passed by Congress.[41] From fiscal policy planning to budget execution, the institutional goal of the 1974 Budget Act was to strengthen Congress's authority against the executive's.

Within Congress, the budget process reforms were designed to limit intrusions on committee prerogatives and to preserve flexibility over spending and revenue decisions. House and Senate Budget Committees were created to prepare the annual budget resolutions, and a new staff agency, the Congressional Budget Office (CBO), was established to provide budget data and analysis. These committees, supported by the CBO, would review and analyze the president's budget, consider the "views and estimates" of spending and revenue committees, and prepare at least two budget resolutions for the upcoming fiscal year—a nonbinding or target resolution to be adopted by May 15 and a binding resolution in the fall. Between the spring and fall resolutions, Congress would act on authorization, appropriations, and tax bills reported out by its committees. The second resolution would allow Congress to reconsider its first resolution and the subsequent decisions on spending and revenue bills. The fall budget resolution would then set a binding ceiling on spending and a binding floor on revenues, and reconciliation legislation would be used, if necessary, to resolve any conflicts between enacted spending and revenue bills and these binding totals. If Congress later decided that additional spending was needed, additional budget resolutions could be enacted. To accommodate these additional stages in the budget process, the fiscal year schedule was changed from July 1–June 30 to October 1–September 30.

The short-term effect of this flexible and ostensibly policy-neutral version of budget reform was to advance congressional Democrats' spending priorities. The budget resolutions adopted in 1975 and 1976 contained deficit and

41. For the current rules and procedures governing deferrals and rescissions, see Allen Schick, *The Federal Budget: Politics, Policy, and Process*, rev. ed. (Washington, D.C.: Brookings Institution, 2000), 250–55.

spending levels well above those recommended by the Ford administration to accommodate additional spending for domestic programs.[42] These budget resolutions also cut the administration's proposed defense budgets. While President Ford managed to moderate the latter, the overall shift in spending policy was pronounced. Between fiscal years 1975 and 1977, inflation-adjusted domestic discretionary outlays rose by nearly 25 percent; defense outlays dropped by 5 percent.

Over time, numerous amendments to and modifications of the congressional budget process have restored some of the initial focus on spending control. By the early 1980s, for example, Congress had abandoned the option of multiple budget resolutions for a given fiscal year, making the spring budget resolution binding and strengthening enforcement of spending totals through allocations to spending committees. An extremely important change, also initiated during the early 1980s, has been the use of reconciliation instructions in the spring budget resolution to direct changes in taxes and entitlements. Budget resolutions set overall spending, revenue, and deficit or surplus totals. Spending allocations for discretionary programs must be complied with by the Appropriations Committees. If budget totals require changes in revenue levels or entitlement spending, the budget resolution includes reconciliation instructions to committees with corresponding jurisdictions to report out legislation implementing these changes. Once the committees have acted, their proposals are organized into reconciliation bills to be considered by the House and Senate. Since budget resolutions and reconciliation bills are protected by special rules governing debate and amendments, filibusters and other delaying tactics cannot ordinarily be used against budget reconciliation initiatives.

Proponents of the 1974 budget reform initiative hailed it as "one of the most monumental reassertions of congressional prerogatives" and "the most significant reform of the 20th century."[43] For the first two years, congressional budgeting was, in fact, a determined and largely successful effort by congressional Democrats to wrest budget policy leadership from the president. Within a few years, however, this imbalance between the legislative and executive branches began to change. In 1981, the Reagan administration took control of the reconciliation process to force major cutbacks in spending and taxes. In 1990, 1993, and 1997, the budget process was used to implement multiyear deficit-reduction agreements negotiated between Congress

---

42. See Ippolito, *Congressional Spending*, 107–8.
43. *Congressional Record*, 93d Cong., 1st sess., 1973, 119, pt. 30: 39344, 39348.

and the executive branch. In 2001, the Bush administration and congressional Republicans employed the budget reconciliation process to enact a $1.35 trillion tax cut. Thus, the policy accomplishments of congressional budgeting have been divergent. And some of that divergence began to emerge, ironically, when the Democratic party recaptured the presidency in 1976.

Divided Democrats: The Carter Presidency

The 1976 election that brought Jimmy Carter to the White House maintained the heavy Democratic majorities in the House and Senate. The 1976 Democratic platform called for new social welfare programs, most notably "comprehensive national health insurance with universal and mandatory coverage" and an income maintenance system with "an income floor both for the working poor and the poor not in the labor market."[44] The domestic policy thrust of the platform was unmistakable, especially by contrast with the defense section that promised to "reduce present defense spending by about $5-billion to $7-billion."[45] And, in what would turn out to be one of the more ironic pledges, the platform promised that "the new Democratic President will work closely with the leaders of the Congress on a regular, systematic basis so that the people can see the results of unity."[46] Instead, the Carter years underscored the serious ideological splits within the Democratic party and the unwillingness of the party's congressional leadership to cede budget policy leadership to the president, regardless of party. The end result was a budget policy record that was vulnerable to attacks from all sides.

The Priorities Dilemma. On spending policy, the Carter administration was repeatedly stymied by budget constraints. The defense budget could not be cut by $5 to $7 billion, or indeed by more modest amounts. Rapidly escalating spending for Medicare and Medicaid convinced administration officials that healthcare cost controls would be needed to make a national health insurance system affordable. In addition, prior liberalizations in other entitlements were proving to be more expensive than expected, undermining congressional support for new spending or welfare reform.

---

44. *Congressional Quarterly Almanac, 1976* (Washington, D.C.: Congressional Quarterly, 1976), 859–60.
45. *Congressional Quarterly Almanac, 1976,* 868.
46. *Congressional Quarterly Almanac, 1976,* 855.

These constraints were reinforced by a mutual reluctance to retrench existing programs. The Food Stamp Act of 1977 eliminated the cash purchase requirement and consolidated the income deductions used in determining need.[47] The result was a sharp increase in the number of beneficiaries that drove spending above the ceilings that Congress established. In 1978, Congress made higher education student aid much more widely available, removing entirely the income eligibility requirements for guaranteed student loans and almost doubling the income qualification standard for cash grants (Basic Education Opportunity Grants). In 1979, eligibility rules were eased further, and the interest subsidy for the guaranteed student loan program was raised. Housing assistance programs received similar liberalizations in eligibility and in benefit formulas. These piecemeal and largely uncoordinated changes raised program costs dramatically. From 1977 to 1981, outlays for food stamps, student aid, and housing assistance grew from $15 billion to $27 billion.[48] Over the same period, cash assistance for the poor went up by only $1.6 billion. One of the principal arguments against additional cash assistance, to say nothing of the Carter administration's proposed guaranteed income plan, was that welfare costs were already too high. None of the House committees with direct jurisdiction over President Carter's 1977 welfare package endorsed it.[49] Democrats had criticized the imbalance between cash assistance and in-kind benefits for the poor under Nixon and Ford, but the imbalance became even more pronounced during the Carter presidency.[50]

The Defense Retreat. Relations between the Carter administration and Congress received an early jolt over the defense budget, setting the stage for several years of policy reversals and acrimony. President Carter's revisions in the Ford administration's FY 1978 budget included $20 billion in additional domestic spending and a $0.4 billion cut in defense. When the House Budget Committee proposed additional defense cuts as part of its FY 1978 budget resolution, the administration sought unsuccessfully to amend the proposal on the House floor. The Democratic leadership then castigated the administration for "not knowing the procedures of Congress," with House Budget Committee chairman Robert M. Giaimo warning that the president

47. Ohls and Beebout, *The Food Stamp Program,* 17.
48. *Historical Tables, Budget of the United States Government, Fiscal Year 2002,* 205–7.
49. Ippolito, *Uncertain Legacies,* 178.
50. Ippolito, *Uncertain Legacies,* 179.

was no longer dealing with "the Georgia legislature" but "the United States Congress where the Democratic majority is going to write the legislation."[51]

By 1978, Carter had moved to boost the defense budget, calling for "prudent real growth" in defense spending.[52] Concerned that Democratic liberals in Congress might attack his defense program, Carter called for even larger increases in domestic spending. The administration also tried to mollify its liberal critics by stressing that its defense proposals were "considerably more moderate than those . . . [of] the previous administration."[53]

The administration's shift on defense, however, was rooted in some harsh realities regarding the U.S. military. The post-Vietnam assault on the defense budget had seriously weakened military capabilities, particularly the balance of forces with the Soviet Union. An influential 1976 Congressional Research Service study commissioned by the Senate Armed Services Committee had identified serious asymmetries between the United States and the Soviet Union with regard to strategic and tactical nuclear forces, along with ground and naval forces. The report concluded that "U.S. budgetary projections point to a bleak picture when related to pressing U.S. problems" in force levels and force quality.[54] Shortly after this report was released, the Central Intelligence Agency (CIA) made public its analysis of U.S. and Soviet defense spending. According to the CIA, the Soviets had moved ahead of the United States in 1971, and by 1975, the Soviet defense spending advantage was estimated to have grown to 40 percent.[55] The disparity for strategic forces was even greater, with the CIA assessing the Soviet advantage at 9 to 1.

The Carter administration came to a roughly similar conclusion. In 1979, Secretary of Defense Harold Brown conceded that Soviet defense spending was 25 to 45 percent higher than that of the United States.[56] This was especially troublesome, Brown stated, since "relative defense spending, annual or cumulative, is the best single crude measure of relative military capabili-

51. *Congressional Quarterly Weekly Report* 35 (April 30, 1977): 776–77.

52. *Budget of the United States Government, Fiscal Year 1989* (Washington, D.C.: Government Printing Office, 1988), 68.

53. *Budget of the United States Government, Fiscal Year 1989*, 68.

54. U.S. Senate, Committee on Armed Services, *United States/Soviet Military Balance: A Frame of Reference for Congress* (Washington, D.C.: Government Printing Office, 1976), 32.

55. Central Intelligence Agency, *A Dollar Comparison of Soviet and U.S. Defense Activities, 1965–1975* (Washington, D.C.: CIA, 1976), 2, 5.

56. *Department of Defense Annual Report, Fiscal Year 1980* (Washington, D.C.: Government Printing Office, 1979), 5.

ties."[57] The obvious problem was that the budget increases being proposed by the administration did not materially reduce the Soviet edge.

Nevertheless, efforts to boost defense funding split congressional Democrats, particularly in the House, and President Carter's tentative embrace of his own defense program did nothing to encourage his supporters. On September 18, 1979, the Senate adopted a budget resolution calling for 5 percent annual increases in defense budgets for fiscal years 1981 and 1982. The administration opposed this commitment as too costly but then failed to garner support for its preferred 3 percent figure in the House. Before Congress could act on its final budget resolution, however, U.S. embassy personnel in Teheran were seized by the Iranian government, and the criticism over U.S. military capabilities and funding rose to new heights. Several weeks after the Iranian debacle, President Carter announced that a 5.6 percent real increase would be recommended for the FY 1981 defense budget, with similarly large additions programmed through 1985. Then, on December 27, 1979, the Soviet Union invaded Afghanistan, dooming Carter's already unpopular Strategic Arms Limitation Treaty (SALT II) in the Senate and raising the stakes once again on defense budget increases.

The administration's FY 1981 budget acknowledged that "large increase in Soviet defense capability" had made it "essential" to upgrade U.S. strategic and conventional forces, but pledged that the president's new defense program "exceeds that objective."[58] Two months later, the administration agreed to revise its budget proposals and to raise its defense spending levels once again. At this point, even the House had moved ahead of the administration in supporting a comprehensive and costly military buildup.

The 1976 Democratic platform had attacked Presidents Nixon and Ford for their "undue emphasis on the overall size of the defense budget as the primary measure of . . . the proficiency of our armed forces."[59] The 1980 Democratic platform denounced "the Nixon-Ford Administration" for the "steady decline of 33 percent in real U.S. military spending between 1968 and 1976."[60] The responsibility for that decline clearly rested with congressional Democrats, but antidefense sentiments continued to have real potency

57. *Department of Defense Annual Report, Fiscal Year 1980*, 5.

58. *Budget of the United States Government, Fiscal Year 1981* (Washington, D.C.: Government Printing Office, 1980), 90.

59. *Congressional Quarterly Almanac, 1976*, 868.

60. *Congressional Quarterly Almanac, 1980* (Washington, D.C: Congressional Quarterly, 1981), 114-B.

within the party throughout Carter's presidency. To accommodate these sentiments, Carter could not assign a higher priority to defense than to domestic programs. Over the FY 1977–80 period, real defense spending increased by about 7 percent. The growth in real spending for discretionary domestic programs was more than 12 percent.

The absence of decisive leadership on discretionary spending typified the budget policy frustrations of the Carter era. The administration had quickly recognized that large defense cuts were simply not feasible, but the defense funding program it then advanced was too limited to remedy the shortfalls that were compromising U.S. military capabilities. In 1977, Carter strongly recommended large increases in discretionary domestic programs. Then in 1979, the Carter budget called for real cuts in many of these programs. Carter's pro-defense critics found his defense policy leadership timid and ineffective. His liberal foes complained that he had abandoned the party's domestic agenda. In his refusal to make clear-cut choices on discretionary spending priorities, Carter wound up satisfying neither the conservative nor liberal factions in his party, and his record on social welfare proved to be similarly feckless.

Social Welfare Stalemate. The overriding social welfare goal of the Carter administration was to correct the growing imbalance between aid to the elderly and aid to the poor. National health insurance and a guaranteed income program were the most important elements in what was expected to be a comprehensive overhaul and expansion of assistance programs, but both initiatives failed to break the liberal-conservative deadlock on welfare reform. National health insurance became inextricably, and fatally, intertwined with healthcare cost controls that Carter proposed to Congress on April 25, 1977. On August 6, the administration's "Program for Better Jobs and Income" was unveiled and was instantly attacked for its costs and philosophy.

By the mid-1970s, healthcare cost inflation had become a serious problem for the federal government and also for the states. Medical costs were growing at an annual rate of 15 percent, much higher than general price inflation, and the expanding beneficiary population for Medicare was driving up costs as well.[61] When Carter took office, the federal government was paying nearly one-third of the nation's healthcare bills, and the states were picking up a growing share as a result of Medicaid's expansion.[62] According

61. *Congress and the Nation, 1977–1980* (Washington, D.C.: Congressional Quarterly, 1981), 601.
62. *Congress and the Nation, 1977–1980,* 604.

to Carter, "The cost of [health] care is rising so rapidly it jeopardizes our health goals and our other important social objectives."[63] Carter's first cost-control initiative, which was presented as a prerequisite for national health insurance, was limited to hospital costs, but the ninety-fifth Congress refused to impose cost regulation or other controls on public and private hospitals. In 1979, the administration introduced a scaled-down version of its original bill, but it too failed.

Under pressure from organized labor and prominent congressional liberals, most notably Senator Edward M. Kennedy, Carter retreated from his demand that Congress act on cost controls before considering national health insurance. On May 14, 1979, Kennedy introduced his labor-backed Health Care for All Americans Act, a mandatory and comprehensive health insurance scheme. One month later, the president unveiled his proposal, a limited, first-phase plan to provide catastrophic coverage. Estimated first-year costs were substantial—$29 billion in new federal spending for Kennedy's proposal and $18 billion for the catastrophic coverage alternative.[64] In addition to new federal funding, employers were required to fund most of the premium costs for their employees' insurance. Employer expenses under Kennedy's bill were projected at $11 billion during the first year, nearly double the premium expenditures for the Carter plan.

The huge costs associated with comprehensive national health insurance quickly doomed the Kennedy bill in Congress, but labor and other interest groups that had worked with Kennedy decided to oppose catastrophic coverage, even when it stood as the only option. Kennedy, who had attacked Carter's early insistence on cost controls as a "failure of leadership," criticized the administration's 1979 plan as too limited, potentially too expensive, and a perpetuation of the nation's "separate and unequal" healthcare system.[65] The Kennedy-Carter split helped to extinguish whatever unity Democrats might have had on healthcare reform, and, by 1980, the party's number one legislative priority was still mired in committee.

This all-or-nothing approach on the part of congressional liberals carried over to welfare reform, although here conservatives were even more eager to

63. *Congress and the Nation, 1977–1980*, 605.
64. *Congress and the Nation, 1977–1980*, 637.
65. *Congressional Quarterly Almanac, 1978* (Washington, D.C.: Congressional Quarterly, 1979), 630; *Congressional Quarterly Almanac, 1979* (Washington, D.C.: Congressional Quarterly, 1980), 540.

bury the Carter administration's "Program for Better Jobs and Income."[66] Formally announced on August 6, 1977, this proposal included a basic cash benefit for those unable to work (the aged, blind, disabled, and parents with young children) and a second, or lower-tier, benefit for the working poor. These new cash benefits, which ranged from $2,500 to $4,200 in 1978 dollars, were to replace AFDC, food stamps, and SSI. Other parts of the proposal included funding for 1.4 million public service jobs and reductions in the non-federal governmental share of public assistance costs. According to administration spokesmen, the welfare initiative would increase the number of persons receiving aid to 32 million—compared with 30 million for one or more of the various programs the new welfare system would replace. While Carter had originally promised that welfare reform would have "no higher initial cost than the present system," the $31.1 billion program he submitted to Congress contained nearly $6 billion in new spending.[67] Even this cost estimate was viewed skeptically, since it did not include Medicaid coverage for the expanded beneficiary population. Moreover, the administration's calculations assumed a variety of program savings, on both the spending and revenue sides of the budget, which were highly problematical.

The highly touted welfare reform proposal of 1977 failed to pass either the House or Senate. A much smaller plan was introduced in 1979 and managed to get through the House, but the bill stalled in the Senate Finance Committee. The cost issue was a major obstacle, since programs such as Medicaid, food stamps, and SSI were already soaring under the impact of high inflation and high unemployment. Faced with much larger beneficiary populations and high outlay growth in the indexed programs, legislators were loath to raise cash benefits at all. With Congress and the states refusing to adjust AFDC benefit levels, the real value of those benefits dropped significantly during the late 1970s. Under such unfavorable economic and political conditions, there was little support for a guaranteed income plan or, indeed, for any enlargement of the federal government's commitment to the poor.

For Social Security and Medicare, the political conditions were quite different, and the congressional response more generous. Faced with deficits in the retirement and disability trust funds, Congress did not even consider

---

66. *Congressional Quarterly Almanac, 1977* (Washington, D.C.: Congressional Quarterly, 1977), 471–78.

67. This total includes $2.8 billion in additional costs and $3 billion in expanded earned-income tax credits. *Congressional Quarterly Almanac, 1977,* 474.

slowing the rate of growth in future benefits. Instead, Social Security taxes were substantially raised in 1977. The tax rate and tax base were increased well above the scheduled adjustments set by previously enacted Social Security laws. By 1987, the new payroll tax rates were scheduled to reach 7.15 percent (compared with 5.85 percent in 1977), and the wage base, which was $16,500 in 1977, was to be more than $42,000. The ten-year revenue effect of the bill was $227 billion, making it at that point the largest peacetime tax increase in history.[68] Along with higher taxes, Congress approved several benefit extensions that the administration had argued were too costly. Among these were lessened penalties for retirees who continued to work and strengthened eligibility protections for widowed and divorced beneficiaries. Congress did reject other benefit extensions and finally "decoupled" the Social Security benefit formula, but the magnitude of the 1977 tax increase demonstrated that Congress was determined to protect the existing Social Security benefit system.

Despite even more serious spending control problems associated with Medicare benefits, Congress took no action on proposals that would in any way curtail benefits. Legislation was approved in 1977 that increased the penalties for fraud and abuse in the Medicare and Medicaid programs, but Congress refused to limit payments for legitimate charges by hospitals or healthcare providers. As part of reconciliation legislation passed in 1980, Congress altered Medicare payment schedules and strengthened program administration, but the expected savings from these changes were minor. Moreover, Congress included new benefits, primarily for medical services received in beneficiaries' homes and in physicians' offices and clinics, as part of this legislation. The only Medicare restriction of note during this period was a 1977 decision by the Department of Health, Education and Welfare (HEW) to require Medicare recipients to pay a greater share of their hospital costs. This adjustment, which HEW was authorized to make under existing law, was intended to force Congress to take action on hospital cost controls, but Congress failed to approve any restrictions on Medicare or on Medicaid and other federally subsidized health programs.

The Carter administration's ambitious goals for reforming and redirecting social welfare policy were not achieved. Instead, programmatic trends that had taken hold under Nixon and Ford became even more pronounced. Plans for substituting more generous cash assistance for in-kind benefits

68. *Congress and the Nation, 1977–1980*, 235.

were rejected by Congress, and the Medicaid, food stamp, and housing pro-grams actually became larger relative to cash programs.[69] National health insurance, in both the comprehensive and scaled-down versions, never came close to passage, nor was substantial progress made in regulating federal healthcare costs in existing programs. Perhaps most surprising, given the Democratic critiques of the Nixon-Ford period, the gap between federal assistance for the elderly and for the poor did not narrow. Instead, Social Security and Medicare spending went up much more rapidly than did entitle-ments for the poor. From 1977 to 1981, the GDP share for Social Security and Medicare grew from 5.3 to 5.8 percent.[70] The accompanying rise in all means-tested entitlements was almost nonexistent—from 1.7 to 1.8 percent. Since means-tested entitlements had climbed from 0.9 percent of GDP to 1.7 percent under eight years of Republican administration, the Carter record was particularly unimpressive. It was also increasingly apparent that Congress was much more sensitive to cost issues when programs for the poor, rather than the elderly, were under scrutiny.

Tax Cuts and Tax Reform. The Carter presidency began with a $32 billion economic stimulus plan, a major portion of which was dedicated to one-time tax rebates for taxpayers and their dependents and to equivalent payments for Social Security recipients and other recipients of federal aid. The rebate plan was withdrawn after a lukewarm endorsement by the House, and the 1977 Tax Reduction and Simplification Act that Congress passed bore little resemblance to the initial plan proposed by Carter. The measure extended a number of temporary individual and business tax cuts from 1975 and perma-nently raised the standard deduction for individual taxpayers. The tax-cutting message was blurred, however, by the much larger Social Security tax increase that was passed later in the year.[71]

The most significant tax bill during Carter's presidency was the 1978 Revenue Act, and this measure was distinctly at odds with both Carter's rec-ommendations and conventional Democratic tax philosophy. The Carter tax program, which was aimed at offsetting some of the rising Social Security and income tax burdens affecting individuals and businesses, included a 2 percentage point reduction in marginal rate brackets, new individual tax credits, and a permanent, more flexible, investment tax credit for corpora-

---

69. Ippolito, *Uncertain Legacies,* 179–80.

70. Congressional Budget Office, *The Budget and Economic Outlook: Fiscal Years 2002–2011,* 151.

71. The 1977 tax cut had an estimated cost of less than $35 billion over three years. The Social Security tax increase was estimated at more than $225 billion over ten years.

tions and small businesses. Carter also called for changes in the tax treatment of capital gains, fringe benefits, and itemized deductions that would compensate for a portion of these revenue losses and would, he argued, fulfill his pledge to make the tax system more progressive.[72] As Congress moved toward a larger tax cut than Carter had requested, the prospects for progressive reform steadily dwindled. The House Ways and Means Committee, which suspended its markup for three months in a failed attempt to negotiate a compromise with the White House, reported out a bipartisan initiative that shifted tax relief to middle- and upper-income taxpayers. One of the major provisions in the Ways and Means bill, and the sharpest rebuff to Carter, was a reduction in maximum capital gains tax rates from 49 to 35 percent. This reduction was modified in conference, but the bill that Congress approved, and Carter reluctantly signed, contained an increase in the capital gains exclusion that distributed more than 80 percent of estimated tax benefits to upper-income taxpayers.[73] The individual income tax cuts in the final bill were, with few exceptions, approximately proportional for all income groups, with an average reduction of 7.2 percent.[74]

The Democratic party's internal divisions over tax policy continued to surface for the remainder of Carter's tenure. In September 1978, Congress blocked the Treasury Department from issuing new regulations on the taxation of fringe benefits. The Treasury Department had, for a number of years, considered changes in its definition of taxable income to make more employee benefits subject to taxation. Congress had forced the department to withdraw proposed new rules in 1976, and it imposed a two-year ban in 1978. A 1979 windfall profits tax, which was passed in response to oil price deregulation, weakened an inheritance tax rule that had been one of the featured Democratic reforms in the 1976 tax bill. In 1980, Congress enacted several minor tax bills, including a phaseout of the use of tax-free state and local bonds to subsidize home mortgages, but no agreement could be reached on the size and distribution of an election-year tax cut.

A Decade of Confusion

The course of budget policy during the 1970s was replete with contradictions. The congressional budget reforms of 1974, for example, were hailed

---

72. *Congress and the Nation, 1977–1980,* 239.
73. *Congress and the Nation, 1977–1980,* 244.
74. *Congress and the Nation, 1977–1980,* 242.

as major improvements in coordinating spending and revenue decisions and in establishing a coherent congressional position on fiscal policy and budget priorities. The 1974 reforms were designed to be "policy neutral" but were not institutionally neutral.[75] Their purpose was to add "a new and comprehensive budgetary framework to the existing [congressional] decisionmaking process" so that Congress could compete more effectively with the president in directing budget policy.[76] During the Ford presidency, the predictable result of congressional budgeting was to sharpen partisan and ideological differences over spending policy and deficit control. Congress prevailed on most of the important budget policy conflicts with the Ford administration, in no small measure because of the large Democratic majorities that controlled the House and Senate after 1974. These triumphs, however, were soon overshadowed by some unpleasant and unanticipated policy results.

The social welfare expansions during and after Vietnam had increased the sensitivity of the budget to cyclical movements in the economy. When economic growth slowed in the 1970s, precipitated in part by explosive increases in oil prices, budgets moved into deficit. Social welfare commitments could not be easily or quickly changed, while demographic and economic forces, such as inflation, were pushing spending higher and higher. Neither these social welfare expansions, nor the economic slowdown and resulting deficit-control problems, were unique to the United States. Similar patterns had emerged in other industrialized democracies.

In the United States, however, there were some unusual complications. The balanced-budget tradition was still alive, in Congress and in the public's mind, making deficit spending politically hazardous. The expanded welfare system in the United States was still less comprehensive and less generous than systems in Western Europe, with the unavailability of national health insurance an especially glaring deficiency for social welfare proponents. At the same time, the United States had to maintain a military with global war capabilities and to respond to an aggressive and destabilizing Soviet military buildup.

These complications overwhelmed the Carter administration and Congress, with the result that budget policy trends in the late 1970s frustrated

75. As one leading study concluded, the congressional reforms had put in place "a process that is neutral on its face. It can be deployed in favor of higher or lower spending, bigger or smaller deficits. Its effects on budget outcomes will depend on congressional preferences rather than on procedural limitations." Allen Schick, *Congress and Money* (Washington, D.C.: Urban Institute, 1980), 73.

76. See Ippolito, *Uncertain Legacies*, 18.

the Democratic party's agenda. The level of total spending under Carter was unusually high, averaging well above 20 percent of GDP annually, but these spending levels could not accommodate the new programs that the party had long championed. Instead, Social Security and Medicare helped to push the costs of existing entitlements steadily upward, but neither the administration nor Congress was willing to consider reductions or targeting of benefits for the elderly. With the largest and fastest-growing entitlements effectively cordoned off, public assistance for the poor could not be expanded. The level of social welfare spending rose during the Carter years, but the rate of growth under Nixon and Ford had actually been much greater (Table 6.4). In addition, the disparity between means-tested entitlements and non-means-tested entitlements widened during the late 1970s, as did the gap between in-kind benefits for the poor, particularly Medicaid and food stamps, and cash assistance. This latter trend was precisely the opposite of what welfare reformers had envisioned when Carter took office.

The discretionary portion of the budget yielded additional frustrations. Democrats had hoped that defense cuts would supply the funding for new discretionary domestic programs. When these hopes evaporated, Democrats were unable to raise discretionary spending levels because social welfare costs were rising so rapidly. The liberal-conservative standoff in Congress and the absence of clear direction from the executive branch under Carter left the size and composition of discretionary spending essentially unchanged (Table 6.5). This result satisfied neither the pro-defense nor the domestic reform blocs in Congress.

Revenue trends during the 1970s were equally devoid of clear direction and satisfactory results. Congress repeatedly cut individual income taxes, but tax burdens still became greater for large numbers of taxpayers. Inflation-induced "bracket creep" was pushing taxpayers into higher marginal rate brackets, the declining real value of personal exemptions was raising the relative burden on taxpayers with dependents, and payroll tax increases for Social Security were large for virtually all income groups.[77] From 1970 to 1981, individual income taxes and payroll taxes grew much faster than personal income.[78] In FY 1981, individual income taxes were 9.3 percent of GDP, the highest level since World War II, while social insurance taxes had climbed to 6.0 percent.[79]

77. See Steuerle, *The Tax Decade*, 21–24.
78. Ippolito, *Uncertain Legacies*, 53.
79. *Historical Tables, Budget of the United States Government, Fiscal Year 2002*, 33.

Table 6.4 Entitlements and Mandatory Spending, 1969–1981 (as a percentage of GDP)

Fiscal Year	Means-Tested Programs			Non-Means-Tested Programs			
	Medicaid	Other	Total Means-Tested	Social Security and Medicare	Other Retirement and Disability	Other	Total Non-Means-Tested
1969	0.2%	0.7%	0.9%	3.5%	0.6%	1.8%	5.9%
1970	0.3	0.7	1.0	3.6	0.7	2.0	6.2
1971	0.3	0.9	1.2	3.9	0.8	2.1	6.8
1972	0.4	1.0	1.4	4.0	0.8	2.2	7.2
1973	0.4	0.9	1.2	4.4	0.9	2.4	7.6
1974	0.4	0.9	1.4	4.5	1.0	2.3	7.7
1975	0.4	1.2	1.6	5.0	1.2	3.0	9.2
1976	0.5	1.3	1.7	5.2	1.1	3.0	9.2
1977	0.5	1.2	1.7	5.3	1.1	2.3	8.6
1978	0.5	1.1	1.6	5.3	1.1	2.4	8.7
1979	0.5	1.1	1.6	5.2	1.1	1.9	8.3
1980	0.5	1.2	1.7	5.5	1.2	2.3	9.0
1981	0.6	1.2	1.8	5.8	1.2	2.3	9.3

SOURCE: Congressional Budget Office, *The Budget and Economic Outlook: Fiscal Years 2002–2011* (Washington, D.C.: CBO, 2001), 151.

High inflation, large payroll tax increases, and structural tax changes also adversely affected the progressivity in federal tax burdens. An extraordinary number of new tax preferences were adopted during the 1970s, but these benefits reduced tax burdens most among very low- and very high-income taxpayers.[80] For the vast majority of middle-income taxpayers, new tax preferences were roughly proportional to tax liabilities. The net effect of proliferating tax preferences, then, was to lessen progressivity in individual income taxation.

Revenue levels in the late 1970s were extremely high, as were the tax burdens on individuals, but the budget was still in deficit. In 1980, the Carter administration's election-year budget program promised an end to deficits in three years, but the road to a balanced budget was politically treacherous. The Carter plan proposed to balance the budget at about 23 percent of GNP, a revenue level that had not been reached even during World War II.[81] To attain that goal, revenues would have to grow at an annual rate

80. Witte, *The Politics and Development of the Federal Income Tax*, 305–6.
81. Ippolito, *Uncertain Legacies*, 55.

Table 6.5 Discretionary Spending, 1969–1981 (as a percentage of GDP)

Fiscal Year	Defense	Domestic	International	Total
1969	8.7%	3.2%	0.4%	12.4%
1970	8.1	3.4	0.4	11.9
1971	7.3	3.7	0.3	11.3
1972	6.7	3.8	0.4	10.9
1973	5.9	3.7	0.4	10.0
1974	5.6	3.6	0.4	9.6
1975	5.6	4.0	0.5	10.1
1976	5.2	4.5	0.4	10.1
1977	4.9	4.6	0.4	10.0
1978	4.7	4.8	0.4	9.9
1979	4.7	4.6	0.4	9.6
1980	4.9	4.7	0.5	10.1
1981	5.2	4.5	0.4	10.1

SOURCE: *Historical Tables, Budget of the United States Government, Fiscal Year 2002* (Washington, D.C.: Government Printing Office, 2001), 126.

of nearly 20 percent, with individual income taxes and Social Security taxes growing even faster. The administration and the Democratic leadership in Congress were uneasy about this strategy, but their opposition to domestic spending retrenchments left them with an unpalatable choice between high deficits or high taxes.

The Reagan "Retrenchment"

Ronald Reagan, like his predecessor, pledged to balance the budget, but the fiscal path he proposed was very different. In March 1981, the Reagan administration presented a budget program to Congress that called for large tax cuts, defense spending increases, and domestic spending reductions.[82] The contrasts between the Carter and Reagan budgets were striking. Reagan's "balanced budget" was nearly 3 percent of GNP smaller than Carter's—its 1984 goal was to match outlays and revenues at 19.3 percent of GNP—and the defense share of Reagan's budget was more than one-third of total outlays.[83]

The Reagan program called for large cutbacks in many discretionary domestic programs and sharply decelerated rates of growth in social welfare

82. *Fiscal Year 1982 Budget Revisions* (Washington, D.C.: Government Printing Office, 1981).
83. *Fiscal Year 1982 Budget Revisions*, 6, 125.

entitlements. The spending criteria proposed for the latter targeted entitlement policies rooted in the Great Society expansion.

> The first criterion is the preservation of the social safety net . . . those programs, mostly begun in the 1930's, that now constitute an agreed-upon core of protection for the elderly, the unemployed, and the poor, and those programs that fulfill our basic commitment to the people who fought for this country in times of war.
>
> The second criterion is . . . to eliminate unintended benefits . . . [from] newer Federal entitlement programs and related income security programs that have undergone rapid growth during the last 20 years. The criterion also applies to certain aspects of social safety net programs that have been added unnecessarily or have grown excessively.
>
> The third criterion is the reduction of benefits for people with middle to upper incomes. . . . This criterion directly challenges the drift toward the universalization of social benefit programs.[84]

The spending priorities, and principles, of the Reagan administration were controversial from the outset, and the record of success was mixed. On defense spending, Reagan generally prevailed, substantially boosting defense budget shares and GDP ratios. Reagan's 1981 Economic Recovery Tax Act was, at the time, the largest tax cut in history, with $750 billion in individual and corporation tax reductions for FY 1981–86. The Omnibus Budget Reconciliation Act of 1981 that the administration engineered narrowed eligibility and reduced benefits for all of the major public assistance programs and laid the philosophical groundwork for work requirements and other welfare restrictions that would be hotly debated but ultimately adopted over the next two decades. The "universalization of social benefit programs," however, became even more entrenched during the Reagan presidency. Congress refused to consider major cutbacks in Social Security and Medicare, approving instead a large Social Security tax increase in 1983 to preserve existing benefits. With non-means-tested entitlements largely immune to budget-reduction efforts, the level of total spending remained unusually high during Reagan's tenure, and the imbalance between spending and revenues soared.

84. *Fiscal Year 1982 Budget Revisions*, 8–9.

Table 6.6 Discretionary Spending, 1981–1989 (as a percentage of GDP)

Fiscal Year	Defense	Domestic	International	Total
1981	5.2%	4.5%	0.4%	10.1%
1982	5.8	3.9	0.4	10.1
1983	6.1	3.8	0.4	10.3
1984	5.9	3.5	0.4	9.9
1985	6.1	3.5	0.4	10.1
1986	6.2	3.3	0.4	10.0
1987	6.1	3.2	0.3	9.6
1988	5.8	3.1	0.3	9.3
1989	5.6	3.1	0.3	9.0

SOURCE: *Historical Tables, Budget of the United States Government, Fiscal Year 2002* (Washington, D.C.: Government Printing Office, 2001), 126.

Reordering Discretionary Spending

The most important Reagan victories on spending policy were achieved within the discretionary portion of the budget. The GDP share of discretionary outlays continued its long-term decline, but this decline was entirely at the expense of domestic programs (Table 6.6). For defense, each of the relevant indexes—GDP shares, real outlays, budget shares—moved sharply upward. Real defense spending during the 1980s was raised to levels comparable to Korean and Vietnam wartime peaks, thereby erasing the cutbacks of the preceding decade. By the end of Reagan's presidency, the domestic discretionary budget and GDP shares were at pre–Great Society levels.

The Defense Buildup. The Ford and Carter administrations did manage to halt what had been a precipitous fall in real defense spending, but upward adjustments in their defense budgets were marginal. Under Reagan, however, real growth in defense was immediate and substantial. During Reagan's first two years, real defense outlays went up nearly 20 percent. While growth rates then slowed, the overall increase for Reagan's two terms was close to 50 percent.

Several aspects of the Reagan defense program were noteworthy in terms of budget policy. First, the administration's focus on the size of the defense budget was a marked departure in presidential defense policy. Reagan's defense planners set out to close the "dollar gap" between U.S. and Soviet military spending, to do so as quickly as possible, and to ensure that "investment spending"—procurement, research and development, and military construction—would be sustained over time.[85] Reagan's first Secretary of Defense, Casper W. Weinberger, later explained that there had been no time for "a lengthy conceptual debate" in 1981.[86] Rather, "the overriding priority" had been "to restore military parity with the Soviet Union." That parity was contingent on investing "roughly as much in our defenses as our primary competitor invests in its forces."[87]

Second, Reagan continued virtually all of the conventional and strategic weapons programs from the Carter years but greatly accelerated development and procurement schedules. The Reagan program also embraced significantly higher force levels. The shipbuilding goal for the Navy called for a six hundred-ship fleet, with the procurement rate in the Defense Department's fiscal year 1983–87 submission 50 percent higher than the Carter naval plan.[88] Carter had called for less reliance on large aircraft carriers and extremely expensive carrier battle groups; Reagan proposed construction of two large-deck carriers and an increase to fifteen deployable carrier groups. A similar preference for more, and costlier, weapons systems was to be found in Army and Air Force procurement planning.

There were, of course, some important policy changes under Reagan. The Carter administration's cancellation of the B-1 strategic bomber program was reversed. Reagan persuaded Congress to fund development of an upgraded B-1B version and then to authorize procurement of a full complement of B-1Bs. In 1983, Reagan announced the Strategic Defense Initiative, which had enormously significant implications for deterrence policy and for defense funding. Within the defense budget, moreover, strategic force modernization was a much higher priority for Reagan than it had been for Carter. Overall, however, there was a great deal of continuity in weapons system development and procurement between their administrations. What the Reagan program provided was a level of budgetary support that Carter had been unwilling to commit.

Third, deliberate efforts were undertaken to protect the defense budget against the possible erosion of congressional support. The administration sought from the outset to lock in long-term budget authority commitments for investment accounts that would drive budget growth in future years.

---

85. Ippolito, *Uncertain Legacies*, 136–37.
86. *Annual Report to the Congress, Fiscal Year 1987* (Washington, D.C.: Department of Defense, 1986), 13.
87. *Annual Report to the Congress, Fiscal Year 1987*, 18.
88. Ippolito, *Uncertain Legacies*, 139.

This budget strategy proved to be prescient. After the FY 1983 budget cycle, Congress became increasingly wary of the administration's escalating defense requests. Large cuts in these requests soon became routine, with enacted budget authority for FY 1983–86 averaging $20 billion per year less than Reagan's requests and outlay differentials only slightly smaller.[89] During Reagan's second term, congressional concerns about deficits and domestic funding needs heightened disagreements over the size and growth of the defense budget. With congressional cuts becoming larger and larger, the administration reluctantly scaled down its modernization initiatives. The FY 1989 defense plan included force structure cutbacks and weapons system cancellations, with the Pentagon warning: "Resource constraints have forced us to accept increased risks to our security and a smaller force structure as we strive to preserve required levels of readiness and sustainability."[90]

Nevertheless, defense budget growth during Reagan's presidency was impressive. Real growth slowed after 1983, but constant-dollar defense spending still climbed to more than $370 billion in FY 1989, the highest level in more than twenty years (Table 6.7). Moreover, Reagan's goal of matching Soviet military spending was reached. A 1988 Department of Defense report concluded: "In 1987, as a result of the continued growth of U.S. outlays, primarily for procurement, the annual difference in the cost of the [Soviet and U.S.] military programs was virtually eliminated."[91]

Domestic Tradeoffs. The Reagan administration's budgets and philosophy called for dismantling a substantial portion of the domestic programmatic framework it inherited. Some programs were slated for termination, others for greatly reduced funding, and still others for devolution to the states. In addition, the New Federalism proposal of 1982 called for a broad transfer of spending and tax resources to the states. While Congress rejected most of Reagan's recommendations for program terminations and never seriously contemplated full-scale programmatic devolution, domestic spending proved vulnerable to the administration's attacks.

The first, and most successful, of Reagan's efforts to retrench domestic programs was the Omnibus Budget Reconciliation Act of 1981, which terminated public service jobs programs under the 1973 Comprehensive Employment

89. Ippolito, *Uncertain Legacies,* 143.

90. *Annual Report to the Congress, Secretary of Defense, Fiscal Year 1989* (Washington, D.C.: Government Printing Office, 1988), 15.

91. Department of Defense, *Soviet Military Power: An Assessment of the Threat, 1988* (Washington, D.C.: Government Printing Office, 1988), 32.

Table 6.7 Defense Outlays, 1981–1989 (in billions of dollars)

Fiscal Year	Current Dollars	Constant Dollars (FY 1996)
1981	$ 158.0	$ 260.1
1982	185.9	283.2
1983	209.9	305.0
1984	228.0	310.1
1985	253.1	331.0
1986	273.8	354.2
1987	282.5	361.1
1988	290.9	365.2
1989	304.0	370.3
Average Annual Percentage Increase	8.6%	4.6%

SOURCE: *Historical Tables, Budget of the United States Government, Fiscal Year 2002* (Washington, D.C.: Government Printing Office, 2001), 123–24.

and Training Act; sharply reduced funding for economic development, transportation subsidy, and housing construction programs; and consolidated numerous health and education programs into block grants. Although the administration's reform proposals were more encompassing than the legislation that Congress finally approved, the reconciliation initiative of 1981 was hailed even by Reagan's critics as "clearly the most monumental and historic turnaround in fiscal policy that has ever occurred."[92]

Congress did not, in later years, accept similarly comprehensive cutbacks in domestic programs, but the authorization and appropriations processes that determined discretionary domestic spending provided Reagan with multiple opportunities to go after individual programs. For example, Reagan did not succeed in abolishing the Department of Energy, but he managed to curtail the alternative energy supply programs and regulatory initiatives that the previous administration had championed. Funding constraints were equally effective in reducing the federal role in non-capital investment domestic grant-in-aid programs. After blocking congressional efforts to increase authorizations for revenue-sharing aid to local governments, the administration finally succeeded in phasing out the $4 billion program in 1986.

The domestic program area that proved to be most resistant to Reagan's ideological and budgetary redirection was agriculture. Initial hopes that fed-

92. *Congressional Quarterly Almanac, 1981* (Washington, D.C.: Congressional Quarterly, 1982), 256.

eral intervention in the agricultural sector could be greatly diminished proved illusory. A deteriorating agricultural economy in the early and mid-1980s made it politically impossible to change the credit and subsidy programs that had been in place for many years. The periodic authorizations required to continue these programs allowed for some adjustments in federal supports and controls, but these adjustments were overwhelmed by an unexpectedly weak farm economy. Federal government payments accounted for nearly 25 percent of farm income in 1983 and 1984, almost four times the level under Carter.[93] From 1981 to 1986, agriculture outlays almost tripled, rising to over $31 billion. Over this same period, other domestic program categories grew minimally if at all.

Of particular importance, the Reagan administration's determination that the federal government should and would define its domestic responsibilities much more narrowly effectively foreclosed ambitious new programs. National industrial policy, which had been high on the Democratic party's agenda during the Carter presidency, had no prospects at all under Reagan, and the push for other "national" approaches on domestic issues suffered a similar fate. Finally, the deficits that occurred under Reagan had a disproportionate impact on discretionary domestic programs. With Reagan's strong commitments to defense and tax cuts and Congress's opposition to reductions in entitlements, there was no margin to accommodate new or expanded domestic initiatives.

During the 1960s and 1970s, discretionary domestic programs had prospered, as the Democratic party steadily widened the scope of federal government commitments. Between 1965 and 1980, discretionary domestic outlays increased by over 500 percent; real growth was over 200 percent. The 1980s, however, were very different. During Reagan's two terms, current dollar growth slowed, while real spending actually fell (Table 6.8). The Reagan presidency clearly demonstrated that strong, consistent leadership could have a pronounced impact on the level and composition of discretionary spending.

The Social Welfare Divide

The Reagan administration's March 1981 budget proposals included major policy reductions in the food stamp program and in federal housing assistance, along with lesser changes in other public assistance programs. Despite

93. Ippolito, *Uncertain Legacies*, 222–24.

Table 6.8 Discretionary Domestic Outlays, 1981–1989 (in billions of dollars)

Fiscal Year	Current Dollars	Constant Dollars (FY 1996)
1981	$ 136.3	$ 236.5
1982	127.1	206.6
1983	129.8	202.8
1984	135.1	200.8
1985	145.3	208.4
1986	147.0	204.4
1987	146.5	197.1
1988	157.8	205.5
1989	168.2	212.3
Average Annual Percentage Change	2.8%	−1.2%

SOURCE: *Historical Tables, Budget of the United States Government, Fiscal Year 2002* (Washington, D.C.: Government Printing Office, 2001), 123–24.

strong Democratic criticism, many of the administration's proposals were adopted. Significant Social Security reforms, including penalties for early retirement and less generous benefit formulas, were submitted to Congress on May 12, 1981. These reform proposals, however, met with fierce and immediate congressional opposition. On May 20, House Democrats unanimously approved a resolution condemning the administration's "unconscionable breach of faith" and pledging to protect the Social Security "program [and] a generation of retirees."[94] That same day, the Senate unanimously approved a statement of opposition to the Social Security proposals, with Republican leaders complaining that they had not been adequately consulted. The administration then quickly retreated.

The contrasting fates of these initiatives set the stage for social welfare policy change during the rest of Reagan's presidency. Means-tested entitlements were tightly controlled, and basic reforms, such as work requirements and tightened eligibility, could be put forward with at least a reasonable chance for legislative success. Social Security and Medicare, however, were politically untouchable. Even though the massive 1977 Social Security tax increase had failed to solve the system's funding problems, Congress was not inclined toward serious benefit adjustments.

94. *Congressional Quarterly Almanac, 1981*, 119.

Public Assistance. The initial thrust of the Reagan administration's public assistance policy reductions was to target cash and in-kind benefits on the demonstrably poor. The eligibility adjustments in the 1981 Omnibus Budget and Reconciliation Act, for example, eliminated food stamps and AFDC benefits for large numbers of households with incomes above the official poverty level. An estimated 1.1 million beneficiaries were removed from food stamp rolls by lowering the income standard to 130 percent of the federal poverty level, and nearly 700,000 households lost some or all of their cash benefits in a similar fashion.[95] In addition, the food stamp benefit formula was tightened, as was the program's income measurement and reporting system for beneficiaries. Congress rejected the administration's recommendation for mandatory "workfare" requirements for AFDC but did permit states to establish "community work experience programs."

Congress also refused to reduce Medicaid spending growth by setting a fixed ceiling, or cap, on federal cost-sharing. The administration had called for a 5 percent increase in federal Medicaid spending for the first year of the cap, with subsequent increases tied to the government's official inflation index. Congress approved instead a reduction in payments to the states but waived that reduction for states with high unemployment or with cost-savings programs. These provisions had a modest impact on Medicaid spending for several years, but outlay increases after FY 1984 averaged more than 10 percent annually.[96] Medicaid absorbed a growing share of the total public assistance budget over the FY 1981–89 period, and it was the only major means-tested entitlement that generally outpaced inflation.

In fall 1981, the administration proposed further cutbacks in the food stamp, AFDC, and housing assistance programs and reiterated the necessity for stricter Medicaid controls. Congress rejected additional entitlement reductions and, in 1982, began to ease some of the restrictions approved in 1981. Extended unemployment compensation benefits were partially restored in 1982, AFDC eligibility was broadened in 1984, and food stamp eligibility and benefits were increased in 1985. Congress also dismissed Reagan's 1982 New Federalism Plan that would have converted Medicaid into an entirely federal program in exchange for the states taking over food stamps and AFDC.

For the remainder of Reagan's presidency, attention focused on work requirements for welfare recipients. The initial congressional response to

95. *Congressional Quarterly Almanac, 1981,* 461.
96. *Historical Tables, Budget of the United States Government, Fiscal Year 2002,* 129–30.

Reagan's call for mandatory training and work obligations was unfavorable, but the National Governor's Association endorsed the concept in 1987 as part of a plan for expanding the AFDC-UP (unemployed parent) program nationwide. A bipartisan compromise was then fashioned, with Democratic Senator Daniel P. Moynihan playing a leading role, and the Family Support Act was cleared by Congress on September 30, 1988.[97] This legislation required states to establish job training and employment programs for "employable" AFDC recipients and provided transitional child care and Medicaid benefits for welfare-to-work participants. Work requirements were attached as well to the AFDC-UP program, and an important step was taken with regard to AFDC eligibility for teenage parents. States were permitted to deny benefits to parents under the age of eighteen not living with their parents or other adult relatives and to direct assistance payments for these minors to their parents or adult guardians.

The 1988 welfare reform legislation was more limited than the Reagan administration had hoped, but it still represented a departure from the welfare initiatives of the 1960s and 1970s. By the mid-1980s, there was little support in Congress for a guaranteed income or for substantial expansions in the existing mix of cash and in-kind programs. Instead, concerns about cost and about welfare dependency left the public assistance component of the social welfare budget vulnerable to retrenchment initiatives.

Social Security and Medicare. The Reagan administration managed to incorporate several cost-cutting provisions affecting retirement and healthcare programs into the 1981 reconciliation measure. The semiannual cost-of-living adjustments (COLA) in federal civilian and retirement benefits were replaced by an annual COLA, and the monthly minimum benefit for Social Security recipients was eliminated. For Medicare, premiums and deductibles for Part B–insured medical services were raised, and hospital reimbursement limits were imposed. Congress rejected, however, other elements in the administration's Social Security "reserve plan" and, in December 1981, overwhelmingly voted to restore the minimum benefit provision it had terminated several months earlier.

With no realistic prospect for curbing Social Security benefits, the Reagan administration agreed to establish a bipartisan commission on Social Security and to charge it with finding a politically acceptable solution to the Social Security financing crisis. The fifteen-member National Commission

97. Ippolito, *Uncertain Legacies,* 182–83.

on Social Security Reform was appointed on December 16, 1981, and its report and recommendations were released in January 1983. Congress acted quickly and favorably on these recommendations, and, on April 20, the president signed into law the Social Security Act Amendments of 1983, a package of immediate tax increases and future benefit cuts that was expected to keep the Social Security system solvent for the next several decades.

The 1983 Social Security bill increased payroll taxes for both employers and employees by raising the tax rate on earnings from 6.7 to 7.51 percent by 1988. Higher rates were also imposed on the self-employed. Mandatory Social Security coverage was instituted for all new federal employees and for employees of nonprofit organizations, while state and local governments were no longer permitted to withdraw their employees from the Social Security system. All of these provisions were aimed at infusing more revenues into the Social Security trust funds. On the benefit side, a six-month delay in the 1983 COLA was approved, and Social Security benefits were made taxable for high-income recipients. In addition, Congress agreed to raise the Social Security retirement age to sixty-six (between 2003 and 2009) and then to sixty-seven (between 2021 and 2027). This particular provision was the focus of a fierce battle in the House, but the higher retirement age was finally supported by nearly all House Republicans and a large number of conservative and moderate Democrats. Long-term financing pressures were further eased by early retirement penalties. The option for retirement at age sixty-two was maintained, but the benefit reduction for early retirees was increased to 25 percent by 2009 and 30 percent by 2027.

These 1983 Social Security tax increases quickly restored the solvency of the main Social Security trust fund (OASI). Within several years, the OASI trust fund had repaid its previous borrowings from other trust funds and had begun to accumulate large reserves. With the trust funds secure, Social Security benefits were immune from further budget-cutting efforts. In his 1984 reelection campaign, President Reagan pledged to preserve existing Social Security benefits, and the 1985 Gramm-Rudman-Hollings legislation exempted Social Security from any automatic spending cuts. During Reagan's second term, COLA delays were considered on occasion, but neither the administration nor Congress attempted to revisit the basic compromises agreed to in 1983.

For Medicare, where spending was rising more rapidly than for Social Security, the benefits problem could not be completely ignored. The growing shortfall between premiums and costs in the Medicare Part B supplemental insurance program led Congress to raise premiums in 1981 and 1982, albeit with the limited goal of covering only 25 percent of Part B benefit payments. Congress also began to impose health provider cost controls as a way to reduce overall Medicare spending growth. Hospital reimbursements and physicians' charges were repeatedly curbed during the 1980s, usually through partial freezes on year-to-year cost increases. These efforts helped to lower Medicare spending growth rates, but Part A and Part B program spending still continued to rise sharply, particularly in comparison with the non-healthcare portion of the budget.

The widespread disquiet over Medicare costs had a more decisive impact on proposals for expanded coverage. For a number of years, Congress had debated the addition of catastrophic illness protection to Medicare. In 1988, the administration and Congress agreed to implement this new coverage but required the program to be self-financing. Participants would pay premiums based on their income for coverage, but this experiment in linking benefits and income quickly failed. The new Medicare surtax was so unpopular with elderly citizens that Congress repealed the catastrophic coverage program in 1989. This particular example notwithstanding, Congress remained generally opposed to reducing Medicare benefits or increasing cost sharing by middle- and upper-income retirees.

Revenues and Deficits

There were numerous tax bills during the Reagan presidency, but the two most important measures—the Economic Recovery Tax Act of 1981 and the Tax Reform Act of 1986—made it impossible to match revenues with the high spending levels that remained in place during the 1980s. The administration's 1982 economic report conceded that "a strategy of reducing taxes in advance of spending cuts implies that it will take some time to achieve the desired level of deficits."[98] Nevertheless, tax cuts were "an essential part of a long-term strategy of reducing the scope of the Federal Government."[99]

In fact, the deficits that followed the 1981 tax cut were much larger than anyone had expected, but the Reagan administration rejected major modifications in its tax program. The 1986 tax bill that it steered through Congress

---

98. James Tobin and Murray Weidenbaum, eds., *Two Revolutions in Economic Policy: The First Economic Reports of Presidents Kennedy and Reagan* (Cambridge: Massachusetts Institute of Technology Press, 1988), 420.

99. Tobin and Weidenbaum, *Two Revolutions in Economic Policy*, 420.

was, at best, deficit-neutral, despite deficit levels that had averaged nearly 5 percent of GDP since 1982. In his final budget, Reagan confessed that he was "disappointed" by the failure to control deficits, but he insisted that "higher taxes are not needed . . . [rather] genuine deficit reduction through moderating the growth in spending is essential."[100]

Supply-Side Tax Cuts. The Reagan administration's 1981 tax-cut plan was presented to Congress in February, expanded during several months of negotiations with Congress, and signed into law on August 13. The Economic Recovery Tax Act of 1981 (ERTA) contained an estimated $750 billion in reduced individual and corporate taxes for fiscal years 1981–86.[101] The cost of this tax bill greatly exceeded any previous tax cut, and its central theme was economic growth. Its "historic changes in the structure of taxation" were "expected to lead to a significant long-term rise in the private business capital stock and increases in labor supply."[102] The individual income tax cuts under ERTA included marginal rate reductions of 23 percent over three years for all taxpayers, along with a reduction in the top marginal rate from 70 to 50 percent. As Reagan emphasized, "Unlike some past 'tax reforms,' this is not merely a shift of wealth between different sets of taxpayers . . . [but] an equal reduction in everyone's tax rates."[103] In addition, the 1981 tax bill indexed all income tax brackets, as well as the personal exemption, standard deduction, and zero-bracket amounts, thereby eliminating inflation-driven increases in tax liabilities. On the corporate side, the major changes included liberalized rules on depreciation and write-offs. The reductions in corporate income taxes totaled approximately $150 billion over five years, or about 20 percent of the total revenue loss under ERTA.[104]

The supply-side rationale for the 1981 tax cut assumed that higher rates of economic growth would yield additional revenues, but there was no expectation that revenues could increase sufficiently to balance existing spending. The revenue-GDP levels that the Reagan administration projected through the mid-1980s were more than two percentage points below the level in place in 1981.[105] Reducing the size of future deficits was

---

100. *Budget of the United States Government, Fiscal Year 1990* (Washington, D.C.: Government Printing Office, 1989), 1–5, 1–15.
101. Ippolito, *Uncertain Legacies,* 58.
102. Tobin and Weidenbaum, *Two Revolutions in Economic Policy,* 450.
103. *Weekly Compilation of Presidential Documents* 17 (February 23, 1981): 135.
104. Ippolito, *Uncertain Legacies,* 59.
105. Tobin and Weidenbaum, *Two Revolutions in Economic Policy,* 397.

therefore dependent on lowering spending-GDP levels below 20 percent of GDP.

The extremely large first-term deficits of the Reagan presidency resulted from two factors. First, revenue-GDP levels dropped more sharply than expected as a result of the recession during 1981–82. Second, spending remained very high, averaging more than 22 percent of GDP from 1981 to 1985. As these huge deficits mounted, Congress responded by trimming some of the revenue losses from the 1981 tax cut. The Tax Equity and Fiscal Responsibility Act of 1982, which reversed some of the corporate tax breaks from 1981, boosted estimated revenues by nearly $100 billion for fiscal years 1983–85.[106] The Deficit Reduction Act of 1984, which repealed or narrowed individual and corporation tax preferences, was expected to yield more than $70 billion in additional revenues over five years.[107] The Social Security Amendments of 1983 contained more than $55 billion in Social Security tax increases over the same period.[108] These tax increases and the several minor tax bills enacted during 1982–84 cut the ERTA revenue losses by about one-third.[109] In terms of revenue levels, however, net reductions remained extremely large. And in terms of tax policy, the marginal rate cuts for individuals were preserved, despite the large deficits.

Tax Reform. Reagan's second term produced the most comprehensive structural tax reforms of the modern era, but there was virtually no change in relative tax levels. The Tax Reform Act of 1986 (TRA) produced net revenue losses after its first year, and other tax legislation Reagan signed yielded relatively small increases in tax levels (Table 6.9). The lowest revenue-GDP levels of Reagan's tenure were registered from 1983 to 1986, with an average ratio of slightly more than 17.5 percent.[110] Over the next four years, the annual average was slightly more than 18 percent.

The Reagan administration's commitment to low tax levels was critical to the overall design of the 1986 Tax Reform Act (TRA). The impetus behind structural tax reform began to take shape during 1984, with a comprehensive Treasury Department plan that called for major cutbacks in tax preferences in exchange for greatly reduced top marginal tax rates for individuals and corporations. During the 1984 presidential campaign, the Democratic nom-

106. Ippolito, *Uncertain Legacies*, 67.
107. Ippolito, *Uncertain Legacies*, 74.
108. Ippolito, *Uncertain Legacies*.
109. Ippolito, *Uncertain Legacies*, 73.
110. *Historical Tables, Budget of the United States Government, Fiscal Year 2002*, 24–25.

Table 6.9 Revenue Effects of Major Legislation Enacted During the Reagan Presidency, 1987–1991 (in billions of dollars)

| | Estimated Direct Effect for Fiscal Year | | | | |
	1987	1988	1989	1990	1991
First-Term Tax Legislation					
ERTA 1981	−$241.7	−$260.8	−$285.5	−$315.7	−$350.2
All Other	+ 95.2	+ 111.5	+ 118.7	+ 116.0	+ 122.9
Net Change	−146.5	−149.3	−166.8	−199.7	−227.3
Second-Term Tax Legislation					
TRA 1986	+ 21.5	−4.5	−17.2	−13.5	−9.5
All Other	+ 7.6	+ 20.2	+ 25.6	+ 26.7	+ 25.6
Net Change	+ 29.1	+ 15.7	+ 8.4	+ 13.2	+ 16.1
Total Revenue Effect	−117.4	−133.6	−158.4	−186.5	−211.2

SOURCE: *Budget of the United States Government, Fiscal Year 1989* (Washington, D.C.: Government Printing Office, 1988), 4-4.

inee, Walter Mondale, called for a tax increase, and the party's platform pledged to "cap the effect of the Reagan tax cuts for wealthy Americans and enhance the progressivity of our personal income tax code."[111] The Republican platform rejected the need for increased taxation, promised further reductions in tax rates, and endorsed a "modified flat tax."[112] With Reagan's landslide victory, the administration pressed forward with an even more ambitious reform proposal.

It took seventeen months for Reagan's tax reform package to work its way through Congress. Democrats pressed repeatedly for a tax increase to reduce the high deficits and criticized the distribution of the proposed tax cuts for individuals. Republicans were concerned about shifting tax burdens to corporations to fund the individual tax cuts. Members of both parties were nervous about the proposed cutbacks in tax preferences for both individuals and corporations.

Nevertheless, the Reagan plan ultimately prevailed. The top marginal rate for individuals was cut from 50 to 28 percent, while the top corporate

111. *Congressional Quarterly Almanac, 1984* (Washington, D.C.: Congressional Quarterly, 1985), 78-B.

112. *Congressional Quarterly Almanac, 1984*, 42-B.

rate was scaled back from 46 to 34 percent. The 1986 Tax Reform Act also eliminated or curtailed numerous tax preferences for individuals and corporations. The tradeoff between lower tax rates and a broader tax base, however, worked differently for individual taxpayers and corporations. For individuals, this tradeoff produced a net tax cut. For corporations, the reductions in tax preferences outweighed the effects of lower rates.[113] In addition, TRA nearly doubled the personal exemption and substantially raised the standard deduction, thereby eliminating all income tax liabilities for an estimated 6 million low-income taxpayers.[114] For high-income taxpayers, a phase-out provision for the bottom marginal rate bracket (15 percent) meant a flat tax of 28 percent on all taxable income. And for all individual taxpayers, indexing provisions were applied to personal exemptions, standard deductions, and marginal income brackets.

Passage of TRA marked the end of major tax legislation during the Reagan presidency. Minor tax increases were passed in 1987 and 1988, but these did not alter the tax rates, indexing provisions, or major structural reforms under TRA. The basic elements of Reagan's tax program—lower revenue-GDP levels and structural tax reforms to promote economic growth—continued in place despite extremely high deficits. The traditional subordination of tax policy to spending and deficit-control requirements was reversed under Reagan, as tax cuts were employed, albeit unsuccessfully, to press for "smaller government."

Gramm-Rudman-Hollings. During 1985, Congress and the administration attempted to negotiate a deficit-reduction agreement, with the Senate Republican leadership taking the lead on a comprehensive package of entitlement and defense cuts and a tax increase. The Senate Republican plan included reductions in scheduled benefit increases for federal retirement programs, including Social Security, a partial freeze for defense spending, and a three-year, $60 billion tax increase. When Reagan met with House and Senate leaders during July, he rejected the defense cuts and tax increase, and House Democrats refused to support the entitlement cutbacks. A second Senate initiative to combine spending cuts and tax increases was also rejected by Reagan.

This impasse over deficit reduction led to the enactment of a fallback measure intended to force the president and Congress to reach future agree-

113. Ippolito, *Uncertain Legacies*, 83.
114. Ippolito, *Uncertain Legacies*, 78.

ments by threatening automatic cuts in spending to bring the budget into balance. The Gramm-Rudman-Hollings (GRH) bill was introduced on September 25 and, after protracted conference committee negotiations, passed by both chambers on December 11. The following day, Reagan signed the Balanced Budget and Emergency Deficit Control Act of 1985 into law.

Under GRH, the president and Congress were required to comply with deficit ceilings during each year's budget process, beginning with a $172 billion limit in FY 1986 and with successively lower ceilings until the budget was balanced in FY 1991. Failure to comply would lead to "sequestration"— automatic spending cuts to meet the deficit ceiling. These automatic spending cuts, however, were largely restricted to discretionary programs. Social Security and most means-tested entitlements were entirely exempt from sequestration, while Medicare was partially exempt. For discretionary programs, automatic cuts were to be divided equally between defense and nondefense accounts. Revenues were excluded completely from the enforcement mechanism under GRH.

Described by one of its sponsors as "a bad idea whose time has come," the GRH approach to deficit reduction was never seriously tested under Reagan.[115] An approximately $12 billion sequester was imposed during FY 1986, but the Supreme Court then invalidated a key provision of the GRH enforcement mechanism.[116] In 1987, the law was rewritten to resolve this constitutional defect, but the deficit-reduction schedule then had to be extended through FY 1993. As a result, no major sequestration threats were posed during the remainder of Reagan's second term, removing any serious pressure on the administration to negotiate a comprehensive deficit-reduction agreement that included higher taxes.

Reagan's tax program thus remained largely intact despite high deficits. The steeply progressive marginal rates in place since World War II had been replaced by a modified flat tax, and indexing had been extended to the revenue side of the budget. The individual and corporation income tax bases had been substantially broadened through cutbacks in tax preferences. In terms of economic efficiency and equity, the structural tax reforms of the

---

115. This description was by Senator Warren B. Rudman (R-NH). The other Senate sponsors were Phil Gramm (R-TX) and Ernest F. Hollings (D-SC). *Congressional Quarterly Almanac, 1985* (Washington, D.C.: Congressional Quarterly, 1986), 459.

116. Under GRH, the comptroller-general (head of the General Accounting Office) issued the binding sequestration order. The Supreme Court held that this provision violated the separation of powers. *Bowsher v. Synar,* 92 L. Ed. 583 (1986).

Reagan presidency were generally positive, but their revenue effects were extremely costly.

Reagan's tax program, however, was also the centerpiece of an ambitious attempt to reduce the size and domestic scope of the federal government. By cutting revenue levels so radically in 1981, Reagan effectively guaranteed that high deficits would continue unless and until massive reductions in spending were implemented. When these reductions were rejected by Congress, Reagan refused to reverse course on tax policy. The inevitable result of this policy deadlock was an uninterrupted series of enormous deficits and a huge increase in the federal debt.

Spending and Deficit Control

During the 1970s and 1980s, the federal budget occupied the center of the political stage. The policy stakes in annual budget battles were continually raised, as Congress and the president competed for influence over the spending and revenue sides of the budget and over how to achieve balance between them. The 1974 congressional budget reforms made this competition with the president more formal and explicit, but these reforms also revealed serious differences within Congress over whether and how to control deficits.

The central problem that policymakers faced during this period was the rising level of federal spending, particularly the cumulative impact of a social welfare expansion that began in the mid-1960s and accelerated during the next decade. Between the end of World War II and 1975, outlay-GDP levels averaged approximately 18 percent annually. Only twice during this time—the peak wartime spending years of Korea and Vietnam—did outlays climb above 20 percent of GDP. From 1975 to 1990, by comparison, spending never fell below 20 percent, and the average outlay-GDP level was nearly 22 percent annually.

These higher spending levels reflected the growing weight of mandatory spending commitments. Discretionary spending accounted for more than two-thirds of the budget before Vietnam and, in 1970, was still more than 60 percent. Two decades later, the discretionary share of the budget had fallen to under 40 percent. Within the mandatory spending portion of the budget, three large programs—Social Security, Medicare, and Medicaid—accounted for much of this shift. Mandatory programmatic spending increased by more than $550 billion from 1970 to 1990; more than $355 billion of this increase was in Social Security, Medicare, and Medicaid.[117] As a percentage of GDP, these three programs climbed from 3.9 percent in 1970 to 6.9 percent in 1990. All other entitlements were, in terms of GDP ratios, almost flat over this period.

By the 1980s, the spending policy dilemma was reasonably straightforward but difficult to resolve. Either the growth of large, politically popular entitlements had to be reversed or discretionary spending programs had to absorb disproportionately large reductions. Reagan did manage to cut discretionary domestic outlay-GDP levels to pre–Great Society levels, but these reductions were partly offset by his defense buildup. When Reagan's call to retrench social welfare entitlements to pre–Great Society levels found virtually no support in Congress, the only deficit-reduction option that remained was higher taxes. This option was unacceptable to Reagan, who continued to insist that excessive domestic spending was the real cause of deficits.

The stalemate over budget policy during the 1980s was not, of course, total. Congress did, after all, support Reagan's defense buildup, although there were efforts to reduce the rate of increase in defense spending after 1982. On entitlements, existing programs were preserved, but no attempt was made to enact costly new programs. With tax policy, the Reagan administration's major concern was individual tax rates; the administration did accept increases in corporate tax levels and social insurance taxes after 1982. Nevertheless, deficits over this period remained at extremely high levels. Hopes that the Gramm-Rudman-Hollings deficit ceilings would force the Reagan administration and Congress to compromise further on taxes and spending proved illusory, but George Bush soon faced the stark choices Reagan had avoided.

---

117. This increase excludes deposit insurance outlays. *The Budget and Economic Outlook: Fiscal Years 2002–2011*, 150.

RECONCILIATION AND BALANCED BUDGETS

(1990–2001)

In December 1987, the Reagan administration and Congress agreed to create an independent National Economic Commission and charged it with proposing a bipartisan solution for balancing the budget. The Commission's final report, released on March 1, 1989, was intended to provide "political cover" for the next administration and Congress, enabling them to "adopt the commission's recommendations en bloc, arguing not only that the problem at hand must be solved but that the commission—and not the elected officials—should be blamed for the unpopular scheme."[1] The Commission found itself divided, however, over the same basic issues that had long frustrated elected policymakers. A bare majority of the fourteen-member Commission concluded that deficits could be eliminated without raising taxes. The minority report criticized this solution as inequitable and impractical. Since these contrasting positions mirrored those of Reagan's successor, George H. Bush, and the Democratic-controlled 101st Congress, it appeared that the deadlock over deficit politics would continue.

1. Lawrence J. Haas, "A Budget Commission Side Step," *National Journal* 21 (March 11, 1989): 592.

In 1990, however, the Bush administration and Congress successfully implemented a five-year budget reconciliation measure that raised taxes, lowered spending, and reduced projected deficits by nearly $500 billion. Three years later, President Bill Clinton persuaded his Democratic colleagues in the House and Senate to expand and extend the 1990 budget agreement. Then, in 1997, with Republicans in control of Congress, Clinton signed the third deficit-reduction pact of the 1990s. In 1998, the budget registered its first surplus in nearly thirty years. Two years later, the surplus had climbed to more than $235 billion.

This unexpected finish to the prolonged period of deficit politics owed a great deal to the end of the Cold War and the high level of economic growth the United States enjoyed for most of the 1990s. In addition, the remarkable improvement in the nation's fiscal outlook resulted from significant changes in spending and tax policy. These changes were accomplished under difficult political circumstances, including divided control of government, and would have been impossible without the creative use of reconciliation procedures that allowed congressional majorities to develop and enforce comprehensive budget agreements. Budget reconciliation proved, in the end, to be an enormously effective deficit-reduction weapon.

For a time, however, many in Congress doubted that the policy differences on deficit reduction could be resolved without a constitutional mandate. During the early 1990s, numerous balanced-budget constitutional amendments were introduced in Congress, but none was able to attract the necessary two-thirds support in the House and Senate. In 1995, however, Republicans controlled both chambers and made the balanced-budget amendment their top legislative priority. Congressional Republicans failed to pass the amendment but did manage to enact a presidential line-item veto that they claimed would curb wasteful spending. This statute, however, had little impact before being held unconstitutional two years later.

The real breakthrough in deficit-reduction politics ultimately came through presidential leadership. The 1990 Omnibus Budget Reconciliation Act that President Bush signed contained politically costly concessions to congressional Democrats on tax policy. Bush was denounced by conservative Republicans for these concessions and never regained the initiative on tax policy. In 1993, President Clinton's budget plan sacrificed parts of his party's domestic spending agenda and featured tax increases that further alarmed congressional Democrats. Unanimous Republican opposition magnified the political risks in Clinton's plan, and it finally passed the Democratic-controlled Congress by the barest of margins. For Bush and Clinton, the compromises required for deficit reduction caused enormous strains within their own parties and helped to unify their opponents.

The electoral rewards for this commitment to fiscal discipline were not especially reassuring, in part because it took years for deficit-reduction programs to yield results. George Bush certainly received no credit in 1992 for his efforts to bring the deficit problem under control. Unlike Bush, Clinton won his reelection bid, but, one year after his budget program was enacted, Republicans gained control of Congress and kept it through the remainder of his presidency. Moreover, the disappearance of deficit politics found Democrats and Republicans once again at odds, this time over how to apportion surpluses among tax cuts, spending increases, and debt reduction. The politics of surplus budgeting that emerged in the late 1990s was simply a new chapter in the long-standing argument over the level at which budgets should be balanced.

The Prelude to Deficit Reduction

During the 1988 presidential campaign, George Bush pledged to oppose any attempt to increase taxes. In his acceptance speech at the Republican convention, Bush declared, "And I'm the one who will not raise taxes. . . . And the Congress will push me to raise taxes, and I'll say no, and they'll push, and I'll say no, and they'll push again. And I'll say to them: Read my lips. No new taxes."[2] This famous declaration came back to haunt Bush when he agreed to raise taxes as part of the 1990 budget agreement, but the budget program that Bush brought to the presidency contained other policy priorities that were equally problematical. Bush had promised to support defense budget increases for both strategic and conventional force modernization and had also promoted domestic initiatives in education, environmental protection, and law enforcement that would boost discretionary spending even more. Because Bush had not advocated offsetting entitlement cuts, it was unclear how substantial deficit reduction could be achieved. Moreover, congressional Democrats had suffered painful reversals on spending priorities under Reagan, so that there was the strong possibility of pitched battles over domestic discretionary spending. With tax increases and defense cuts

---

2. *Congressional Quarterly Almanac, 1988* (Washington, D.C.: Congressional Quarterly, 1989), 43-A.

supposedly unacceptable to Bush, the deficit-reduction options appeared limited.

The 1989 Bipartisan Experiment

Nevertheless, the first year of the Bush presidency opened with considerable optimism about presidential-congressional cooperation. On February 9, 1989, when his FY 1990 budget program was presented to a joint session of Congress, Bush vowed to "work with the Congress, to form a special leadership group, to negotiate in good faith . . . to meet the budget targets, and to produce a budget on time."[3] Although Bush reiterated his opposition to higher taxes, he distanced himself from his predecessor on two key points. He agreed in advance to "a one-year freeze in the military budget" and called for increased spending on a number of social programs.[4] Despite this conciliatory approach, partisan splits over budget policy quickly surfaced in Congress.

The Reagan Benchmark. Ronald Reagan's final budget had called for substantial deficit-reduction savings in nondefense discretionary programs and in retirement, health, and public assistance entitlements. The Reagan administration's FY 1990 budget showed nondefense discretionary programs declining, in real dollars, by more than 10 percent over five years, with constant-dollar defense spending growing by a slightly smaller amount.[5] Proposed entitlement cutbacks were estimated at $17 billion for FY 1990 and almost $120 billion over five years.

Reagan's budget was well below the $100 billion Gramm-Rudman-Hollings (GRH) II deficit ceiling for 1990 and projected a balanced budget by the FY 1993 deadline. The Congressional Budget Office (CBO), however, concluded that deficit targets would not be met under the Reagan program. According to the CBO, the administration's economic assumptions were too optimistic, and its deficit-reduction proposals overstated. Instead of a balanced budget in 1993, the CBO's projections showed an $80 billion deficit.[6] In addition, Reagan's budget-balancing scenario contained domestic spending cuts that congressional Democrats were almost certain to reject.[7]

---

3. *Congressional Quarterly Almanac, 1989* (Washington, D.C.: Congressional Quarterly, 1990), 10-C.

4. *Congressional Quarterly Almanac, 1989*, 12-C.

5. Congressional Budget Office, *An Analysis of President Reagan's Budgetary Proposals for Fiscal Year 1990* (Washington, D.C.: CBO, 1989), 30–39.

6. Congressional Budget Office, *An Analysis of President Reagan's Budgetary Proposals for Fiscal Year 1990*, 4.

7. As the CBO noted, "Only small revenue increases are proposed, and defense spending would be increased. As a result, nondefense spending would bear the brunt of deficit reduction.

The Bush Revisions. The starting point for talks between the incoming Bush administration and Congress was the $100 billion deficit target for FY 1990. The administration did not submit a full-scale revision of the Reagan budget but instead proposed overall spending and revenue guidelines that would comply with the deficit limit and provide flexibility for budget policy discussions with congressional leaders. Since the economic forecasts for the upcoming fiscal year remained favorable, official estimates of deficit-reduction requirements were modest. The administration, for example, projected GRH compliance costs at under $30 billion.

After more than two months of negotiations, White House and congressional leaders announced agreement on a "budget framework" for the FY 1990 budget, which included $28 billion in deficit reduction roughly split between spending cuts and revenue increases. A congressional budget resolution based on the agreement was passed fairly quickly by the House and Senate, but the reconciliation legislation needed to implement the agreement was not enacted until late November. This delay, caused in part by Democratic opposition to an administration-sponsored capital gains tax cut, triggered automatic spending cuts under GRH when the fiscal year began on October 1.[8] When the reconciliation bill was finally passed, it incorporated a portion of these automatic cuts to achieve the necessary deficit reduction.

What finally emerged from the bipartisan agreement in 1989 was modest by any standard. The original deficit-reduction goal that the administration and Congress had set was not achieved. Appropriations, sequestration, and reconciliation measures produced deficit savings of only about $15 billion.[9] If the administration's accommodations on discretionary domestic programs were intended to encourage Democratic compromises on revenues

---

Almost half of the savings would come from cuts in entitlement spending, a third from holding down nondefense discretionary appropriations, and most of the rest from lower debt service costs." Congressional Budget Office, *An Analysis of President Reagan's Budgetary Proposals for Fiscal Year 1990*, 25.

8. The capital gains tax cut was controversial for policy and budgetary reasons. The original agreement between the administration and Congress included an unspecified $5.3 billion increase in new revenues. Other additional revenues were to be raised by tax-enforcement programs, user fees, and asset sales. The administration contended that most of the new revenues would be generated by the increased economic activity following a capital gains tax cut. Many congressional Democrats opposed the cut as objectionable policy and disputed the notion that it would raise, rather than lower, revenues.

9. Under GRH procedures, the final calculation of required deficit cuts took place just before the fiscal year began on October 1. At that point, an estimated $16.2 billion was required for compliance, not the $28 billion deemed necessary earlier in the year. *Congressional Quarterly Almanac, 1989*, 94–95.

and entitlements, the results were disappointing. The only substantial deficit savings that ultimately were realized came from defense cuts and revenue increases. Moreover, by the time that budget-related legislation had been enacted, technical reestimates had wiped out virtually all of the anticipated deficit reduction for future years. According to the CBO, annual baseline deficits for fiscal years 1991–93 remained above $140 billion. Since the GRH timetable required the budget to be balanced over this period, the administration and Congress faced an enormous deficit-reduction challenge, and the halting progress of Bush's first year was not encouraging.

The 1990 Deficit Miscalculation

The FY 1991 budget was submitted to Congress on January 29, 1990, and the administration raised no alarms about GRH compliance. The deficit target for FY 1991 was $64 billion, and the "President's Policy Deficit" proposals promised to meet this goal and to achieve a budget surplus by FY 1993. There would be no necessity, moreover, for "major legislative action" to correct the deficit problem.[10] Instead, President Bush called on Congress to hold spending growth to 3 percent (3.4 percent for nondefense programs and 1.9 percent for defense). Revenues would increase by 9 percent, the president reported, not as a result of new taxes but "on the strength of economic growth."[11] The administration's budget estimated revenues at 19.9 percent of GNP, the highest level in ten years, while outlays were projected at 20.1 percent, the lowest level since the late 1970s.

The economic assumptions in the administration's budget were more optimistic than those of the CBO and leading private-sector forecasters.[12] The administration acknowledged these differences and included "alternative economic scenarios."[13] Its "lower-growth scenario," however, projected the FY 1991 deficit at only $77.5 billion, just slightly above the GRH deficit ceiling. Moreover, the administration reassured Congress that the deficit problem had, at worst, been "stabilized," and "the pattern of continuous erosion that characterized the early- and mid-1980s [seemed] to have been broken."[14]

---

10. *Budget of the United States Government, Fiscal Year 1991* (Washington, D.C.: Government Printing Office, 1990), 9.

11. *Budget of the United States Government, Fiscal Year 1991*, 10.

12. Congressional Budget Office, *The Economic and Budget Outlook: Fiscal Years 1991–1995* (Washington, D.C.: CBO, 1990), xix–xxii.

13. *Budget of the United States Government, Fiscal Year 1991*, 12.

14. *Budget of the United States Government, Fiscal Year 1991*, 14.

Within just a few weeks, however, these reassurances were fading. In March 1990, the CBO's analysis of the president's budget showed a rapid deterioration in the deficit picture. The CBO claimed that the administration's faulty economic assumptions had resulted in very large revenue overestimates and in substantial spending underestimates.[15] The administration had grossly underbudgeted for interest costs on the debt, for deposit insurance outlays to cover savings and loan insolvencies, and for other economically sensitive spending programs. The CBO projected a $130 billion deficit, more than double the administration's deficit forecast, assuming full enactment of Bush's deficit-reduction proposals. Since many, if not all, of these proposals were likely to be ignored by Congress, the politically realistic deficit was even higher.

As these deficit reestimates were being digested, the economic and budgetary situation was worsening. By June, the CBO's baseline deficit for FY 1991 had climbed above $230 billion, and the FY 1992 estimate was even higher.[16] With deficits this large, sequestration was not a feasible option. A $100 billion FY 1991 sequestration, for example, would have required close to a 40 percent reduction in discretionary domestic programs and a 25 percent cut in defense.[17] Then, to meet the GRH balanced-budget deadline, additional cuts would have been required in 1992 and 1993.

Amid this economic turmoil, President Bush invited congressional leaders to meet with administration officials for budget negotiations with "no preconditions."[18] GRH sequestration had to be avoided, but Bush did not want to call for an outright repeal of the GRH statute. To maintain the pressure for deficit reduction, the administration hoped to replace GRH with a comprehensive and practical multiyear budget agreement. Congressional Democrats agreed to participate in a budget summit but insisted that Bush first renounce his "no new taxes" pledge, stalling negotiations for nearly two months. Finally, on June 26, the president conceded that "tax revenue increases" would be necessary given "the size of the deficit problem and the need for a package that can be enacted."[19] Bush's statement placated Democratic leaders, but congressional Republicans reacted angrily, foreshadowing

15. Congressional Budget Office, *An Analysis of the President's Budgetary Proposals for Fiscal Year 1991* (Washington, D.C.: CBO, 1990), 1–10.

16. Congressional Budget Office, *The Economic and Budget Outlook: An Update* (Washington, D.C.: CBO, July 1990), xiii.

17. Congressional Budget Office, *The Economic and Budget Outlook: An Update* (1990), 56.

18. *Congressional Quarterly Almanac, 1990* (Washington, D.C.: Congressional Quarterly, 1991), 130.

19. *Congressional Quarterly Almanac, 1990*, 131.

problems that Bush would have within his own party when the budget pact was sent to Congress for approval in the fall. To make matters worse, Democratic negotiators quickly made clear their intent to pursue "tax equity" by raising income tax rates for upper-income taxpayers.

What the Democratic leadership hoped to accomplish was a replay of the battles they had fought with the Reagan administration over income tax policy, albeit with a different outcome. Although Reagan had agreed to deficit-reduction tax increases in 1982, 1983, and 1984, he had successfully opposed all attempts to raise marginal rates for individual taxpayers, and the Tax Reform Act of 1986 had then put into place the lowest marginal rate structure of the modern era. For President Bush, the political risks of a tax increase would be magnified if individual tax rates were raised, and congressional Democrats were eager to exploit this vulnerability.

The Budget Summit and Its Aftermath

The budget summit of 1990 lasted nearly five months in its various incarnations, with an agreement between administration and congressional representatives finally announced on September 30. The agreement contained approximately $500 billion in deficit reduction spread over fiscal years 1991–95. Included were spending savings in discretionary and mandatory programs of almost $290 billion; increases in revenues and fees of nearly $150 billion; and lower interest costs (because of reduced future deficits) of $65 billion.[20]

During the on-again, off-again negotiations during summer 1990, deficit projections continued to climb. In addition, the Iraqi invasion of Kuwait on August 2 triggered a mass deployment of U.S. troops to the Persian Gulf. On September 11, President Bush addressed a joint session of Congress on the Persian Gulf situation and concluded with a plea that Congress quickly enact "a five-year program to reduce the projected debt and deficits by $500 billion . . . [so that] we can avoid the ax of sequester—deep across-the-board cuts that would threaten our military capacity and risk substantial domestic disruption."[21] Action had repeatedly been blocked because of splits within

---

20. *Congressional Quarterly Almanac, 1990,* 134. For a detailed examination of these discussions and their results, see Daniel P. Franklin, *Making Ends Meet: Congressional Budgeting in the Age of Deficits* (Washington, D.C.: Congressional Quarterly, 1993).

21. *Congressional Quarterly Almanac, 1990,* 133.

and between the Republican and Democratic parties in Congress. While agreement had been reached fairly early on the parameters of the deficit-reduction package—$50 billion in FY 1991 and $500 billion over five years—it had not been possible to resolve the differences over spending cuts and tax increases needed to achieve these savings.

On the Republican side, the tax issue overshadowed everything else. Neither the White House negotiating team nor President Bush himself could pacify conservative Republicans, especially in the House, who opposed increased taxes. The Democratic congressional leadership, in turn, was constrained by liberal opposition to domestic spending cuts, particularly in entitlements. Thus, the small group of executive branch officials and congressional leaders who endorsed the September 30 agreement found themselves facing a fractious Congress. From an objective standpoint, the tradeoffs in the leadership agreement appeared to be balanced. Democrats had protected discretionary domestic programs from significant cuts but had agreed to entitlement spending curbs, including higher beneficiary cost sharing for Medicare services. The administration had accepted tax increases but had managed to spread these across a range of revenue sources—energy taxes, Medicare payroll taxes, and individual income taxes. The increase in individual tax liabilities, moreover, did not involve higher marginal rates. Instead, White House negotiators agreed to limit deductions for upper-income taxpayers. On defense, the budget agreement specified that defense cuts would account for all discretionary spending savings for at least three years but prohibited additional defense transfers to domestic programs. Important compromises had also been reached on user fees, credit program reforms, and, most important, multiyear budget process controls.

Whether these and related policy changes would actually yield $500 billion in deficit savings was arguable, given the optimistic economic and policy assumptions that accompanied the budget agreement, but the House's overwhelming rejection of the agreement on October 5 had nothing to do with accurate accounting. A last-minute effort by President Bush to rally public support failed miserably, and a majority of House Republicans also ignored personal entreaties by the president to support the negotiated tax increases. On the Democratic side, spending cuts proved equally unacceptable to many members. After the budget agreement was rejected, the House and Senate passed a continuing resolution to provide stopgap funding and to suspend GRH cuts for the upcoming fiscal year, but President Bush vetoed the measure.

Rewriting the Budget Agreement

With a government shutdown looming, the Bush administration unexpect-edly withdrew from the next stage of budget talks, and House Republicans likewise decided to disengage. The congressional Democratic leadership decided at that point to formulate a budget package that could pass without Republican support. A revised budget resolution was quickly moved through the House and Senate, FY 1991 appropriations bills were cleared, and a budget reconciliation measure was passed in record time.[22] The Omnibus Budget Reconciliation Act of 1990 (OBRA 1990) was very different from the original agreement between the administration and Congress. The change in tax policy was pronounced, as Democrats voted to impose heavier tax bur-dens, including a higher marginal rate, on upper-income taxpayers.[23] Of an estimated $160 billion in additional revenues from OBRA 1990's Title XI tax provisions, nearly $70 billion was accounted for by higher marginal rates, reduced deductions and personal exemptions, and higher Medicare payroll taxes affecting high-income taxpayers.[24] The Medicare savings that had been included in the original agreement were greatly reduced and tilted more heavily toward lower reimbursement rates for providers. Other entitlement reductions followed a similar pattern, being either cut back or eliminated in the final reconciliation bill. In addition, the appropriations bills that Congress passed and the discretionary spending limits in OBRA 1990 fully protected domestic programs at the expense of defense.

The 1990 deficit-reduction legislation that Congress passed, and Presi-dent Bush reluctantly signed, was a clear victory for Democrats on the major policy issues, but the administration could claim some credit for new budget enforcement provisions.[25] For the FY 1991–95 period covered by the 1990

22. Less than three weeks elapsed between approval of the FY 1991 congressional budget res-olution and passage of the 1990 reconciliation bill. The latter was cleared by a House vote of 228 to 200 (Democrats 181 to 74; Republicans 47 to 126) and a Senate vote of 54 to 45 (Democrats 35 to 20; Republicans 19 to 25) on October 27.

23. The 1986 Tax Reform Act had two basic rates—15 and 28 percent. A so-called bubble rate (33 percent) was used to phase out personal exemptions and the 15 percent rate for upper-income taxpayers. However, after those benefits were eliminated, the top marginal rate was a flat 28 per-cent. The 1990 reconciliation bill repealed the "bubble rate" but added a 31 percent marginal rate for upper-income taxpayers. It also continued the phaseout of personal exemptions for these tax-payers and limited their personal deductions.

24. Congressional Budget Office, *The Economic and Budget Outlook: Fiscal Years 1992–1996* (Washington, D.C.: CBO, 1991), 67.

25. These budget enforcement provisions were included in Title XIII of the 1990 reconcilia-tion bill and designated as the Budget Enforcement Act of 1990.

reconciliation bill, several restrictions were put in place to ensure that the deficit-reduction savings would not be dissipated: (1) five-year statutory ceilings were established for discretionary spending programs, covering both budget authority and outlays; (2) "pay-as-you-go" (PAYGO) limits were mandated for entitlement and revenue legislation—in a given fiscal year, combined tax policy and entitlement benefit changes could not increase the deficit; and (3) separate sequestration procedures were prescribed for violations of either the discretionary spending ceiling or the PAYGO restrictions. In addition, much stricter budget accounting was required for the costs of federal credit programs, including direct loans, loan guarantees, and federal insurance.[26]

Under the discretionary spending caps, discretionary outlays were reduced by nearly $200 billion below baseline levels.[27] Congress could increase these savings by appropriating less than the specified amounts, but could not appropriate more or, for fiscal years 1991–93, transfer funds between the defense and nondefense spending categories. In contrast to these appropriations restrictions, the PAYGO limits did not directly control entitlement spending. Instead, Congress could not increase entitlement outlays above the OBRA 1990 baseline without a corresponding offset in taxes. Increases resulting from unanticipated economic or demographic factors, however, were completely unrestricted. In addition, the OBRA 1990 baseline for entitlements contained only a small reduction of $75 billion, most of which was accounted for by lower Medicare reimbursements to doctors and hospitals and by new fees.[28]

These new budget process controls were considered to be more workable than the GRH deficit ceilings, but they left in place high rates of growth in the largest social welfare entitlements. For discretionary programs, by comparison, cuts would have to be made in existing commitments to meet the outlay ceilings. The combined effect of the appropriations decisions and multiyear spending limits in 1990 was to continue the long-term shift of the budget toward mandatory spending programs.

For the Bush administration, the politically costly policy concessions in the final 1990 budget agreement were made more difficult to defend by a

---

26. Congressional Budget Office, *The Economic and Budget Outlook: Fiscal Years 1992–1996*, 104–9.

27. For fiscal years 1991–95, including enacted appropriations for FY 1991. Congressional Budget Office, *The Economic and Budget Outlook: Fiscal Years 1992–1996*, xvii.

28. Congressional Budget Office, *The Economic and Budget Outlook: Fiscal Years 1992–1996*, xvii, 66.

deteriorating economic situation that was pushing deficits to unprecedented levels. In FY 1991, for example, the estimated $33 billion in deficit reduction from revenue increases and spending cuts was almost immediately overwhelmed by new deficit pressures (Table 7.1). Post-OBRA deficit projections were even higher than the pre-OBRA estimates, and actual deficits for fiscal years 1991–95 exceeded even these disappointing initial projections.[29] The absence of any visible improvement in the deficit problem was especially troublesome in FY 1992, which extended right up to the presidential election.

Implementing OBRA 1990

Compared with the first two years of the Bush presidency, budget policy disputes were fairly muted during 1991 and 1992. Disagreements between Congress and the executive branch involved primarily the discretionary domestic spending ceilings and accompanying moratorium on defense transfers, both of which survived repeated attacks by liberal Democrats. In 1991, for example, the Senate rejected several attempts to raise domestic spending under the recession escape-clause in the budget agreement.[30] Although the Bush administration was able to moderate defense budget reductions and to protect the deficit savings mandated in 1990, it failed to gain congressional support for entitlement reforms to expand these savings.

The FY 1992 budget debate was, of course, overshadowed by the Gulf War during the first few months of 1991, the outcome of which insulated the defense budget from any serious congressional attacks for the remainder of the year. The Gulf War also boosted President Bush's public approval rating to the highest level ever recorded in a Gallup Poll, but the administration refused to commit this political capital to an ambitious new agenda. Instead, differences between the administration's budget program and congressional action remained concentrated in the discretionary domestic spending category. Within the spending limits set by the 1990 budget act, the Bush administration's 1992 budget proposed a substantial reordering of priorities, which Congress promptly rejected.[31] Congress was forced, however, to limit

29. The actual deficits for fiscal years 1991–95 totaled close to $1.2 trillion, almost $200 billion more than the January 1991 projections and $250 billion more than the CBO's pre-OBRA baseline deficit projections.

30. *Congressional Quarterly Almanac, 1991* (Washington, D.C.: Congressional Quarterly, 1992), 74.

31. The Bush budget called for increases in 250 programs, cuts in 109, and terminations of 238 existing programs. *Congressional Quarterly Almanac, 1991*, 55.

Table 7.1 Pre- and Post-OBRA 1990 Changes in Deficit Projections (in billions of dollars)

	1991	1992	Fiscal Year 1993	1994	1995	Cumulative Five-Year Changes
July 1990 Baseline Deficit	$ 232	$ 238	$ 196	$ 145	$ 138	N/A
Budget Agreement: Policy Changes						
Revenues	−18	−33	−32	−37	−39	−158
Entitlements and Other Mandatory Spending	−9	−12	−16	−19	−19	−75
Enacted Appropriations	−6	−6	−9	−12	−13	−46
Required Reductions in Discretionary Spending	N/A	−13	−22	−46	−62	−144
Debt Service Savings	−1	−4	−10	−17	−27	−59
Subtotal	−33	−69	−89	−131	−160	−482
Economic Assumptions	50	63	63	70	79	N/A
Technical Reestimates						
Deposit Insurance	23	20	7	32	−44	N/A
Other	26	30	36	42	43	N/A
Subtotal	49	50	43	74	−1	N/A
Credit Reform	0	2	3	2	0	N/A
Net Changes	66	46	19	15	−81	N/A
January 1991 Deficit Estimate	298	284	215	160	57	N/A

SOURCE: Congressional Budget Office, *The Economic and Budget Outlook: Fiscal Years 1992–1996* (Washington, D.C.: CBO, 1991), xvii.

spending in numerous programs because of the discretionary spending caps. Although the appropriations process in the House and Senate was completed on schedule, nonbudgetary issues delayed final action on several FY 1992 appropriations measures.

The president's budget also contained proposals for targeting, or means-testing, entitlement benefits in a wide variety of programs. While the immediate savings from these proposals were minor—an estimated $6.3 billion out of more than $700 billion in FY 1992 mandatory spending—their long-term impact was potentially important. With the mandatory spending share of the budget having risen to more than 50 percent, the substantive case for entitlement reform might have seemed inescapable, but Congress simply ignored the administration's proposals. Moreover, congressional Democratic leaders criticized Bush for attempting to resurrect entitlement cutbacks that had been rejected in 1990, particularly with regard to Medicare. For its part, the administration employed the new PAYGO rules to block for six months a Democratic initiative to extend unemployment benefits. The amount at issue was under $6 billion, but Bush refused to agree to an emergency spending waiver, eventually forcing Democrats to find offsetting revenues to pay for the measure. Whether this fight was worthwhile, however, was another matter. In the midst of a serious recession and with deficit projections hovering around the $300 billion mark, an unemployment compensation bill was a political inevitability, as even congressional Republicans recognized. The president finally signed a compromise measure in November, giving the Democrats a huge political victory and underscoring the uncertain legislative strategy in the executive branch.

During 1992, the administration attempted to step up its challenge to congressional Democrats on domestic spending priorities, to renew the call for tax cuts to stimulate savings and investment, and to press for entitlement reforms and healthcare cost controls. In each of these areas, however, the bright lines the administration attempted to draw were, in the end, easily blurred. Its FY 1993 budget, for example, called on Congress to reduce discretionary spending below the statutory caps. For defense, the administration proposed a nearly $7 billion cut below the FY 1993 budget authority limit as part of a $50 billion multiyear reduction in its defense program. For domestic programs, the proposed cutback was substantially less, amounting to a freeze in spending for FY 1993 and for later years as well.

The administration's scaled-back defense program allowed congressional Democrats to avoid the antidefense label that had plagued the party since the Vietnam War. House and Senate Democrats endorsed the administration's post–Cold War defense strategy and called for only modest cuts in its multiyear defense plan.[32] The congressional Democratic leadership also decided to avoid any serious confrontations over domestic spending. When President Bush revived his demand for a domestic spending freeze at the 1992 Republican convention and threatened to enforce it with vetoes if necessary, Democratic leaders calculated that a prolonged fight over spending was a probable political loser. Instead, appropriations measures were trimmed to comply with the freeze, and all of the regular appropriations bills were signed by the president.

On tax policy, Democrats felt little pressure to compromise with the administration. Democratic leaders joined Bush in calling for a tax cut, but their version emphasized middle-class tax relief paid for by increased taxes on upper-income taxpayers. Congress included few of the administration's tax-cut proposals in a $77.5 billion measure that passed on March 20, and the president promptly vetoed it. A second tax-cut measure, which started out as an urban aid initiative in the wake of the Los Angeles riots, was broadened to include dozens of targeted tax cuts and offsetting revenue increases and was also vetoed. In both cases, the administration was adamant that it would not accept higher tax burdens on upper-income taxpayers, but its efforts were clearly overshadowed by the increases enacted two years earlier.

During 1992, two of the Republican party's strongest issues in prior presidential elections—defense and tax policy—were neutralized. In addition, the administration's attempt to challenge Democrats over entitlement policy reform failed miserably. The FY 1993 budget, for example, highlighted annual, enforceable ceilings on mandatory spending programs.[33] In the political environment of 1992, however, even congressional Republicans had no enthusiasm for attacking entitlement spending.

The Bush Record

There were some truly unusual twists in the course of budget policy during the Bush presidency (Table 7.2). An administration that was, in fact, strongly

---

32. On the Democratic party's defense budget alternative, the Force C option developed by House Armed Services Committee chairman Les Aspin and adopted by the Clinton campaign, see Dennis S. Ippolito, *Budget Policy and the Future of Defense* (Washington, D.C.: Institute for National Strategic Studies/National Defense University Press, 1994), 84–97.

33. The proposal included annual adjustments in entitlement programs based on the growth in beneficiaries and prices, along with a specified increment for real growth. When projected

Table 7.2 Composition of Outlays and Revenues, 1989–1993 (as a percentage of GDP)

	Fiscal Year				
	1989	1990	1991	1992	1993
Revenues:					
Individual Income Taxes	8.2%	8.1%	7.9%	7.7%	7.8%
Social Insurance Taxes	6.6	6.6	6.7	6.6	6.5
Other	3.4	3.2	3.3	3.2	3.3
Total	18.3	18.0	17.8	17.5	17.6
Outlays:					
Discretionary Defense	5.6	5.2	5.4	4.9	4.5
Discretionary Nondefense	3.4	3.5	3.6	3.7	3.8
Entitlements and Mandatory	10.2	10.9	11.8	11.5	11.2
Net Interest	3.1	3.2	3.3	3.2	3.0
Offsetting Receipts	−1.2	−1.0	−1.8	−1.1	−1.0
Total	21.2	21.8	22.3	22.2	21.5
Deficits	2.8	3.9	4.5	4.7	3.9

SOURCE: Congressional Budget Office, *The Economic and Budget Outlook: Fiscal Years 2002–2011* (Washington, D.C.: CBO, 2001), 143, 145, 147, 149.

committed to spending control and deficit reduction presided over the largest peacetime deficits in history. Under Bush, spending-GDP levels remained extremely high, and the composition of the spending budget shifted even further toward entitlement spending programs. The 1990 tax increase, shaped by congressional Democrats, did not appreciably raise revenue-GDP levels for several years, but Bush nevertheless absorbed all the political costs associated with raising taxes. And, of course, the deficit reduction that was finally achieved as a result of the 1990 budget act wound up benefiting the Clinton administration.

The 1990 budget act imposed greater discipline on the budgetary process, but its procedural reforms came at a heavy political price for Bush. The Reagan administration had been able to cut real spending for discretionary domestic programs and to block entitlement expansions without any multi-year controls. During the Bush presidency, by comparison, real spending in

---

growth exceeded this adjustment, legislative reductions were mandated in the form of reconciliation. Failure to act would trigger automatic sequestration in mandatory programs other than Social Security. See *Budget of the United States Government, Fiscal Year 1993* (Washington, D.C.: Government Printing Office, 1992), 15–17.

both categories rose sharply. It can be argued, of course, that the new spending controls proved their true worth when the Clinton administration and a Democratic Congress were forced to scale back their spending programs, but the Bush administration simply did not have a coherent strategy for dealing with the domestic policy agenda.

President Bush perhaps misjudged the motives and partisanship of the Democratic congressional majority, assuming that they shared his willingness to depoliticize the budget policy debate in the interests of deficit reduction. Instead, the Democrats repeatedly used budget policy to attack and weaken the Bush presidency, whether the issue was tax rates, Medicare cost controls, or unemployment benefits. The administration gained no credit with congressional Democrats for its conciliatory approach to domestic spending, and it sacrificed any advantages it might have gained from direct confrontations over defense spending and tax policy. Moreover, the refusal to commit political capital after the Gulf War on behalf of a serious domestic reform agenda protected congressional Democrats, and eventually Bill Clinton, from having to defend their positions, while giving them broad license to attack the administration's domestic priorities.

When the Bush administration took office, the evidence was clear that deficit problems were not unique to the United States. In virtually all of the industrialized democracies, large structural deficits had emerged during the 1980s as a result of the social welfare expansion of the preceding two decades. The Reagan defense program and tax cuts had certainly increased deficits in the United States, but the fiscal problems Bush inherited were also caused by the high costs of retirement and healthcare programs. While the administration's budgets forthrightly described this problem, there was no serious attempt to elevate entitlement reform to the top of the legislative agenda. Instead, the administration settled for piecemeal adjustments in defense spending and in revenue levels. Given the political realities of divided government, this narrow approach was less risky than a comprehensive deficit-reduction program, but it also deprived the administration of any overarching principles that would clearly define its policy leadership. Facing a difficult campaign for reelection in 1992, the Bush administration could not offer voters a distinctive budget policy program. The contrast between the administration's principled, aggressive, and remarkably successful foreign policy leadership and its inchoate domestic record was especially glaring. In a year when economic and domestic concerns predominated, the contrast proved fatal.

Table 7.3 The Clinton Administration's 1993 Deficit-Reduction Proposals (in billions of dollars)

	1994	1995	Fiscal Year 1996	1997	1998	Total 1994–98
Baseline Deficit	$ 301	$ 296	$ 297	$ 346	$ 390	$1,630
Spending Proposals:						
Defense	−7	−12	−20	−37	−36	−112
Nondefense Discretionary	−4	−10	−15	−20	−23	−73
Entitlements	−6	−12	−24	−34	−39	−115
Debt Service	—	−3	−7	−14	−22	−46
Investment Spending	+15	+22	+33	+39	+45	+153
Total	−2	−15	−33	−66	−75	−191
Revenue Proposals:						
Tax Increases*	−49	−57	−72	−90	−90	−358
Stimulus Tax Cuts	+13	+17	+15	+15	+17	+77
Total	−36	−40	−57	−75	−73	−281
Net Deficit Reduction	−39	−54	−92	−140	−148	−473
Projected Deficit	−262	−242	−205	−206	−241	−1,157

* Includes Social Security tax increase.

Source: *Congressional Quarterly Almanac, 1993* (Washington, D.C.: Congressional Quarterly, 1994), 88. Copyright 1994 by Congressional Quarterly, Inc. Reproduced with permission of Congressional Quarterly, Inc. in the format Trade Book via Copyright Clearance Center.

Clinton's Deficit-Reduction Triumph

Although the third-party candidacy of Ross Perot raised the salience of deficit politics during the 1992 presidential campaign, neither George Bush nor Bill Clinton proposed detailed deficit-reduction programs. By the time that Clinton took office, however, deficit projections had become so alarming that the president made deficit reduction the centerpiece of his economic recovery program. In an address to a joint session of Congress on February 17, 1993, Clinton warned, "If we just stay with the same trends of the last four years, by the end of the decade the deficit will be $635 billion a year, [debt will be] almost 80 percent of our gross domestic product, and paying interest on that debt will be the costliest government program of all."[34] The administration's five-year budget program, formally submitted to

34. *Congressional Quarterly Almanac, 1993* (Washington, D.C.: Congressional Quarterly, 1994), 10-D.

Congress on April 8, contained more than $700 billion in spending cuts and tax increases; the budget also called for new "investment" spending and tax incentives totaling $230 billion. The net deficit reduction in Clinton's plan was estimated at $470 billion, leaving the projected deficit for its final year, FY 1998, at more than $240 billion.[35]

Most of Clinton's investment proposals did not survive what turned out to be more than four months of contentious debates in the House and Senate, but, in early August, Congress cleared a nearly $500 billion deficit-reduction measure. The Omnibus Budget Reconciliation Act of 1993 (OBRA 1993) passed the House by a vote of 218 to 216, with all 175 Republicans voting against it. In the Senate, the margin was equally narrow, with Vice President Al Gore casting the tiebreaking vote in a 51 to 50 outcome. As in the House, all Republicans voted no. Congressional Republicans were united by their opposition to the size and types of tax increases advanced by the administration, particularly proposals to raise marginal rates and income tax liabilities for upper-income taxpayers. In the end, nearly one-third of the projected deficit reduction in OBRA 1993 was the result of higher tax burdens for these individuals.[36]

Spending Versus Taxes

The original Clinton administration fiscal program was directed toward increased taxes and defense cuts (Table 7.3). The entitlement "savings" that the administration recommended were, for the most part, continuations of Medicare cost controls approved in 1990—restrictions on payments to health-care providers and Medicare premium increases. The only benefit "cut" was, in effect, a tax increase for Social Security recipients whose postretirement income exceeded certain thresholds. In 1983, the tax exemption for Social Security benefits had been partially repealed.[37] For high-income retirees, up to 50 percent of Social Security benefit payments was made taxable as part of regular income. The Clinton administration recommended that the percentage subject to taxation be raised to 85 percent, with estimated revenues from this change totaling nearly $30 billion over five years.[38]

Proposed individual income tax increases included a 36 percent marginal rate on taxable income and an additional 10 percent income surtax for upper-income

---

35. *Congressional Quarterly Almanac, 1993*, 88.
36. The revenue projections for increased marginal rates were $124.5 billion over five years. The lifting of the Medicare cap for payroll taxes was estimated at $29.2 billion.
37. See Steuerle, *The Tax Decade*, 63–65.
38. *Congressional Quarterly Almanac, 1993*, 88.

taxpayers. The surtax, which congressional Democrats had unsuccessfully promoted in 1990, constituted a fifth marginal rate bracket of 39.6 percent. Finally, Clinton recommended that Congress impose a broad-based energy tax, affecting most types of energy, with an additional surtax on petroleum products.

The stimulus and investment package that Clinton sent to Congress was, unlike the deficit-reduction program, heavily weighted toward spending. Most of the new or increased spending was targeted for education and training programs, as well as for energy and environmental initiatives. Additional outlays, totaling approximately $25 billion over five years, were tied to an expanded earned-income tax credit for the working poor, including families without children. The tax stimulus in the administration's proposal featured an investment tax credit, primarily for small businesses, and special tax treatment for investments in economically distressed areas of the country.

Taking into account proposed new outlays for discretionary domestic programs and entitlements, the spending savings in Clinton's deficit-reduction plan fell to under $200 billion, with defense cuts and debt service interest savings accounting for most of this net reduction. The defense budget program that the Clinton administration proposed was more than $125 billion below the Bush administration's planning levels for fiscal years 1994–98.[39] The defense cutbacks were also considerably larger than those that Clinton had advocated during the presidential campaign. Congressional Republicans were critical of the scale of the defense retrenchment and of the administration's failure to provide a strategic rationale or justification for its defense cuts. While the administration had announced its intention to lower the active-duty military force level to 1.4 million, compared with 1.6 million under the Bush program, it had not provided Congress with detailed five-year plans for adjusting force levels and weapons programs.[40] These plans were not made available until well after Congress had acted on its 1993 budget resolutions and reconciliation legislation. Moreover, there was widespread concern that congressional Democrats would eventually impose additional cuts on defense to expand domestic spending margins in future years.

Although few congressional Democrats joined Republican efforts to moderate defense cutbacks, there was considerable Democratic unease about the

39. See Ippolito, *Budget Policy and the Future of Defense*, 97–99.

40. Congressional Budget Office, *An Analysis of the President's February Budgetary Proposals* (Washington, D.C.: CBO, March 1993), IV-1–IV-9.

imbalance between the spending cuts and revenue increases in the president's program. One of the first casualties of this Democratic disunity was the Senate's rejection of a FY 1993 supplemental appropriation to fund Clinton's short-term economic stimulus package. The president had called for immediate action on this measure as the first installment of his economic recovery plan, and the House approved a $16.3 billion "emergency" appropriation that was exempt from the discretionary spending cap for the year. Senate Republicans then mounted a successful filibuster against the bill, forcing the Democratic leadership and the administration to accept only a $4 billion appropriation to fund extended unemployment benefits.

Congressional Democrats took the lead in boosting spending savings in the FY 1994 budget resolution that gained final approval on April 1, 1993. The $1.5 trillion budget plan endorsed most of the president's deficit-reduction initiatives but included an additional $50 billion in spending cuts for domestic programs. With adoption of the budget resolution, the stage was set for action on reconciliation legislation to implement the multiyear deficit-reduction program. More than two dozen House and Senate committees were issued reconciliation instructions for spending and revenue deficit-reduction targets, with the primary responsibilities resting with the Ways and Means and Finance Committees.

As House and Senate committees debated spending and tax changes, important modifications were made in the Clinton administration's proposals—the $71.5 billion energy tax was dropped, as was much of the investment spending that Clinton had proposed. The individual income tax increases, however, survived intact, and the $500 billion deficit-reduction goal was maintained. Since Republicans refused to support the tax increases and were hoping to hand Clinton an embarrassing defeat on his most important legislative priority, there was little bipartisan cooperation in formulating alternatives to the Clinton program. Instead, Democratic leaders in the House and Senate focused on limiting defections in their party, and the negotiations within and between the two chambers were arduous. The House finally managed to pass its version of the reconciliation bill on May 27 by a narrow 219 to 213 margin. The Senate's vote of 50 to 49, with Vice President Gore casting the tiebreaking vote, came on June 25.

The House and Senate then had to resolve major differences in their approaches to deficit reduction, particularly since the House bill contained substantially higher tax increases and lower spending cuts. When conferees dropped the House-passed energy tax in favor of the Senate's motor fuel tax, the loss in revenues required offsetting spending savings that threatened to unravel the shaky majority in the House. The situation in the Senate was equally uncertain, since several conservative Democrats had repeatedly called for much deeper spending retrenchments in Medicare and other entitlements than the conferees were willing to consider. On August 2, House and Senate Democratic leaders announced that agreement had been reached on the conference report, and the administration launched an intensive lobbying campaign, including a nationwide television speech by the president, to try to hold wavering Democrats in line. Last-minute promises were made by Clinton to take additional steps to control future spending, including entitlement limits, but no binding commitments were attached to the reconciliation conference report.[41] Even so, the Democratic majorities barely held together on the House and Senate floor votes. The importance of these votes was made abundantly clear by Democratic Senator Bob Kerrey, whose decision to support Clinton was announced just before the Senate vote took place. Kerrey declared, "I could not and should not cast the vote that brings down your presidency."[42] Kerrey's vote produced the tie that the vice president then broke, providing Clinton with perhaps his most crucial legislative victory.

OBRA 1993 Policy Changes

Deficit reduction from the 1993 reconciliation bill was calculated by the administration at more than $500 billion for fiscal years 1994–98.[43] The CBO estimate was only $433 billion, primarily because CBO excluded discretionary spending savings for 1994 and 1995 that had already been required under OBRA 1990.[44] With this exception, there was agreement on the size and distribution of the policy changes in OBRA 1993. In particular, revenue increases were by far the largest element in the deficit-reduction package, with these increases weighted toward higher tax burdens for high-income taxpayers (Table 7.4). According to the CBO, 80 percent of the net tax increases under OBRA 1993 would be paid by families with incomes of

---

41. On August 4, for example, Clinton signed an executive order establishing a "deficit-reduction trust fund." The order stated that none of the deficit savings in the reconciliation bill would be used for future new spending but solely for deficit reduction. *Congressional Quarterly Almanac, 1993,* 124.

42. *Congressional Quarterly Almanac, 1993,* 123.

43. *Congressional Quarterly Almanac, 1993,* 108.

44. Congressional Budget Office, *The Economic and Budget Outlook: An Update* (Washington, D.C.: CBO, September 1993), 28–29.

$200,000 or more.[45] In addition, the earned-income tax credit (EITC) expansion under OBRA 1993 greatly decreased effective tax rates for low-income taxpayers. When EITC changes were fully phased in, effective tax rates for the 20 percent of families with the lowest incomes were expected to fall to their lowest levels since the 1970s.

The Clinton administration had largely succeeded in redistributing tax burdens, a Democratic priority since the Reagan presidency. What the administration failed to achieve was approval for a major new revenue source, in the form of an energy tax, which could be used to offset its investment spending initiatives. The spending policy outcomes in 1993 were largely a continuation of the approach taken in OBRA 1990. The strictest controls, and most predictable deficit savings, were in discretionary programs. For fiscal years 1994–98, discretionary outlays were capped at, or slightly below, FY 1993 spending. The stringency of these caps was acceptable to Clinton and congressional Democrats, because their impact was expected to fall almost entirely on defense. The administration's 1993 budget program, and the corresponding congressional budget resolution, called for multiyear defense cuts that would permit real increases in domestic programs despite these discretionary caps.

Under OBRA 1993, mandatory spending savings did not appreciably affect entitlement benefits. In sharp contrast to discretionary spending, mandatory outlays were projected to grow by more than $300 billion between 1992 and 1998 (Table 7.5). The major entitlement savings under OBRA 1993 were healthcare cost controls that limited reimbursements to healthcare providers under Medicare and curtailed payments to the states for Medicaid. The 1990 reconciliation bill had assumed substantial savings from these same controls. Although initial results had been disappointing, it was hoped that heightened regulatory effectiveness would yield better results over time.

The absence of meaningful entitlement reforms in OBRA 1993 meant that deficit reduction depended on discretionary spending cuts and higher taxes. Unless Congress and the president violated the spending caps, discretionary spending savings would be fully realized. Higher revenue levels, however, were contingent on favorable economic conditions. Despite these limitations and uncertainties, the 1993 budget agreement had a greater impact than its Democratic supporters or Republican critics had anticipated.

---

45. These are estimates of comprehensive net effects of the tax policy changes. Congressional Budget Office, *The Economic and Budget Outlook: An Update* (1993), 31.

Table 7.4 Estimated Deficit Reduction Under OBRA 1993 (in billions of dollars)

			Fiscal Year			Five-Year Total
	1994	1995	1996	1997	1998	
Revenues						
Increase in Tax Rate for High-Income Individuals	$-15.4	$-22.8	$-25.7	$-24.6	$-26.3	$-114.8
Repeal of Cap on Earnings Subject to Medicare Tax	-2.8	-6.0	-6.4	-6.8	-7.2	-29.2
Increase in Taxable Portion of Social Security Benefits	-1.9	-4.6	-5.3	-6.0	-6.7	-24.6
Extension and Increase of Motor Fuels Tax	-4.4	-4.5	-7.4	-7.5	-7.5	-31.3
Increase in Corporate Tax Rate	-4.4	-2.8	-2.9	-3.1	-3.2	-16.4
Reduced Business Meal and Entertainment Deduction	-1.8	-3.1	-3.3	-3.4	-3.6	-15.3
Other	4.3	0.4	-0.5	-9.3	-4.0	-9.1
Subtotal	-26.4	-43.5	-51.5	-60.7	-58.5	-240.6
Mandatory Spending						
Medicare	-2.1	-5.5	-11.6	-16.4	-20.2	-55.8
Federal Employee Retirement and Health Benefits	-0.4	-0.8	-2.9	-3.7	-4.0	-12.0
Medicaid	*	-1.0	-1.6	-2.1	-2.5	-7.1
Federal Family Education Loans	-0.6	-0.4	-0.8	-1.2	-1.2	-4.3
Veterans' Benefits	-0.2	-0.4	-0.4	-0.4	-1.2	-2.6
Farm Programs	-0.1	-0.7	-0.5	-0.6	-0.5	-2.5
Refundable Earned Income Tax Credit	0.2	2.0	4.4	6.1	6.4	19.1
Food Stamps	*	0.2	0.4	0.8	1.0	2.5
FCC Electromagnetic Spectrum Auction	-1.7	-1.8	-1.7	-1.0	-1.0	-7.2
Other	-0.3	-0.2	-1.8	-2.4	-2.5	-7.2
Subtotal	-5.3	-8.5	-16.6	-20.9	-25.7	-76.9
Discretionary Spending	0	0	-7.7	-23.0	-37.9	-68.5
Debt Service	-0.9	-3.4	-7.5	-13.6	-21.3	-46.8
Total Deficit Reduction	-32.6	-55.5	-83.3	-118.1	-143.4	-432.9

* Less than $500 million.

Source: Congressional Budget Office, *The Economic and Budget Outlook: An Update* (Washington, D.C.: CBO, September 1993), 29.

Table 7.5 Baseline Spending Projections Under OBRA 1993 (in billions of dollars)

			Fiscal Year				
	Actual	Estimated	Projections				
	1992	1993	1994	1995	1996	1997	1998
Discretionary Outlays (Caps)	$536	$547	$542	$542	$548	$547	$547
Mandatory Outlays (Excluding Deposit Insurance)	712	764	808	855	901	969	1,035

Source: Congressional Budget Office, *The Economic and Budget Outlook: An Update* (Washington, D.C.: CBO, September 1993), 38.

The drop in the FY 1994 deficit was $50 billion more than projected, and the decline was even greater the following year, when the deficit fell to its lowest level since 1989. Nevertheless, after the Republican party captured control of the House and Senate in the 1994 midterm elections, the deficit issue returned to center stage.

The Government Shutdown and 1997 Balanced-Budget Accord

When the 104th Congress convened on January 4, 1995, the centerpiece of the Republican agenda was a balanced budget, but Republicans did not announce a specific plan to eliminate deficits. Instead, House and Senate leaders pressed for quick approval of a constitutional balanced-budget amendment. The version of the amendment introduced in the House required a balanced budget by 2002.[46] A three-fifths vote of the House and Senate would be needed to waive this requirement, except in the case of a declared military emergency, or to increase the publicly-held debt limit. In addition, a three-fifths vote of the House and Senate would be required to raise taxes, signaling the Republicans' determination to balance the budget through spending cuts. Republicans were forced to drop this last provision, and the House then proceeded to pass the balanced-budget amendment, HJ Res 1, by a 300 to 132 vote on January 26.

The brief House debate revealed, however, the pitfalls of a balanced-budget requirement unaccompanied by a detailed fiscal plan. The Clinton administration and congressional Democratic leaders charged that funding for Social

46. The balanced-budget deadline was 2002 or two years after ratification, whichever was later.

Security, Medicare, and education programs would be threatened once the balanced-budget amendment took effect. The Social Security issue was especially sensitive. Despite Republican pledges to protect Social Security benefits, Senate Democrats insisted that the Social Security trust funds be excluded from deficit calculations. When their proposals were rejected, thirty-three of the forty-seven Senate Democrats voted against the balanced-budget amendment on March 2, and it failed by a single vote.[47]

Republican efforts to strengthen controls over spending did succeed, however, with passage of a presidential line-item veto. Giving the president authority to veto individual items in appropriations bills could not possibly solve the deficit problem, but proponents of the line-item veto claimed that it would curb wasteful spending. Ronald Reagan had called for a line-item veto during his presidency and had endorsed a constitutional amendment as the "most effective" means of instituting it.[48] The amendment route, however, had proved too difficult, so sympathetic members of Congress turned to a statutory line-item veto.

A variety of line-item veto bills had been considered during the late 1980s and early 1990s, but none had come close to passing both chambers.[49] Opponents had argued that the line-item veto represented a transfer of power from Congress to the executive branch that was unwise in principle and, if accomplished by statute, an unconstitutional violation of the separation of powers between the branches. Republican leaders nevertheless decided to make the veto a legislative priority in 1995. Line-item veto bills were then passed by the House and Senate but in very different forms, and serious difficulties in reconciling these versions delayed final enactment until April 9, 1996, when President Clinton signed the Line-Item Veto Act.

The law signed by Clinton provided for "enhanced rescission" authority: the president was authorized to send Congress rescission proposals canceling previously enacted appropriations, as well as certain tax benefits and limited types of entitlement spending. Rescission proposals would take effect automatically, unless Congress passed a special disapproval bill. Any disapproval

---

47. The official vote was 65 to 35. Majority leader Robert Dole, who suggested the amendment, voted against it to have the opportunity to call for a re-vote. He did so on June 6, 1996, but the amendment failed again, this time by a 64 to 35 vote. The only Democratic provision that Republicans added to the amendment text was a prohibition against judicial enforcement.

48. *Congressional Quarterly Almanac, 1984*, 6-E.

49. On this background and the constitutional arguments, see Louis Fisher, *Congressional Abdication on War and Spending* (College Station: Texas A&M University Press, 2000), 137–53.

bill, however, could then be vetoed by the president, and a two-thirds vote of the House and Senate would be required to override the veto.

The line-item veto took effect on January 1, 1997, and was soon challenged in the courts. It was overturned by the Supreme Court the following year as an unconstitutional violation of the legislative procedures set forth in the Constitution.[50] In the interim, President Clinton had used it sparingly, particularly after Congress blocked his vetoes of approximately $290 million in FY 1998 military construction appropriations.[51] A second cancellation package, affecting the federal civilian retirement system, was withdrawn by the administration. Only about $355 million in FY 1998 cancellations survived, and the administration made almost no use of the veto authority over targeted tax benefits.[52]

The demise of the line-item veto evoked surprisingly little reaction in Congress. Efforts to revive it in constitutionally acceptable form were ignored, in part because its irrelevance to serious deficit reduction had been amply demonstrated during its brief existence. The balanced-budget constitutional amendment had been much more important in Republican plans to reshape the federal budget, and their failure to pass the amendment in 1995 launched a series of budget battles with the Clinton administration that dominated the legislative agenda for almost two years. The opening round was a sweeping Republican alternative to Clinton's FY 1996 budget.

The "Train Wreck": FY 1996

On May 18, 1995, the House adopted a FY 1996 budget resolution that called for spending cuts sufficiently large to bring the budget into balance during a seven-year period, while exempting both Social Security and defense and permitting a large tax cut. The spending reductions in the House plan totaled $1.04 trillion, with Medicare ($288 billion) and Medicaid ($187 billion) providing nearly half of the savings. The tax cuts exceeded $350 billion, with the largest elements being reduced capital gains taxes and a $500-per-child tax credit for families. These spending cuts and tax cuts were scaled down by the Senate, but the final version of the FY 1996 budget resolution

---

50. The vote was 6 to 3, affirming a ruling by a federal district court. *Clinton v. City of New York*, 118 S. Ct. 2091 (1998).

51. These estimated savings were over a five-year period. Fisher, *Congressional Abdication on War and Spending*, 149.

52. Fisher, *Congressional Abdication on War and Spending*, 150.

still included almost $900 billion in reduced spending along with a $245 billion tax cut.

The Republicans' balanced-budget plan put the Clinton administration on the defensive, at least temporarily. President Clinton's FY 1996 budget, sent to Congress on February 6, had contained only minor deficit-reduction proposals. Under the president's budget, deficits were projected to remain at the $200 billion level through FY 2000. With Republicans uniting behind their ambitious and aggressive balanced-budget program, the president decided to scrap his original budget. On June 13, President Clinton announced a ten-year plan to balance the budget by 2005, a timetable that allowed him to offer smaller spending cuts than Republicans had endorsed, particularly for Medicare and other social welfare entitlements.

Clinton's announcement was condemned by Democratic liberals, who insisted that the additional spending cuts in the administration's new program were unacceptable. Meanwhile, congressional Republicans decided that the president's timetable was too long and his policy prescriptions too limited. Republicans seized on a CBO critique of the president's program to argue that the budget could not be balanced without the types of spending cuts they had demanded.[53] Republican leaders believed that public support for a balanced budget was sufficiently strong to permit major cutbacks in politically popular spending programs, and they were convinced that Clinton would eventually be forced to accept their proposals.

The FY 1996 budget resolution was adopted on June 29 by party-line votes in the House and Senate.[54] With the congressional budget plan in place, Republicans began to work on a reconciliation bill incorporating both spending and tax cuts, and House and Senate committees were given specific reconciliation instructions for fiscal years 1996–2002. While Medicare and Medicaid cuts were the largest and most controversial element of these reconciliation instructions, numerous other entitlements, from farm subsidies to federal employee pensions to the earned-income tax credit, were also slated for substantial reductions. There were, not surprisingly, difficulties in holding Republicans together as entitlement programs were reviewed by House and Senate committees, and neither chamber met the September 22

53. According to the CBO, the president's budget program would have resulted in a $200 billion deficit in 2005. *Congressional Quarterly Almanac, 1995* (Washington, D.C.: Congressional Quarterly, 1996), 2–29.

54. The Senate vote was 54 (Republican) to 46 (Democrat). In the House, one Republican and eight Democrats crossed party lines.

deadline for having all reconciliation proposals in the hands of their respective budget committees. Nevertheless, the House Budget Committee was able to send a complete reconciliation package to the floor of the House on October 20, and the Republicans passed the bill by a comfortable 227 to 203 margin on October 26. The Senate adopted its version of the reconciliation bill on October 28, with only one senator crossing party lines. Over the next three weeks, House and Senate conferees put together a compromise reconciliation bill that cleared Congress on November 20.

As the reconciliation bill proceeded through Congress, President Clinton joined congressional Democrats in denouncing the policy changes that Republicans were pressing. The Medicare cutbacks were the most inviting target, as Democrats repeatedly charged that social welfare retrenchments were being used to finance Republican tax cuts. Clinton's threat to veto the Republican reconciliation package was carried out on December 6, with the president's veto message citing "profound differences with the extreme approach that the Republican majority has adopted."[55]

The deadlock on reconciliation had no immediate repercussions, but Republicans were also challenging President Clinton on other fronts. The first was a threat to block needed increases in the statutory debt limit unless the president agreed to their balanced-budget plan. In September, House Speaker Newt Gingrich had declared that Republicans were ready to risk a government default if Clinton refused to accept their tax and spending proposals. On November 10, Republicans passed a short-term debt extension but coupled it to multiple provisions that the administration opposed, including a commitment by the president to balance the budget by 2002 using congressional economic assumptions and spending estimates.[56] Clinton vetoed the debt-limit extension, and Secretary of the Treasury Robert E. Rubin then orchestrated a series of debt refinancing actions that allowed the government to circumvent the looming debt-limit problem.

There was no room for maneuver, however, on the appropriations front. Republicans were confident that they could cut domestic discretionary outlays well below the president's budget requests, since the president would not risk vetoing reduced appropriations and thereby shutting down agencies and programs. The FY 1996 budget resolution ordered the appropriations

55. *Congressional Quarterly Almanac, 1995*, D-37.

56. One of the persistent Republican demands was that CBO, rather than OMB, estimates be used in any balanced-budget plan calculations.

committees to cut nondefense discretionary outlays by $10 billion below the 1995 level and specified larger reductions in future years. The House and Senate Appropriations Committees then proceeded to expand these cuts and to attach numerous policy riders to domestic appropriations bills. Abortion restrictions, environmental deregulation, and other challenges to Democratic legislative commitments sometimes overshadowed funding debates within the Appropriations Committees, and disagreements among Republican appropriators over just how far to push these riders delayed action on all but two FY 1996 spending bills beyond the October 1 start of the fiscal year.[57]

The administration and Congress averted this first deadline with a six-week continuing resolution that gave the Republicans a partial victory on funding levels. Continuing programs, for example, were limited to the average of the House- and Senate-passed bills minus an additional 5 percent. Programs that Republicans had zeroed out, however, were allowed to continue at 90 percent of their FY 1995 appropriations, and the policy riders that had been added to the House and Senate bills were not included in the continuing resolution. Both sides also agreed to protect federal employees from any spending cutbacks. The continuing resolution included language authorizing additional spending to ensure that agencies would not be forced to furlough their employees.

The first FY 1996 continuing resolution expired on November 13, and, by that time, Republicans were intent on forcing the president to accept much more stringent conditions for another continuing resolution. Only three of the thirteen regular appropriations bills had been signed, a fourth had been vetoed, and several others contained policy riders that the president had said were unacceptable. With their reconciliation bill facing a presidential veto, Republican leaders hoped to force the president to negotiate an alternative budget agreement that would include all disputed appropriations bills and a compromise reconciliation measure, while adhering to the seven-year balanced-budget timetable. On November 13, Congress sent the president a new continuing resolution, which committed the administration to spending cuts in domestic appropriations, to Medicare premium increases, and to a balanced-budget deadline. This continuing resolution was vetoed, and a six-day government shutdown followed, with 800,000 federal workers affected.

---

57. The military construction and legislative branch appropriations were cleared on September 22. Clinton signed the military construction bill but vetoed the legislative branch appropriation.

The shutdown created problems for the Republicans and for Clinton. Public opinion polls indicated that Republicans were considered more at fault for the shutdown than the president, but congressional Democrats were becoming uneasy that the administration might lose the more important debate over when and how to balance the budget. When Congress passed a new continuing resolution, which dropped the Medicare proposals but retained the balanced-budget requirements, forty-eight House Democrats and seven Senate Democrats voted with the Republicans. Although Republican leaders still lacked enough votes for an override, the number of Democratic defections was much higher than expected. If not for the startling admission by House Speaker Gingrich that the ongoing shutdown had been precipitated by personal animosities toward Clinton, the White House might have faced a much more decisive erosion in Democratic support.[58]

A compromise continuing resolution was finally worked out on November 20. The four-week extension provided funding for all agencies and programs whose budgets had not been passed, including programs that Republicans had scheduled for termination, and the White House agreed to meet with congressional representatives to formulate a seven-year balanced-budget plan by the end of December. Republicans pledged that their balanced-budget proposals would "protect" designated programs, including Medicare and Medicaid; reform public assistance programs; and implement tax policies to help working families and stimulate economic growth. The White House accepted the Republican demand that CBO spending estimates and economic assumptions be used to certify any balanced-budget plan, although CBO was instructed to consult with the Office of Management and Budget (OMB) and other budget analysts in its certification process.

On December 15, this second continuing resolution expired. By this time, the reconciliation bill had been vetoed, and budget talks between the administration and Congress had broken down. Six appropriations bills were still blocked, and the government shutdown that ensued sent 300,000 federal employees home and closed down numerous domestic agencies. Clinton held firm, vetoing three disputed appropriations bills on December 18, and House Republicans threatened to continue the shutdown until a balanced-budget agreement was reached. In the Senate, majority leader Robert Dole publicly broke with House leaders and called for immediate action to reopen the government, but House Republicans only agreed to allow the District of

58. See *Congressional Quarterly Almanac, 1995,* 11-5.

Columbia government to keep running and veterans' and welfare benefit checks to be issued through January 3. Then, with 260,000 federal employees still locked out, Congress adjourned for the Christmas recess.

By the time Congress reconvened in early January, most Republicans recognized that their shutdown strategy had been a political debacle. The poll data were indisputable, reflecting public anger over the shutdown and public blame toward the Republicans for having caused it. Majority leader Dole, who was seeking the Republican presidential nomination in 1996, insisted that the government be reopened, and House Republicans finally relented, approving several continuing resolutions that completely restored government operations on January 6.

The budget battle was not entirely over. Additional continuing resolutions had to be passed before the appropriations process for FY 1996 could be completed, and Republicans tried to revive the balanced-budget talks. In the end, all the Republicans had gained was a modest cutback in discretionary domestic spending; Clinton had prevailed on the most controversial policy riders and managed to preserve funding for programs that the Republicans had vowed to eliminate. Clinton had also managed to blunt the Republicans' broader attempt to reshape federal spending policy as part of their balanced-budget program. Two government shutdowns, fourteen continuing resolutions, and seven months after the fiscal year began, the last of the FY 1996 appropriations disputes was finally resolved. With only five months left to deal with FY 1997 appropriations and the fall election looming, Republicans had to decide whether to renew their assault on domestic spending. After some dispirited attempts to revive their balanced-budget challenge, Republicans abandoned their efforts to cut domestic programs and to pass large tax cuts. With President Clinton having regained the offensive on budget policy, congressional Republicans had to settle for limiting their losses.

The FY 1997 Budget Round

The appropriations battles in 1995 were about domestic spending cuts and conservative policy riders that congressional Republicans hoped to impose on a politically vulnerable president. One year later, President Clinton's public standing had improved dramatically, Republicans were nervous about their chances of retaining control of Congress, and the administration was pressing for increased spending and liberal policy riders. By early September, two FY 1997 appropriations bills, the agriculture and District of Columbia funding measures, had been passed, and several others were on the verge of being cleared. The remaining domestic appropriations bills, however, were tied up because of administration demands for additional funding.

To expedite the appropriations process, Republican leaders offered to work out an omnibus appropriations package, including all of the pending domestic bills, with the administration. On September 16, White House representatives met with the congressional leadership and presented Clinton's demand for a $6.5 billion increase in domestic appropriations, primarily for elementary and secondary education aid and job training and employment services. When Republicans agreed, new spending demands were introduced, along with policy riders that Clinton insisted be included in the omnibus appropriations package.

The administration's tactics succeeded. Funding for the White House's domestic priorities was well above the previous year's levels.[59] The Labor-Health and Human Services-Education spending bill contained a 10 percent increase for the Labor Department and close to a 15 percent increase for the Education Department. Appropriations for elementary and secondary education programs were more than $600 million above Clinton's initial budget request, and Congress also agreed to add funds to several public health programs. The Interior Department appropriations bill, which had been the target of funding cuts and policy riders in 1995, was treated much more gingerly in 1996. Hostile environmental riders were rejected, and final funding actually exceeded the administration's budget request. The Commerce Department, which Republicans previously had tried to terminate, had its FY 1996 appropriation increased by $100 million, and the combined Commerce-Justice-State appropriation was more than $2.2 billion above what Congress had approved the year before.

White House negotiators also prevailed on controversial policy riders. A number of Republican-sponsored riders had been dropped as bills moved from the House to the Senate, and additional ones were removed as the omnibus appropriations talks proceeded. The president's representatives then used the appropriations measure to rewrite a pending bill on immigration.[60] Republicans were forced to drop provisions that would have denied

59. *Congressional Quarterly Almanac, 1996* (Washington, D.C.: Congressional Quarterly, 1997), 10-20–10-92.

60. *Congressional Quarterly Almanac, 1996*, 5-3.

government benefits to legal immigrants, imposed new income tests for sponsors of legal immigrants, and barred public education for the children of illegal immigrants.[61]

Republicans managed to boost defense spending above Clinton's budget, adding nearly $10 billion to the FY 1997 defense appropriation bill. The president also reluctantly signed a military construction appropriation that was approximately 10 percent higher than his budget request. The combined effect of domestic and defense appropriations increases was to exceed the spending limits that Republicans had set in their FY 1997 budget resolution.[62] Although Republican leaders claimed that they had complied with the limits, they were forced to use accounting gimmicks to accommodate the additional spending.

During the 104th Congress, Republicans failed to cut the level and change the composition of discretionary spending. Domestic discretionary outlays had risen, in constant dollars, by more than 25 percent from 1988 to 1995, while inflation-adjusted defense outlays had dropped by almost 30 percent. During FY 1996, after the tumultuous Republican attacks on spending, domestic outlays fell by under 4 percent, while defense dropped by 6 percent. The following year, real spending for discretionary domestic programs increased, while defense spending was flat. If Democrats had retained control of Congress in 1994, the defense decline would probably have been more pronounced and the domestic growth somewhat greater, but the Republican takeover did not yield the discretionary spending changes the party had advocated so strenuously. Instead, the domestic discretionary spending levels that Clinton had targeted in 1993 remained largely in place.

Republicans also failed in their efforts to cut the rate of growth in Medicare and Medicaid. Neither of these programs was substantially revised in 1995 and 1996. In 1996, however, Congress did manage to pass a historic welfare reform bill that ended the Aid to Families with Dependent Children (AFDC) welfare entitlement and revised other public assistance programs. President Clinton, who had previously vetoed two Republican-sponsored welfare reform measures, signed the Personal Responsibility and Work Opportunity Reconciliation Act on August 22, 1996. This compromise bill contained projected savings of $55 billion in cash welfare payments, food

61. *Congressional Quarterly Almanac, 1996*, 5-17.
62. *Congressional Quarterly Almanac, 1996*, 10-20.

stamps, Supplemental Security Income (SSI), and related benefits for fiscal years 1997–2002.[63]

The most important change in the 1996 welfare bill was the substitution of block grants to the states for Temporary Assistance to Needy Families (TANF) as a replacement for AFDC. This change allowed the states to exercise much greater control over eligibility and benefits, while also establishing time limits and work requirements for welfare recipients.[64] Work requirements were also applied to the food stamp and Medicaid programs. The projected welfare reform savings were based on the block grant authorizations for TANF and on eligibility and benefit restrictions for food stamps and SSI benefits.

The 1996 welfare compromise, however, did not include Medicaid program changes Republicans had proposed. The welfare reform-Medicaid bill that Republicans introduced in May 1996 had included the termination of the Medicaid entitlement and the establishment of fixed-sum federal grants to the states to fund health insurance programs for the poor. Projected Medicaid savings were $72 billion, or approximately 10 percent, over six years. The Clinton administration and congressional Democrats insisted that these Medicaid provisions be removed, and they also made Republicans drop additional non-AFDC program revisions. In particular, benefits for working families under the EITC were fully protected. With Medicaid and EITC benefits unchanged, the budgetary impact of the 1996 welfare overhaul was limited, but the changes in program philosophy were far-reaching. Work requirements, time limits, and eligibility restrictions redefined the federal government's relationship to the poor and set new and ambitious goals for welfare policy reform.

A third Republican objective, large tax cuts, was blocked by Clinton's veto of the 1995 reconciliation bill. Included in that measure were a $500-per-child tax credit for families, a capital gains tax cut for individuals and businesses, and a phaseout of the alternative minimum tax for corporations. The net reduction in revenues that Republicans had sponsored in 1995 was estimated at $245 billion over seven years. What Republicans finally succeeded in passing was a 1996 tax cut for small businesses as part of an increase in the minimum wage. This tax cut was estimated at $10 billion over five years.[65]

63. Congressional Budget Office, *The Economic and Budget Outlook: Fiscal Years 1998–2007* (Washington, D.C.: CBO, 1997), 21–22.

64. *Congressional Quarterly Almanac, 1996*, 6-6.

65. *Congressional Quarterly Almanac, 1996*, 2-34.

The 1997 Reconciliation Bills

With the 1990 and 1993 tax increases still fully in effect, revenue levels were beginning to climb more rapidly than had been anticipated.[66] As a result, the deficit for 1996 was lower than had been projected, and the deficit outlook for FY 1997 was even more positive, when the 105th Congress, still controlled by Republicans, faced a newly reelected President Clinton in 1997. Nevertheless, CBO and administration projections still showed future deficits beginning to climb unless additional deficit-reduction measures were adopted. Against this backdrop, the administration sent to Congress its plan for balancing the budget by FY 2002. Unlike the partisan clashes that had erupted over Clinton's budgets in the previous two years, the 1997 budget negotiations began with pledges of bipartisanship by both sides. While a number of disputes over tax cuts and healthcare entitlements threatened to derail the talks at several points, a general agreement between the White House and Republican leaders was announced on May 2. On May 15, a detailed budget plan was ratified, followed by the passage of a congressional budget resolution and, in August, two reconciliation bills.

The initial impetus behind the 1997 budget pact was President Clinton's acceptance of the 2002 balanced-budget deadline that Republicans had championed. His FY 1998 budget message declared that "much of the hard work of reaching balance in 2002" had been accomplished, and Clinton called on Congress "to help . . . finish the job."[67] The task that remained, according to administration projections, was much less prepossessing than the deficit situation in 1990 or in 1993. The administration's proposed changes for FY 1998–2002 totaled approximately $235 billion in deficit reduction, with an additional $15 billion in debt-service savings. Thus, the size of the initial deficit-reduction package in 1997 was about half that of the 1990 and 1993 efforts, and it had the added attraction of being reasonably likely to produce an actual balanced budget.

The improved fiscal outlook in 1997 was the result of strong economic growth and favorable budget trends. Spending growth rates had begun to

66. The baseline deficits for fiscal years 1996 and 1997 dropped by nearly $85 billion during the latter part of 1996. Approximately half of this amount was the result of revised revenue estimates. Much of the remainder reflected revised technical assumptions for Medicare and Medicaid. Congressional Budget Office, *The Economic and Budget Outlook: Fiscal Years 1998–2007*, xxi.

67. *Budget of the United States Government, Fiscal Year 1998* (Washington, D.C.: Government Printing Office, 1997), 3, 7.

Table 7.6 Revenue and Outlay Growth, 1991–1997

	Percentage Increase over Previous Year	
Fiscal Year	Revenues	Outlays
1991	2.2%	5.7%
1992	3.4	4.3
1993	5.8	2.0
1994	9.0	3.7
1995	7.4	3.7
1996	7.5	3.0
1997	8.7	2.6
Average Annual Percentage Increase	6.3	3.6
Total Increase, 1991–97	49.7	20.9

SOURCE: *Historical Tables, Budget of the United States Government, Fiscal Year 2002* (Washington, D.C.: Government Printing Office, 2001), 22.

slow during the early 1990s, primarily as the result of defense cuts and deposit insurance stabilization. Between 1991 and 1997, net outlays for these two spending categories fell by nearly $130 billion.[68] Then, beginning in 1993, revenue growth rates began to climb (Table 7.6). By the mid-1990s, revenues were outpacing economic growth, while the reverse was occurring with spending.

The 1997 budget negotiations were eased by budget projections that became more optimistic as the talks proceeded. As the deficit-reduction requirements became smaller and smaller, the necessity for major policy adjustments disappeared. Politically difficult choices still remained, however, over tax and spending cuts. Republicans could not hope to achieve tax cuts remotely comparable to those that had been advanced in 1995, but they still were committed to selective tax reductions. The Clinton administration, in turn, could not expect to avoid spending concessions, but the president's legislative priorities had to be accommodated as well. These competing priorities gave the 1997 balanced-budget agreement its unusual twist. Its tax provisions provided immediate relief, but spending cuts were phased in at a later date. An estimated 70 percent of the net spending cuts were postponed

68. Defense outlays dropped from $320 to $272 billion. Deposit insurance outlays were $66 billion in 1991 but –$14 billion in 1997. Negative outlays were the result of deposit insurance receipts exceeding spending. *Historical Tables, Budget of the United States Government, Fiscal Year 2002*, 123.

Table 7.7 Projected Deficits Under the May 1997 Budget Agreement (in billions of dollars)

	Fiscal Year				
1997 (est.)	1998	1999	2000	2001	2002
$ −67.0	$ −90.4	$ −89.7	$ −83.0	$ −53.3	$ +1.3

SOURCE: *Congressional Quarterly Almanac, 1997* (Washington, D.C.: Congressional Quarterly, 1998), 2–18.

until fiscal years 2001 and 2002, while the tax reductions were spread much more evenly over the five years covered by the agreement.[69] As a result, the deficit projections for the agreement actually showed a short-term rise in deficit levels (Table 7.7). Not until FY 2001, the fourth year of the agreement, was the deficit expected to fall below its 1997 level, and the projected surplus for 2002 was minuscule.

The Parameters. The deficit-reduction goal for the 1997 budget agreement was approximately $200 billion. This total included $85 billion in net tax relief for fiscal years 1998–2002 and $280 billion in net spending reductions.[70] The spending savings combined $140 billion in discretionary program savings, tied to the extension of discretionary spending caps through 2002, with $140 billion in mandatory program reductions. The largest reductions in mandatory spending affected Medicare, with projected savings of $115 billion over five years. The budget agreement further specified, however, that more than $30 billion in additional funding would be provided for designated presidential priorities—children's health insurance, welfare benefits for disabled legal immigrants, food stamps, and a number of discretionary domestic programs. Tradeoffs were used on the revenue side as well. The capital gains tax cut, child tax credit, and other revenue-loss provisions that Republicans supported had a five-year cost of $135 billion. Republicans agreed to offset $50 billion of this amount with "revenue raisers," primarily airline ticket and excise taxes.

With the presidential-congressional budget pact in place, the House and Senate adopted the FY 1998 congressional budget resolution as the first step in implementing the agreement. The resolution contained reconciliation

69. *Congressional Quarterly Almanac, 1997* (Washington, D.C.: Congressional Quarterly, 1998), 2–18.

70. *Congressional Quarterly Almanac, 1997*, 2–20.

instructions for authorizing and tax-writing committees, with the requirement that the tax and spending reconciliation bills be considered separately.[71] Included as well were discretionary spending limits for the Appropriations Committees. There were scattered challenges to the House and Senate versions of the budget resolution, but majorities of both parties finally lined up in support, and the conference report was approved by equally wide margins on June 25.

Over the next several weeks, House and Senate committees worked on detailed reconciliation proposals, with the Budget Committees monitoring and coordinating these efforts. The House and Senate passed their versions of both reconciliation bills by the end of June, but important differences then had to be resolved in conference. The conference negotiations were further complicated by the president's repeated veto threats. Before the conference meetings were concluded, a final round of negotiations took place between Republican leaders and White House representatives. To secure the president's agreement to sign the final bills, Republicans had to make additional concessions on healthcare spending and tax credits. By incorporating these concessions into the conference report, the Republican leadership ensured overwhelming bipartisan support during the House and Senate floor votes. The only opposition at this point came from liberal Democrats, who were still upset with the distribution of tax benefits.

Spending. The spending reconciliation bill, entitled the Balanced Budget Act of 1997, cleared Congress on July 31 and was signed into law on August 5. The budget enforcement provisions in the bill included extension of discretionary spending caps and PAYGO rules through 2002.[72] The actual levels set under the caps provided small increases in nominal spending for three years and slight reductions thereafter (Table 7.8). To provide some protection for defense and to defuse partisan conflicts over upcoming appropriations, "firewalls" between defense and nondefense spending were set for the first three years.[73] In addition, discretionary spending cuts were backloaded so

71. The unusual two-bill implementation had been insisted on by the White House. The purpose was to allow Clinton and congressional Democrats to block tax cuts that had unacceptable distributive effects. Clinton also insisted that his backing of the budget agreement was contingent on majority support of the budget resolution by congressional Democrats. *Congressional Quarterly Almanac, 1997*, 2-24.

72. The PAYGO enforcement procedures, that is, sequesters, applied through 2006. *Congressional Quarterly Almanac, 1997*, 2-53.

73. A separate category was also created for "violent crime reduction" budget authority and outlays for FY 1998–2000. These were approximately $5 billion annually. The remainder under

Table 7.8 1997 Balanced Budget Act Discretionary Spending Caps and Savings, 1998–2002 (in billions of dollars)

	Fiscal Year				
	1998	1999	2000	2001	2002
Outlay Cap	$ 556	$ 561	$ 566	$ 565	$ 561
Estimated Deficit Savings	10.8	−1.1	−13.8	−31.4	−53.3

SOURCE: Congressional Budget Office, *The Economic and Budget Outlook: An Update* (Washington, D.C.: CBO, September 1997), 30, 40.

that decisions about program cutbacks could be postponed until after the Clinton administration had left office.

The projected deficit savings in the Balanced Budget Act were slightly below the levels in the budget agreement that the administration and Congress had announced several months earlier. Final discretionary spending savings were estimated at approximately $90 billion over five years, while net mandatory savings were approximately $105 billion.[74] Medicare program changes accounted for almost all of the mandatory spending cuts. Medicare reductions were estimated at more than $110 billion between 1998 and 2002, primarily through lower payment rates for healthcare providers. There were additional, but much smaller, cutbacks affecting Medicaid, veterans' programs, and several other entitlements, as well as more than $20 billion in deficit reduction from increased receipts tied to electromagnetic spectrum broadcast auctions by the Federal Communications Commission. The reconciliation bill offset a portion of these spending savings, however, with a new block grant to the states for children's health insurance and with increased spending for SSI, food stamps, and welfare-to-work grants. The largest of these was the Children's Health Insurance Program, with five-year costs of approximately $20 billion. An additional $14 billion in public assistance spending was targeted toward restoring benefits that had been denied under the 1996 welfare reform law.

---

the caps was for all nondefense spending. For fiscal years 2001 and 2002, however, the caps for discretionary spending applied to all defense and nondefense programs. The defense-nondefense firewalls had first been used under OBRA 1990 for FY 1991–93. *Congressional Quarterly Almanac, 1997*, 2-52.

74. Congressional Budget Office, *The Economic and Budget Outlook: An Update* (Washington, D.C.: CBO, September 1997), 40–41.

The most important spending retrenchments in the reconciliation bill, therefore, affected discretionary programs and Medicare. For the former, defense and nondefense programs were to be held at stable current-dollar levels, which translated into a 10 percent or greater drop in real spending over five years.[75] For Medicare, spending growth would continue but at a slower pace. The various Medicare reimbursement curbs were expected to bring annual outlay growth down from 8.5 percent to 6 percent over the FY 1998–2002 period.[76] There were, however, no major benefit changes in the Medicare program. The Senate had included a phased increase in the eligibility age for Medicare and an income-based, or means-tested, formula for Medicare Part B premiums in its spending reconciliation bill, but these provisions were dropped during conference. Nevertheless, there was greater balance between discretionary and mandatory spending cutbacks in 1997 than there had been in either the 1990 or 1993 reconciliation bills.

Tax Cuts. The Taxpayer Relief Act constituted the tax portion of the 1997 reconciliation package, and the net tax reductions it provided were reasonably close to the parameters of the spring agreement. Five-year revenue losses were projected at $80 billion, with the ten-year cost expanding to more than $240 billion (Table 7.9). The largest tax reduction was the child tax credit ($400 in 1998 and $500 beginning in 1999) that Republicans had long promoted. Under pressure from Clinton and congressional Democrats, Republicans modified the tax credit to include a phaseout for upper-income taxpayers, and benefits to low-income families were also made available through refundable earned-income tax credits. Tax credits for educational expenses were another administration victory, and both the Hope and Lifetime Learning benefits included upper-income phaseouts. Altogether, eleven new education tax incentives were established in 1997, with a five-year revenue cost of almost $40 billion.

The Republican leadership succeeded in reducing capital gains tax rates for long-term investments and in raising the tax exemption for estates and gifts. The tax treatment of individual retirement accounts (IRAs) was liberalized, with higher-income limits for deductible IRAs and new, nondeductible Roth IRAs. Tax relief for businesses included easing of alternative minimum tax rules, particularly for small companies. The short-term revenue effects of most of these changes were relatively small, although costs did begin to

75. Congressional Budget Office, *The Economic and Budget Outlook: An Update* (1997), 41.
76. Congressional Budget Office, *The Economic and Budget Outlook: An Update* (1997), 41.

Table 7.9 1997 Taxpayer Relief Act Revenue Changes, 1997–2007 (in billions of dollars)

	Fiscal Year Totals	
	1997–2002	1997–2007
Provisions That Reduce Revenues		
Child Tax Credit	$ −73	$ −155
Education Incentives	−39	−99
Estate and Gift Tax Reductions	−6	−34
Capital Gains Rate Reductions	—	−21
IRA Expansions	−2	−20
All Other	−20	−43
	−141	−373
Provisions That Increase Revenues		
Airport and Airway Taxes	33	80
Increase in Cigarette Tax	5	17
All Other	21	36
	60	131
Net Change, All Provisions		
	−80	−242

SOURCE: Congressional Budget Office, *The Economic and Budget Outlook: An Update* (Washington, D.C.: CBO, September 1997), 36.

accelerate after 2002. To meet the $80 billion revenue loss target, however, several offsetting tax increases were added, notably taxes on cigarettes and air travel, totaling $60 billion from 1998 to 2002.

Both the size of the tax cut and its distributional effects were different from the plans that congressional Republicans had advanced in 1995. The estimated revenue loss from the Taxpayer Relief Act was approximately 1 percent of revenues in any given year or less than 0.3 percent of GDP.[77] With revenue levels during 1996 and 1997 well above 19 percent of GDP, the revenue impact of the tax-cut package was relatively minor. In addition, the child tax credit and education incentives, which accounted for the largest share of the multiyear tax reduction, were targeted at low- and middle-income taxpayers.

Deficits and Surpluses. When action was completed on the 1997 reconciliation bills, baseline budget projections still showed deficits remaining in place for several years.[78] Moreover, the so-called on-budget deficits—budget

77. Congressional Budget Office, *The Economic and Budget Outlook: An Update* (1997), 35.
78. Congressional Budget Office, *The Economic and Budget Outlook: An Update* (1997), 30.

totals that excluded Social Security trust funds—remained large.[79] Even the balanced budget projected for 2002 was the result of a Social Security surplus that offset a nearly $90 billion deficit for the rest of the budget, and on-budget deficits of similar magnitude were expected to continue indefinitely.

During FY 1998, however, the budget outlook began to improve much more rapidly than anyone had expected. The major cause of disappearing deficits was a surprising rise in revenue levels accompanied by an equally unforeseen drop in spending growth. As these trends became more pronounced, the FY 1998 budget moved into surplus, and revised forecasts showed progressively larger surpluses over time. These improvements, moreover, extended even to the on-budget accounts, which were moving from deficit to surplus.

The magnitude of these forecasting swings became even greater over the next two years, as revenue levels continued to surge.[80] The rise in revenues was particularly steep for individual income taxes. From FY 1993 to FY 1998, individual income tax receipts grew at an annual rate of more than 10 percent.[81] In FY 2000, individual income tax revenues went up more than 14 percent, and the individual income tax-GDP ratio was 10.2 percent, well above the previous peak set in World War II.

Changes on the spending side of the budget also contributed to the abrupt shift from deficits to surpluses. The rate of growth in spending slowed significantly during the mid-1990s, and, in FY 1997, the outlay-GDP level dropped below 20 percent for the first time since the early 1970s. With spending growth rates lagging well behind GDP increases and even further behind revenue growth, the projected deficits in 1998 and 1999 gave way to surpluses. When the Clinton administration sent its FY 2000 budget to Congress on February 1, 1999, it trumpeted "decades of surpluses to come."[82]

These remarkable improvements in the fiscal outlook had actually begun well before the 1997 balanced-budget agreement was reached. As shown in Table 7.10, the combined effects of the 1990 and 1993 reconciliation efforts started to take hold during the mid-1990s. Before then, revenue levels were falling below projections. Beginning in 1996, however, these revenue shortfalls

79. Congressional Budget Office, *The Economic and Budget Outlook: An Update* (1997), 30.

80. On explanations for this phenomenon, see Congressional Budget Office, *The Budget and Economic Outlook: Fiscal Years 2002–2011* (Washington, D.C.: CBO, 2001), 55–58.

81. Congressional Budget Office, *The Budget and Economic Outlook: Fiscal Years 2002–2011*, 54.

82. *Budget of the United States Government, Fiscal Year 2000* (Washington, D.C.: Government Printing Office, 1999), 3.

began to disappear. On the spending side, outlays were generally below projected levels, but the differentials were small until 1997. The confluence of mounting spending savings and escalating revenues in 1997 and later years yielded much greater deficit reduction than had been projected.

Clinton Versus Congress: Surplus Budgets

With budget surpluses suddenly available, the Clinton administration was intent on raising domestic spending while blocking Republican tax cuts. The former proved relatively easy, since even congressional Republicans were developing an appetite for increased spending on domestic programs. The latter was more difficult, since revenue levels remained exceptionally high. The strategy that Clinton employed, with considerable success, was to insist that tax cuts be postponed until a Social Security reform package was in place. In the interim, Social Security surpluses would be used only for debt reduction. By walling off most of the projected surplus to "protect" Social Security, Clinton was able to blunt the Republican pressures for tax cuts through the remainder of his second term.

The investigation and impeachment of President Clinton by the House of Representatives in 1998 obviously overshadowed the debates over budget policy. Despite the scandals and distractions, the administration's budget program fared remarkably well. In February, Clinton's budget message to Congress declared that "the Administration and Congress should not spend a budget surplus for any reason until we have a solution to the long-term financing challenge facing Social Security."[83] This declaration was a warning to Republicans that attempts to push large tax cuts would be portrayed as a threat to Social Security's future solvency. Clinton also called for additional spending on domestic programs, and the lure of additional spending proved irresistible.

Congress failed to pass a budget resolution, primarily because of House-Senate differences over domestic spending.[84] These spending disputes carried over onto appropriations bills, most of which had failed to pass by the October 1 deadline. When Republican leaders tried to expedite action by packaging these bills into an omnibus appropriations measure, Clinton threatened a veto unless additional funding was provided. The president

---

83. *Budget of the United States Government, Fiscal Year 1999* (Washington, D.C.: Government Printing Office, 1998), 3.

84. This was the first time that Congress had failed to enact a budget resolution since the 1974 Budget Act was passed.

Table 7.10 Projected and Actual Budget Totals Under the 1990, 1993, and 1997 Reconciliation Bills (as a percentage of GDP)

			1990 OBRA			
	Revenues		Outlays		Deficit (−)/Surplus (+)	
Fiscal Year	Projected	Actual	Projected	Actual	Projected	Actual
1991	19.4%	17.8%	24.7%	22.3%	−5.3%	−4.5%
1992	19.5	17.5	24.2	22.2	−4.7	−4.7
1993	19.5	17.6	22.9	21.5	−3.4	−3.9
1994	19.5	18.1	21.9	21.0	−2.4	−2.9
1995	19.5	18.5	20.3	20.7	−0.8	−2.2

			1993 OBRA			
	Revenues		Outlays		Deficit (−)/Surplus (+)	
Fiscal Year	Projected	Actual	Projected	Actual	Projected	Actual
1994	19.1	18.1	23.0	21.0	−3.9	−2.9
1995	19.4	18.5	22.3	20.7	−2.9	−2.2
1996	19.4	18.9	22.0	20.3	−2.6	−1.4
1997	19.4	19.3	22.0	19.5	−2.6	−0.3
1998	19.4	19.9	21.9	19.1	−2.5	+0.8

			1997 OBRA			
	Revenues		Outlays		Deficit (−)/Surplus (+)	
Fiscal Year	Projected	Actual	Projected	Actual	Projected	Actual
1998	19.6	19.9	20.3	19.1	−0.7	+0.8
1999	19.5	20.0	20.1	18.6	−0.6	+1.4
2000	19.2	20.8	19.7	18.4	−0.5	+2.4
2001	19.1	19.6	19.4	18.4	−0.4	+1.3
2002 (est.)	19.1	19.2	18.8	19.4	+0.3	−0.2

Sources: The projected figures are from CBO reports issued after these agreements were enacted: *The Economic and Budget Outlook: Fiscal Years 1992–1996* (Washington, D.C.: CBO, 1991), 63; *The Economic and Budget Outlook: An Update* (Washington, D.C.: CBO, September 1993), 27; *The Economic and Budget Outlook: An Update* (Washington, D.C.: CBO, September 1997), 31. The actuals for these years are from *The Budget and Economic Outlook: Fiscal Years 2003–2012* (Washington, D.C.: CBO, 2002), 3, 159.

obtained the spending he demanded, and Congress exceeded by more than $20 billion the discretionary appropriations cap it had enacted just one year before.[85]

85. The spending was designated as "emergency" to avoid a deliberate violation of the spending cap. See Congressional Budget Office, *The Economic and Budget Outlook: Fiscal Years 2000–2009* (Washington, D.C.: CBO, 1999), 34.

Republicans retained control of the House and Senate in the 1998 midterm elections but still could not alter the dynamics of surplus budgeting. In 1999 and again in 2000, Clinton used the "Save Social Security First" arguments against large tax cuts. Indeed, Clinton expanded the argument, insisting that Medicare as well as Social Security trust fund surpluses be used solely to reduce the publicly-held debt. When Republicans settled for small, targeted tax cuts, including estate tax reductions and changes in the tax treatment of married couples, Clinton vetoed them.

On spending, Clinton managed to maneuver around the discretionary spending caps and even to evade the PAYGO limits on entitlements. Discretionary outlays during FY 2000 were more than $50 billion above the statutory caps, and the excess spending the following year was close to $80 billion.[86] Approximately one-third of the increased discretionary spending for fiscal years 1998–2001 was for defense; the remainder was directed toward non-defense domestic programs, including the Clinton administration's priorities in education and health.[87]

Congress also approved several entitlement expansions. Medicare reimbursement rates for healthcare providers, which had been curbed by the 1997 Balanced Budget Act, were raised by more than $50 billion in 1999 and 2000.[88] The healthcare entitlement for military retirees was broadened, at an estimated cost of $60 billion over 10 years.[89] Smaller increases were authorized for veterans' benefits and children's health programs.

The administration and Congress could not agree, however, on Social Security or Medicare reform plans. Clinton's proposal that interest savings from debt reduction be transferred to the Social Security trust funds was rejected by Republican leaders, as was his recommendation for investing a portion of these transfers in equity markets.[90] Republicans also refused to enact "lockbox" measures that would have formally designated future surpluses for debt reduction. In turn, Clinton and congressional Democrats rejected Republican proposals for private retirement accounts as the corner-

---

86. The original caps for 2000 and 2001 were approximately $565 billion. FY 2000 discretionary outlays were more than $615 billion; FY 2001 outlays were more than $645 billion. Congressional Budget Office, *The Budget and Economic Outlook: Fiscal Years 2002–2011*, 75.

87. Congressional Budget Office, *The Budget and Economic Outlook: Fiscal Years 2002–2011*, 75.

88. *Congressional Quarterly Weekly Report* 58 (December 16, 2000): 2860.

89. *Congressional Quarterly Weekly Report* 58 (December 16, 2000): 2877.

90. *Budget of the United States Government, Fiscal Year 2001* (Washington, D.C.: Government Printing Office, 2000), 37.

stone of a reformed Social Security system. On Medicare, neither the administration nor Congress showed any enthusiasm for debating structural reforms.

The politics of surplus budgeting during the last years of the Clinton presidency produced no dramatic changes. Republicans failed to pass targeted tax
cuts over Clinton's vetoes, and they could not get broader tax-cut measures
through the House and Senate. The statutory limits on discretionary spending
were ignored, but discretionary budget shares and GDP ratios still remained
low. Entitlement policy stayed largely intact. As a result, the composition of
spending policy changed very little over Clinton's second term (Table 7.11).
Most of the surpluses were used for debt reduction, as Clinton had demanded.
Between 1997 and 2001, the publicly-held debt fell by almost $600 billion,
while the debt holdings in the Social Security and other government
accounts rose by more than $850 billion.[91]

Policy, Procedure, and Balanced Budgets

While congressional Republicans claimed credit for ending the era of deficit
politics, the policy changes behind the fiscal turnaround of the 1990s were
heavily tilted toward Clinton administration and Democratic priorities.
Between 1990 and 2000, revenue levels increased by 2.8 percent of GDP,
while outlay-GDP levels fell by 3.4 percent. By far the biggest factor behind
higher revenue levels was the growth in individual income taxes, particularly
among high-income taxpayers. On the spending side, the most important
change was the decline in defense.

The Democratic victory on tax policy was clear cut. Approximately 80
percent of the increase in revenue-GDP levels came from individual income
taxes, and most of the remainder was accounted for by corporation income
taxes. The most important tax law changes in 1990 and 1993—higher marginal rates, phaseouts of exemptions, limits on deductions, removal of the
earnings cap for Medicare payroll taxes—were aimed at high-income taxpayers. These changes, along with an unexpectedly sharp rise in income
among upper-income households, significantly shifted income tax burdens.
The share of individual income taxes paid by the top 1 percent of households
climbed from 22.3 percent in 1991 to 32.9 percent in 1997; for the top 10
percent, the increase was from 53.9 percent to 63.8 percent.[92] By FY 2000,

91. *Historical Tables, Budget of the United States Government, Fiscal Year 2002*, 117.
92. Congressional Budget Office, *Effective Federal Tax Rates, 1979–1997* (Washington, D.C.:
CBO, 2001), 74.

Table 7.11 Spending Category Allocations, 1993–2001 (as a percentage of total outlays)

Fiscal Year	Discretionary		Mandatory	
	Defense	Nondefense	Programmatic*	Net Interest
1993	20.7%	17.5%	47.6%	14.1%
1994	19.3	17.7	49.1	13.9
1995	18.0	17.9	48.7	15.3
1996	17.0	17.1	50.4	15.4
1997	17.0	17.2	50.6	15.2
1998	16.4	17.1	52.0	14.6
1999	16.2	17.4	52.9	13.5
2000	16.5	17.9	53.1	12.5
2001 (est.)	16.1	18.8	53.9	11.1

* Includes offsetting receipts.

SOURCE: Historical Tables, *Budget of the United States Government, Fiscal Year 2002* (Washington, D.C.: Government Printing Office, 2001), 125.

individual income tax receipts were 10.3 percent of GDP, the highest level ever recorded, and effective tax rates for high-income taxpayers were much higher than during the 1980s.[93] As a result, the progressivity of the income tax, and the federal tax system generally, was greater during the 1990s than it had been during the Reagan presidency.

Despite their takeover of Congress in 1995, Republicans were unable to reverse these revenue trends. The Taxpayer Relief Act of 1997, which they sponsored, had almost no impact on revenue levels or progressivity. Long-term capital gains taxes were lowered, but much of the tax relief in 1997 was in the form of tax credits for dependent children and education expenses that primarily benefited low- and middle-income groups. During Clinton's second term, congressional Republicans never came close to restoring the income tax policies of the Reagan presidency.

The central budget battle of the 1990s—whether to balance the budget at high- or low-revenue levels—was won by Clinton and congressional Democrats, and their victory carried over to spending policy. The outlay-GDP levels for discretionary domestic programs and social welfare entitlements changed very little during the 1990s. Defense outlays, however, dropped from 5.2 percent of GDP to 3.0 percent, the lowest level since the late 1940s. The programmatic spending savings that produced surpluses came from defense;

93. Congressional Budget Office, *Effective Federal Tax Rates, 1979–1997*, 2.

the remaining savings, from deposit insurance and interest, were substantial but held no policy implications.

Given these policy outcomes, it is not surprising that Democrats were becoming fervent advocates of balanced budgets and debt reduction, while Republicans were losing their enthusiasm for what had been traditional party goals. When Republicans had promoted a constitutional balanced-budget amendment in 1995, their assumption was that a prohibition against future deficits would inevitably force huge cutbacks in domestic spending. Democrats shared that assumption and feared the cutbacks would eventually include Social Security and Medicare. The abundance of surplus revenues by the late 1990s, however, shattered these assumptions. For Republicans, the chances of slashing "big government" in the future depended on tax cuts that would eliminate surplus revenues and restore the spending discipline they associated with the balanced-budget rule. For Democrats, the preservation of surplus revenues would permit budgets to be balanced while expanding domestic spending programs. Thus, the key budget policy issue in the 2000 elections was tax cuts.

Finally, the procedural path to balanced budgets was the reconciliation process. Budget reconciliation allowed the executive branch and Congress to negotiate multiyear deficit-reduction programs and to implement these programs through comprehensive legislative packages of tax increases and spending cuts. Reconciliation legislation also put in place discretionary spending caps and PAYGO controls on revenues and entitlements to preserve deficit-reduction gains over time. Without this expanded reconciliation process, it is unlikely that either Bush or Clinton would have been able to redirect budget policy so decisively from deficits to surpluses.

BUDGETING FOR THE FUTURE

The 2000 election was, in part, a contest over the future size of government. One dimension of this contest was comparatively short term—what to do with the burgeoning surpluses expected during the next decade. During the election campaign, the Congressional Budget Office (CBO) had projected a surplus of more than $230 billion for the FY 2000 budget and even larger surpluses over the next ten years.[1] According to the CBO, total surpluses for 2001–10 could exceed $4.6 trillion.

The Bush and Gore campaigns issued competing plans for allocating these surpluses, with the biggest and most important difference between them being the size and distribution of tax cuts. George W. Bush called for a massive $1.6 trillion tax cut over ten years, with sharply lower marginal rates on individual income and broad-based tax relief.[2] For Bush and his congressional Republican allies, the first priority was to lower revenue levels and eliminate

---

1. Congressional Budget Office, *The Budget and Economic Outlook: An Update* (Washington, D.C.: CBO, July 2000), 1–2.

2. The exact cost of the Bush tax cut was complicated by a dispute over whether to include the increased interest costs that would accompany smaller surpluses. The Bush administration's FY 2002 budget, however, called for "$1.6 trillion in tax relief over 10 years." *Budget of the United States Government, Fiscal Year 2002* (Washington, D.C.: Government Printing Office, 2001), 7.

part of the surplus that would otherwise be available to support new domestic spending programs. Al Gore, whose proposed tax cuts were about one-third as large as Bush's and more narrowly targeted, had a much more ambitious domestic agenda. For Gore, and most congressional Democrats, large and permanent tax cuts would mean less room for new and expanded domestic spending. The central issue in surplus budgeting, as it had been in deficit budgeting, was whether to balance budgets, and accommodate spending demands, at high- or low-revenue levels.

A second, less publicized dimension to this conflict involved demographic trends and long-term entitlement policy.[3] In 2000, the budget outlook for the next decade was favorable, but there was growing apprehension about the post-2010 costs of federal retirement and healthcare programs. After 2010, the large baby-boom generation begins to reach retirement age, and the Social Security and Medicare programs become much more expensive. At the same time, there are expected to be fewer workers for each of these retirees, shrinking the tax base to support their benefits. Among budget policy analysts, there is concern that unless entitlement commitments are reduced, these demographic trends "will overwhelm the surplus and drive us back into escalating deficits and debt."[4]

The issue of tax cuts played a role here as well. To the extent that projected surpluses over the next decade could be saved—that is, used to retire publicly-held debt—future interest costs would be lower, more spending would be available to support retirement and healthcare entitlements without excessive deficits or debt, and the need for reforming entitlements would be less urgent. The Bush-Gore dispute over tax cuts, then, had implications for long-term social welfare policy: Bush advocated Social Security reforms that would limit future spending and keep tax levels low, while Gore vowed to preserve the existing system of retirement benefits.

Bush's victory in the 2000 presidential race, along with the narrow (if temporary) Republican majorities in Congress, settled the tax issue. Despite an economic slowdown that threatened future surpluses, President Bush and congressional Republicans pushed through a tax cut early in 2001 that significantly lowered revenue levels for at least ten years. Then, the events of

---

3. On the transition from short-term to long-term policy problems, see General Accounting Office, *Long-Term Budget Issues: Moving from Balancing the Budget to Balancing Fiscal Risk* (Washington, D.C.: GAO, 2001), 5–11.

4. General Accounting Office, *Long-Term Budget Issues*, 1.

September 11 transformed the political landscape, triggering a war against terrorism the costs of which have already risen enormously and the duration of which is unknown. Just one year after George Bush took office, the budget was in deficit, the on-budget surpluses projected for the next decade had evaporated, and the long-term entitlement financing problem had grown worse.

Because the budget and the economy are so closely linked, budgeting for the future is always uncertain, but the situation facing policymakers today is unusually demanding. In addition to the usual questions about the economy, there are pressing issues concerning war costs and domestic spending needs over the next decade. Policymakers must also deal with entitlement financing problems that loom far on the horizon but that constitute a fiscal risk in terms of flexible and sustainable budget policy. Balancing current needs and demands against long-term spending commitments is obviously a complex policy challenge. It is a political challenge as well, since the president and Congress will be determining the future size and role of the federal government.

The Uncertainties of Multiyear Budgeting

Since the 1970s, Congress and the executive branch have increased their reliance on multiyear budget forecasts and plans to strengthen budget controls. The initial objective behind multiyear budgeting was to make it more difficult to disguise the long-term costs of spending and tax bills. Under the 1974 Budget Act, the CBO was given the responsibility of estimating the five-year costs of legislation reported by House and Senate committees and monitoring comparisons between spending and tax bills and congressional budget resolutions. Over time, however, Congress has moved toward more elaborate and lengthier budget planning and enforcement, and the use of multiyear forecasts has become much greater in the executive branch as well.

The 1990 and 1993 deficit-reduction bills placed enforcement controls on discretionary spending, revenues, and entitlements to prevent any legislative actions that might increase deficits during the five-year periods covered by the legislation. The 1997 Balanced Budget Act then extended the enforcement controls on revenues and entitlements to ten years.[5] The 1997 Act also required future congressional budget resolutions to cover a minimum of five years, but permitted the House and Senate Budget Committees to recommend resolutions covering even longer periods. Since the late 1990s, the CBO has issued

---

5. *Congressional Quarterly Almanac, 1997*, 2-52–2-53.

ten-year budget and economic projections at the beginning of each congressional session, and recent presidential and congressional budgets have featured multiyear plans.[6]

Deficit Versus Surplus Budgeting

When policymakers were still dealing with deficits, multiyear budgeting helped to curb legislative initiatives that would have made the deficit problem worse. With the advent of surpluses, however, the discipline in multiyear budgeting began to weaken. Proponents of tax cuts and spending increases found they could justify immediate action on the basis of surpluses projected far into the future. When surplus projections began to climb into the trillions, the temptation grew to ignore the uncertainties of these forecasts and to reap some current benefits. In the final years of the Clinton presidency, discretionary spending limits were ignored, as were the controls on minor entitlements, but the deadlock over tax cuts and entitlement reform kept surplus balances largely intact.

When the Bush administration first took office, the budget outlook was still positive. The CBO's current policy projections showed a FY 2002 surplus of more than $300 billion and a $5.6 trillion surplus for fiscal years 2002–11.[7] Both the administration and Congress agreed to reserve the Social Security, or off-budget, portion of this surplus—estimated at $2.5 trillion—exclusively for reductions in the publicly-held debt. The remaining $3.1 trillion, however, provided the administration with a persuasive argument for cutting taxes substantially and permanently.

House and Senate Republicans then passed a congressional budget resolution that incorporated a ten-year, $1.35 trillion tax cut and used reconciliation procedures to speed enactment of the actual tax bill. Two features of the 2001 tax-cut legislation were highly unusual. First, most of the tax reductions were phased in gradually, with the scale of annual revenue losses rising sharply after 2005.[8] The biggest portion of the tax cut was scheduled to take effect when surplus projections were least certain, but Republicans rejected Democratic proposals that would have tied future-year tax cuts to continued surpluses. By the time that the tax bill cleared in May 2001, surplus projections were

6. See Rudolph G. Penner, "Dealing with Uncertain Budget Forecasts," *Public Budgeting and Finance* 22 (Spring 2002): 12.

7. Congressional Budget Office, *The Budget and Economic Outlook: Fiscal Years 2002–2011*, 2.

8. Congressional Budget Office, *The Budget and Economic Outlook: An Update* (Washington, D.C.: CBO, August 2001), 8.

indeed beginning to fall, but the Bush administration never wavered from its tax-cut strategy.

Second, because the size of the 2001 tax cut threatened to violate reconciliation process rules and Congress's own budget plan, Republicans were forced to limit the tax cut's duration.[9] At the end of calendar year 2010, all of the 2001 tax law changes will expire, and pre-2001 tax policy will be reinstated.[10] While they no doubt would have preferred a permanent tax-law change, the Bush administration and congressional Republicans succeeded in passing an enormous tax cut that remains in effect for a decade regardless of whether the surpluses used to justify it ever materialize.

In his FY 2003 budget, President Bush acknowledged that "attempts to look out a decade in the future have varied wildly from year to year . . . 2001 showed finally how unreliable and ultimately futile such estimates are."[11] The president announced an end to the "experiment with 10 year forecasting" and an "appropriate focus on five year figures." Of course, the administration had already achieved its most important budget policy priority with the 2001 tax cut, and it probably could not have done so without relying on ten-year surplus projections.

The time periods used in multiyear budgeting are an important consideration. There is clearly a need for multiyear estimates to help evaluate current and proposed spending and tax policies. Extremely long-term projections, however, may undermine budget discipline, especially when those projections promise large, but uncertain, surpluses. The first five years of budget forecasts usually contain sizable errors; projections for the second five years are even less reliable.[12] Using the latter as the basis for significant and permanent changes in current policies increases the fiscal risks in multiyear budgeting.

Economic Uncertainties

One of the main uncertainties in multiyear budgeting, even with relatively short time horizons, involves assumptions about the economy's performance.[13]

---

9. Congressional Budget Office, *The Budget and Economic Outlook: An Update* (2001), 5.

10. Some provisions expire earlier. See Congressional Budget Office, *The Budget and Economic Outlook: An Update* (2001), 11.

11. *Budget of the United States Government, Fiscal Year 2003* (Washington, D.C.: Government Printing Office, 2002), 6.

12. See Penner, "Dealing with Uncertain Budget Forecasts," 13.

13. For comparisons of government and private economic forecasts, see Congressional Budget Office, *CBO's Economic Forecasting Record* (Washington, D.C.: CBO, February 2002).

Economic variables such as growth, productivity, and inflation directly affect spending and revenue estimates, and unanticipated changes in these and other key variables can have a dramatic effect on even short-term forecasts. As budget outlooks are extended to five or ten years, the potential for estimating errors is heightened. The CBO has emphasized the uncertainty associated with economic trends in its recent reports, pointing to the singular difficulty of making accurate forecasts when the economy is at "cyclical turning points"—moving from expansion to recession or in the opposite direction.[14]

The budget forecasts of the past two decades provide some perspective on the estimating errors attributable to economic variables. The average absolute difference in the CBO's surplus and deficit projections over this period, for example, has been large—more than 2 percent of GDP for the third year of a projection, rising to more than 3 percent for the fifth year.[15] In terms of current forecasts, this average difference represents a potential swing of about $350 billion in the surplus projection for FY 2007.[16] The forecasting record also reveals a pattern—estimates for deficits and surpluses in the initial year of a five-year forecast have tended to be "slightly pessimistic," while estimates for the final years have been "slightly optimistic."[17]

Revenues are extremely sensitive to economic fluctuations and therefore especially unpredictable when economic conditions are changing. During the late 1990s, revenues grew more rapidly than expected; in the 1980s and early 1990s, revenue growth had lagged behind estimates. From 1981 to 2001, the average absolute difference between a fifth-year revenue projection and the actual revenues for that year was more than 2 percent of GDP.[18] In general, revenue overestimates are greatest just before recessions, while underestimates tend to be highest in the early stages of an expansion.

Outlay estimating errors have usually been smaller than revenue errors, particularly for the outyears in multiyear projections. Still, the average absolute difference between outlays projected five years ahead and actual spending has been more than 1 percent of GDP in CBO forecasts between 1981 and 2001.[19] Spending estimates have been much less reliable, however, for health-

---

14. Congressional Budget Office, *The Budget and Economic Outlook: Fiscal Years 2003–2012* (Washington, D.C.: CBO, 2002), 90.

15. These estimates take into account the effects of policy changes. Congressional Budget Office, *The Budget and Economic Outlook: Fiscal Years 2003–2012*, 92.

16. Congressional Budget Office, *The Budget and Economic Outlook: Fiscal Years 2003–2012*, 92.

17. Congressional Budget Office, *The Budget and Economic Outlook: Fiscal Years 2003–2012*, 93.

18. Congressional Budget Office, *The Budget and Economic Outlook: Fiscal Years 2003–2012*, 92.

19. Congressional Budget Office, *The Budget and Economic Outlook: Fiscal Years 2003–2012*, 92.

care entitlements, particularly Medicare and Medicaid, which will account for a growing share of future budgets.[20]

Finally, the uncertainties in multiyear budget projections that relate to the performance of the economy are greatest for the on-budget revenue and spending accounts. Alternative economic assumptions therefore have an enormous impact on revenue and spending projections. Midrange economic assumptions used for current forecasts for fiscal years 2002–12 produce a baseline surplus of $2.2 trillion.[21] Economic performance over this period that instead mirrors the late 1990s would inflate the surplus to almost $6 trillion; a reversion to pre-1996 economic trends—in GDP growth and productivity, the composition of personal income, and healthcare cost inflation—would eliminate the surplus and yield instead a $2 trillion deficit.

As the president and Congress budget for extended periods, the uncertainties in revenue, spending, and deficit or surplus projections represent a fiscal risk. The risk is heightened when a multiyear budget program assigns equal weight to a current-year spending or revenue projection and a projection ten years ahead. Unless policymakers are cautious, they can easily make major miscalculations about the size and balance of future budgets.

Policy Uncertainties

The controllable element in multiyear budgeting involves legislative changes, but there are uncertainties here as well. The course of future legislation is subject to events and political factors that are not easy to predict. Legislative changes in the first twelve months of the Bush presidency, for example, reduced projected surpluses over the next decade by approximately $2.4 trillion.[22] The tax-cut portion of this surplus reduction was intentional; much of the spending portion was unexpected.

The Bush administration's 2001 tax program had two goals—lowering future revenue levels to discourage new spending and rolling back the individual income tax increases enacted in 1990 and 1993. The Economic Growth and Tax Relief Reconciliation Act of 2001 is expected to reduce revenues by 1 percent of GDP in 2006 and to maintain this lower level for the next several years.[23] These revenue losses are almost entirely attributable to lower marginal

---

20. On these problems, see Penner, "Dealing with Uncertain Budget Forecasts," 9–10.

21. Congressional Budget Office, *The Budget and Economic Outlook: Fiscal Years 2003–2012*, 100.

22. Congressional Budget Office, *The Budget and Economic Outlook: Fiscal Years 2003–2012*, 8–9.

23. Congressional Budget Office, *The Budget and Economic Outlook: An Update* (2001), 8.

rates and other forms of tax relief for individuals. When fully phased in, the 2001 tax law will cut the lowest marginal rate on individual income from 15 to 10 percent and the top rate from 39.6 to 35 percent.[24] Tax rate changes account for two-thirds of the ten-year revenue reductions from the 2001 tax bill; lesser, but substantial, tax relief is provided by increased child tax credits, estate and gift tax reductions, and tax law changes affecting married couples, retirement savings, and education expenses.[25]

The administration's plan for limiting discretionary spending growth, however, has been buffeted by events and checked by Congress. Through much of the 1990s, discretionary spending was tightly controlled, but once the deficit problem eased, there was growing support for additional funding in defense and domestic programs. Between 1991, the first year of the statutory caps on discretionary outlays, and 1998, total discretionary spending increased by less than $20 billion. Over the next three years, defense outlays went up by $35 billion, and nondefense discretionary spending rose by more than $60 billion.[26]

The Bush administration's FY 2002 budget recommended approximately $690 billion in discretionary outlays, an increase of more than $40 billion over 2001, with about half of the additional funding directed toward defense.[27] The Bush budget also called for moderating the "recent explosive growth in discretionary spending."[28] New discretionary spending limits were proposed for fiscal years 2003–6, with annual outlay increases limited to about $20 billion over this period.[29]

Whether these funding levels were politically realistic before September 11 was questionable, but the post–September 11 discretionary spending path is on an entirely different trajectory. Emergency supplemental appropriations in September and December 2001 totaled $40 billion.[30] With these additional funds, discretionary spending for FY 2002 was raised to approximately $730

24. The 10 percent rate was made retroactive to January 2001. The 35 percent rate takes effect in 2006.

25. The 10 percent bracket rate reduces estimated revenues by $421 billion for fiscal years 2001–11. The cuts in all other rates reduce revenues by an equal amount. See Congressional Budget Office, *The Budget and Economic Outlook: An Update* (2001), 8.

26. Congressional Budget Office, *The Budget and Economic Outlook: Fiscal Years 2003–2012*, 71.

27. *Budget of the United States Government, Fiscal Year 2002*, 230, 238.

28. *Budget of the United States Government, Fiscal Year 2002*, 7.

29. *Budget of the United States Government, Fiscal Year 2002*, 230.

30. The September 2001 Emergency Supplemental Appropriations Act for Recovery from and Response to Terrorist Attacks on the United States made $20 billion in budget authority

billion; defense outlays have been increased to more than $350 billion. The discretionary spending-GDP ratio for 2002 is projected at 7.1 percent, the highest level since the mid-1990s.

The higher discretionary spending baseline in place by January 2002 reduced projected surpluses by approximately $550 billion for fiscal years 2002–11.[31] This baseline, however, may be much too conservative. Planning for homeland security programs is not fully developed, and additional emergency spending might prove necessary if there are new terrorist attacks on the United States. In addition, the policy assumption for discretionary spending projections is that defense and defense programs will grow only at the rate of inflation. If these programs are budgeted for real growth, the spending baseline is elevated, and surplus projections are decreased. The effects over time are substantial. Over ten years, the inflation-only baseline for discretionary programs totals $8.6 trillion; if spending instead grows at the rate of GDP, discretionary outlays are $1.2 trillion higher.[32]

The size and composition of the discretionary portion of the budget are particularly hard to predict, given the growing differences between Congress and the Bush administration over domestic spending. Congress has supported the administration's requests for additional defense funding in fiscal years 2001–2, and the proposed increase in defense budget authority for FY 2003— $45 billion or nearly 13 percent—is even larger.[33] To compensate for these new defense commitments, however, the administration is proposing tight restraints on domestic spending that Congress may find difficult to accept. The administration's FY 2003–7 recommendations for nondefense discretionary outlays are nearly $70 billion below baseline levels.[34] The House and Senate, which were unable to agree on an overall FY 2003 budget, were in accord on nondefense spending targets well above the administration's budget request, and appropriations leaders from both

available for immediate obligation. In December, the Department of Defense and Emergency Supplemental Appropriations made another $20 billion available. Congressional Budget Office, *The Budget and Economic Outlook: Fiscal Years 2003–2012*, 71.

31. Congressional Budget Office, *The Budget and Economic Outlook: Fiscal Years 2003–2012*, 8.

32. Congressional Budget Office, *The Budget and Economic Outlook: Fiscal Years 2003–2012*, 74.

33. Congressional Budget Office, *An Analysis of the President's Budgetary Proposals for Fiscal Year 2003* (Washington, D.C.: CBO, 2002), 24.

34. Congressional Budget Office, *An Analysis of the President's Budgetary Proposals for Fiscal Year 2003*, 24.

Table 8.1 The Effects of Policy and Economic Changes on Surplus Projections, 2002–2011 (in billions of dollars)

	Fiscal Years	
	2002–2006	2002–2011
January 2001 Total Surplus	$2,007	$5,610
Policy Changes:		
Tax Cuts	−452	−1,205
Discretionary Spending Increases	−255	−550
Debt Service Costs	−114	−562
Other	−49	−102
Total	−870	−2,420
Economic and Technical Changes:		
Economic	−530	−929
Technical	−356	−660
Total	−886	−1,589
Impact on the Surplus	−1,757	−4,008
January 2002 Total Surplus	250	1,602

SOURCE: Congressional Budget Office, *The Economic and Budget Outlook: Fiscal Years 2003–2012* (Washington, D.C.: CBO, 2002), 8–9.

parties have insisted that actual cutbacks in FY 2003 and later years are impossible.[35]

Politically difficult choices about discretionary spending policy are further complicated by the large on-budget deficits now expected for the next several years. Continued high rates of discretionary spending growth will swell these deficits and cut even further into off-budget surpluses. Nevertheless, the Bush administration could find that large increases for defense will require concessions to Congress on domestic spending.

Surplus Uncertainties

The budget outlook for the next decade has changed markedly over a brief period. Surplus projections for FY 2002–11 have fallen by more than $4 trillion (Table 8.1). Policy changes—the 2001 tax cut and discretionary spending increases—account for approximately one-half of the surplus drop over the next five years and 60 percent of the decline over the ten-year projection period. The impact of the 2001 tax cut is roughly double that of the discretionary

---

35. On the efforts to bypass the budget resolution and come up with a nondefense spending total, see *Congressional Quarterly Weekly Report* 60 (April 13, 2002): 953–57.

spending increases, but both have additional costs in terms of debt service, which further reduce projected surpluses.

In addition to the changes in the total surplus, the on-budget surpluses projected in January 2001 have been entirely erased. On-budget spending and revenues are expected to be in deficit by more than $720 billion from 2002 to 2006 and approximately $740 billion from 2002 to 2011. These deficit levels may not be terribly large in terms of GDP levels or other measures of relative size, but they will make it more difficult to fund new programs that seemed politically inevitable a short time ago. On-budget deficits will also speed up the timetable for debates over entitlement reform.

The Uncertainties of Entitlement Reform

The post-2010 budget outlook is dominated by questions about three programs—Social Security, Medicare, and Medicaid.[36] Spending for these programs now accounts for approximately 8 percent of GDP, nearly double the level of just thirty years ago. If the current programs are left in place, costs are expected to rise moderately over the next decade but to grow much more rapidly thereafter. In 2040, for example, Social Security, Medicare, and Medicaid spending projections range from 15 to 20 percent of GDP.[37] These long-term funding requirements have focused attention on entitlement reform. There is widespread concern that unless retirement and healthcare policies are changed, it may prove increasingly difficult to fund other essential federal programs and to avoid unacceptable levels of deficits and debt. What lends urgency to this concern is that any major changes in retirement or healthcare benefits would have to be made fairly soon, to allow future retirees ample time to adjust their financial planning.[38] Proponents of entitlement reform, then, are looking to make immediate policy adjustments that will strengthen long-term budget control.

36. The treatment of these three programs as a category is based in part on the fact that approximately one-third of Medicaid spending is devoted to the elderly. In addition, both Medicare and Medicaid spending are affected by healthcare cost inflation. See C. Eugene Steuerle and Jon M. Bakija, *Retooling Social Security for the 21st Century* (Washington, D.C.: Urban Institute Press, 1994), 55.

37. The "midrange" projection is approximately 17 percent. Congressional Budget Office, *The Long-Term Budget Outlook* (Washington, D.C.: CBO, 2000), 3–5.

38. These adjustments would affect planned age of retirement, private savings, and consumption levels. See Steuerle and Bakija, *Retooling Social Security for the 21st Century*, 65.

Entitlement Growth: Short Term

A complicating factor in the politics surrounding entitlement reform is that the costs of current programs are not a serious problem over the short term. Between 2002 and 2012, the baseline projection for entitlements increases by almost $835 billion, but the spending-GDP ratio remains stable (Table 8.2). Social Security, Medicare, and Medicaid, however, will grow more rapidly than other entitlement programs and, by 2012, will account for almost 80 percent of total mandatory spending.

The sources of short-term entitlement growth include more beneficiaries, but the impact of rising caseloads is relatively small. Only about one-fifth of additional spending for entitlements reflects demographic changes in the beneficiary population.[39] More important in terms of projected growth over the short term are automatic increases in benefits that are required by law. These include cost-of-living-adjustments (COLAs) in retirement benefits and healthcare reimbursement rates. Other programmatic increases reflect the volume and types of medical services used by Medicare and Medicaid beneficiaries.

Over the next decade, the costs of existing entitlement commitments increase steadily but at about the same rate as the overall economy. Indeed, it would be possible to fund new Medicare prescription drug benefits or liberalized cash and in-kind benefits in other programs without drastically changing the GDP share or budgetary allocation for social welfare programs. Any new commitments, however, would have a much greater impact when the demographics of entitlement spending begin to change.

Entitlement Growth: Long Term

To prepare for the new demographics of entitlement spending, Congress has scheduled future adjustments in Social Security retirement benefits. Under the 1983 Social Security Act Amendments, the normal retirement age for Social Security goes from sixty-five to sixty-six over a six-year period ending in 2009. A second increase, to sixty-seven, is scheduled for another six-year period ending in 2027. Early retirement at age sixty-two remains in place but at reduced benefits. At age sixty-two, retirees now receive 80 percent of full retirement benefits. This percentage falls to 75 percent by 2009 and to 70 percent by 2027, with the reductions phased in alongside increases in the normal retirement age. Eligibility for Medicare benefits, however, remains at

39. Congressional Budget Office, *The Budget and Economic Outlook: Fiscal Years 2003–2012*, 81.

Table 8.2 Baseline Projections of Mandatory Spending, 2002–2012 (in billions of dollars)

							Fiscal Year						Total, 2003– 2012
	2002	2003	2004	2005	2006	2007	2008	2009	2010	2011	2012	
Means-Tested Programs												
Medicaid	$143	$152	$164	$179	$194	$211	$230	$250	$272	$296	$323	$2,271
Other	138	145	147	152	155	156	163	167	173	184	168	1,612
Total	281	297	311	331	349	367	393	417	445	480	491	3,883
Non-Means-Tested Programs												
Social Security	451	470	493	518	545	574	606	642	682	724	771	6,026
Medicare	249	263	279	302	318	346	374	404	435	471	498	3,690
Other	207	218	209	210	215	220	229	237	247	258	262	2,306
Total	907	951	981	1,030	1,078	1,140	1,209	1,283	1,364	1,453	1,531	12,022
All Mandatory Spending												
Percentage of GDP	11.5	11.5	11.2	11.2	11.2	11.2	11.3	11.4	11.5	11.7	11.7	11.4

SOURCE: Congressional Budget Office, *The Budget and Economic Outlook: Fiscal Years 2003–2012* (Washington, D.C.: CBO, 2002), 3, 77.

Fig. 8.1 Spending for Social Security, Medicare, and Medicaid Under Midrange Assumptions, 1970–2040

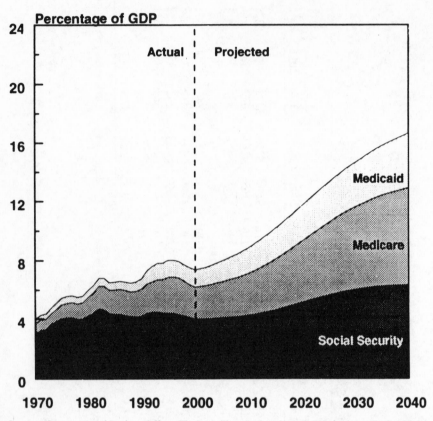

SOURCE: Congressional Budget Office, *The Long-Term Budget Outlook* (Washington, D.C.: CBO, 2000), 3.

age sixty-five. Despite these changes, the number of Social Security beneficiaries will grow very rapidly after 2010, and retirement costs will quickly escalate. In addition to the growing number of retirees, per-beneficiary costs are expected to climb because of longer life expectancy. Average life expectancy at age sixty-five is currently about sixteen years for males and twenty years for females.[40] The Social Security Administration predicts that life expectancy will grow by an additional two years over the next several decades.[41] These

40. Steuerle and Bakija, *Retooling Social Security for the 21st Century*, 41–42.
41. Steuerle and Bakija, *Retooling Social Security for the 21st Century*, 41–42.

demographic changes will affect healthcare costs as well as retirement benefits. Longer life expectancy, for example, is likely to raise healthcare spending even more rapidly than retirement costs.

Spending Composition. Under current policy, the budget shares and GDP ratios for Social Security, Medicare, and Medicaid would grow by sizable amounts over an extended period. Recent projections show the spending-GDP ratio for Social Security, Medicare, and Medicaid more than doubling between 2000 and 2040 (Fig. 8.1). By 2050, the GDP ratio could be even higher—more than 20 percent according to General Accounting Office (GAO) projections.[42]

Funding requirements anywhere close to these levels leave little room for other programs without large tax increases or high deficits. The portion of the budget directed toward the elderly has been expanding for several decades, while the budget shares for discretionary programs and entitlements for the non-elderly have declined. If future spending budgets tilt even more heavily toward the elderly, the constraints on other programs would tighten still further. Moreover, current baselines exclude some emerging commitments likely to require substantial new spending—homeland security, environmental cleanup obligations, and contingent liabilities for federal insurance programs—so that the lack of flexibility in heavily encumbered budgets presents additional problems.

The composition of spending policy serves as a reasonable approximation of federal priorities. In the recent past, social welfare has emerged as the dominant priority, and, within the social welfare category, programs for the elderly have enjoyed the broadest political support and the strongest commitment in terms of funding. The needs of the elderly, however, inevitably have to be balanced against other federal responsibilities. As the GAO has warned, "Absent changes in the structure of Social Security and Medicare, some time during the 2040s government would do nothing but mail checks to the elderly and their health-care providers. Accordingly, substantive reform of Social Security and health programs remains critical to recapturing our future fiscal flexibility."[43]

Deficits and Debt. Another uncertainty about the long-term budget outlook is fiscal sustainability—whether spending commitments can be maintained without triggering unacceptable deficit and debt increases. The starting point here involves assumptions about future revenue levels. Long-term budget

42. General Accounting Office, *Long-Term Budget Issues*, 10.
43. General Accounting Office, *Long-Term Budget Issues*, 10.

projections incorporate a revenue baseline of approximately 20 percent of GDP.[44] This baseline represents current tax policy; it also reflects a widely held belief among policy analysts, however, that there is a ceiling on tax levels in terms of political feasibility.

There is some historical support for this belief. During the past sixty years, revenues have generally been well below 20 percent of GDP, with the major exceptions being World War II and the late 1990s. In 1944 and 1945, when wartime spending was more than 40 percent of GDP, revenues were just slightly above 20 percent. The deficit-reduction tax increases of the early 1990s were expected to raise revenue levels to approximately 19.5 percent of GDP. Revenues eventually climbed above 20 percent in 1999 and 2000—matching the revenue levels of World War II—but this was the result of economic factors rather than deliberate tax policy.

If political considerations and economic policy needs impose a comparable ceiling on future revenue levels, maintaining current spending commitments would lead to sharp increases in deficits and debt. When these increases actually begin to emerge depends on further assumptions, particularly those about the size and disposition of short-term budget surpluses (Fig. 8.2). If the large surpluses originally projected for the next decade had been entirely devoted to reducing the publicly-held debt—the "save total surpluses" scenario—lower interest costs and related savings would have offset increased spending for a time, postponing serious problems with deficit and debt levels until after 2050. Saving only the off-budget surpluses would still have kept deficit-debt levels under control for several decades. Now, with on-budget deficits for at least the next few years, off-budget surplus savings are evaporating, and potential deficit and debt problems are drawing closer.

Regardless of short-term reductions in the publicly-held debt, the projected growth of retirement and healthcare benefits would eventually threaten sharp increases in debt levels. In addition, the large trust fund balances that Social Security is expected to accumulate over the next ten to fifteen years are misleading in terms of the potential gap between revenues and spending. When Social Security benefits begin to exceed payroll tax receipts, which the Social Security Board of Trustees expects will occur around 2016, the difference must be funded through higher taxes, reductions in other spending,

---

44. General Accounting Office, *Long-Term Budget Issues*, 10. See also Congressional Budget Office, *The Long-Term Budget Outlook*, 15–18.

Fig. 8.2 Projections of Debt Held by the Public Under Different Assumptions About Saving Surpluses, 1990–2070

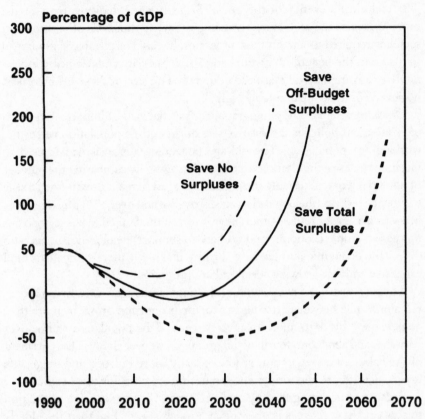

SOURCE: Congressional Budget Office, *The Long-Term Budget Outlook* (Washington, D.C.: CBO, 2000), 8.

or borrowing.[45] Trust fund surpluses make Social Security's claim on budgetary resources stronger, since the government owes interest and principal payments on securities held by the trust funds, but the actual funds to satisfy these claims must still be provided. The same conditions apply to the Medicare trust fund. Like Social Security, the Medicare trust fund is expected to have a negative balance between payroll tax revenues and benefit payments beginning around 2016.[46] Since the Medicare trust fund surplus is smaller

45. For trust fund solvency projections, see *Congressional Quarterly Weekly Report* 59 (March 24, 2001): 665.
46. *Congressional Quarterly Weekly Report* 59: 665.

and the projected imbalance between revenues and spending greater, its projected insolvency is forecast for 2029, compared with 2038 for Social Security. The technical solvency of the Social Security and Medicare trust funds, however, is not the real issue. More important are the levels of taxation and spending required to support these programs. It would be possible, for example, to maintain the benefit obligations for Social Security and Medicare indefinitely by raising payroll taxes accordingly.[47] The size of these tax increases, however, could be unacceptably high.

Dependency Ratios. The demographic factor that is most important in terms of entitlement policy is the relative size of the retiree population versus the working-age population. The old-age dependency ratio is widely used to illustrate the fiscal implications of population aging by comparing the number of potential workers (usually the population aged sixteen to sixty-four) to the number of retirees (the population aged sixty-five and over).[48] With large numbers of workers per retiree—more than 5 to 1 in the United States in 1960[49]—there is an ample economic and tax base to support the elderly. As this ratio drops, the economic and tax base shrinks, making it more difficult to fund expensive and fast-growing social welfare programs.

 Through 2010, the proportion of the population aged sixty-five and over remains stable; between 2010 and 2030, the proportion grows by more than 50 percent.[50] By 2030, more than 20 percent of the population will be over sixty-five, and about one-fourth of this group will be over eighty. The retirement of the baby-boom generation produces many more retirees, and longer life expectancy adds to the retirement and healthcare costs for these retirees.

Because of declining fertility rates, however, the working-age population to support these retirees is growing at a much slower rate than the elderly population.[51] Fertility rates after World War II were well above 3.0 for nearly two decades but then began to drop. By the mid-1970s, the rate had fallen to less than 1.75; current rates are around 2.0 and expected to remain at or slightly below this level over the next twenty years. The effect of these contrasting demographic trends is a falloff in the number of workers per beneficiary. By

47. See Joseph White, "Budgeting for Social Security or: When Are Savings Really Savings?" *Public Budgeting and Finance* 20 (Fall 2000): 1–23.

48. Organisation for Economic Co-Operation and Development, *Reforms for an Ageing Society*, 34.

49. *National Journal* 33 (July 14, 2001): 2236.

50. Organisation for Economic Co-Operation and Development, *Reforms for an Ageing Society*, 216. The U.S. population aging projections are similar to the OECD average.

51. Steuerle and Bakija, *Retooling Social Security for the 21st Century*, 45–47.

Fig. 8.3   Ratio of Persons 65 and Over to Working-Age Population and to Number of Employed, 1980–2030

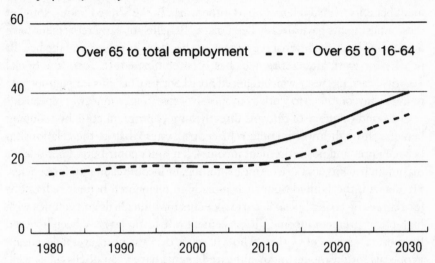

Source: Organisation for Economic Co-Operation and Development, *Reforms for an Ageing Society* (Paris: OECD, 2000), 217. OECD Copyright 2000.

2030, the ratio of persons aged sixty-five and over to the working-age population is expected to be above 35 percent (Fig. 8.3). The ratio to actual workers would be about 40 percent, which means a worker-to-beneficiary ratio of 2.5 to 1. In 2060, the projected ratio is even lower—approximately 2 to 1.[52]

The fiscal problems associated with population aging are not confined to the United States. Most industrialized democracies are facing dependency ratios considerably worse than those of the United States; these ratios will necessitate proportionally greater retrenchments in social welfare commitments to the elderly.[53] Indeed, a number of countries have already begun to implement reforms designed to reduce future obligations in their public pension systems.[54] The common themes in these reform efforts are demographic adjustments and structural changes in social welfare systems.

Policy and Budgetary Reforms. The most straightforward demographic adjustment to population aging is to encourage people to work longer. The options

52. Based on the 2001 Social Security Trustees Report. *National Journal* 33 (July 14, 2001): 2236.

53. Organisation for Economic Co-Operation and Development, *Reforms for an Ageing Society*, 33–34.

54. Organisation for Economic Co-Operation and Development, *Reforms for an Ageing Society*, 35–41.

here include penalizing early retirement, raising the normal retirement age, and providing extended transitions to full retirement through partial government benefits that supplement part-time work. In the United States, some of these adjustments have already been made. Benefits for early retirement have been scaled back, the normal retirement age has been increased, and the benefit penalty for work after retirement has been eliminated. In 2000, the Social Security "earnings test," which reduced Social Security benefits for high-income retirees who continued to work from ages sixty-five to sixty-nine, was repealed.[55]

A second category of reforms directly targets program costs by reducing benefits through lower income replacement rates (that is, the relationship between pre- and postretirement income), lengthier contribution periods for maximum benefits, and stricter means-testing, or income eligibility, for benefits. Here again, the United States has already implemented benefit reductions for retirees by taxing Social Security benefits for individuals and couples with high postretirement incomes. Replacement rate formulas have been lowered for most categories of workers who will retire over the next several decades.[56] Proposals for means-testing healthcare benefits have been discussed as well, but thus far there has been extremely strong opposition to means-testing benefits under Medicare Part A or premiums for medical insurance under Medicare Part B. When catastrophic health insurance coverage was added to Medicare in 1988, premiums were based on retirees' incomes, but intense reaction against this "surtax" led to the program's repeal the following year. It is possible that the addition of prescription drug benefits to Medicare would incorporate a means-test formula, but similar provisions for current Medicare program benefits appear unlikely.

These policy reforms and adjustments in the United States, however, are already reflected in the long-term cost projections for Social Security and Medicare. To lower costs still further, more extensive changes would be required in both programs. For Social Security, the Bush administration has taken the lead in promoting individual investment-based retirement accounts, funded by a portion of Social Security payroll taxes, which would supplement a basic (and lower) Social Security benefit available to all retirees.[57] This partial privatization would not affect current or near-term retirees, but diverting

55. These changes did not apply to early retirees and to these receiving Social Security disability payments.

56. Steuerle and Bakija, *Retooling Social Security for the 21st Century*, 95–98.

57. For a review of existing and proposed retirement reforms in other countries, see Organisation for Economic Co-Operation and Development, *Reforms for an Ageing Society*, chap. 4.

payroll taxes to private retirement accounts for future retirees would necessarily lead to sizable transition costs in terms of funding current benefits. In addition, privatization raises complicated policy problems. The Social Security system now in place has both income replacement and income redistribution components. Low-wage earners receive a higher Social Security benefit, relative to pre-retirement earnings, than do high-wage earners. In addition, low-wage earners are more likely to depend heavily or even exclusively on Social Security benefits for their retirement income. One of the major concerns about privatization is that the redistributive nature of the current system would be weakened. A related issue is the extent to which a combined basic Social Security benefit and private retirement account could guarantee retirement incomes comparable to those under the current system.

The complexities of Social Security reform, however, pale in comparison to those associated with healthcare. The Medicare system is open ended, with budgetary requirements determined by healthcare demands and costs. The two basic coverages—hospital insurance and outpatient coverage—are financed differently. The Medicaid program is administered by the states and financed by both the federal government and the states. Since Medicaid covers a large share of nursing home care and other long-term care for the elderly, it further complicates efforts to control benefit allocation, taxpayer costs, and budgetary effects. Moreover, the enormous growth in federal and state healthcare expenditures has not remedied serious gaps in coverage for the elderly, particularly for prescription drugs and catastrophic care.

No single reform can solve the demographic problems confronting Medicare and Medicaid, but a comprehensive restructuring of the system now in place could provide needed improvements in efficiency and equity. Long-term budgetary costs could also be lowered by raising the Medicare retirement age to match Social Security and through means-testing of benefits. The political difficulties of making these types of changes and reducing the federal government's role in funding healthcare services are formidable, but the gap between promised benefits and budgetary resources will inevitably need to be addressed.

Fiscal Choices

The decision-making framework for federal budget policy has changed a great deal in recent decades. The congressional budget process has become more centralized and coordinated through budget resolutions and reconciliation. New fiscal controls and multiyear budget agreements have enabled the federal government to limit spending, deficits, and debt much more effectively. The problem of large and chronic structural deficits has been largely eliminated.

Policymakers still face, however, difficult and serious choices about budget policy. The war against terrorism is the federal government's highest priority, but it is not the only priority. Cold War defense programs were subject to budgetary constraints, and these constraints have not disappeared. Over the short term, new national defense and homeland security requirements must be balanced against other domestic needs and available revenues. Inevitably, this balancing will occur as the president and Congress determine annual budgets, amid the economic, policy, and political uncertainties that make the budget process so unpredictable.

Policymakers will also have to decide what to do about entitlements. The impact of demographic changes on retirement and healthcare entitlements is a pressing concern for which there are no easy or painless solutions. The United States is, fortunately, better equipped to deal with these long-term problems than most industrialized democracies. The relative size of the social welfare system, and of government generally, is considerably smaller in the United States than elsewhere, and demographic pressures are less severe.

The United States has also been at the forefront of fiscal consolidation—the shift toward budget balance and debt reduction after the era of deficit politics. Publicly-held debt levels have been greatly reduced and are likely to remain relatively low for least the next decade, and interest costs have fallen sharply from the high levels of the 1980s and 1990s. The success of fiscal consolidation efforts in the past provides much greater flexibility in responding to any unexpected budget-control problems that may arise.

At some point, however, the United States must revisit the perennial question of the size and role of the federal government. The defining issue today is the future of the entitlement state. The federal government's commitments to the elderly and, to a much lesser extent, the poor account for more than half of its budget. As the costs of entitlements in general and retirement and healthcare benefits in particular expand even further, the president and Congress must be able to fund defense and other domestic needs at adequate levels and to maintain revenue levels that are politically and economically viable. Balancing the budget is, in this context, only one consideration. More important, and more difficult, is determining the levels of spending and taxation at which balance can be achieved.

SELECTED BIBLIOGRAPHY

Adams, Henry. *The Life of Albert Gallatin.* New York: Peter Smith, 1943.

Adams, Henry C. *Public Debts: An Essay in the Science of Finance.* New York: D. Appleton and Company, 1887.

Amenta, Edwin. *Bold Relief: Institutional Politics and the Origins of Modern American Social Policy.* Princeton: Princeton University Press, 1998.

Berkowitz, Edward D., and Kim McQuaid. *Creating the Welfare State: The Political Economy of Twentieth-Century Reform.* Rev. ed. Lawrence: University Press of Kansas, 1992.

Betts, Richard K. *Military Readiness: Concepts, Choices, Consequences.* Washington, D.C.: Brookings Institution, 1995.

Bolles, Albert S. *The Financial History of the United States from 1789 to 1860.* 2d ed. New York: D. Appleton and Company, 1885.

———. *The Financial History of the United States from 1861 to 1885.* New York: D. Appleton and Company, 1886.

Boskin, Michael J. *Too Many Promises: The Uncertain Future of Social Security.* Homewood, Ill.: Dow Jones-Irwin, 1986.

Brown, E. Cary. "Episodes in the Public Debt History of the United States." In *Public Debt Management: Theory and History,* edited by Rudiger Dornbusch and Mario Draghi. Cambridge: Cambridge University Press, 1990, 229–54.

Brownlee, W. Elliott. *Federal Taxation in America.* Cambridge: Cambridge University Press, 1996.

Buchanan, James M., and Richard E. Wagner. *Democracy in Deficit.* New York: Academic Press, 1977.

Burkhead, Jesse. *Government Budgeting.* New York: John Wiley and Sons, 1956.

Campbell, Ballard C. *The Growth of American Government: Government from the Cleveland Era to the Present.* Bloomington: Indiana University Press, 1995.

Commager, Henry Steele, ed. *Documents of American History.* 6th ed. New York: Appleton-Century-Crofts, Inc., 1958.

Cooke, Jacob E., ed. *The Reports of Alexander Hamilton.* New York: Harper & Row, 1964.

Deering, Christopher J., and Steven S. Smith. *Committees in Congress.* 3d ed. Washington, D.C.: Congressional Quarterly, 1997.

Dewey, Davis Rich. *Financial History of the United States.* 6th ed. New York: Longmans, Green and Co., 1918.

Farrand, Max, ed. *The Records of the Federal Convention of 1787.* 2 vols. New Haven: Yale University Press, 1911.

Fenno, Richard F., Jr. *The Power of the Purse: Appropriations Politics in Congress.* Boston: Little, Brown and Company, 1966.

Ferguson, E. James. *The Power of the Purse: A History of American Public Finance, 1776–1790.* Chapel Hill: University of North Carolina Press, 1961.

Fisher, Louis. *Presidential Spending Power.* Princeton: Princeton University Press, 1975.

———. *Congressional Abdication on War and Spending.* College Station: Texas A&M University Press, 2000.

Forsythe, Dall W. *Taxation and Political Change in the Young Nation, 1781–1833.* New York: Columbia University Press, 1977.

Franklin, Daniel P. *Making Ends Meet: Congressional Budgeting in the Age of Deficits.* Washington, D.C.: Congressional Quarterly, 1993.

Friedman, Benjamin M. *Day of Reckoning: The Consequences of American Economic Policy Under Reagan and After.* New York: Random House, 1988.

Gilbert, Charles. *American Financing of World War I.* Westport, Conn.: Greenwood Press, 1970.

Gordon, John Steele. *Hamilton's Blessing.* New York: Wallace and Company, 1997.

Haas, Lawrence J. "A Budget Commission Side Step." *National Journal* 21 (March 11, 1989): 592.

Hamilton, Alexander, James Madison, and John Jay. *The Federalist Papers.* New York: New American Library, 1961.

Hamilton, John C., ed. *The Works of Alexander Hamilton.* Vol. 4. New York: Charles S. Francis and Company, 1851.

Hammond, Paul Y. "NSC-68: Prologue to Rearmament." In *Strategy, Politics, and Defense Budgets,* edited by Warner R. Schilling, Paul Y. Hammond, and Glenn H. Snyder. New York: Columbia University Press, 1962, 267–378.

Harris, Joseph P. *Congressional Control of Administration.* Washington, D.C.: Brookings Institution, 1969.

Ippolito, Dennis S. *Congressional Spending.* Ithaca: Cornell University Press, 1981.

———. *Hidden Spending: The Politics of Federal Credit Programs.* Chapel Hill: University of North Carolina Press, 1984.

———. *Uncertain Legacies: Federal Budget Policy from Roosevelt Through Reagan.* Charlottesville: University Press of Virginia, 1990.

———. *Budget Policy and the Future of Defense.* Washington, D.C.: Institute for National Strategic Studies/National Defense University Press, 1994.

Jillson, Calvin, and Rick K. Wilson. *Congressional Dynamics: Structure, Coordination, and Choice in the First American Congress, 1774–1789.* Stanford: Stanford University Press, 1994.

Kahn, Jonathan. *Budgeting Democracy: State Building and Citizenship in America, 1890–1928.* Ithaca: Cornell University Press, 1997.

Kearny, John Watts. *Sketch of American Finances, 1789–1835.* New York: G. P. Putnam's Sons, 1887.

Keech, William R. *Economic Politics.* New York: Cambridge University Press, 1995.

Keller, Morton. *Regulating a New Economy: Public Policy and Economic Change in America, 1900–1933.* Cambridge: Harvard University Press, 1990.

Kendrick, M. Slade. *A Century and a Half of Federal Expenditures.* New York: National Bureau of Economic Research, 1955.

Kettl, Donald F. *Leadership at the Fed.* New Haven: Yale University Press, 1986.

Kimmel, Lewis H. *Federal Budget and Fiscal Policy, 1789–1958.* Washington, D.C.: Brookings Institution, 1959.

King, Ronald F. *Money, Time, and Politics: Investment Tax Subsidies and American Democracy.* New Haven: Yale University Press, 1993.

Lenkowsky, Leslie. *Politics, Economics, and Welfare Reform.* Washington, D.C.: American Enterprise Institute, 1986.

Letwin, William, ed. *A Documentary History of American Economic Policy Since 1789.* New York: Norton, 1972.

Mackenzie, G. Calvin, and Saranna Thornton. *Bucking the Deficit: Economic Policymaking in America.* Boulder, Colo.: Westview Press, 1996.

McAdoo, William G. *Crowded Years.* Boston: Houghton Mifflin, 1931.

Mitchell, Wesley Clair. *A History of the Greenbacks, with Special Reference to the Economic Consequences of Their Issue, 1862–65.* Chicago: University of Chicago Press, 1903.

Morgan, Iwan W. *Eisenhower Versus "The Spenders": The Eisenhower Administration, the Democrats, and the Budget, 1953–1960.* New York: St. Martin's Press, 1990.

Morris, James M. *America's Armed Forces: A History.* 2d ed. Upper Saddle River, N.J.: Prentice-Hall, 1996.

Morse, Jarvis M. *Paying for a World War: The United States Funding of World War II.* Washington, D.C.: U.S. Savings Bonds Division, Department of the Treasury, 1971.

Murphy, Henry C. *The National Debt in War and Transition.* New York: McGraw-Hill, 1950.

Myers, Roy T. *Strategic Budgeting.* Ann Arbor: University of Michigan Press, 1994.

Neustadt, Richard E. "Presidency and Legislation: The Growth of Central Clearance." *American Political Science Review* 48 (September 1954): 641–71.

Noyes, Alexander Dana. *Forty Years of American Finance: A Short Financial History of the Government and People of the United States Since the Civil War, 1865–1907.* New York: G. P. Putnam's Sons, 1898.

Ohls, James C., and Harold Beebout. *The Food Stamp Program.* Washington, D.C.: Urban Institute Press, 1993.

Organisation for Economic Co-Operation and Development. *Reforms for an Ageing Society.* Paris: OECD, 2000.

Paine, Thomas. *Basic Writings of Thomas Paine: Common Sense, Rights of Man, Age of Reason.* New York: Willey Book Co., 1942.

Patterson, James T. *America's Struggle Against Poverty, 1900–1994.* Cambridge: Harvard University Press, 1994.

Patterson, Robert T. *Federal Debt-Management Policies, 1865–1879.* Durham: Duke University Press, 1954.

Pechman, Joseph A. *Federal Tax Policy.* 5th ed. Washington, D.C.: Brookings Institution, 1987.

Penner, Rudolph G. "Dealing with Uncertain Budget Forecasts." *Public Budgeting and Finance* 22 (Spring 2002): 1–18.

Plehn, Carl C. "Finances of the United States in the Spanish War." *University Chronicle* 1 (October 1898): 419–63.

Porter, Kirk H., and Donald B. Johnson, eds. *National Party Platforms, 1840–1968.* Urbana: University of Illinois Press, 1970.

Ratchford, B. U. *American State Debts.* Durham: Duke University Press, 1941.

Savage, James D. *Balanced Budgets and American Politics.* Ithaca: Cornell University Press, 1988.

———. "Budgetary Collective Action Problems: Convergence and Compliance Under the Maastricht Treaty on European Union." *Public Administration Review* 61 (January/February 2001): 43–53.

Schick, Allen. *Congress and Money.* Washington, D.C.: Urban Institute, 1980.

———. *The Federal Budget: Politics, Policy, and Process.* Rev. ed. Washington, D.C.: Brookings Institution, 2000.

Schortheimer, Frederick E. *Rededicating America: Life and Recent Speeches of Warren G. Harding.* Indianapolis: Bobbs-Merrill, 1920.

Skocpol, Theda. *Protecting Soldiers and Mothers: The Political Origins of Social Policy in the United States.* Cambridge: Harvard University Press, 1992.

Skowronek, Stephen. *Building a New American State: The Expansion of National Administrative Capacities, 1877–1920.* Cambridge: Cambridge University Press, 1982.

Smithies, Arthur. *The Budgetary Process in the United States.* New York: McGraw Hill, 1955.

Spaulding, E.G. *History of the Legal Tender Paper Money Issued During the Great Rebellion.* 1869. Reprint. Westport, Conn.: Greenwood Press, 1971.

Stabile, Donald R., and Jeffrey A. Cantor. *The Public Debt of the United States.* New York: Praeger, 1991.

Stein, Herbert. *The Fiscal Revolution in America.* Chicago: University of Chicago Press, 1969.

———. *Presidential Economics.* New York: Simon and Schuster, 1984.

Steuerle, C. Eugene. *The Tax Decade.* Washington, D.C.: Urban Institute Press, 1992.

Steuerle, C. Eugene, and Jon M. Bakija. *Retooling Social Security for the 21st Century.* Washington, D.C.: Urban Institute Press, 1994.

Stewart III, Charles H. *Budget Reform Politics: The Design of the Appropriations Process in the House of Representatives, 1865–1921.* Cambridge: Cambridge University Press, 1989.

Studenski, Paul, and Herman E. Kroos. *Financial History of the United States.* 2d ed. New York: McGraw-Hill, 1953.

Surrey, Stanley S., and Paul R. McDaniel. *Tax Expenditures.* Cambridge: Harvard University Press, 1985.

Tanzi, Vito, and Ludger Schuknecht. *Public Spending in the 20th Century: A Global Perspective.* Cambridge: Cambridge University Press, 2000.

Timberlake, Richard H. *Monetary Policy in the United States: An Intellectual and Institutional History.* Chicago: University of Chicago Press, 1993.

Tobin, James, and Murray Weidenbaum, eds. *Two Revolutions in Economic Policy: The First Economic Reports of Presidents Kennedy and Reagan.* Cambridge: Massachusetts Institute of Technology Press, 1988.

Weaver, R. Kent. *Automatic Government: The Politics of Indexation*. Washington, D.C.: Brookings Institution, 1988.

Webber, Carolyn, and Aaron Wildavsky. *A History of Taxation and Expenditure in the Western World*. New York: Simon and Schuster, 1986.

West, Robert C. *Banking Reform and the Federal Reserve, 1863–1923*. Ithaca: Cornell University Press, 1977.

White, Joseph. "Budgeting for Social Security or: When Are Savings Really Savings?" *Public Budgeting and Finance* 20 (Fall 2000): 1–23.

Wildavsky, Aaron. *The New Politics of the Budgetary Process*. Glenview, Ill.: Scott, Foresman, 1988.

Wildavsky, Aaron, and Naomi Caiden. *The New Politics of the Budgetary Process*. 3d ed. New York: Longman, 1997.

Willoughby, W. F. *The National Budget System*. Baltimore: Johns Hopkins University Press, 1927.

Witte, John F. *The Politics and Development of the Federal Income Tax*. Madison: University of Wisconsin Press, 1985.

INDEX

spending (*continued*)
  estimates of, 296–97
  federal trends in, *80*
  Great Depression and, 130–31
  Hoover program, 131–32
  Johnson administration, 176–77
  Nixon-Ford years, 199–203, *200*
  OBRA 1993 and, *265*
  oversight of by Congress, 90–93
  post–Civil War, 62–63, 83–86
  post–Vietnam War, 186
  post–World War I, 120–23, *122*
  post–World War II, 156–60, *157*
  Reagan administration, 8, 222, 223–27, *228*
  F. Roosevelt program, 132–38, *138*
  transition in, 7–8, *8*
  World War I and, 101, *102*
  World War II and, 145–48, *149*, *150*
Sputnik, 170
State and Local Fiscal Assistance Act (1972),
  199
states
  banks and, 55
  borrowing by, 59–60
  Constitutional Convention and, 32
  corruption, political, 90
  debt of, 25–26, 27, *28*, 36–37, *37*, 59–60
  direct taxation of, 41–42
  internal improvements, federal aid for,
    45–46, 53–54
  public assistance programs, 136
  requisitions and, 25
  sovereignty of, 29–30
  spending post–Civil War, 85
  spending post–World War I, 123–24
  unemployment compensation plans, 136
Stevens, Thaddeus, 71
Strategic Defense Initiative, 224
strategic parity, doctrine of, 179–80
sugar, duties on, 86, 87
Supplemental Security Income (SSI), 201
surpluses
  Clinton administration and, 284–87, *288*
  Democratic party and, 289
  effects of policy and economic changes on,
    300
  FY 1997 reconciliation bills and, 282–84,
    285
  multiyear budgeting and, 294–95, 300–301
  in 1998, 242

post–Civil War, 78–79
Republican party and, 116
2000 election and, 291–93

Taft, Robert A., 170
Taft, William Howard, 85, 89, 94, 95
Tariff Act (1864), 66
tariffs
  budget surpluses and, 78–79
  Civil War and, 66
  Democratic party and, 76
  national, 26–28
  post–Civil War, 74, 75, 86–88
  post–World War I, 119
  pre–Civil War, 22
  protectionism and, 42, 50, 51–53
  Republican party and, 76–77
  revenue productivity of, 52–53
Tax Adjustment Act (1966), 176
taxation. *See also* corporations, taxes on;
    payroll tax; tax cuts; individual income
    tax
  G. H. Bush administration, 243–44
  Carter administration, 214–15, 216–17
  Chase program, 65
  Civil War and, 65–69
  Clinton administration, *258*, 259–63, *264*
  Constitutional Convention and, 30–32
  Democratic party and, 86–87, 287–88
  Eisenhower administration, 164–65
  equity and, 154
  Federalist era, 41–42
  Ford administration, 204–5
  Hoover administration, 138–39
  Johnson administration, 174–75
  Kennedy administration, 173–74
  Nixon administration, 203–4
  post–Civil War, 74–75, 89
  post–World War II, 152–56
  Reagan administration, 9, 234–36
  F. Roosevelt administration, 139–41, 146,
    147–48
  World War I and, 101–5, *106*
  World War II and, 145–48, *149*, *150*
tax cuts
  G. W. Bush administration, 292, 294–95,
    297–98
  Clinton administration, 275, 281–82
  countercyclical, 166
  Eisenhower administration, 165–66